SUSSEX
WRITERS
IN THEIR LANDSCAPE

SELF-FULFILMENT IN THE AGE OF THE MACHINE

PETER BRANDON
EDITED WITH ADDITIONAL MATERIAL
BY BRIAN SHORT

The
History
Press

Publisher's Note

The beneficiaries of the late Peter Frank Brandon's estate have agreed to transfer the copyright of his unfinished text for this book to Professor Brian Short.

First published 2023

The History Press
97 St George's Place, Cheltenham,
Gloucestershire, GL50 3QB
www.thehistorypress.co.uk

British Library Cataloguing in Publication Data.
A catalogue record for this book is available from the British Library.

ISBN 978 1 80399 364 5

Typesetting and origination by The History Press
Printed and bound in Great Britain by TJ Books Limited, Padstow, Cornwall.

Trees for LYfe

CONTENTS

ILLUSTRATIONS

Figures

Plates

Dedication by Peter Brandon

To my Mother's humble forebears whose skills helped shape the Sussex landscape, the inspiration to the writers mentioned in this book.

What is the fascination about Sussex that it should inspire book after book to be written in its praise and honour … that it should capture the hearts and fill the imagination of those who cannot even lay claim to be its own sons and daughters?

Thurston Hopkins, The Lure of Sussex *(1928)*

EDITOR'S PREFACE

By Brian Short

Most of the original text for this book was written by Peter Brandon prior to his death in November 2011, but the book remained unfinished. As time allowed, I have edited the text, researched suitable images and added the footnotes that Peter indicated but never wrote, always conscious of preserving, as far as possible, the energetic text so characteristic of the man. As well as this introduction I have also added a brief final chapter to further contextualise Peter's work, and where appropriate, I have inserted references to work published since 2011. He was still writing this book during his last period of hospitalisation. The visitor to his hospital bedside in Worthing would see a pile of books (mostly from the London Library) and assorted manuscripts scattered across his meal tray as he searched vigorously for the *mot juste* to include.

A pandemic and another European war have arrived upon us since Peter's death. This book is concerned with the discovery of the Sussex countryside before the Second World War, in what now seems, by contrast and at least superficially, like an innocent, indeed charming age in which writers welcomed the countryside surrounding them. So, we vicariously contemplate another time, seemingly another world, one with its own looming problems, of course, but through the writers' skill with words, we too can embrace rural Sussex, visit the haunts described and partake in something of the sense of environing nature offered to them.

Peter Brandon was, above all, an outdoors man, who found pleasure and a professional pride in the countryside of his adopted Sussex. As a landscape historian and historical geographer, he certainly looked to the past and drew inspiration from his scholarly investigations. But his interests in the environment also caused him to consider the future, to support countryside planning and to emphasise the importance of the humanities in revealing the complexities of human–nature interrelationships. Hence this book.

His text is not overtly theoretical but, in many ways, he was at the forefront of what has come to be called ecocriticism, the study of the relationship between literature and the physical environment.[1] This not a term he used himself, but it is applicable perhaps in that our lives, and those of the writers considered here, were lived *in a place*. He saw the Sussex countryside phenomenologically, as a lived experience – a two-way interrelationship between the writer and their surroundings. In this light Jonathan Bate has written, 'The poet's way of articulating the relationship between humankind and environment, person and place, is peculiar because it is experiential, not descriptive.'[2]

Of course, politics intrude, as does chronology and passing time. Was there a different landscape experience to be had from the depths of the late-nineteenth century farming depression, compared with, say, that experienced during the Great War? Certainly, the latter coloured many experiences, as is so well known, and therefore perhaps we should not get overly concerned with striving to find any unchanging essence of human–environment relations in any supposedly pure form. Context, place and time are all, and always, important.

So, to contextualise the rest of this book, I hope that a brief biography of Peter Frank Brandon will help to characterise his writings.[3] He was born on 16 July 1927 at his maternal grandmother's home in Shoreham, the only son of Frank and Doris, whose father Frederick Parsons was a sand and beach merchant. As a child, Peter's grandmother had picked up flints from Shoreham beach, work which frequently entailed fording the Surrey Hard (next to the modern Sussex Yacht Club) at low tide with horse and cart, filled with flint cobble and shingle, for dispatch by train to London, for ballast and building purposes. Peter regularly visited his maternal grandparents in Shoreham.

Frank was a master butcher in Twickenham, marrying Doris in 1925 and living over the shop in Hampden Road, Peter's home for more than twenty-five years (Figure 2). Peter attended secondary school at Twickenham, but soon moved on to Clark's College, Putney, where he studied accountancy for his intended career. He did, in fact, look after the shop's accounts and, together with his younger sister Gill, worked in the shop and made deliveries by bicycle, which Peter later claimed gave him a sense of place and feel for the local landscape. He was also inspired by Richard Jefferies, whose nature writing he devoured, and who had also lived briefly in nearby Surbiton. Jefferies offered a way into writing that was to remain with Peter throughout his life.

He was called up for war service in 1945, at the very end of the conflict, serving in the RAF but without either flying or demonstrating any real enthusiasm. Instead, he undertook a three-year teaching qualification at Borough Road Teacher Training College, finishing in 1951, aged 24, and in the following year being also awarded an External London general degree in

FAMILY BRANDON BUTCHER

ESTABLISHED 1903

F. BRANDON

Geography, English and History, which he had undertaken concurrently by private study.

He began teaching in Hampton but following his father's death in 1957 he gave this up to briefly take on the family shop. Peter as a shopkeeper is an interesting thought for those of us who knew him. However, within a year or so, the family had sold up and moved to Kingston Buci, Shoreham. Gill married shortly after, and Peter continued to live with his mother until her death in 1991 and thereafter lived alone.

This Sussex location imbued him with a passion for both the South Downs and the Weald. But while still at Twickenham, he had visited Juniper Hill Field Centre where he was introduced to the techniques of geography by S.W. Wooldridge (1900–63), first Professor of Geography at King's College London, whose own book on the Weald was to be such an influence, not only on Peter, but on generations of post-war Wealden enthusiasts. This is perfectly captured in the opening lines to the editors' preface:

> It would be difficult to find anywhere in the world an area of comparable size which exhibits so perfectly the responses of plant, animal and human life to the stimuli of varied physical environments as the Weald which Londoners have at their doorstep.[4]

Peter had also enrolled for a part-time degree at Birkbeck College and in 1959, the year of moving to Shoreham, he achieved a first-class honours degree in geography. He then proceeded to a PhD in historical geography, also at Birkbeck, for a thesis on Sussex medieval common fields and common lands (Plate 1).[5] In 1961, he was appointed to teach geography at North Western Polytechnic, Kentish Town, and commuted from Shoreham to north London for twenty-six years, until taking early retirement in 1987 and taking on the role as a sessional tutor in the Centre for Continuing Education at the University of Sussex, where he quickly became a popular lecturer on the Landscape Studies interdisciplinary BA degree.

Peter never published anything that might be regarded as conceptual or abstract, preferring thought-provoking empirical work. But one abiding influence was undoubtedly the French geographer, Paul Vidal de la Blache (1845–1918), the founder of French human geography, who held that the role

Opposite: Fig. 2: Frank Brandon and the family shop in Twickenham.
(Family photograph collection, by permission of Mrs Gill Hooker, née Brandon)

of people is not passive, since within limits they can modify their environment to advance their own ends. People and land were inseparable, expressed through culture – building materials and styles, food and drink, language, costume, etc. – 'like a snail moulded to its shell'. Vidal was the moving force behind a spate of French regional monographs and Peter's life work reflected this, translating it into a south-eastern English landscape, revealing how the interactions between culture and topography, or between farming and soil, resulted in differing histories and human landscapes.

By the early 1980s he had produced scholarly articles in many of the leading national geography, history and regional journals, as well as producing, in 1974, his highly acclaimed *The Sussex Landscape* under the editorship of W.G. Hoskins. With this and his edited *South Saxons* and his *History of Surrey*, he became increasingly known to a wider audience.[6] The 1974 volume became a standard fixture on reading lists accompanying undergraduate and adult education courses, and in the introduction he wrote, 'I have written this book in the hope that readers will take to the by-roads, footpaths, bridleways, coastal creeks and waterways, and so savour the real essence of the Sussex scene'.[7]

But in 1979 there was, in retrospect, a significant shift in Peter's writing when he published a chapter in an edited volume, *Change in the Countryside: Essays in Rural England, 1500–1900*. Now there was a newer emphasis: the infusion of artistic creativity into the landscape through the spread of designed gardens and parklands in the south-east, and the theme of creative cultural endeavour and its links to the environment stayed with him for the rest of his life.[8]

And with its greater emphasis on the eighteenth century and beyond, there was also a shift from his earlier concern with the medieval period, underlined by a 1981 article on the designer Philip Webb and his links with Sussex and William Morris *c.*1900, together with a paper investigating the impact of London's proximity on the Wealden landscape and the interpretations of that landscape by nineteenth-century artists.[9]

The last twenty years of his life were extremely productive. And another theme in his interests now also emerged strongly: a fierce resistance towards any development threatening to spoil rural landscapes, whether the iconic South Downs or the more 'ordinary' (and thus less protected) areas such as the Sussex Low Weald. Never content to shut himself in his study, he became engaged with a variety of conservation organisations: a member of the Society of Sussex Downsmen (now the South Downs Society) from 1987 and president from 2004 until his death; chairman of the Sussex branch of the Campaign for the Protection of Rural England (as it then was) from 1986 to 1999, and from 1992, he and I were both among the founder members of the Sussex Downs Conservation Board, the forerunner of the present national park.

Perhaps his most accessible work was the trilogy of books concerned with the South Downs (1998), the Kent and Sussex Weald (2003) and the North Downs (2005). All demonstrated his characteristic verve and depth of feeling, with much of the books' charm emanating from their synthesis of historical and contemporary, artistic and literary themes. A final major publication (and for me, his best work) was *The Discovery of Sussex* (2010), in which he was quite clearly working towards the themes that would be developed in this present volume, his last book.[10]

Through these books and his prolific lectures and media appearances – television, radio and local newspapers – over many years, he had established himself as the distinguished authority on the landscape history and protection of rural Sussex. So, these are his last words.

Asked on the day before he died from kidney failure, 'What present advice would you pass onto folk?'

He replied, 'We must fight to keep what countryside we have left!'

ACKNOWLEDGEMENTS

I am indebted to Peter's longstanding friend, Ann Winser, who had indexed many of his books and whose photographs of their many local trips as slides were gifted to me but deposited in January 2022 at the West Sussex Record Office, Chichester. I am only sorry that Ann died before this book could be published. She also deposited an unfinished version of this present book in the library of the Sussex Archaeological Society, and I am grateful for the ready assistance of the late Esme Evans in allowing me access to the typescript, thereby enabling me to digitise and edit the text.

I am also pleased to acknowledge the ready support of Peter's sister, Mrs Gill Hooker, and her daughter, Alison Livesley, who have allowed me to reproduce the photographs of Peter and Frank Brandon. When he died, Peter left a veritable Aladdin's Cave of books, notes, slides and sundry material that oozed out of every corner and lurked in every cupboard. To help clear this, I worked with Dr Geoffrey Mead, another longstanding devotee and colleague of Peter, and I acknowledge his help with the production of this text.

I do not myself have literary training, and I therefore happily also acknowledge the help of Dr Hope Wolf of Sussex University and Dr Miles Leeson (University of Chichester). Many others have helped me at various stages: Kathryn Aalto, Damian Atkinson, Colin and Judy Brent for initial discussions about this project; Sara Cooper (Towner Gallery Eastbourne), Evelyn Dodds, Alan Grey, Chris Hare, Oliver Hawkins (literary executor to the estate of Wilfrid and Alice Meynell), Martin Hayes, Matthew Jones (West Sussex Record Office), Mark Lynch (National Portrait Gallery), Lord and Lady Lytton, Robin Maclear, Peter McLeod, Harry Meynell, Eisha Neely (Cornell University, New York), Joleene New (Ditchling Museum of Arts & Crafts), Janet Pennington, Sue Ray, Helen Rogers, Sue Rowland, Janet Such, Norman Vance, Michael Vickers, Lucy Williams and Martin Wingfield.

In the references all publications are assumed to be from London publishers unless otherwise shown. Where the publisher and place of publication are shown in the bibliography this is not repeated in the footnotes. I have endeavoured to acknowledge all sources for the illustrative material, but some have proven difficult, and I apologise if I have inadvertently omitted the correct attribution. I trust that all such use of illustrative material is non-infringing and in accordance with all applicable copyright laws. The communal spirit of the brilliant Geograph website within the commons.wikimedia.org project is gratefully acknowledged for making available Creative Commons images, which are so much better than I could ever have produced myself.

My thanks also go to the late Michael Packard, who was an understanding and enthusiastic supporter in bringing this volume towards publication. It was to him that Peter Brandon initially brought an early version of this book, seven months before he died.

Nicola Guy has been an understanding, patient and most helpful contact at The History Press, along with project editor Ele Craker. As always, I remain eternally thankful that I have technologically knowledgeable sons, David and James, and an understanding wife, so deepest love and thanks go to Valerie, whose respect and affection for Peter in his later years matched my own.

ABBREVIATIONS

ODNB – Oxford Dictionary of National Biography
NPG – National Portrait Gallery
SAC – Sussex Archaeological Collections
SCM – Sussex County Magazine

INTRODUCTION

Take of English earth as much
As either hand may rightly clutch.
In the taking of it breathe
Prayer for all who lie beneath –
Not the great nor well-bespoke,
But the mere uncounted folk
Of whose life and death is none
Report or lamentation.
Lay that earth upon thy heart,
And thy sickness shall depart!

It shall sweeten and make whole
Fevered breath and festered soul;
It shall mightily restrain
Over-busy hand and brain;
It shall ease thy mortal strife
'Gainst the immortal woe of life,
Till thyself restored shall prove
By what grace the Heavens do move.[1]

Rudyard Kipling urges readers to find themselves in nature and familiar
places. Most Sussex poets and writers have always been country lovers.
Generations of Sussex writers have itched to demonstrate in verse and prose
the life they saw before them and the pleasures and values of country living.
The dominant strand in Sussex literature has been the writers' predilection
for the outdoors, its landscape, rural places, natural things, rural pursuits and
country lore. As poets in the English lyric tradition, their keynote was praise
or celebration of the peace and beauty resulting from their self-discovery
of the countryside. In prose, there is a strong, persistent, elegiac undertow.
And so, poets and writers created a radiant vision of England's pleasance
in Sussex's inexpressibly beautiful countryside. We shall not follow in the
footsteps of a Clare, or a Wordsworth, or a Hardy, but Sussex writers,
including some of the best loved in the English language, actively amassed
an unrivalled and much-prized body of literature in a rural setting.

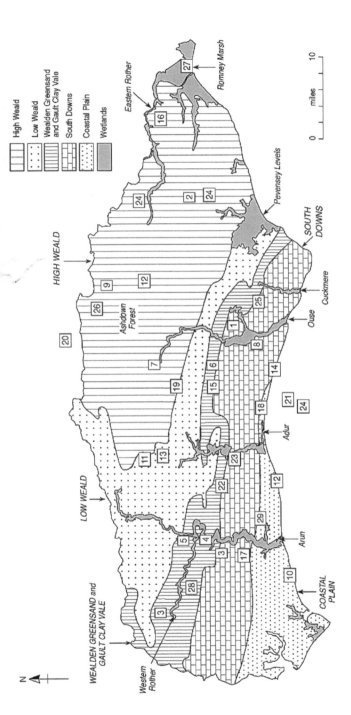

Fig. 3: Sussex writers in their landscape: 1. William Hay (Mount Caburn); 2. Reverend James Hurdis (Burwash); 3. Charlotte Smith (Bignor and Woolbeding); 4. D.H. Lawrence and the Meynell family (Greatham); 5. Ford Madox Ford (Bedham); 6. Eric Gill and Amy Sawyer (Ditchling); 7. John Halsham (Lindfield); 8. Virginia and Leonard Woolf (Rodmell); 9. Lady Dorothy Wellesley (Withyham); 10. William Blake (Felpham); 11. Wilfrid Scawen Blunt (Shipley); 12. Richard Jefferies (Crowborough and Goring) and Arthur Conan Doyle (Crowborough); 13. Hilaire Belloc (Shipley); 14. Rudyard Kipling (Rottingdean and Burwash); 15. Habberton Lulham (Hurstpierpoint); 16. Sheila Kaye Smith (Northiam); 17. Eleanor Farjeon (Houghton); 18. S.P.B. Mais (Southwick); 19. Ernest Raymond (Haywards Heath); 20. Stella Gibbons (Hampstead, north London); 21. Arthur Stanley Cooke (Brighton); 22. Arthur Bell (Storrington); 23. Charles Dalmon (Washington); 24. Andrew Young (Hove and Stonegate); 25. Julian Bell (Charleston); 26. A.A. Milne (Cotchford, Hartfield); 27. Henry James (Rye); 28. H.G. Wells (Midhurst); 29. John Cowper Powys (Burpham). (Map by Sue Rowland)

In time, this became a veritable counterculture, nurtured by writers who had been estranged from cities in the years between the two world wars and concerned by the alienation of city dwellers from nature with the relentless spread of urbanisation, and its accompanying economic attitudes and values. From this perspective, they presented a rousing case for the preservation of the heritage of rural Sussex, anticipating lively issues of sustainability and harmony, which have been reawakened in our own day in a global context. Locally, they became profoundly concerned about deterioration, particularly worried at the loss of 'place' through suburbanisation and a general 'dumbing-down' of the Sussex coastline with every field striped with imitation Tudor villas. They regarded the time in which they lived as one of confusion, not untouched with despair, very wearied and awaiting change for the better.

This book deals with the poets and writers who fell under the charm of rural Sussex and left a literary legacy. Their primary locations, together with the physical divisions of Sussex, are recorded in Figure 3.

However, the writers who lived among fields, woods and muddy lanes would have enjoyed nature in ways we cannot readily do today. They felt a breeze from the Downs with a scent of thyme, experienced silence and the glorious night sky, listened to the murmur of waves on an uninhabited seashore and heard a louder chorus of birds singing in the trees than we do. It seems now that theirs was a pre-urban world in the glow of its last sunset, without a care or doubt, in which it seemed as if nothing could ever come to harm. Here was their version of that ideal world that has haunted the dreamer, rebel and pastoral poet for centuries.

But visions of a rural Arcadia were not for everyone. There was no electricity or gas in rural districts and a day's work might be measured out in pails of water drawn from a pump or well. It was also a world of ramshackle cottages with appalling sanitation and utilities, the workhouse, low wages, a life of drudgery and hardship, especially for women, restricted education and few opportunities for self-advancement for working people. Unsurprisingly, many of those who could do so vanished to London and other towns and cities, including Brighton, and by the 1960s an older Sussex-born generation had almost become extinct. So, reading earlier Sussex authors is a reminder of the Sussex that has largely disappeared.

The best way to soak oneself in the scenery and places spiritualised by Sussex writers is to search a map and walk or cycle into the outdoors, always trying for the byways with grassy verges and roses in the hedges and bridleways and footpaths leading to fields, meadows, woods and brooks. And stop often, following the Golden Rule of getting off the beaten track and over the first stile you can find. This brings the satisfaction of discovering at first hand the places where Sussex writers found deep and lasting happiness in gathering their quickly changing scene into a few inches of paper. To Richard Jefferies, for example, this gave a sense of a seventh heaven, 'a spirit land seemingly scarce fit to be touched or long watched lest it should fade away'.[2]

The practice of purposeful walking made writers so intensely local in their inspiration that places they visited, generally very ancient and picturesque ones, often enter penetratingly into their works to form its whole substance and constitute a record of their wanderings in search of views, trees, rivers, flowers, animals, birds, hills, fields and ruins. This means that, in some ways, this is a geography book as well as a literary history.[3]

On account of this strong sense of place in Sussex writers, often their motivating force, the *where* of a poem or a story is often its most important element, not simply because it sets the predominant atmosphere, creates the appropriate tone or leads to associated thoughts, but rather because the place *is* the story, the fabric of the literature itself. Landscapes of a writer's mind, of course, can be some imagined locale, no less than a real one, but they were created out of real fields, woods and streets and, however inaccurate or falsi-fied, they are not entirely divorced from the real world, for there needs to be a reality behind it for the myth itself to take a hold on a reader's imagination.

Many discoveries are to be made. The imaginative impulse and visualising emotions writers drew from these places can also be explored; how they handled their material, sometimes by combining separate effects or monitor-ing and altering details like a landscape painter, or describing what is tran-sient, for example. Knowing a writer's art in seeing, imagining, interpreting and transforming a landscape familiar to them also reveals to the reader much of the county's presences and past character. This can add greatly to the enjoyment of an author's work and is also a delightful way of absorb-ing unconsciously the cultural history and geography of Sussex as well as gaining a greater knowledge of the vast changes in the Sussex landscape since the end of the last war.

We also learn something of the personalities of the writers themselves for, as C.E. Montague remarked in *The Right Place*, an attempt to describe a place may well be a description of it, but also as certainly, something of a description of the person who made it.[4]

One can enjoy, of course, Rudyard Kipling's 'The Way Through the Woods' or 'The Ballad of Mine Pit Shaw' without discovering the real places near his home at Burwash, which inspired him to write about them. But by following in the poet's footsteps to such actual sites, one is introduced not only to the extraordinary charm of the beautiful, wooded landscape but also to something of his creative processes and emotions that produced his works.

This is the exhilaration that Edmund Blunden experienced crouching behind the wicket at Horsham when distracted by music welling within him to the refrain 'Here Shelley lived', which came from 'wooded knoll to knoll, from leaning spire to lime-tree avenue'. Between overs, Blunden looked upon the rising ground of parkland at Denne, whose long tracts of softest greensward and spiky oaks are believed to have been among Shelley's first memories and which Blunden liked to think had stirred him in childhood to his later extraordinary poetic flights.[5]

These examples can be multiplied: Hilaire Belloc at the remote Gumber on the downland; Charles Dalmon among the cottages and orchards of Washington; Virginia Woolf at Alciston, inspired to write her last novel, *Between the Acts*; or John Keats, inspired by the stained-glass windows in the Vicars' Hall in Chichester and in Stanstead Chapel nearby, beginning 'The Eve of St Agnes' in the Hornet Square at Eastgate Chichester in 1819, and the first lines of 'The Eve of St Mark', also inspired by Chichester and giving a sense of people walking to evening prayer in an old county town on a coolish evening.[6]

The literary and landscape story is taken in this book to 1939, which marks the end of Sussex's predominance in English rural writing and creatively its best years. To most modern readers, several of the writers included are perhaps half-forgotten and others unknown, but they had a certain degree of fame in their day and deserve to be rescued from oblivion.

1

A SECOND EDEN

From this proud eminence the ravish'd eye
Sees Earth and Heav'n and Heav'n and Ocean vie,
To form a second Eden ...[1]

As an aircraft from the Continent loses height nearing Gatwick Airport the view from its windows reveals a large, intimate patchwork of small fields separated by thick hedges rolling to the bevelled edge of the long, grey wall of chalk hills closing the distant view. The powerful visual appeal of this singular landscape with its capacity to arouse strong emotional responses was the venue of the Sussex poet and writer in 'Secret Sussex', still somewhat detached from the rest of England. Despite creeping urbanisation, the landscape differs absolutely from the stark, hedgeless, linear and seemingly dehumanised, utilitarian, Mondrian-like landscape of northern France, over which the aircraft had just flown.

But ever since the seventeenth century, people with a liking for the magic of great scenery have resorted to Box Hill on the North Downs, 'the busiest spot in the world', to drink in the immense view of the Weald and the long bare line of the South Downs on the horizon, the view made famous by Tennyson's four well-known lines:

You came, and look'd and loved the view
Long known and loved by me,
Green Sussex fading into blue
With one grey glimpse of sea.[2]

For this is one of the great landscapes of England, reckoned among the loveliest hill, dale and coast that England can show. And for those with a special sensibility to landscape, the rippling wooded folds ending in that dreamful line of distant undulating chalk hills so deeply affected the eye that here was something of a second heaven. The view has relieved low spirits, banished grey moods and stirred the deepest human emotions. Here was love, beauty,

awe, wonder and reverence, meditation, consolation, fortitude and humility, and thus it has entered vividly into the artistic imagination and by its
marked individuality has impressed itself on the public's mind. Yet, do what
poets and writers will, there remains an unknown quality. Arthur Bell was
probably correct in remarking that the very best verse in the world, set to
the very best music, would still fail to give a full appreciation of this world
of loveliness.[3]

By the accidents of geology, south-east England is moulded in a striking
earth architecture. From Leith Hill, although it only rises to 1,000ft with the
aid of the folly on its top, twelve counties could be seen before the modern
growth of trees, and it is still possible to view the great sweep of country
from the English Channel to the south and the Dunstable Downs, far
beyond, to the north. The chalk upland of the Chilterns dips under London,
rises again to form the North Downs and reappears in the South Downs, the
overarch of chalk having been subsequently eroded away to expose the broad
levels of the intervening Weald. Within the departed crest are panoramas as
grand as they are beautiful.

These views are diverse almost to the point of absurdity and they change
quickly. On account of this differing series of rocks there was a corresponding diversity of plant, animal and human life. This led to Sussex historically
having sharply distinctive little economies 'joined at the hip', each with
different faces and rural cultures, and the field scientist's habit of observing
its topography, fauna and wildlife has led to enormous leaps in perception
over the last 200 years.

In the Weald, a remnant of old Europe, every feature, whether natural or
made by humans, tended to be tiny and seemingly laid together in a Lilliputian
plan, with secluded nooks – the perfect place for withdrawal to a haven or a
healing sanctuary, for it had the intimacy of a cradle and all the homeliness
of a home. Here too, there is always a river or shallow brook within sight
or hearing, and much of the Wealden charm emanates from the delightful
stragglement of nature and dense network of 'secret' bridleways and footpaths
traversing secluded copses, little fields and streams. Many were old 'iron ways',
tracks used to move ore and products of furnace and forge such as those from
around the site of Burwash Forge or from the old ironworks at Stream Farm in
Chiddingly. For some, such things at close range were too enthralling to leave
much time for the wider prospect. And one of the most mystical of 'secret'
places is Amberley Wild Brooks, of which C.E.M. Joad has written, 'Here, if
anywhere, one feels, the nature gods still stayed'.[4]

Filling Veins with Life

Although they never consciously set out to be regional writers, the Sussex poets and writers developed a passionate attachment to their particular piece of country and to its particular pleasures. And it was nostalgia for the Sussex past in which writers principally indulged, which Jonathan Bate has cynically suggested 'must be a sign of the sickness of the present'.[5]

Sussex seemed to lack modernity. The nostalgia, an unavoidable human trait, was a sense of a lost past, but time and place were conjoined: to be in Sussex was to be conscious of the past all around them, so it was easy for writers to convey the myth of an England irredeemably rural and unchanging. Thus, as we shall see, Kipling found at Burwash a landscape so 'alive with ghosts and shadows', such a 'site of memory' that it could tell the nation's history.[6]

Almost half-forgotten is the character of the Sussex countryside, which was the inspiration to the writers considered here. So tremendous has been the transformation of Sussex from around 1900 that no one alive can recall, or even imagine, what that countryside was like and what were the habits, attitudes, outlooks and everyday life of its people. There is far more

Fig. 4: Habberton Lulham, photograph accompanying his 'Amberley and her Wild Brooks'. (*SCM* 13, 1939, p. 598)

difference between life in Sussex today and 100 years ago than there was between the life of our great-grandparents and the days of the first Queen Elizabeth, for in 1900, Sussex, apart from the seaside resorts, had more in common with the Sussex of 1800, or even 1700, than today's Sussex with all its modern appliances, post-industrial and cultural shifts.

In 1900 villages were still collections of farmsteads and their attendant farm workers' cottages. There were also the crafts of the millwright, ploughwright, blacksmith, saddler, harness-maker and shoemaker. The church, inn and village store/post office were lively centres. Horse power still ruled the pace of life: as late as 1939 Amberley residents could still hear the teams of farm horses, a farm boy sitting astride the leading horse with a string of others, each one tied to the next, making for the Wild Brooks in the evening (Figure 4). Ways of farming had seemingly changed little for centuries: Southdown sheep flocks thickly dotted the turf of the Downs and thistledown floated down on visitors in high summer. Hundreds of small family farms still existed in the Sussex Weald. Hazel and chestnut coppices were regularly cut and were the preferred home of the nightingale. Men had not left off singing and the tuneful note of sheep bells, the swish of the scythe and the melody of the bell-team of wagon horses on the road were familiar sounds.

So, newcomers encountered a region that retained more than vestigial survivals of a people's cultural inheritance. On the Downs sheep-farming practices extended back to biblical times. The lean soils of the Weald still sharpened the wits of small family farmers, who have since disappeared, though many of their small fields remain. To a considerable degree, speech, manners, customs and country wisdom handed down over many generations still prevailed among Sussex country people up to the time when the motor car had barely intruded. Moreover, weighted with tradition, Sussex was still a place saturated in legends and folklore, sham ghosts and bristling with relics – prehistoric earthworks, abbeys, castles, ancient manor houses, old villages and market towns.

All these were naturalised into the landscape and imbued with the slow rhythm of old country life and seclusion. History writing, landscape paint-ing, photography and film, as well as poetry and literature, all popularised the past, building on Sussex's beguiling identity and continuity in contrast with the fast-changing times over most of Britain. The overall effect tended to give a false sense of an enduring, unchanging, 'timeless' Sussex landscape, therapeutically valued by a reader who was disturbed at the speed and extent of change.

The Sussex landscape itself was an extended record of the county's history. A revelation in the 1920s and 1930s was provided by the thrilling archaeological excavations of the Curwens and their followers on the South Downs, which revealed a legacy of human occupation extending over more than 5,000 years. Before the ploughing up of the Downs during and after the Second World War, the complex of prehistoric earthworks everywhere inscribed on the turf was something physical, tangible. Edward Thomas remarked how potent was the appeal of 'sheep-walk scarred with a thousand tracks and memorials of a people of uncharted antiquity', and his wife, Helen, wrote of her thrill at encountering this prehistoric landscape and of the wave of patriotism that came over her when she felt she was 'in the heart of England's being'.[7]

This glory of the Downs has almost disappeared since the ploughing up from 1940. The old chalk grassland is now one of the rarest habitats in Western Europe. This makes it difficult, if not impossible, for readers who did not know them in childhood to understand fully the inspiration derived by earlier generations of poets and writers. The soft, velvety nature of the short, springy turf made walking delightful. Unwearied, everyone was fleeter of foot, sturdy ramblers donned seven-league boots and strode, or leapt for joy, and when cyclists ground their pedals, they had the sensation of flying through the air. Horses, hounds, foxes and hares ran faster than anywhere else and the turf was superb on which to play cricket. It is not surprising that Goodwood celebrated in 2002 the third centenary of its first cricket match and the second of its race meeting.

Thus, Sussex was a place where landscape and history were inextricably fused. In still summer heat, the visitor could associate Sussex in their minds with one of the quintessential English scenes, that of the ploughman and his ox team, shaven turf, a flock of sheep clustering on a hillside with the strange music of tinkling sheep bells gradually moving away into silence, larks spiralling overhead. These scenes depicted the way of life on which Sussex had been founded for centuries, and writers' evocative descriptions travelled all over the English-speaking world.

The most explicit book to deal with the Sussex past was Arthur Beckett's *The Wonderful Weald* (1911), in which the reader never seems to leave the historical pageant of a medieval wonderland. But the past, as we shall see, was also the core of Belloc's *The Four Men* and Kipling's Burwash period, and it was the inspiration for Amy Sawyer's preservation of Sussex dialect. Both Yorkshire-born 'John Halsham' and Virginia Woolf came to recognise the local people as the true bearers of the identity and values of Sussex rather than the 'townee' visitors and residents who sketched, photographed and ogled them.[8]

'Halsham' was the pseudonym of George Forrester Scott, grandson of a stockbroker and whose father was the secretary of a national insurance company and his mother the daughter of a banker. Although never very wealthy, he dug steadfast, even hermetic roots into the mid-Sussex country-side, leaving an unsurpassed record of changes in the landscape and society of the Sussex Weald at a time of transition between old and new ways of living. He also came to champion landscape protection in Sussex and was the first in the county to apply his acute seeing eye to the transience of beauty in the shifting light of day and season. This earned him the description of 'the perfect countryman'.

Trumpeting Sussex with Religious Fervour

Northerners might find the chalk odd, rather like finding an albino black-bird, and prefer their rugged uplands to the flaccid, soft, smooth Downs. But the Sussex man or woman never saw the friendly and familiar Downs and distant sea without a lift of happiness in their hearts, and in the breeze from the sea the visitor felt strangely refreshed. The magnificent prospect of the long line of the Downs westward from the summit of the Devil's Dyke, was suggested by James Thorne as early as 1844 as being perhaps unequalled in any of the southern counties.[9]

Indeed, the South Downs became the most celebrated range of hills in England between around 1900 and 1939. Written of, poetised, painted, photographed, advertised and mimicked, their fame spread worldwide. Numerous writers absorbed them into their very being, and Richard Jefferies, D.H. Lawrence and Virginia Woolf were transported into rapturous ecstasy. Another was the poet Laurence Binyon, who was mesmerised by the harmonious beauty of the wave-like Seven Sisters cliffs, an iconic view of the outline of England that has certainly won worldwide acclaim, and he thought of the hearts that had ached to see it:

> What eyes have waked
> Ere dawn to watch those cliffs of long desire
> One after one rise in their voiceless choir
> Out of the twilight over the rough blue
> Like music![10]

And there were the striking views to the patterned coastal plain and to the water meadows in the gaps between the chalk, flooded in winter, where the Arun, Adur, Ouse and Cuckmere wandered aimlessly about the level land, seemingly with no idea of the sea's direction.

The writers' deep devotion to their particular landscape cannot be questioned. Richard Jefferies' attachment to the South Downs amounted to the mystical. Wilfred Scawen Blunt found it difficult to recognise natural beauty other than that of the deep oakwoods and sheltering hedgerows of his native Weald and frankly confessed that it meant more to him than all the English colonies put together. The Ditchling calligrapher Edward Johnston recalled the enlightened, blessed moment when he found its surroundings, to which he gave more love than to any woman. Eleanor Farjeon confessed that the Downs meant more to her than any human being. All took pleasure in learning about an entirely new way of life, and the many commonplace authors, perpetually on the stretch with their obsessive scrutiny of nature, could actually weary the reader.

The astonishing beauty and ceaseless variation of the Sussex landscape might also be the subject of Christian reverence and religious awe as if it was gifted with a special place in God's scheme. Considered as divine a landscape as the Vale of Tempe, eyes and heart were lifted up to a 'heavenly geography' spreading ethereally to a heaven on earth, which would have been sacrilege to link with ordinary landscapes. Its celestial grandeur was viewed as one of the sacraments prepared for man and to be discovered by him as a heavenly vision where one could see and walk with God and heaven alike.

To Belloc, in whom the land was always expressed in religious terms, Sussex was a 'holy place' where God shone all around, as if a star like that which shone over Bethlehem marked out Sussex as blessed. Villages such as Washington under the Downs were also 'holy'. Looking down from Chanctonbury Ring upon the Weald was to see the 'Plains of Heaven' in contrast to the Babylon of London. Vera Arlett saw the Weald as her friend and 'heavenly blue' and 'holy ground' and where beauty put a 'diadem of holiness' on it. Maurice Hewlett, scanning the distant Weald, found the 'truce of heaven', while Michael Fairless envisaged the Downs as 'lone heavenward hills'. The sculptor Eric Gill thought of paradise in his family's evening excursions through Poynings, under Newtimber Hill and by the round hill of Wolstonbury to Clayton. Numerous other writers saw the landscape as all but divine and to them, looking down on the earth from the Downs was like looking upwards to heaven.

In their uplifting sense of openness to beauty and goodness, few landscape writers can have been more eloquent advocates of the benefits of faith.

The Reverend F.W. Orde Ward discovered a little nook on a summer's day whose beauty was like 'Heaven's gate to things supernal'. His vivid awareness of the beauty and goodness of Sussex enter into the religious feelings of his *Songs of Sussex* (1910), poems in praise of Sussex with the spiritual message, singularly appropriate for the needs of a generation being herded into towns, that Sussex was a green sanctuary as God had made it. Here, sinners from the world outside could repent in tune with nature, their souls shriven in secluded valley altars washed in Sussex dews and purified in the 'precious greeting of Sussex hills'.

His songs are essentially simple and sincere religious verses written with many gracious and tender touches in a poetical calendar of sea, downs, woodland and heath. They were inspired by his love of place: Eastbourne, Seaford, Ashburnham, Wilmington, Willingdon, Herstmonceux and Jeving-ton. At each, he sought God and found him. At Bayham Abbey, he declares his brotherhood as priest of the bracken glades and woodland spirit, the briar and brake dearer to him than is a nestling baby to a mother, and the wonder of the world mingles in him at that holy place where he saw the living heart of God laid bare. Sussex has skies that look down bluer, woods are greener, its waters more musical, the sheen of woman's brow more beautiful, and its toiling people happy. Altogether, his verses recall the mood Wordsworth conveyed in his 'Lines written above Tintern Abbey'.[11]

There were other specifically spiritual messages. The Reverend Francis Rosslyn Bruce (1871–1956), naturalist, writer and Rector of Herstmonceux, collected in *Sussex Sacred Songs* (1927) religious verses from parishioners. And a religious tone infuses other books, such as Michael Fairless' *The Roadmender*, which envisaged Sussex nature in a secular light as a womb where dwelt the happy, the wise and the unconceived.

Sussex authors were not modest about their beloved landscape. One of their undeclared aims was to redefine and maintain Sussex as a special geographical place with a separate individuality. This was done by building on its history and traditional ways of life against a background of timeless-ness. Many were never free from a self-conscious pride in Sussex and, like all patriots could, by even the simplest statement inflame the mind and heart of a reader. Hyperbole could be infectious and Arthur Beckett, founder and first editor of the *Sussex County Magazine*, was perhaps the most insistently assertive of all (Figure 5).

In his hubris can be seen a cause of the hurrying feet seeking the Sussex scene in the interwar years. In *The Wonderful Weald* he explains that it had been his mission to 'teach' readers to love the region. In fact, as a newcomer

Fig. 5: (Left) Arthur Beckett (1872–1943), founder of the Society of Sussex Downsmen, and his brother-in-law, R. Thurston Hopkins (1884–1958), as president. Hopkins had recently published *Sheila Kaye-Smith and the Weald Country* (1925) and in the year the photograph was taken, *Sussex Pilgrimages* (1927). (*SCM* 1 [2], 1927, p. 84)

himself, he was learning the traditions of the 'old' Sussex in order to restore knowledge of them to the new town-bred arrivals. He became a strong propagandist, and in glorying Sussex he declared that it had the best hills, the springiest turf, the sweetest sunshine, the purest air and the most famous sheep in England, and averred that he had never met man nor woman who did not envy those bred or nurtured in the county. His boisterous note continued in his songs. One version by Beckett of Kipling's poem appeared thus:

> For it's good to live in Sussex, the land 'o brave and free,
> Where men are bruff and honest – such men as you an' me.
> If you weren't born in Sussex, whoever you may be
> Then come and die in Sussex land, sweet Sussex by the sea.[12]

In such reactions, the county's writers were forever searching, transforming and measuring against other parts of Britain a new image of Sussex as if they were trying to create from Sussex a new sense of English national identity, much as Lambarde, Camden, Drayton and others had proffered Kent to sixteenth-century England.

The suggestion was that Sussex was both singular and secretive, yet at the same time the platonic idea of England, so identified with English qualities as to fill one with a sense of England itself. The glorification of the Sussex landscape, through synecdoche, aroused patriotism for England. It is found in Charles Crocker's Kingley Vale, and very explicitly in Binyon's 'Thunder on the Downs' (see page 65).

Such meditations on nationhood, as expressed in pastoral images, were led by the fear of invasion and disruption by Napoleonic France in Crocker's case.[13] For the early twentieth-century writer, the impetus came from the disquieting news from the Continent in the interwar years, which contrasted so strongly with the peaceful landscape they saw around them. And these feelings could easily spill over into extremely jingoistic praise of England as the most beautiful and best country in the world. Their passionate patriotic feeling flooded their hearts with a thankfulness. Back-slapping exercises in regional pride could reach extraordinary heights of enthusiasm that Belloc, with the flamboyant braggadocio of a Bergerac de Cyrano, claimed had turned the county into one of England's minor religions.

The literary notion was created that the essential England was not London or the industrial Midlands and north. This spirit pervades Walter Wilkinson's *A Sussex Peep-Show* (1933), in which he does not disguise his distaste for modern civilisation. He had two objectives in his journey across Sussex, one to reach the Downs and the other to avoid Brighton.[14] This was regarded by Weiner as a sign of a fundamental unwillingness to accept an industrial and commercial modern society, a symptom he took to be one of British economic decline.[15]

This insistence on the significance of the south country aroused considerable clatter. Southerners, in the main, were amused at the arrogance, but it was not in the best interests of the county. In the Midlands and north, not to mention other delightful places, it was an irritant to be mocked and scorned. The most significant literary reaction, as we shall see, was Stella Gibbons' *Cold Comfort Farm*, a parody, indeed almost a kind of hymn, of hate against Sussex.[16] The cultural effect was to be profound. The remedy for the passionate love of Sussex was yet more love. But love does have a dynamic, dangerous side, and it was to transform Sussex or, as some insisted, destroy it.

2

SUSSEX PLACES AND
THE ARTISTIC IMAGINATION

Wild Arun too has heard thy Strains,
And Echo, 'midst my native Plains,
Been soothed by Pity's Lute.[1]

In the Beginning

The earliest Sussex poets normally wrote only about the local landscapes they could see, ride or walk over from their manor houses and parsonages, the focus of their daily lives and what was nearest and most interwoven with them. They saw the landscape from the back of a horse, struggling through mire and ruts, and knew it intimately. Their poems tended, therefore, to be of familiar, loved places and not the broader aspects of Sussex landscapes they infrequently visited but this may be one reason why, to modern taste, much is insipid.

This parochial restriction began to change with improved roads from the mid-eighteenth century, a notable consequence being Elizabeth Hitchener's 'The Weald of Sussex' (1822), but it was the facility of travel by railway that really first opened the door on the Sussex landscape.[2] So, ironically, without the modernity of trains, especially on local lines where they ambled along slowly, poets, writers and artists could never have appreciated Sussex's beautiful changing scene, discovered much of its ancient past or readily compared and contrasted one landscape with another. Consequently, some of the most useful insights into landscape by Victorians and their successors are attributable to railway travel.

Early passengers of the Brighton Railway, for example, were astonished to find themselves within 35 miles of London whirling through wild and beautiful country around Balcombe Station. And as the rail network was later extended, Sussex became even more accessible, and therefore more known, to urban travellers who were introduced for the first time to a slower tempo of life in beautiful scenery (Figure 6).

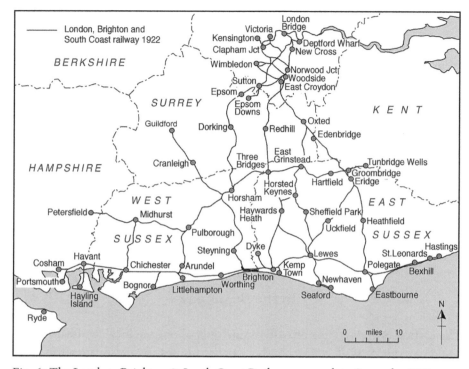

Fig. 6: The London, Brighton & South Coast Railway network in Sussex by 1922.
(Map by Sue Rowland)

Paradoxically, it was the railway that also gave writers rural seclusion, enabling them to reach their refuges in which to write but equally to run up to the hurly-burly of London whenever they liked. Clearly, from the moment of the building of the first railway line across Sussex in 1841 it was a love-match between people, landscape and transport, which has been as significant in the history of Sussex's cultural history as it has in that of communication. Even more significant was the coming of the motor car, which was to make accessible even the most remote parts of the countryside. But by the 1930s, Sussex was becoming subtly suburbanised in the way of all Sunday afternoon motoring areas around cities and much of its literature of that period has a flavour of 'beauty spots' and 'Olde Tudor' tearoom.

Seeing the Light in the West

We can survey a broad picture of the history and geography of literary creativity in the county, and of the underlying landscapes that produced an intellectually exhilarating effect on the mind, by imagining two separate vantage points overlooking the countryside. To seek the locale of most of the Sussex writers up to the eighteenth and early nineteenth centuries one would make for St Roche's Hill (now better known as the Trundle), high on the Downs above Chichester and about 1 mile from Goodwood House. There are few eminences from which the eye can take in so much beauty as in this extensive and variegated panorama. Rolling downland passes into the highly cultivated coastal plain which, in turn, meets the sea in the headlands and creeks of Chichester Harbour and leads the eye to the distant Isle of Wight (Plate 2). The focal point of this exquisite view is the spire of Chichester Cathedral.

Early Victorians and their eighteenth-century predecessors rode to the hill to gorge on this view that, to Horace Walpole, resembled 'in no slight degree that kind of horizon with which Claude was accustomed to bound the finest of his pictures'.[3] Such a commendation gained the view a special fame in an age when 'fashionables' saw landscape through the eyes of Claude Lorrain and other seventeenth-century painters of Italian scenery. Guests and visitors to Goodwood House banqueted at Carne's Seat in the park for the sake of this view.

Some later authors also derived inspiration from much the same prospect. Hilaire Belloc's love of Sussex initially came from Gumber Corner on the Downs above Slindon, which he called the 'watch tower of England'.[4] The favourite view of the famed ecologist Sir Arthur Tansley was from Bow Hill, the dramatic backdrop to the Kingley Vale National Nature Reserve, which also affords much the same beautiful view but also extends eastward along the coast to Highdown Hill, near Worthing, and northward into the Surrey Hills. This was the subject of Charles Crocker's 'Kingley Vale' (1837), the earliest poetic statement from that numinous place.

These broadly similar views disclosing western Sussex fading into Hampshire, more or less encompass the locale of almost all of the inspiration for the literary, artistic and musical creativity in the whole of Sussex up to around 1900. Like all cathedral cities, Chichester bubbled with intellectual and religious life, which overflowed into literature and the arts. The wooded western South Downs were then more favoured scenically than the bare downs eastwards, and the Arun was their fairest Sussex stream.

Moreover, this district was a nobleman's Arcadia with the age-old 'business with pleasure' atmosphere then so conducive to the arts. The patronage of the elite was a crucial requirement for authors, and here were William Hayley of Eartham and Felpham, the MPs William Huskisson and William Wilberforce, the Dukes of Richmond and Norfolk and the 3rd Earl of Egremont – the 'Maecenas of the age' in Crocker's phrase. The gentry also included the brothers Burrell of Knepp and West Grinstead, and clergy sufficiently disposed to the arts to have been beneficed by a number of these distinguished patrons.

This was the world of Chichester's Thomas Weelkes, organist of the cathedral and composer of charming madrigals; Jasper Mayne, the Dean, who wrote with the intensity of John Donne; Bishop Henry King, whose moving exequy to his wife was a tale of married love during bloodshed and civil rebellion; and the composer of church music and diarist, John Marsh. Here, too, had been the earliest Sussex writers, James Taylor, the Water Poet, Thomas Otway of Trotton, William Collins, Charlotte Smith, Hayley and William Blake. And we have already noted the poet Keats' productive visit to the Chichester district. But there were also painters such as the brothers Smith of Chichester, and Stubbs, admired by the 2nd Duke of Richmond, and Turner, famously at Petworth and Copley Fielding around Arundel and the South Downs.

The same district was also the homeland of humble Charles Crocker and William Hersee from Coldwaltham, the nearest Sussex equivalents of the poet Robert Bloomfield, the Suffolk 'Farmer's Boy'. Hersee (1786–1854) had a patron in Hayley, and his volume of verses, *Poems, Rural and Domestic* (1810), was sponsored by the Prince Regent, Lords Egremont, Mahon and Carrington, William Huskisson, the brothers Burrell and other West Sussex celebrities.[5] Later, the western Weald had also claimed Wilfrid Scawen Blunt as its first major writer and in the first third of the twentieth century, incomers Hilaire Belloc, Habberton Lulham, Esther Meynell, Eleanor Farjeon, Galsworthy and Tickner Edwardes, together with Ivon Hitchens and numerous painters.

The dominance of these western landscapes in early verses can be illustrated by examining James Taylor's anthology, *The Sussex Garland*, published in 1851, to discover the particular places that inspired the earliest Sussex verse.[6] The South Downs emerge overwhelmingly with thirty-eight poems (including Lewes), but the western downland was more favoured than the eastern Downs (twenty-five poems to thirteen). This is partly accounted for by the prolific Charlotte Smith, together with the preference for wooded landscapes compared with bare downs, but perhaps mainly, as we have seen, the presence of the great landed patrons.

Of the waters, the Arun earned fond praise from William Collins, and its beautiful hangers, flowery meadows and woods were also beloved by Charlotte Smith. The stream winds its way through places lined with willow, alder, poplar and sycamore, backed by the hanging woods of beech and yew that thrilled Constable on his visit to Arundel in 1834, and its banks are clothed with waterside plants seen at their best in summer, such as the great hairy willowherb, balsam and tansy, commemorated in the novel of that name by a local naturalist-parson, Tickner Edwardes of Burpham. A walk along the Arun's banks between Pulborough and Arundel reveals one of the most beautiful and least-changed valleys in Sussex.

The poetic spirit also touched the coastal towns in Taylor's collection: St Leonard's and Rye are represented with one each, Hastings with two, Chichester with three, and Brighton, although still a fledgling watering place, scored twelve. The cliffed coast of Sussex inspired four. The Weald is represented by twelve poems, including Taylor's own appreciation of the 'green hills' of Newick, where he lived. He wrote of the green lanes (old drove ways) carpeted with primroses in spring, the tinted foliage and the brown fallows in autumn and of his rambles along the banks of the River Ouse.

The East Comes into View

Yet, if we search for the places in Sussex that dominated the arts from around 1900 to 1939, we should move across Sussex and ascend to another vantage point, Firle Beacon, which has one of the most distinctive profiles in the whole of the South Downs (Plate 3). The magnificent panorama from its summit includes the rounded summit of Mount Caburn, below which Lewes nestles, and there is the distant view of the Forest Ridge of the Weald as well as the cliffs at Seaford Head. There are views of Glyndebourne, which became the site of the internationally famous opera house, and a glimpse across the River Ouse to Rodmell, which held Virginia Woolf's home.

On a warm day in high summer, a fresh breeze sometimes blows on Firle Beacon while a heat haze hangs over the great expanse of Downs and Weald. Chalk headlands repeating themselves westwards disappear into a boundless infinity as they merge and enlarge into one unbroken line in the water vapour. Northwards, the Weald fades away in the misty light and Lewes is lost to sight in its river valley. In all this silent treeless country, there are few buildings visible and there seems to be no sign of human activity, the road traffic along the A27 being hidden by hedges. There is almost an eerie time-lessness, making one feel that this is an entry to another world, somehow central to Sussex's history, and it also helps to explain why twentieth-century and earlier writers sang Sussex's praises with such strong feelings and why people aspired to follow their example and go to live there. The scene also largely explains why this book has been written.

A radius of less than 10 miles from Firle Beacon circumscribes most of the creative activity in Sussex in the forty years before the Second World War and could be seen as the cradle of modern Sussex literary and artistic endeavour. Once again, the associated names are legion. In the wake of Kipling's arrival at Rottingdean in 1897 came Alfred Noyes, Enid Bagnold and Angela Thirkell, together with painters Henry George Hine and William Nicholson. Just beyond is the scene of the evocative watercolours of Eric Ravilious and Peggy Angus' interiors. Then we recall Cyril Connolly, Arthur Beckett, Ernest Raymond and Alfriston artist Frank Wootton. The 'Bloomsberries', Virginia and Leonard Woolf, Vanessa Bell and Duncan Grant, Clive Bell and Maynard Keynes need no effort of memory. And just over Mount Caburn was the Ditchling colony of the sculptor and letter-cutter Eric Gill, which also housed Brangwyn, Charles Knight, Amy Sawyer and etcher Edgar Holloway, while Brighton was exciting Graham Greene and Patrick Hamilton.

Such a list is not comprehensive; it omits many contemporaries in journal-ism and the arts, but the ascent of Mount Caburn or Firle Beacon serves to introduce most of the countryside that inspired the extraordinary flowering of creativity in the Sussex Downs near Lewes, which made Sussex probably the leading county in English literature before 1939.

Lewes was a focus for creative landscape writing for the eastern and central parts of the county. This modern flowering was foreseen by John Halsham in his book *Idlehurst* (1898). He walked through the breakneck lanes of Lewes down to the Cliffe and up the steep hill above the great chalk pits and sat on the top in still, hot afternoon air.

Apart from the railway sidings below, the scene was one of amazing beauty.[7] Looking down, he found Lewes a compact, busy hive, 'not alto-gether out of tune with the quiet heaven', where people from downland and Weald were doing business with little hurry, noise, smoke or stench. The smell of the sea and Downs pervaded even the inmost streets. He yearned for the saving of English towns like Lewes, which were not too big and dense for swallows to nest in the eaves.

In the warm air, he drowsily fell into a kind of daydream: in the direction of London were going the thrusters, the vulgar, 'heavy-fingered intellects' and 'Progressive spouters'. Coming back from the capital's clubs and cab ranks were 'the geniuses, the poets and painters, all the nice and pretty people'. In his dream, they were conserving the town, forming distinct schools of letters and art in a kind of countryside Athens, quite different from that of the 'smoke-ingrained Cockney mind' which was spreading universally.

Halsham's half-dream was in several respects to be strikingly fulfilled. Whether the 'spouters' vanished or not is still in question, but the town's radicalism had perhaps declined and there was an invasion of artists, writers and intellectuals into the heart of Lewes' rural hinterland, perhaps searching for some kind of terrestrial paradise, thereby reversing the rural exodus that Halsham deplored. Their search for the right place was over.

It was not only the novelist Mrs Henry Dudeney who would have described Lewes just before the Second World War as the 'most divine spot on earth', or Edmund Blunden as a place where one would not find an 'unproved loaf, a badly-shod horse, a weakly-bound book or knife that would not cut'. It still throbs with intellectual life, with two neighbouring universities, art galleries, museums, historic buildings and independent bookshops, and offers that priceless gift of sitting still which has mostly gone out with modern life. This it advertised until recently to all by the simple expedient of removing hands from one clock and ensuring that not another single public or hotel clock told the proper time.

Lewes' spectacular site on a spur of the Downs, the amphitheatre of surrounding grey-green hills, its compact size, the intricate and intimate crooked lanes and twittens, its castle tower and rich meadows have resounded in its praise ever since Elizabeth Hitchener described it as a 'Town more pleasing boasts not Albion's Isle'. William Morris considered Lewes 'set down better than any town I have seen in England'.[8] It is likely that the beauty of Chichester sweeps up at once and irresistably, whereas Lewes' steals gradually and insensibly, yet both have proved enduring.

The Unsought Sussex Landscapes

Sussex writers cried out for space, sweet air and clean rain, and detested the reeking urban streets. But not every part of Sussex was quiet or green enough nor bereft of charabancs. Presumably, the absence up to 1939 of a 'Haywards Heath' or 'Crawley Road' school of writers suggests that they could not honestly attempt to write pastorals there. Nor could one laze easily to write a desultory piece within earshot of the steam whistles of the Brighton expresses and the sight of advertisements in the fields lining the tracks before the late 1920s. Nor was there poetry in Peacehaven, and likewise, no poets wooed the Downs at the funfair on the Devil's Dyke – and those who found joy in the countryside had to shut at least one eye and ear along the coast road between Brighton and Littlehampton. E.V. Lucas was never to discover that where he once scented hay had become the Holmbush megamarket outside Shoreham-by-Sea, and only poor Richard Jefferies' ghost knew what befell Goring-by-Sea through suburbanisation.

FORGING THE SUSSEX LITERARY TRADITION

How did a Sussex literary tradition evolve? We might look first at the context and preconditions for its growth from its seedbed in the eighteenth century, then the later urge to escape and gain self-fulfilment by writers, the importance of London's presence, the processes of authorship, particularly country walking, and the employment of literary devices to illustrate the beauty of their Sussex countryside. Above all, they all struggled, with varying degrees of success, to articulate the affect and emotion of that beauty and its impact upon them as individuals.

Garlanding Downland Verse

Robert Bloomfield, on approaching Worthing, wrote:

> Are these the famed, the brave South Downs,
> That like a chain of pearls appear?
> Their pale-green sides and graceful crowns;
> To freedom, thought and peace, how dear!
> To freedom, for no fence is seen;
> To thought, for silence soothes the way;
> To peace, for o'er the boundless green
> Unnumber'd flocks and shepherds stray.[1]

The South Downs promoted an avalanche of painting and literature and some music throughout the interwar years. This has tended to eclipse completely those who were inspired by the downland earlier. W.H. Hudson rightly remarked in *Nature in Downland* of 'Sussexians' that there had been to that point, 'no genius to stamp its lineaments on our minds'.[2] The Sussex historian M.A. Lower had noted this a generation before and prayed that some literary giant would inform and inspire people worldwide with the magical qualities of the Downs, a prayer answered threefold by the almost simultaneous appearance of Hudson, Kipling and Belloc, and shortly to be followed by Alfred Noyes.

Where Hudson went quite astray, however, was by remarking that earlier the Downs had not figured greatly in artistic and literary imagination:

> Curiously enough, Sussex, or any part of it, can hardly be said to exist in literature; or if it has any place there and in our hearts it is a mean one, far, far, below that of most counties.[3]

Hudson could not have been more wrong. In fact, the corpus of topographical literature from the early eighteenth century is so substantial that the selection of the best amounts to over 150 pages in Taylor's *The Sussex Garland* in 1851.

Through the clergymen poets, one becomes conscious of the depth of the literary tradition around the Sussex Downs. Some of their poetry was execrable or insipid to modern taste, but others so expressive of their neighbourhoods in their profound eighteenth-century calm as to deserve an honourable place in the English tradition of topographical verse before Wordsworth and the Romantic movement. Proud Sussex landowners and country parsons, together with one or two poets of humble origin, such as William Hersee, wrote in blank verse or rhyming couplets about their hills, valleys, fields, woods, and the ways of life long before 1900. C.F. Cook's anthology, *Another Book of Sussex Verse* (1928), for example, includes poems by Blake, Crocker, Gideon Mantell, Mortimer Collins on Brighton, and Charles Townsend's epitaph on Otway, all writers before the mid-nineteenth century.[4]

In this respect, Sussex is quite unlike the Lake District, which hardly figures in literature before Wordsworth. The outpourings of the early imaginative history of the South Downs should be of considerable interest to the student of literature and the social historian for it is an invaluable source of material for unravelling changing attitudes to the environment and the spirit of place, illustrations of what a thinking person *felt* at a particular time about their surroundings. These early literary works are not English national treasures, but we would be poorer spiritually without some knowledge of early writers on the Downs and of the subjects they chose to celebrate.

The early poets wrote with the calm authority of those who had lived long among their landscapes. Venerable men worked in old country rectories by candlelight. They were concerned about their localities' credit, but they avoided hyperbole in praise or distaste, but rather described what they had admired over a lifetime. This is not to deny that the Downs were exempt from the dictates of fashion. The bare, treeless and waterless Downs between Brighton and Beachy Head were unappreciated by fashionable Regency visitors. Dr Johnson detested the 'Brighthelmstone Downs' and was famously quoted as saying, 'It was a country so truly desolate that if one had a mind to hang one's self for desperation at being obliged to live there it would be difficult to find a tree on which to fasten the rope.'[5]

Instead, they were under the thrall of William Gilpin's Picturesque notions: for a scene to be called Picturesque it should be like the work of a great master, Claude Lorrain or Salvator Rosa. John Keats found tourists hunting for the Picturesque 'like beagles' at Shanklin Chine in 1819 but he would have found the Downs around Brighton virtually empty.[6] The anonymous author of *Excursions in the County of Sussex* (1822) warned visitors to Brighton that it had 'a want of trees' and, because of the nature of the chalk soil, it was 'monotonous, and in a degree, even arid' – disadvantages, the author remarked, that only royal patronage could overcome.[7]

However, there is, in fact, little trace of any influence from Gilpin upon the Sussex poets writing at the end of the eighteenth century and into the early nineteenth. They paid no heed to the new rules of taste. Instead, we find Elizabeth Hitchenor praising the wild thyme of Ditchling Beacon in her 'native downs' and the Reverend Charles Dunster of Petworth and Tillington gazing longingly on the Downs' 'steeps sublime' and 'changeful scenery ever new'. They were sensible to the romance of scenery without Gilpin's dogma.

William Hay (1695–1756)

William Hay was a Whig landowner from Glyndebourne, long-serving MP for Seaford and a supporter of the Duke of Newcastle. In his own words, he was a man 'who loved his native country and his friends'. In writing 'Mount Caburn' in 1730, he may justly be considered the father of Sussex verse.

His inspiration came from another hill poem, Sir John Denham's 'Cooper's Hill' (1642), of which, he conceded, his poem was a 'spiritless imitation … a bad copy of the noblest original'. Denham's was the begetter of all English 'descriptive-cum-moralizing' hill poems that became a tradition for more than a century, when climbing a hill to obtain the 'prospect' became part of genteel English taste. Geoffrey Grigson has rightly remarked, of the 300 or so English hill poems, that although most have hardly enough genuine poetry 'to fill an eye-bath', they nevertheless give evidence of the growth of admiration for landscape.[8]

Hay's is possibly the first full English poem portraying the countryside in its own right and was written eighteen years before James Thomson's 'The Seasons' and John Dyer's 'Grongar Hill'. Hay's poem had some eighteenth-century popularity, and it can thus be judged to have spread an appreciation of Sussex scenery. It was anthologised in Taylor's *Sussex Garland* and there is an extract in Cook's *The Book of Sussex Verse*.[9]

Fig. 7: Hay's countryside – Mount Caburn, overlooking Glynde Reach, with the village of Glynde beyond. (*Britain From the Air: The Weald and its Environs* [Macmillan Education Ltd, 1971])

So, Caburn is the first place in Sussex to have inspired the significant creative writing of landscape (Figure 7). As we have discussed, from the summit
of Caburn there is an extended view of the downland landscape. Its summit,
capped by the ramparts of an Iron Age hillfort, soars to no more than 500ft
but the hillfort is visible for miles around. Below lies the Vale of the Brooks,
drained by the Glynde Reach, a little left-bank tributary of the River Ouse,
which is today as agriculturally productive as when Hay wrote his poem.
The slopes of Mount Caburn are threaded with cornfields and pastures,
grazed more by alpacas now than sheep or cattle, and on its eastern flanks
descending gently through the village of Glynde to Glynde Place and the
square-built eighteenth-century church.

Despite writing in the conventional pastoral style of his age, the poem
can still be read with pleasure. He proudly reproduces his birthplace around
Glynde, with its rich agriculture and abundant beauty, and he illustrates his
contemporaries' growing passion for extensive and variegated views, where
beauty and plenty are hand in hand. He extolls a valley golden with corn and
filled with grazing sheep and cattle, a scene that was to him the embodiment
of a good and generous life. Apart from topographical description, he is
quite uninhibited in weaving into his long poem his sketchy history, legends
and folklore. And in bidding farewell to his beloved hill, there is a delicious
sense of irony in his modest hope that a better poet would ultimately do
greater justice to the scene 'in an immortal line', in strains more lasting than
the oaks and as smooth as the currents glide.

Notably, he explicitly celebrates the smoothly configured chalkland and
its springy turf:

Thrice happy mountains! Which no outward Storm,
Or foul Eruptions from within, deform.
No Rocks, like rags in poverty, they wear,
But a rich verdant Mantle through the Year.

Looking down, he muses over the great flocks of sheep and looks benignly
on the labourers:

Beneath me, all around the happy soil,
I see a thousand sturdy mowers toil;
Each seems, from hence, small as the lab'ring ant,
And, like him too, provides for winter's want.

In short, Hay's notion of beauty was never dissociated from that of actual or potential human well-being. Accordingly, he praises his hill and vale, not for their peace and solitude or as a picture gallery or pleasure resort for the visitor, but as the heart of a prosperous and flourishing mixed-farming community of which he was proud to be a member. Furthermore, in addition to writing verse, the preface to Hay's collected works attributes to him experiments in diversifying his fields with walks and plantations and producing silk for Spitalfields from silkworms bred on his estate.[10] He was also an antiquarian, Keeper of the Records in the Tower and, according to an admiring M.A. Lower, 'one of the greatest souls, though enshrined in the smallest of bodies, that it has been the lot of Sussex to produce'.[11]

The Reverend James Hurdis (1763–1801)

To John Betjeman, the Reverend James Hurdis, the friend of the poet Cowper, was the most melodious, observant and interesting of the early English poets.[12] Born in Bishopstone, near Seaford, as a self-confessed 'silent, shame-faced, hesitating boy', he was educated in Chichester before going up to Oxford in 1780.[13] Thanks to his involvement as a tutor with the Pelham family at Stanmer House, he was appointed to the curacy of Burwash, a Pelham living, in 1786 and happily remained there for six years (Figure 8). He lived on Spring Lane in a shallow vale about half a mile north of the village.

Fig. 8: Reverend James Hurdis (1763–1801). ('Anon., 'The Hurdis-Cowper Letters: Some Correspondence of a Sussex Poet'. (*SCM* 1 [2], 1927, p. 317)

His 'Village Curate' (1788) portrays his quiet and cultured life and the three sisters in his household, somewhat in the manner of Cowper's 'The Task', to which he was introduced by William Hayley. To many contemporaries, indeed, he was seen as a pale imitation of Cowper. 'The Village Curate' is, in essence, a love poem to the Burwash Wealden landscape. He shows the beautiful views from his front door, still today small, hedged fields rising to woodland above a little brook, although the hop fields have disappeared and the former open heathland on the ridge has been enclosed and cultivated. He then describes his rooms: the plainly furnished inner room containing half a dozen shelves heavy with books, his violin, and his greatest joy, a battered old harpsichord.

The poem records views of the varied countryside through which he walked with his sisters, using not the public highways but the footpaths across meadows, fields and woods, discovering the full charm of their accompanying wildlife (Plate 4). This remains an enchanting place, with its myriad of droveways and twisting byways, some of them hollow ways with foliage still overarching, which Hurdis thought 'not unlike a cathedral aisle completely roof'd with boughs'.

Hurdis' account appears to be the first record of rural walking in Sussex. He tells us of Burwash Forge, watching cricket and a lively description of the fair on the village street. The parish bells jingled loudly, young men turned out in their 'Sunday frock', Nell tripped along, boys shouted, dogs barked and the 'clam'rous drum called to the puppet show'. There was a dancing girl, a quack, a juggler and other amusements for children and infants in a street full of booths and stalls for gingerbread and beer.

Hurdis did not approve of all the goings-on. He was most concerned at his fellow countrymen's indifference to his fellow creatures, savagely denouncing their hunting in the autumn when 'the fields are thronged with licenced murderers who slay for sport'.[14] He would later also free wheatears that had been trapped by downland shepherds, leaving coins in their place.

But he says nothing otherwise of the darker and harder sides of life in the rumbustious parish of his day. For the other side of the story, we need to read John Coker Egerton, a later incumbent of Burwash, who noted that 'as far as wood and hill and dale could give contentment he [Hurdis] had it here, no doubt to a high degree'. But Egerton himself offers a more realistic impression of Burwash life in mid- and late-Victorian times.[15]

In 1791, he was appointed to the living at Bishopstone, but the following year he was devastated by the death of his favourite sister Catherine. This was followed in 1793 by his appointment as Professor of Poetry at Magdalen College Oxford. In April 1800, shortly before his death, he self-published 'The Favourite Village', a eulogy of his birthplace and the downland, often seen as his best work.[16]

This still unspoilt downland village, which has shrunk since Hurdis' time, lies in a shallow vale in a cul-de-sac. His family home was Little Halland (later enlarged and Gothicised), in the hamlet of Norton, then known as Norton Cottage. Hurdis takes us past the village pond and along his beloved elms, a sawyer's pit, the church, the Pelham mansion (demolished in 1831 but

with silent cellars and walled garden visible as late as 1947) and past several
cottages to his own house where he was born, and up to the 'brow of brows'
rising above the loose string of tenements.

   Much detail was included on the farming, customs, flora and fauna.
Although socially removed from his flock, he was clearly fond of them. He
watches dancing at the harvest festival and listens to the sound:

> Of the brisk viol challenging the foot.
> And of the foot respondent, and to see
> The village maid and village hind alert
> Pacing the giddy labyrinth of joy,
> Each in the trim of holiday attir'd.

He also gives vivid detail of the farming:

> … Let the slow team
> Of steers reluctant pressing on the yoke.
> With down-sunk forehead and depending tongue,
> With winding shoulders and slow-pacing foot,
> Pant as it ploughs along the mountain side…

The public reception of Hurdis' poetry was extraordinary. His sisters
published a posthumous collected edition in 1808 with over 1,200 subscribers, including the queen and seven princesses, and 200 signatories from
Sussex alone. Another edition appeared in 1810.

   His strengths as a poet were summed up in 1838 by Robert Willmott,
who wrote, 'His poetical merit is to be sought for only in the truth of his
descriptions of scenery, and rustic employments.'[17] He died in December
1801, and an imposing memorial tablet was erected in Bishopstone Church
with an epitaph by William Hayley (Plate 5).[18]

Charlotte Smith (1749–1806)

Charlotte Smith (née Turner) was initially educated in Chichester and
genteelly brought up in London and at Bignor Park near Petworth (Figure
9). But her father, following her mother's death, squandered his inheritances,
leaving Charlotte and two siblings in some poverty. She was unsuccessfully
married, at still not quite 15, to the violent and profligate Benjamin Smith

in 1765 becoming, in her own later words, 'a legal prostitute' and the victim of 'personal slavery'. She began to write professionally in the humiliating circumstances of her husband's debts and mismanagement.

Mismarried and misplaced, she drew from considerable literary gifts and, in her own words, existed 'to live only to write and write only to live', in order to provide for her large family. She bore twelve children, of whom only six survived her. Fortunately, she found a champion in William Hayley, the prominent patron and poet of Eartham, who introduced her to the publisher of her first volume of poetry, *Elegiac Sonnets* (1784). This was written while staying with her husband in King's Bench debtor's prison.[19]

Fig. 9: 'Charlotte Smith (née Turner)' by Samuel Freeman, after George Romney stipple engraving, published 1808. (NPG D17828)

Her fame was instant and the poems went through repeated editions. The family fled to France to escape further debtors, returning to England the following year and moving to Woolbeding House near Midhurst (Plate 6). However, the marriage deteriorated and, in 1787, she left her adulterous husband but had to wait for a settlement of her father-in-law's will, which was to help provide for her and her family but only materialised after her death.

She turned her hand to children's as well as adult books, a play, translations and fiction. In all, she wrote nine novels, including *The Manor House*, now regarded as her best. A second collection of *Elegiac Sonnets* appeared in 1797 and two long Sussex poems followed. A sense of her 'Sussexness' was always central to her entire being, drawing on her childhood memories in the South Downs.

Charlotte Smith is a significant writer in several respects. Her poetry speaks of suffering and painful melancholy. For this, she did something new according to an old recipe. She revived the sonnet, influencing Wordsworth and Keats, and writing in a style and with subject matter that now reveals her as among the first Romantics, a fact that Wordsworth himself acknowledged.[20] Indeed, although poor, she mixed with other early Romantics such as Coleridge, Cowper, Hayley and Mary Wollstonecraft, as well as celebrated painters, such as George Smith of Chichester and George Romney.[21]

Drawing on the Sussex landscape, her principal theme in the *Elegiac Sonnets*, and one reappearing in her other poems, is the contrast between her carefree and leisured childhood on the heaths and the Arun or gliding between flowery meadows and the South Downs near Bignor Park, compared with her almost penniless circumstances and despair in adulthood:

> I once was happy when while yet a child
> I learn'd to love these upland solitudes, ...[22]

But later:

> So many years have pass'd,
> Since, on my native hills, I learn'd to gaze
> On these delightful landscapes; and those years
> Have taught me so much sorrow, that my soul
> Feels not the joy reviving Nature brings;
> But, in dark retrospect, dejected dwells ...[23]

She doubts whether the South Downs can ever again bring peace to her troubled mind. She envies the woodmen and the shepherds, whom she regards (unrealistically) as happy and carefree and reveals an extraordinary knowledge of botany. The banks of the Arun come alive with yellow broom and silver birch, willow herb and flags sheltering the reed birds. Unusually for her generation, she also sees beauty in the heath and is knowledgeable about the wildflowers of the chalk, including the various orchids. In addition, she was a talented botanical artist and had an interest in downland geology and archaeology.

In a further development, she also took up a political stance, which must have surprised and probably angered many of her erstwhile genteel supporters and, coming from a woman, was incomprehensible, indeed insufferable. She particularly identified with the French émigrés and 'The Female Exile' was 'written at Brighthelmstone in 1792' and apparently set in Newhaven.[24] Book 1 of *The Emigrants*, written in November 1792, opens on the cliffs east of Brighton, where she compares the fate of the 'wandering wretches, hapless, homeless, friendless' with her own fate, arguing that the much-vaunted freedom, justice and liberty in England is a sham. Even in the view from the cliffs she sees evidence of class warfare in the trees hiding the parish church, 'with care conceal'd/ by verdant foliage, lest the poor man's grave/

Should mar the smiling prospect of the lord'. She compared the shepherd's and the labourer's lot with the parasites who giddily scorn those who are, in reality, superior in worth.

Her aim is to escape from all this and retreat to her native West Sussex downland:

> How often do I half-abjure Society,
> And sigh for some lone Cottage, deep embower'd
> In the green woods, that these steep chalky Hills
> Guard from the strong South-West; where round their base
> The Beach [beech] wide flourishes, and the light Ash
> With slender leaf half hides the thymy turf![25]

'Beachy Head', her last work, which has Wordsworthian influences from his 'Tintern Abbey', is a prospect poem in blank verse (Figure 10). She alternates between South Downs and Weald, the coast and the heath, and muses on history in this 'local poem'. In the pure air on Beachy Head, with the sound of the sea pounding on the cliffs, the harsh cry of the sea birds and the shepherd's baying dog, she surveys the vast expanses of hill and vale and avows that all this is worth more than the sophisticated human society of her age with its 'vague theories, or vain dispute' of science or 'the polluted smoky atmosphere and dark and stifling streets'.

She champions the Sussex peasant in an organic society in the manner of the young Wordsworth – the simple rustics, their humble homes and charming cottage gardens, despite struggling to live on the flinty soil.

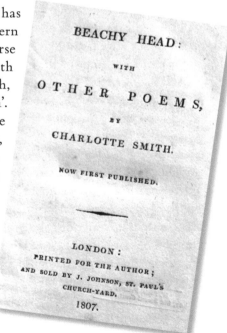

Fig. 10: Charlotte Smith, *Beachy Head: With Other Poems*, published posthumously in 1807.

These Arcadian subjects are compared in their (supposed) contentment with 'the child of luxury/ Enjoying nothing, flies from place to place/ In chase of pleasure that eludes his grasp'.

It is in this poem that she details, again with remarkable Wordsworthian overtones, her passion for nature in childhood:

An early worshipper at Nature's shrine;
I loved her rudest scenes – warrens, and heaths,
And yellow commons, and birch-shaded hollows,
And hedge rows, bordering unfrequented lanes
[…]
I loved to trace the brooks whose humid banks
Nourish the harebell, and the freckled pagil;
And stroll among o'ershadowing woods of beech.

And the flora of the chalk turf is knowledgeably described:

While in the breeze
That wafts the thistle's plumed seed along,
Blue bells wave tremulous. The mountain thyme
Purples the hassock of the heaving mole,
And the short turf is gay with tormentil,
And bird's foot trefoil, and the lesser tribes
Of hawkweed; spangling it with fringed stars.

Her novel *The Old Manor House* (1793) is focused on a large landed estate near her childhood home at Bignor.[26] It is again infused with her sense of a deterioration in government and public life since the halcyon days of her youth as a result of misgovernment, corruption and pauperisation. Her aristocrats are mainly dissolute rakes, lawyers are despicable rogues, and her churchmen vain nepotists. In her general disillusionment, she sides with the Americans in their War of Independence and hints that reforms in France won by insurgents could well be applied to England.

During the last twenty years of her life, she moved frequently, with a general restlessness but also to avoid creditors and as her health fluctuated. Her homes included Chichester, Brighton, Storrington and Frant, and ended at Tilford, Surrey, where she died. Her poetic melancholy is reflected in her monument in Stoke Church across the River Wey near Guildford, which recalls 'a life of great and various sufferings'. This is where she had been baptised in 1749.

Walter Scott wrote that she 'preserves in her landscapes the truth and precision of a painter' and it was also claimed that she was the first to include sustained natural description in novels.[27] And certainly the combination of interior subjectivity with external realities and Sussex environments was an important legacy left to the early Romantic writers.

It must be admitted that much of the verse by the three poets above, like that of its period generally, is dull to modern taste, and therefore unread. But there is little doubt that Charlotte Smith had much success in inspiring her generation about the Downs. In their time, she and Hurdis were regarded as significant and influential poets, the former being accounted one of the best, as well as one of the first, of the Romantic poets. Wordsworth prophetically remarked that she would be 'a lady to whom English verse is under greater obligations than are likely to be either acknowledged or remembered'. She is now becoming better known but her contribution to landscape literature remains largely unrecognised today.

The Preconditions for a Sussex Literature, 1850–1939

The sky is cloudy, yellowed by the smoke.
For view there are the houses opposite
Cutting the sky with one long line of wall
Like solid fog: far as the eye can stretch
Monotony of surface & of form
Without a break to hang a guess upon.
No bird can make a shadow as it flies,
For all is shadow
...
No figure lingering
Pauses to feed the hunger of the eye
Or rest a little on the lap of life.
All hurry on & look upon the ground,
Or glance unmarking at the passers by ...[28]

Most migrants into Sussex by the early twentieth century were stressed towns-people who regarded the city as alienating and were wanting, perhaps at a turning point in their lives, to search for a better society and a better world.

There were the 'push' factors: the worsening conditions of smoke, fog, noise and the incredible filth and pollution. Some hated the unrelenting mechanistic and materialistic atmosphere of modern technology and inter-national capitalism. Even more deeply, as Henry Williamson noted in his autobiographical novels of life in south London, there was a foreboding that people had lost basic human instincts that were now buried under the superimposed industrial civilisation.

Then there were the 'pull' factors: the careworn also felt estranged from natural life owing to the remorseless urbanisation. For those who could afford it, the countryside beckoned, with a seemingly more acceptable moral and social atmosphere. An older experience of time might also be found since, as Richard Jefferies had found, the open spaces immediately on the edge of the capital, although in their way beautiful and richer in wildlife than he had expected, nevertheless left something wanting. The city still exerted a restlessness, and for this reason, he explained, he had added a concluding chapter on the far-away 'lovely downs that overlook the south coast' to his book.[29]

By 1850, many townspeople had come to believe that it was harmful to an individual, and the nation generally, for mankind to be bereft of the spontaneous activity of nature and natural beauty. Instead, opposite tendencies seemed to prevail. J.S. Mill saw human beings, in his well-known phrase, as 'struggling to get on, trampling, crushing, elbowing and treading on each other's heels'.[30] A tremendous rural walker in his youth, he also deplored the prospect that every single yard of English soil would be brought under cultivation.

This mood was intensified by the physical, mental and moral strains of the First World War. Many were traumatised by the experience of appalling slaughter, and after any turmoil and public strife there has generally been a longing for the quiet of rural peace, continuity and homely things. And when the future is uncertain, minds turn to the perceived certainties of the past. Veterans in the aftermath of war conceived of Sussex as a 'Promised Land' where they could pick up life anew; a mood reflected in the tremendous literary output on the landscape and traditions of the county between around 1900 and 1939 and aimed specifically at urban readers.

Also sharing this craving for countryside were worried people during the violence and insecurity of the interwar years – the epidemics that followed the war, the revolutions, the break-up of states, the financial collapse of 1929 and consequent mass unemployment, the rise of autocratic dictatorships, war in Europe and the threat of more to come. To those who needed cheering in an atmosphere that was tense, jumpy and apprehensive, Sussex was a sanctuary, at least for a time. As Charques noted in 1936, to be in Sussex one was delivered from both portents of ruin and theories of Utopia, and far away from war and rumours of war.[31]

Writers' Self-fulfilment in the Age of Anxiety

Writers migrating into Sussex sought to free themselves from the spiritually dislocated world of the Age of the Machine and to seek self-fulfilment where humanitarian concerns took precedence over technological advancement. Of course, this was no new development. Ever since around 1800, when the poet-visionary Blake in his Felpham period had a vision of angels ascending and descending over the South Downs in his quest for inspiration away from London, several generations of authors had taken a similar road and for the same purpose. Blake epitomised such feelings, 'Great things are done when men and mountains meet; This is not done by jostling in the street.'[32]

Whereas most townspeople were caught up in routine and the need to earn a living, writers were freer agents. Central to their aspirations was to live more in tune with nature, and hopefully to aspire to write better and secure a growing reputation. In this manner, Sussex became a principal locus for writers. Some doubtless deceived themselves, but the majority appear to have found what they sought, achieving a daily existence that could be cherished for its own sake and which, to them, was a more moral way of living. Mostly, they secured the pleasurable self-fulfilment sought by one of the disaffected, Habberton Lulham:

> What do we ask of you, and asking find?
> That which the glittering cities may not give,
> What in the fields of flowers can never live,
> Nor in the hurrying season leave behind
> Unchanging shelter from the blast unkind
> Refuge and solitude for the unquiet mind.[33]

To many authors, Sussex was the landscape of their dreams. The magic was in the sudden transformation. It was like being born anew into an atmosphere of carefree charm in its 'South Saxon' sleep, in a timelessness that seemingly amounted almost to stasis. The Sussex countryside offered a gateway to a new existence where, in those 'dear little villages under the Downs', for example, or at the sea, they could begin life anew. It symbolised a very English idea of Elysium as a place of transcendent magic. And to late Victorians and Edwardians, Sussex was like a different country, with different folk (but not too many), and as unspoilt, remote and mysterious as de la Mare's 'Arabia'.[34] Ralph Vaughan Williams could claim, following his return from the Sussex/Surrey borderlands, where he had been collecting folk song and music in 1912, 'I am like a psychical researcher who has actually seen a ghost, for I have been among the more primitive people of England and have noted down their songs.'[35]

Such inspirational and restorative effects attracted artists who abandoned historical painting in London for *plein-air* landscapes in London's countryside, together with wealthy industrialists from the Midlands and the north, who saw country living as a social grace where they could consume the countryside rather than grindingly accumulating money. This immersion by incoming writers and poets gave wings to their imagination.

Before the Second World War, the scratch of their pens or click of their typewriters was heard almost uninterruptedly in every village and small town. Sussex literally floated in a sea of words. Ditchling dramatist Amy Sawyer declared Sussex to be 'the Thing' and said its literary efforts put together would circle the globe twice. With the same pardonable exaggeration, G.K. Chesterton described a visit to neighbouring Kent in 1904, 'which looked ancient and innocent enough', but:

> This green England of ours is really bursting with literary men. Short story writers leap from behind hedges, minor poets drop from the trees like ripe fruit; you cannot walk through deep grass without stumbling over Sociologists. I have met in meadows here some of the most beautiful and terrible people of Fleet Street. I have seen a cottage, decent and quiet on the outside, inside which, as I hope for Heaven, there were Burne-Jones's on the wall. In short, we are in the presence of a peculiar phenomenon. The people are not going 'back to the land' but the cultivated classes are.
>
> But there is something about these intellectual people in flannel shirts who come out and live in the country, where they play tennis and read Thoreau which gives me a haunting notion that they do not really belong to the country; they dwell rather than live in it.
>
> Now this is very false.[36]

When *The Poetry Review* published a Sussex number in 1921, 300 poems were submitted for inclusion and a little later it was remarked in the same journal that it was normal to receive on the same day two volumes of Sussex poems, since 'for more than those of any county in England have the beauties of Sussex been sung by poets'. Nor was all this magazine stuff – the Sussex Poetry Society in the mid-1920s, of which Belloc was at one time president, was addressed by John Masefield, Edith Sitwell, Robert Graves, John Freeman and Helen Thomas.

Sussex as London's 'Other' Beyond the Smoke

In the early nineteenth century, Heinrich Heine wrote:

> Send a philosopher to London, but no poet! Send a philosopher there, and
> stand him at a corner of Cheapside, he will learn more there than from all
> the books of the last Leipzig fair; and as the human waves roar around him,
> so will a sea of new thoughts rise before him ... But send no poet to London!
>   This downright earnestness of all things, this colossal uniformity, this
> machine-like movement, this moroseness even in pleasure, this exaggerated
> London, smothers the imagination and rends the heart.[37]

As we have seen, the Sussex landscape would not have acquired its heightened
charm, nor would its literature have blossomed as it did, without the sharp
contrast with its 'other', the crowded, noisy, precincts of the conurbation of
London, acting as a foil on its borders. And nor could it have flourished but
for the peculiar English passion for nature that Ford Madox Ford called in the
1920s the 'cat-dog-wild-bird, wild-flower obsession' that was missing in his new
quarters in Provence. Understandably, therefore, Sussex writers did not get on
with their metropolitan cousins: their feelings for London and other big cities
were always at most equivocal, never very deep, and generally denunciatory.

Instead, their two main themes, the rural environment and their place in
nature, were two concepts emanating from a way of life that writers held to
be of more profound and lasting value. Their imagination was stimulated by
the four main nature elements in Sussex – the sun, the sea, the Downs and
the Weald – each seen to be singularly wild and untampered.

The high priest of the Sussex summer was Richard Jefferies, with his
intense reverence for the 'alchemic, intangible mysterious power' of the sun's
rays, the inspiration for his autobiographical *Story of my Heart*, which tells
of his devotion to the joys of physical existence.[38] And the sea also called to
him, as also to Hilaire Belloc, as we shall see.

The third Sussex element, the Downs, were seen by many as a refuge.
This was certainly the case for the young Edward Carpenter, who initially
knew of no society other 'than that which loafed along the Brighton parade
and tittle-tattled in drawing rooms'. Walter Wilkinson, the travelling Punch
and Judy puppeteer, was so inspired in 1935 by the idea of migrating 'like
sagacious locusts from the place we helped to impoverish' that he took the
road from Storrington towards the Downs, where life to him seemed more
possible, and looked out to the Weald, the fourth element:

We were in the heavens, looking down on a toy, miniature world that was all beauty, and light and colour, a world of loveliness in which all men might live had they but the good taste to embrace it.[39]

Fresh country air was unbesmirched with poisoned city smoke. Henry Williamson's reference to 'smoke drifting from the factories ... and the acid dust in the atmosphere, which hung low with fog from the Thames and slowly poisoned the leaves of the oak. So it was stunted, fighting all the time for pure air' constitutes some of the most evocative description of polluted air in the English language.[40] Contrastingly, Maynard Keynes, writing of his country house at Tilton, near Lewes, reported, 'There is no better air than here for work' and also to unwind and see friends.[41] Little wonder that Sussex writers celebrated the prevailing south-west wind, the only wind not charged with soot, with an almost religious devotion.

The Footpath Way to Literature

To walk on hills is to employ legs
As porters of the head and heart
Jointly adventuring towards
Perhaps true equanimity.[42]

Before the meteoric rise of Manchester, Mrs Gaskell could write in *Mary Barton* of cotton-mill operatives strolling out from their homes to nearby open spaces on summer evenings and at weekends.[43] But Henry David Thoreau cited James Wilkinson, a surgeon, who remarked in 1851 that the inhabitants of the larger English towns were confined for walking almost exclusively to public parks and the highways, because footpaths 'were gradually vanishing under the encroachments of the proprietors'. Wilkinson stressed the importance of providing places for exercise, where pure air and pleasant sights could be found around large towns, but compared strolling in a town park with vigorous walking in the countryside, 'a very different tension of mind and muscle'. He pressed for the statutory designation and mapping of footpaths so that they 'would open new energies of health to the people' and become their rightful inalienable possession. He concluded that 'the whole neighbourhood of towns is a public park ready-made, if only the paths were duly administered'. Thoreau commented that no citizens on the globe could be so limited for walking for pleasure.[44]

In 1851 the national census recorded that, for the first time, a slight majority of the British population lived in towns. Such news was greeted by some with alarm, as many urban areas were already seen by public and philanthropic groups as unhealthy for mind, body and morality. Fresh air and space for recreation was needed and would provide civilising influences. So, in 1865 the Committee on London Commons was formed to enquire into the preservation for the public of the forests, commons and open spaces within 15 miles of London. In the same year, the Commons Preservation Society (CPS) was formed, and in the following year, the Metropolitan Commons Act was passed. The CPS aimed to enhance appreciation of the commons and spaces for public leisure and recreation, rather than for their economic value to local commoners or to the lord of the manor, who might seek enclosure and/or building development.

Long before this, we find the poet-walker Hurdis who, as we have seen, preferred to stroll in the field paths, woods and hop grounds at Burwash rather than in the 'boasted' London gardens of Ranelagh and Vauxhall. Many of his successors were equally enthusiastic walkers whose maxim to 'jog on, jog on, the footpath way' in a landscape threaded with more footpaths than most meant as much to them as it had to Shakespeare.[45]

In the Sussex countryside one could walk freely, fast and far, especially on the great expanse of springy turf on the South Downs, while the Weald was threaded with myriad footpaths and bridleways that opened up its secret places. The third edition of the one-inch Ordnance Survey map, published from 1903 and a masterpiece of world cartography, exquisitely showed in colour much new information for the walker. The diversity of terrain and its corresponding soils meant that a walk could be taken in any direction according to the season when it would be most pleasurable.[46] The many subscribers to the enthusiasm for the open air meant that it became almost a national passion in the interwar years. Ramblers and cyclists abounded at the weekends over much of rural Britain (Plate 7).

Outdoor enthusiasm and literature worked together: one landmark had come in 1844 when James Thorne noted that in large cities almost all the 'care-worn sons of toil' became overwrought, their mind and body overstrained and enervated, unless they sought renewed health and vigour by leisurely walking in the countryside. To assist them, he devised a walk along the Rivers Adur and Arun, then relatively unknown to the tourist, as examples of accessible countryside with a variety of beautiful scenery (Figure 11).

Fig. 11: Bramber Castle. (James Thorne, *Rambles by Rivers: The Duddon, the Mole, the Adur, Arun, and Wey, the Lea*, 1844, p. 67)

Two years later came Gideon Mantell's book on walking in and around Lewes, the first recorded walking guide to the Downs. From Mount Caburn looking onto the Ouse Valley:

> Let us sit down on this verdant tumulus, and briefly consider the nature of those physical changes, by which this chasm through the South Downs has been partially filled up and converted into the rich alluvial pastures now smiling at our feet, and covered with flocks and herds.[47]

A little later, and also prominent in this respect, were Louis J Jennings' *Field Paths and Green Lanes* (1877) followed up by *Rambles on Southern Hills* (1888), both principally concerned with the South Downs and the first books written for jaded walkers from London or some big town, keeping to footpaths and bridleways rather than the increasingly busy highways.

By 1900, the Victorian and Edwardian intelligentsia had been practising 'muscular Christianity', with the conviction that the duty of man was to fear God and walk many miles in a day. There now came a flood of books on walking and songs of the open road, which coincided with the spread of leisure walking among a wider population escaping from what Sydney Smith had called the 'city-poison'. These included Edward Thomas' edited *Pocket Book of Poems and Songs of the Open Road* (1907), Hilaire Belloc's edited *The Footpath Way* (1911) and Sir Arthur Conan Doyle's *Songs of the Road* (1911) with thirty-three poems. Later, in the 1930s, S.P.B. Mais' organised walks for young people living in London made him the supremo of Sussex walkers (see page 201–2).

The exploration of the southern countryside was undertaken in many different ways. Sir Leslie Stephen, author, mountaineer and father of Virginia Woolf, was a founder member of the 'Sunday Tramps' active from 1879 to 1895. The 'Tramps' were:

[U]nited by a late Victorian intellectual vigor, affiliated with many other clubs and groups of the age. While the act of strolling and engaging in intellectual dialogue was an accepted Victorian pursuit, walking past churches and cathedrals on a Sunday was a direct challenge to accepted behavior of the period.[48]

Stephen felt that 'the author is but the incidental appendage of the tramp'.[49] And quite differently, others might come in family outings, perhaps to one of the burgeoning tea rooms dotting around Sussex, and perhaps by charabanc. But by contrast, the poet and writer-walker tended to move and observe nature in solitude, becoming acquainted with objects animate and inanimate that allured and enthralled, as Thomas Hardy had suggested was a prerequisite for a contented life in the country.[50] And so walkers explored, with their legs as well as eyes, the 'spirit' of a country in the best possible way.

R.L. Stevenson neatly observed that 'clear vision goes with a quick foot'.[51] Here was a footpath way to literature gained through sturdy legs and long strides.[52] Galsworthy, in his sixties, strode across the Downs as briskly as when a young man. And Edmund Gosse has left a vivid impression of meeting poet Coventry Patmore on the Parade at Hastings. Gosse kept up by trotting beside him. In Patmore's mid-fifties he had moved to Hastings and this had revitalised him:

His imagination, his mystical and his religious vitalities were simultaneously quickened, and he walked along the sea by Hastings, or over its gorse-clad downs, muttering as a young man mutters, with joy uplifting his pulses and song breaking from his lips.[53]

There are many other examples: Habberton Lulham's 'South Downs', a record of his journey on foot from Ditchling to Amberley; Richard

Jefferies' walks over chalkland in Wiltshire and Sussex exploring prehistoric landscapes; Wilfrid Scawen Blunt, walking on his Crabbet Park estate near Crawley and standing to muse on those generations of farmworkers who had passed that very spot in the making of the beloved landscape. John Halsham appears to have walked daily, returning to his study to write up his impressions of the mid-Sussex Weald, which became *Idlehurst* (1898). Virginia Woolf, noted down ideas caught 'hot and sudden' while meandering on afternoon downland walks.

John Burroughs truly wrote:

> No one else looks out upon the world so kindly and charitably as the pedestrian; no one else gives and takes so much from the country he passes through. Next to the laborer in the fields, the walker holds the closest relation to the soil; and he holds a closer and more vital relation to Nature because he is freer and his mind more at leisure.[54]

We might finally confess that not all walking was joyful. There were those whose outlook on life made it difficult to take in the beauty of the downland. The depressive Scotsman John Davidson (1857–1909), coming to stay in Shoreham in 1898 to escape from the claustrophobia of London, suffered a breakdown and spent many hours walking by himself on the Downs. Styling himself as the itinerant wanderer, he published 'On the Downs' in the *Speaker* and 'Eclogue on the Downs' shortly afterwards, in which three men walk to the Fox and Hounds in Steyning while debating the nature of suffering. He could appreciate the downland winds but regarded Shoreham as 'doleful'.[55]

The Sound of Silence in the Beauty of Sussex

One of the important factors in the promotion of well-being, and a recurrent theme contributing to the Sussex literary tradition during the interwar years, was an overpowering and bewildering blissful silence, sorely needed in an ever more frenetic and noisy world. Poets such as Andrew Young made their silences more silent by creating just the right atmosphere and a choice of vowels, consonants and cadences. The loafer is alone in the noonday stillness with the breeze, a vista and the blue sky in a 'holy calm' in which all vestiges of sordid humanity have disappeared. Prone on their back on the springy downland turf, they hear only the carolling of skylarks and a tinkling of bells from distant flocks, and at night:

How peaceful and magnificent it was to stand in darkness in a quietly breathing night under great glimmering of stars and immense prospects and to hear, of all this fussy world, only tiny, far-way sounds hardly louder than the bursting of bubbles.[56]

The summits of the pre-war South Downs in particular, then almost devoid of people, seem to have embodied silence and any human noise came from workers in the coombes. Nowadays, all has changed: one seems never to see anyone working in the hollows, but instead meets scores of ramblers on the heights. The great sense of freedom, and to some extent, silence, is no longer there.

To an urban readership, who had rarely experienced silence, this provided healing and consolation. The soft sounds such as the wind coursing through woods, mysterious cracklings in the undergrowth, the calls of birds, muffled wings and bats flitting down a village street, or the faintest tinkling of sheep bells, were scarcely sounds at all, in fact, rather 'silence dying'. Such rare, still hours gripped heart and mind. Thus, inaction and contentment with small pleasures came to be part of the tradition of Sussex verse.

A sustained poem on downland silence and repose before thunder is Laurence Binyon's 'Thunder on the Downs' (Figure 12):

Wide earth, wide heaven, and in the summer air
Silence! The summit of the Down is bare
Between the climbing crests of wood; but those
Great sea-winds, wont, when the wet South-West blows,
To rock tall beeches and strong oaks aloud
And strew torn leaves upon the streaming cloud,
To-day are idle, slumbering far aloof.
Under the solemn height and gorgeous roof
Of cloud-built sky, all earth is indolent.
Wandering hum of bees and thymy scent
Of the short turf enrich pure loneliness;
Scarcely an airy topmost-twining tress
Of bryony quivers where the thorn it wreathes;
Hot fragrance from the honeysuckle breathes.

As his eye wanders the wide land below, his heart 'breathes heavenly space' and he cries with patriotic pride, 'And this is England'.[57]

Fig. 12: Laurence Binyon
(1869–1943) in 1934.
(NPG x10379)

Metaphor and Iconography

In searching for the ways in which the Sussex literary tradition was established, we might note that the landscape itself has long been seen as a cultural and symbolic presence. 'Meanings' would be attached and layers of memory built up over time, such that it has become popular to speak of 'reading the landscape' to decode its meanings, and to perceive landscape as representing particular cultural traits. The symbolism of eighteenth-century woodland with its 'hearts of oak' and 'wooden walls' as bulwarks against foreign aggressors is just one example, and the White Cliffs of Dover yet another.[58] And some literary landscapes are humanised to some degree, such that one remembers the gaunt face of Egdon Heath in Hardy's *The Return of the Native* almost as another character within the novel. Landscape here is not just the stage, but integral and at the heart of a story.

Within Sussex literature such traits were long apparent. Metaphor might be used to shape feelings about the landscape by asserting some similarity between a landscape feature and something else. It can convey a frisson, jolting us to consider a landscape differently. There was, for example, the perception of the swelling contours of the Downs, shaped in the curves of human-like forms.

Gilbert White of Selborne noted that the South Downs 'swell and heave their broad backs into the sky so much above the less animated clay of the wild below', and 'the shapely figured aspect of chalk hills', which were 'analagous to growth in their gentle swellings'.[59] The downland was being humanised and the sinuous convex and concave curves, gave the effect of classical nudes. Eric Ravilious constructed a landscape incorporating such muscular combes on Firle Beacon (Plate 8). W.H. Hudson likened the contours to the 'solemn slope of mighty limbs asleep'.

There were many such anthropomorphic allusions, and they were not confined to male writers. Eleanor Farjeon envisaged the Downs as maternal, 'rounded and dimpled like human beings, dimpled like babies, rounded like women. The flow of their lines is like the breathing of a sleeper; you can almost see the tranquil heaving of a bosom.'[60]

Anthony Mario Ludovici's poem 'The South Downs' evoked their shapely forms more explicitly:

Amid the roar of the wind and surf,
Beneath their skins of springy turf,
Tight-fitting to their mighty shapes,
Their deep thyme-scented breath escapes.

They sleep, these giants, side by side,
Their breast right steep, their buttocks wide,
Their arms enlocked, their legs entwined,
Vast rolling leagues of wench and hind.

Patched o'er with brambles, heather, hawth,
Nor heeding man's small joys and wrath,
They've lain serenely in the sun
Since ever England was begun.

And, 'neath the gossamer that takes
Its sluggish flight as daylight breaks,
I almost see a god's great hand
Stretched down to stroke this sweep of land.

Were I a god, and loved smooth skin
Not less but more than anything,
I, too, would drop my hand at night
And stroke those hills until the light.[61]

Many recent scholars have drawn attention to the historical (and contemporary) ubiquity of the 'male gaze' and problematised the sense of male empowerment over females and also over the environment. Such issues went unrecognised historically.[62]

Somewhat differently, poets, as well as visitors, saw a personification of the South Downs in the legendary long-striding shepherd with his keen eye and noble independence (Plate 9). They were an iconic presence. As shepherds and their flocks dwindled from the early nineteenth century so did sentiment for them increase in inverse proportion.

The emblematic shepherd and his flock came, indeed, to symbolise much about steadiness, care and hardiness. As late as 1938, the 16th Duke of Norfolk suggested that the man who was really Sussex was the shepherd, integral to the Downs for 6,000 years or more, a permanent thing in an unstable world. People thrilled at the thought that the shepherd's job, in taking his flock up onto the Downs by day and bringing them down at nightfall to fold on the farm, and spending nights with the sheep at lambing time, was the self-same routine as that of the Old Testament shepherds. The solitary cloaked shepherd standing motionless on some high hillside, his dog at heel, guarding his flock, together with the music of the sheep bells and the crushed scent of thyme, became symbolic of a countryside of the mind up to 1939, which was everything that modern industrial society was not – ancient, stable, slow-moving and spiritual. Sussex was richer culturally as a result.

A most vivid portrait is Alfred Noyes' of 'Old Bramble', a shepherd he met before the First World War:

Now, five years later, while the larks went up
Over the dew-ponds in a wild-winged glory,
And all the Sussex downs, from weald to sea,
Were patched like one wide crazy quilt, in squares
Of yellow and crimson, clover and mustard-flower,
Edged with white chalk, I found him once again.
He leaned upon his crook, unbudged by war,
Unchanged, and leering eagerly as of old.

How should I paint old Bramble the shrewd face,
Brown as the wrinkled loam, the bright brown eyes,
The patriarchal beard, the moleskin cap,
The boots that looked like tree-stumps, the loose cloak
Tanned by all weathers, every inch of him

A growth of Sussex soil. His back was bent
Like wind-blown hawthorn, turning from the sea,
With roots that strike the deeper.
[…]
'Marnin',' he said; and swept away five years.[63]

The Challenge of a Transient Beauty

The ways in which transient Sussex beauty might be caught and expressed in words has challenged generations of writers. Some have declared themselves inadequate to convey landscape in the shifting light of the hour and season, however fast they worked. As we have seen (p.26) Arthur Bell thought that, even by combining all the arts, a full idea of Sussex beauty would not be achieved.[64] Certainly, with a setting sun and an evening calm, many views had a quality of quietness, peace, humility and pathos which could not be caught in words.

The fact that transient beauty was only partly revealed was a problem taken up by John Halsham. In the course of his solitary walks, he was the first Sussex writer to engage with the shifting light of day and season. He describes sudden changes such as a countryside growing progressively darker on an autumnal evening, the breeze driving wheat across fields in elastic curves, the curled crest of a thunder cloud lifting above a downland ridge, light striking on water in disused marl pits and the sunset glow on long light evenings. Indeed, he thought it strange if he could see a landscape twice in the same mood when he went outdoors. In 'Nightfall', the concluding chapter to *Old Standards*, we see him walking home at sunset in fading light, noting the peculiar light produced in a blackbird's bright black eye, the faint bars on its dark breast feathers and the translucent gold-brown of its half-spread wings, and how a foxglove swayed a little at the stroke of the bird's wings and, as it caught the light, showed the paler speckle through the purple of its bell. A little later darkness had fallen.[65]

Virginia Woolf was also much intrigued by capturing the transience of beauty. In her diary, she repeatedly records her surprised rapture at beauty encountered on her journeys through Sussex and of her failure, despite her own extraordinary powers of description, to convey it. 'I cannot hold this – I cannot express this – I am overcome by it – I am mastered,' she wrote on a journey back to Rodmell from Bexhill. In her essay 'Evening over Sussex: Reflections in a Motor Car', she recalls travelling through a beautiful landscape and noting how the veil of evening obliterated buildings and their people, leaving what remained as an outline of 'what there was when William came over from France ten centuries ago'. But then the vision collapsed completely. She resented being overcome by beauty extravagantly greater than she had expected and which was escaping from her all the time at 'one's right hand, one's left; at one's back too'. She registered her impotence at capturing so little so that another person could share it.[66]

Establishing a Tradition

The most obvious trait that developed in the Sussex literary tradition was the unrestrained enjoyment expressed at release from the city to get into the enchanted Sussex countryside. Thus Charles Dalmon:

> I longed to see my Sussex Downs again,
> To breathe the Sussex air,
> And see a Sussex lane,
> And all the fair
> Outspreading of the Sussex Weald,
> And hear the cry
> Of Sussex peewits in a Sussex field
> Beneath a clear blue Sussex sky![67]

But one of the dangers in establishing this tradition was the idealising of 'Old' England in a process Raymond Williams noted as an urban and industrial effort to remake the countryside as a townsman's image.[68] People were now being offered a land and soil worship as a diversion from city streets.[69] The idea of the countryside as a place of relaxation and leisure was separated from the country as a place of production, the first one booming as the latter fell away after about 1880. In the process of creating or recreating Sussex, writers were often content to describe the beauty of the countryside without attempting to draw any deeper meaning from it.

In so selecting their material, the more commonplace writers were loving the county with such an undemanding and uncomplicated passion that they could not write impartially, but applauded only the good of rural living, not seeing the bad. Indeed, by the sheer power and volume of their writing, Sussex itself became a kind of artefact, something that could be shaped and reshaped as writers wanted to see it, not as it really was. A huge gap thereby developed between the materiality of country life and the townsperson's perception of it. Weekenders, trippers and residential incomers might value the countryside as a playground and kind of art gallery set apart for the enjoyment of its beauty and peace, and perhaps seen from a distance, for in close-up reality, it could be horrid. On the other hand, the true countryperson perceived most of rural Sussex as a place for agricultural productivity.

But Sussex could now acquire an element of make-believe and misrepresentation in a nostalgic premodern past that could be at once both true and plainly wrong. And in this process 'Old Sussex' was distorted and magnified into an apparently changeless, immobile, frozen and long-lasting new Eden.

The poetic and lively prose descriptions of landscape were a factor in the growing enchantment and love of the county by outsiders. Sussex literature can be said to have made an important contribution to the reading public's sense of general well-being and makes Sussex a good place to start in a study of the anatomy of modern contentment. But love can take on a dangerous, dynamic power, and in the case of Sussex, it was to work a social and landscape transformation so drastic that it was never to be the same again.

4

LIVING FOR THE OPEN AIR: COTTAGES AND GARDENS

We are not yet ripe for growing up in the streets. Has any good ever come out of the foul-clustering town-proletariat, beloved of humanitarians?[1]

The love of and recourse to country are the most important and persistent things in my life. The country is also the safety valve of my spiritual Taoism.[2]

The Writers' Sussex Cottage

All the walls are white with lime,
Big blue periwinkles climb
And kiss the crumbling window-sill:
Snug inside I sit and rhyme,
Planning poem, book, or fable,
At my darling beech-wood table
Fresh with the bluebells from the hill.[3]

Incoming writers, nostalgic for open spaces and clear views, sought out their Sussex cottage, where they could find a perfect antidote to life in towns. Such cottages, preferably sheltered by high banks or belts of trees, with projecting gables, fancy tiling and massive chimney shafts, were 'almost always eminently picturesque' and 'with their lively groups of pigs, dogs and children about their doors'.[4] The preferred accompaniment was the consolation of an old-fashioned garden (Plate 10). The cottage and garden together could distil an atmosphere of relaxation, coziness and homeliness, continuity of tradition and sense of security.

William Cobbett found much to praise in the Sussex lanes in 1823. He found excellent rose-bedecked cottages with capital gardens and orchards furnished with flowers, vegetables, beehives and much else attractive and useful, 'The houses are good and warm; and the gardens some of the very best that I have seen in England.'[5] There followed the publication of his practical manual *Cottage Economy*, largely written from a small farm at Worth near Crawley, the seventeenth edition of which was republished in 1916, with G.K. Chesterton's foreword, by Hilary Pepler, who had joined the Eric Gill community at Ditchling in that year.

William Blake, who probably had never seen a country cottage before, could not conceive anything more congenial than his little Felpham 'cot'. To the sculptor Flaxman, he wrote in September 1800:

Dear Sculptor of Eternity
We are safe arrived at our cottage, which is more beautiful than I thought it, and more convenient. It is a perfect model for cottages [...] Nothing can be more grand than its simplicity and usefulness. Simple without intricacy, it seems to be the spontaneous expression of humanity, congenial to the wants of man. No other formed house can ever please me so well, nor shall I ever be persuaded, I believe, that it can be improved either in beauty or use.

Mr. Hayley received us with his usual brotherly affection. I have begun to work. Felpham is a sweet place for study, because it is more spiritual than London. Heaven opens here on all sides her golden gates: her windows are not obstructed by vapours; voices of celestial inhabitants are more distinctly heard, and their forms more distinctly seen.[6]

Later writers also dreamt of a little country hermitage where they could live an idyllic, carefree life away from the temptations, strain and provocation of the literary hassle of London. So Hilaire Belloc wrote:

If I ever become a rich man,
Or if ever I grow to be old,
I will build a house with deep thatch
To shelter me from the cold,
And there shall the Sussex songs be sung
And the story of Sussex told.[7]

Such an aspiration is romantically conveyed in the description in 1900 by Sydney Cockerell of the cottage called Caxtons, intended for the retired revivalist architect Philip Webb, his friend and a close associate of William Morris:

Near Three Bridges there is a hill, and on that hill there is a cottage, and in front of that cottage there is a Saxon Church and a forest where the dragon was killed. Lilies of the valley grow where his blood ran, and nowhere else.[8]

Caxtons, near Worth, belonged to Wilfrid Scawen Blunt, and Webb detailed the travails he endured in dealing with the Sussex workmen employed to make the necessary adjustments to the building (Plate 11). He moved into the cottage in early 1901 and was grateful to Cockerell:

Your helpfulness in getting this very lame dog over his awkward stiles is as boundless as the southern horizon of Caxtons; and as – doubtless – I shall often be drunk there, your goodness will be double to me along with the moon.[9]

The writer, local historian and broadcaster Gerard Young loved his Meadow Cottage on Hoe Lane, Flansham, a hamlet near Bognor, and wrote several books about his life there from 1938. He claimed that in almost everyone there was the urge to live, at least periodically, with oil lamps, logs burning in an open hearth and smelling 'your own honeysuckle outside the porch and collect[ing] your milk from the farm across the fields'. In his four books about life in his hamlet, Young admitted his obsession, 'The desire to know everything, everything, literally every tree and field and wood, almost every blade of grass in a particular neighbourhood and never wanting to go anywhere else, or to write about anything else.' But he also remarked, 'When there is no longer a countryside, there will be no city either, we shall have in a quite literal sense shut up shop.'[10]

Although writers might genuinely like the country, living there was also a practical matter of cheapness. The only home many struggling writers could afford in the interwar years was a farm labourer's cottage or a rundown farmhouse on a farm they would not or could not farm for themselves. Laurence Binyon expressed in verse his aspirations for happiness in a dream home in an 'airier and less jostled' world. In familiar south country terms, he envisaged its 'befriending roof' with birds nesting under his eaves sheltered by hanging beech woods on the generous slope of a green hill that opened up views of alluring distances. The garden was to have a walnut and a wild crab and merry children would peer out of a snow of blossom and fiery fruit in the orchard bordering a stream that murmured all day long.[11]

The Meynells at Humphrey's Homestead

One of the most remarkable literary and family colonies ever established in Sussex, and which many found more mellifluous than that of the Bloomsbury group, was founded in 1911 by Wilfrid Meynell (1852–1948), a Catholic convert, journalist and director of the Catholic publishing firm Burns & Oates, and Alice, his wife (1842–1922), the well-known poet and essayist (Figures 13 and 14). The Meynells bought a somewhat dilapidated and unobtrusive farmhouse at Greatham, called Humphrey's Homestead, together with some 80 acres of poorly farmed land in secluded countryside. A converted outhouse was referred to as 'Shed Hall'.

The complex was to be a weekend and holiday home, amid fields in a myriad of lanes hovering over the expanse of the Wild Brooks, with the South Downs always in sight, a view that Alice thought the finest in the world. Although a library was built as an extension, it was never intended to be 'smart', but this was mainly where Wilfrid lived out the last years of his life.

Wilfrid discussed with his good friend Wilfrid S. Blunt (also a Catholic convert) the sites of cottages he intended to build for the occupation of family and friends. A cowshed was converted into a cottage for Wilfrid's daughter and fifth child of the seven surviving, Viola, who was a lover of the Sussex countryside and biographer of her mother and father. The Meynells' son, Sir Francis, was a major literary figure who founded the Pelican and Nonesuch presses (the latter with David Garnett) and was a notable journalist, becoming a film executive and a distinguished industrial designer. Another son, Gerard, who lived at Ditchling, ran the Westminster Press and his wife, Esther (née Moorhouse), wrote several books on Sussex.[12]

Alice Meynell was the rescuer of the metaphysical and mystic poet Francis Thompson, a Catholic opium addict who died in 1907, aged 48, although the family members did what they could to help him. At one stage, in 1889, he was sent off to the French-speaking monastery of the Canons of Prémontré, Priory of Our Lady of England, at Storrington, where he attempted to rid himself of his addiction. Once recovered, he took to walking up the steep track leading onto the Downs to Kithurst Hill, the location venerated in his 'Ode to the Setting Sun'. Meynell sent Thompson's work to Tennyson and Browning, where it was well received.

Fig. 13: Wilfrid Meynell. (NPG Ax39216)

Fig. 14: Alice Meynell. (With permission from Oliver Hawkins. Frontispiece from Damian Atkinson, *The Selected Letters of Alice Meynell: Poet and Essayist* [Cambridge Scholars Publishing, 2013])

On the Downs, Thompson met some children from nearby Cootham who were gathering wild raspberries. He befriended them and wrote the poem 'Daisy', which remains among his better-known poems. And on Kithurst Hill he began his famous essay on Percy Bysshe Shelley, who had been born at Field Place, Horsham, to the north of Storrington. A controversial work, it was only published after his death, when royalties from Thompson's work, which came to the Meynells, helped to fund the house at Greatham.

Furthermore, as the poetic confidante of Andrew Young, Viola introduced him and several other budding poets to a wider public through the Nonesuch Press. Eleanor Farjeon was also a frequent visitor to the Meynells (page 195). *The Week-end Book*, which appeared for several years from 1925, published and edited by Francis and his second wife, Vera Mendel, is perhaps the most notable Sussex book written specifically for urban 'comers-and-goers' with its poems, songs, games and domestic cottage advice.[13]

Uniquely, Humphrey's Homestead remains the centre of the Meynell family to this day.[14] A plaque recording the family tree includes the names of more than 200 members of the Meynell family, running into the fifth generation, who meet in reunions at the house and occasionally holiday there and in its range of dwellings scattered in the grounds. The extraordinary atmosphere of contentment and quiet repose and the homeliness created at Humphrey's Homestead and its surroundings is celebrated by John Drinkwater (1882–1937), the eminent literary figure of that time, in his glad and grateful note addressed to his fellow poet and hostess, Alice Meynell, and by his 1914 poem 'Of Greatham (to those who live there)', following a visit in July, a gesture much appreciated by the family.[15]

For peace, than knowledge more desirable
Into your Sussex quietness I came,
When summer's green and gold and azure fell
Over the world in flame …
[…]
I have known that loss. And now the broken thought
Of nations marketing in death I know,
The very winds to threnodies are wrought
That on your downlands blow.

I sing of peace. Was it but yesterday
I came among your roses and your corn?
Then momently amid this wrath I pray
For yesterday reborn.[16]

Coulson Kernahan has said that 'not even our Sussex-born and Sussex-true poets have painted a more perfect picture' than this poem. Walter Wilkinson thought of the house as a poem itself which had been exquisitely wrested from the hotch-potch of vulgar life.

A Dream Come Real: D.H. Lawrence at Greatham

One author who obtained a new impetus by means of a stay at Greatham was D.H. Lawrence. After a spell of five months near Chesham in Buckinghamshire after the declaration of war in 1914, he felt 'seedy' and 'every moment dead, dead as a corpse in its grave clothes'. He and his wife Frieda leapt at the invitation to join the Meynell family in one of their cottages in January 1915. And within a month at Greatham, the spirit of the Sussex Downs brought inspiration and he began to write with renewed vigour:

> I have got into the stride of my novel, and am working gallantly [...]
> I continue to love this place [...] I have got a new birth of life since I came
> down here [...] Now I feel the waking up, and the thrill in my limbs, and
> the wind blows ripples on my blood as it rushes against this house from the
> sea, full of germination and quickening.[17]

Indeed, within days of arrival at Greatham he was feeling rid of his black despair and was even finding hope beyond the war, which had hitherto eluded him. On leaving Greatham in July 1915, Lawrence thanked Viola for the cottage in a similar mood, 'It has a special atmosphere, and I feel as if I had been born afresh there, got a new, sure, separate, soul' (Plate 12).

Although rejuvenated, Lawrence was in fact caused anguish and disappointment by two literary works completed there. One was the famed short story 'England My England', initially published in the *English Review* of September 1915, which later Lawrence wished 'at the bottom of the sea before even it had been printed', and the other, the revision of his 'beloved book', *The Rainbow*. This was typed by Viola, completed in March 1915 and published on 1 October, but was suppressed and all copies confiscated on the grounds of indecency about a month or so later.

From Lawrence's published letters it is evident that on several occasions he walked to the top of the Downs within half an hour, presumably up Greatham Lane, described as 'wide, grassy, briar-entangled studded with oaks', and this would have taken him by a white track up the escarpment to Rackham Hill. On one occasion, he apparently walked along the ridge of the Downs (now the South Downs Way) to the high point of Amberley Mount. He wrote of that view to Lady Ottoline Morrell:

> It was so beautiful on the downs today, with the sea so bright on one hand
> and the downs so fresh, and the floods so blue on the other hand, away
> below washing at the little villages. I don't know why, but my heart was
> so sad, almost to break. A little train ran through the floods, and steamed
> on so valiant into the gap. And I seemed to feel all humanity, brave and
> splendid, like the train, and so blind, and so utterly unconscious of where
> they are going or of what they are doing.[18]

The lifting of the spirits he experienced on the Downs and the sentiment expressed in the previous quotation had an instantaneous and crucial influence on *The Rainbow*, which he was to finish at breakneck speed. Without any intimation to the reader, Ursula, Lawrence's main character in this part of his story, is transposed from the collieries of Ilkeston and arrives at a friend's Sussex cottage at the foot of the Downs. She yearns to go to the top of the Downs and takes the white track up to the rounded summit, probably Rackham Hill and the site mentioned in Lawrence's letter. Up there, she is entranced by the wide views of a 'high, smooth land under heaven' and she sees idyllic Arundel Castle, the little train pushing through the water meadows, the villages and woods of the Weald, and in the superb stillness lies face downwards on a prehistoric earthwork in 'sun-glowing strength' and cries until tears run down her face.[19]

Presumably this signified Lawrence's own reactions to the Downs. Unsurprisingly, in a Lawrence context, Ursula and her male partner spend a midsummer night on the Downs and take off their clothes to become as 'utterly naked as the downs themselves'. The novel was initially banned, and the 'pots of gold' Lawrence was expecting for the English sale did not materialise, although the censorship objections were later lifted.

Those who chose this life of writing, of living in gardens with beauty and ideas, were an easy target for people who conventionally pursued some work, profession or business, and who might envisage writers who wore long hair and shaggy tweeds and went gadding about on long country walks between pubs, swilling down beer with his bread and cheese and thus ever open to the charge of 'escapism', cowardice and parasitic idleness. This was the theme of the short story 'England, My England', which Lawrence also wrote during his brief Greatham period in 1915. It was also later to cause a literary stir and result in a complete rupture with all members of the large Meynell family.

The tale is set in the lonely Greatham district, evocatively described as a corner of the Old England of hamlets and yeomen amid commons and marshes through which the 'spear of modern invention had not passed', and with the 'savage peace of the commons ... lingering on primeval as when the Saxons came'.[20] The short story was later expanded and republished in 1921 with a more savage denunciation of the war and south country Englishness.

Among the weekenders with the Meynells were the Lucases: Percy, the son of E.V. Lucas, the noted essayist, and Madeleine, one of the daughters of Wilfrid and Alice, whom Lawrence much liked. But Lawrence appears to have taken an instant dislike to Percy, who becomes 'Egbert', portrayed as a handsome and cultured gentleman living in a country cottage and 'tampering' with the arts, literature, painting, music and sculpture as a sort of epicurean hermit, loving the county's past but evading the business world of his well-to-do father-in-law. In Lawrence's words, 'He had no profession:

he earned nothing', and he lacked any ambition or wish to undertake work. According to Lawrence, although initially he had a devoted wife, his failure to make a responsible living to support his family, culminating in an accident to a daughter due to his own negligence that severely injured her leg, caused the marriage to end in failure.

The literary motif of the story was Lawrence's current obsession with the relationship between married men and women. He singled out the Lucases as offering an example of a woman who gave 'honest love' but had rejected her husband, who was a spiritual coward. Lawrence was later to express the view that he should never have visited Greatham, but hoped that if the story, published so hastily, was true, it would do no great damage. It was indeed untrue, a complete fabrication.

The real 'Egbert', Percy Lucas, was an expert genealogist and, as an accomplished Morris Dancer, had edited the *Journal of the English Folk Dance and Song Society*. Lawrence appears to have had only a superficial acquaint-ance with him. He was commissioned into the army and died of wounds at the opening of the Battle of the Somme in July 1916. One of his daughters mentioned in the story became Barbara Wall, the Catholic novelist, and she corrected Lawrence's account in 1961. She observed that the Lucas family was living in London at the time Lawrence wrote the story in 1915, that 'Egbert' was already a volunteer soldier and, furthermore, that the accident falsely attributed to her father had been caused by a visitor's negligence. It appears that at Greatham, Lawrence used the Lucases, whom he hardly knew, as models for his preoccupation with conflicts and crises between men and women, between town and country, and with the revival of an English folk culture. But as Compton Mackenzie remarked, Lawrence had a trick of describing a person and their setting and then putting them into 'an ectoplasm entirely of his own creation'.[21]

Ford Madox Ford Comes to Sussex and a Gingerbread Cottage

Ford Madox Ford (1873–1939) was born Ford Hermann Hüffer but his father had moved from Germany to England in 1869 and Ford Madox Ford was the name his father adopted in 1919, 'partly because a Teutonic name in these days is disagreeable'.[22] Ford's grandfather was the pre-Raphaelite painter Ford Madox Brown and he grew up in a household that was well acquainted with artists and writers. Eloping with his school girlfriend Elsie Martindale in 1894, they left to find a simple life at a substantial cottage, Pent Farm, near Hythe in Kent, one of several such attempts by Ford to find tranquility, including joining the Limpsfield community in eastern Surrey in 1898 for a year, where he met Conrad. In 1901, he and Elsie moved to Winchelsea but by 1909 he had left her.

Associating with avant-garde writers such as Ezra Pound, Hemingway and Joyce, at Pent Farm he associated closely with Conrad, who wrote *Heart of Darkness* there and to whom he sublet the tenancy. Also, there came H.G. Wells, Henry James (at Lamb House, Rye, from 1897) and the consumptive American Stephen Crane (a tenant at the rundown Brede Place from 1899). Kipling was over at Burwash and Galsworthy and W.H. Hudson also visited. Jean Rhys and Rebecca West were mistress-muses, the former with Ford from 1924 and the latter with Wells from 1913. All sought a rural retreat from London.

Ford had joined up at the age of 41, but returned, shell-shocked, to find health and mind in Sussex. In a troop train two days before going into the line in Flanders, Ford had seen what soldiers died for:

[…] I watched our England pass
the great downs moving slowly,
Far away,
The farmsteads quiet and lowly,
But THIS is what we die for … As we ought …
For it is for the sake of the wolds and the wealds
That we die.[23]

And as a returning soldier, now aged 45, it was firstly in deepest Sussex that Ford learned to write again after his physical, mental and emotional wounds and disillusionment with society resulting from the war.

He had clear visionary requirements for the perfect country cottage. Writing for those who yearned for such a place, he warned that it must be desired long before it is acquired. The ideal cottage was to be idyllically set in cherry trees on the edge of a village green, as convenient and habitable as if it had been designed by the most accomplished modern architect. It was to have casement windows in which charming curtains, the size of a pocket handkerchief, would flutter in the breeze and these windows would preferably be set in age-deep thatch. But there must be lots of light and sun and wide views. Cosiness was essential to the perfect cottage and yet there must be space to house many books and a cherished Blüthner grand piano.

His companion Stella Bowen, the Australian portrait artist (1893–1947) wrote in the same vein. At Coopers at Bedham, she found something:

> [...] inexpressibly touching and reassuring about a very old cottage set in a gentle English landscape that has been inhabited for many generations by ordinary country folk. Something that seems to say; if you come inside here, you can live your own true life in peace and security and privacy.[24]

Stella Bowen's role in Ford's writing in the post-war years was a vital one. As a catalyst she organised Ford's life to a great extent and created the conditions in which he could write (Plate 13). More fundamentally, she gave him, or restored to him, two indispensable things, belief in himself as a writer and a real practical sense of the future. The birth of their daughter Esther in November 1920 was also central to his rediscovery of his ability, making it more necessary and dutiful to write.

Ford wrote in 1919 that he was 'occupying a period of invalidishness with writing some stuff about the country – gardening & birds & the like'.[25] Ford's Sussex country homes were far from grand, but to them they were a haven, a safe spot and refuge, a place where they had not even to struggle to earn a living or worry about success. They could escape from the moneyed life.

Originally in 1919, three months after he was demobbed, he rented Red Ford Cottage, Hurston, near Pulborough, before moving to Coopers Cottage in Bedham, where he was joined by Stella in 1920. He had chosen the secluded Red Ford (now Redford Cottage) because it was necessary for him to have a place where he could write undisturbed if he was ever to write again (Plate 14). He described his new home as 'a leaky-roofed, tile-healed, rat-ridden, seventeenthcentury, five-shilling a week moribund labourer's cottage'.[26] It was the sanctuary of this cottage, and later that at nearby Coopers, together with the vital contribution made by Stella Bowen, that got 'all the bits and poison out of my poor old carcase and lungs' and therapeutically restored to him the ability to write again.[27]

His account of his recovery, which led to innovation in the English novel, is a tale of painful reconstruction and one of the most moving accounts of the role of the Sussex landscape as a consolation to one who felt at the lowest ebb of his life. However, he gradually recovered to take up again *No Enemy: A Tale of Reconstruction*. This was partly written, he said, while serving in the line, but the bulk was evidently written immediately after the war at Red Ford. It is a mix of fiction and autobiography. Due to anguish relating to wartime experience and personal reasons, he felt unable to publish the book until ten years later in 1929, when it appeared in the USA. On its belated publication in Britain in 2002, it was recognised as an outstanding book of the First World War genre, but unusual in being concerned with the painful recovery of the writer's mind, and yet also a perfect paean to the English countryside that was his salvation.

Ford was passionately fond of the English landscape and tells us that he first dreamed of a 'green nook' after the war when he saw a 'gingerbread' cottage above the Somme at Albert, where he had received hospitality and which he regarded as 'the Sussex-down landscape of the Somme'. In old and mouldering Red Ford he saw again the little green nook of the earth at Albert in Flanders. Its similarity with Red Ford was so great that it seemed as if a camera had clicked and readjusted itself. Of Red Ford, he wrote:

> The Gingerbread Cottage [...] is, in all but looks, a very bad cottage, with a roof that leaks, walls that used to drip with damp, cupboards that until the advent [of the author], smelled of mould and bred the very largest spiders that can be imagined.[28]

He was so penniless there that he spent some weeks as a jobbing gardener on the tiniest income. He scraped together a few items of furniture, given to him by the son of the composer Arnold Bax, bought a little cutlery from the effects of a lieutenant in the Royal Sussex Regiment who had committed suicide, and an antique brass candlesnuffer with a goose quill pen to stimulate writing. He had moved in the spring and his party of friends at Easter found the cottage still leaking like a sieve through the roof, the walls and floor, but Ford unconcernedly cooked on paraffin stoves and collected wild herbs from the hedgerows. No hard road approached Red Ford with its roof greened over with mossy stains, which stood in a commonplace, rather untrimmed, hidden and yet beautiful countryside of heaths, woods and elm-bordered fields. It was what Ford called 'just country', with no famous views, simply fields that no one had ever heard of. But this was a sanctuary, 'I don't know: there's nothing to it, really. A spray of dog roses; a whitethroat dropping over the hedge; some gorse; the long, rolling land; the high skies and the clouds above the downs.'[29] Yet the invalid Ford's tired mind imagined he could hear the sound of heavy guns above the birds' chorus, and the cry of 'Fall in there!' and of men moving off.

Ford tells the story of his first hours alone at Red Ford in a frankly revealing, entertaining and evocative account. With a lighted candle, he put up his bed and canvas table in the mouldering cottage. His thoughts alternated between remembered events in France and some basic necessities of establishing himself in the cottage and cooking a meal:

> On my first evening in Red Ford, leaning on my elbows on my camp-bed and watching the death of my first fire of twigs and driftwood in a completely empty house. [...] There I lay, the ruined author, in a bare room that shadows were beginning to invade from every corner. With the last light of day I had raked out of the outhouse a cast-iron crock that I had washed and filled at the spring under the oak trees and there, near the fire, from a pot-rack, it hung and was half filled with a stew. The rest of the stew was giving me courage [...] I had said to myself, 'I will never look back'. I had then that night come through Pulborough in a farm-wagon and had brought some haphazard eatables – a neck of mutton, some shallots, bread, salt, and a bottle of port.

He was unsure of how best to proceed in this new situation:

> I had never seen the house before. It had been taken for me by a friend who knew my tastes – and my means. I had no knowledge of the countryside: West Sussex to a Kent minded man is as foreign in speech and habits as is China [...] I had never been so alone.[30]

But it was at Red Ford, often in Ezra Pound's company, that Ford began to consider the change of heart he considered necessary in a world transformed by the Great War. He is of special interest at this point because, years ahead of his time, he practised what we would now call sustainability and 'green' living. He had no truck with what he called the 'dependence society', arguing that one should not eat until being able to cook,

Fig. 15: Ford, the small producer, in 1921 with his champion Angora goat named 'Ezra Pound'. (Courtesy of Oliver Soskice and originally reproduced in Saunders, *Ford Madox Ford*, Vol. 2, facing p. 290)

not live in a house of one's own until one could sweep the floor and should blush if one found something in the house not made by human hand. He was not, however, preaching a Back-to-the-Land crusade, but wanted independence from the machine and the ways of life it created. Many of his ideals would now be acceptable in the present age as ecologically sound, such as avoidance of waste, living near one's work and growing crops that would be called organic. He had become, in fact, a neo-medievalist, who could also set his hand to the various crafts that maintained human existence. He referred to himself as a 'Small Producer', even entering flowers at the local Pulborough show – albeit unsuccessfully (Figure 15).

Ford's poem 'A House', which won an American award for the best poem of 1921, celebrates his and Stella's entire household community: humans and the domestic and farm animals in cottage and barn. It corroborates Stella Bowen's own account of life at Red Ford and Bedham, where she writes of the holding with its vegetables, chicken run, goats and pigs. It is a kind of modern morality play and expressive of the humble simplicity and otherworldliness that was now central to Ford's life and his notion that farm animals, grass, trees and humans were one. The poem conjures up the atmosphere that meant most to Ford and Stella: the rest, security and an escape from money and the moneyed world, although his financial insecurity meant that there were always thunderclouds about.

Appropriately, Ford was making a stake-and-binder hedge to keep his prize sows in when the letter containing his poetry award arrived, and he was also tending his pigs when Sir Edward Elgar, a near neighbour, looked over his hedge.[31] The practical side of kitchen gardening could certainly be useful to Ford. He indefatigably experimented with raising potatoes from seed, and by the end of 1922 had succeeded in creating nine new varieties that he considered disease-free. He named his potato plants after fellow writers and so it could be reported that 'Mr 'Enry James has picked up proper but Mr Conrad is yallowin'.

Red Ford is still accessible only by trackways off public roads. It lies in the tranquil Stor Valley at a point where a bridleway crosses the stream by a footbridge, formerly a ford, giving glimpses of the red staining from the iron in the local sandstone, which is revealed in the hollow way a little uphill and in the cliff of a former stone quarry against which the cottage lay. In early April, wild daffodils, cowslips, primroses, celandines and stitchwort (windflower) make a lovely scene, together with a few bluebells shyly budding among masses to follow. Although the site has been charmingly landscaped and the little brook dammed into a lake, the cottage, although rebuilt, is recognisable behind a modern extension that is in keeping with the traditional Sussex domestic building. On the site of Ford's old kitchen, damp and mould still trouble the present owners, but the elms have been lost to disease. The local countryside he loved is now shaggier but has also suffered less change than the neighbourhood in general.

Cooper's at Bedham has been renamed Cotford. It is a delightful little half-timbered building overlooking a wide and beautiful view of the Weald. Since Ford's days as a 'Small Producer', trees have colonised his paddocks and local coppicing has died out with the death of the last cutter. The room from which Stella Bowen painted has been demolished to make space for a new bedroom and kitchen. But the nightingales still sing, the lanes, although now asphalted, are still completely rural and the neighbourhood retains its feeling of remoteness despite considerable road traffic. Carpets of wild daffodils enhance the scene in spring.

Ford had, through writing in the peace and seclusion of the Sussex landscape, found his way back to health. His *No Enemy* has been described as 'a book which registers the psychological effects of Ford's war by exploring his relationship to landscape' – the way crucial moments of his wartime experience come back to him as visions of the landscape. And in remembering the horrors of landscape destruction and trench warfare, he showed how this caused the mind to turn to fonder images of treasured English scenery.[32] In retrospect, Ford's stay in Sussex was brief but vital to his recovery. In 1922, he and Stella moved to London, and thereafter to France, to Paris and the south. They separated in 1928 and Ford died in Deauville in 1939, three months before the beginning of another European conflagration.

Clearly, both Ford and Lawrence found the tranquility they needed to refresh body and soul and move forward in their literary careers. The Sussex cottage and the cottage garden might well be the perfect cure for angst, and those who could not face the mass movements of the present or the germ of the future took refuge in the past, often into a womb-like romanticism and myth making.

Ditchling Cottagers

A group of cottagers and smallholders who played a distinctive part in Sussex culture before the Second World War, and who felt that the city must be abandoned for the land, were those of the handcraftsmen of the Catholic Arts & Crafts community of St Joseph and St Dominic at Ditchling

Common. This was founded by Eric Gill (1882–1940), described as 'the greatest artist–craftsman of the twentieth century' (Figure 16). He had been born in Brighton but moved to study in Chichester, which he always regarded as the model for the ideal city.[33]

The community at Ditchling was based on the ideals of Belloc's and Chesterton's land-sharing Distributism (see page 131), as expounded from the extremist position of the Dominican Father Vincent McNabb, who held that a brave new world would be impossible unless it drew inspiration from the Gospels and the teachings of the early fathers. By 1922, there were forty-one Catholics living and working in the commune, with each family an independent unit living its own domestic life. Gill and his family originally lived at Sopers in Ditchling village from 1907, then moved to Hopkin's Crank, with outbuildings and farmland, off Ditchling Common, where he lived until he moved to Capel-y-ffin in the Black Mountains, Powys, in 1924, tiring of the 'public spectacle' that the commune had become. Dissension among the adherents thereafter brought the scheme to an end.[34]

The group grew quickly. Hilary and Clare Pepler and their children moved in. Fragbarrow Farm was the home of Hilary Pepler's son, David, who married Betty Gill, Eric Gill's daughter. Commander Herbert Shrove, a keen Distributist, lived at Hallett's Farm. David Jones' home was Woodbarton Cottage, later occupied by Valentine Kilbride, the weaver. Edgar Holloway came to live with his second wife, Jennifer, at Woodbarton, which had been designed and built by Gill in 1920 for Desmond Chute. Joseph Cribb, Donald Maxwell, Dunstan Pruden and the other members of the community also lived in cottages scattered nearby, most of them walking across the fields to and from the workshops.[35] There was a chapel and a calvary near to the London to Brighton railway line.

Fig. 16: 'Eric Gill' by Howard Coster, *c*. 1927. (NPG Ax2305)

All lived in Spartan simplicity. Water was drawn from a pump, oil lamps were used for lighting, there were candlelit tables and, because meals were cooked on open fires, burning logs sent most of the heat up the chimneys and left occupants in winter dining in greatcoats, mufflers and hats.

The main workshop by the 1930s was Pepler's St Dominic's Press, which produced from handpresses, generally in eighteenth-century Caslon Old Face, books that, for all their technical defects, are regarded as examples of beautiful typography.

The search for the perfect resting place on earth was often restless and fraught, no more remarkably than in Eric Gill's case, whose ideal choice of country retreat as a panacea forever eluded him. Having moved to the isolated Black Mountains, he then moved again in 1928 to 'Spiggots', near High Wycombe, so that, ironically, he could be closer to the commissions he sought in London. Increasingly frail, he died in late 1940.

5

'AN ENGLISH GENTLEMAN OF GENIUS': WILFRID SCAWEN BLUNT (1840-1922)

I am no patriot in the modern sense – I mean no imperialist – hardly a
nationalist about black manufacturing England. But I have a passionate
love for my native county with its green oak woods, its deep clay fallows,
its sheltering hedgerows, its ancient forest wastes, and that 'chain of
majestic mountains', its South Downs. These are more to me than all the
British Colonies put together [...] I love also the Sussex farm folk and
indigenous peasantry, so patient of their labour, so able of their hands, so
intelligent in their traditional agricultural work.[1]

A Sussex Squire on a Large Stage

Wilfrid Scawen Blunt was one of the most extraordinary personalities Sussex
has ever produced. As the owner of landed estates, he was a paternalistic
conservative, in politics a radical, though no friend of the Whig arriviste,
and as for that other England, contrasting so strongly with his own peaceful
fields, the 'black manufacturing England', it hardly entered his mind. Politically, he was a born agitator and an out-of-step champion of the exploited
and downtrodden, and in Ireland's cause, he was imprisoned and stood
almost alone in his opinions.

He was an *enfant terrible*, totally at odds with his imperialistic age and with
the sheer energy and incandescence of life, was also an explorer, a Sussex
squire, amateur architect, a poet of distinction, a brilliant diarist, a great
English eccentric, a sportsman with a deep interest in the Arab world. He
was a paradox: as an anti-imperialist, he nevertheless admired Kipling's
stories, and he was a born amorist and compassionate man. All this rolled
into one. His son-in-law Neville Lytton wrote of him, 'His love of nature
inclined him to yield to his instincts, and to have, as it were, a new mate
every spring.'[2]

His career suggests that he would have flourished best in the sixteenth century as an 'ultimate man', ignoring the conventions of his age. His marriage to the heiress Lady Anne Noel in 1869 not only brought substantial wealth, enabling him to build Crabbet Park, a country house near Crawley, and maintain a smaller one at Newbuildings, Shipley, but also gave him a connection with Lord Byron, his wife's grandfather, whose support for the Greeks in their war of independence against the Ottoman Empire had made him famous throughout Europe (Figure 17).

That grand gesture ever remained an inspiration to Blunt in his own anti-imperialism in support of India, Egypt and home rule for Ireland. It is also conceivable that Byron's literary achievements and full-blooded lifestyle had been a model to the youthful Blunt. He seems, as a young man, to have engaged in a delicious round of thinking, seeing, feeling and enjoying, eating, riding and lovemaking, in jolly bonhomie that was put into verse with an uninhibited sensuous enjoyment, contrasting him with the 'respectable' Victorian traits of his contemporaries. In personality, he was a man of confident and commanding presence and authority and was also, by common consent, one of the handsomest of men, irresistible to ladies and the terror of husbands. E.M. Forster denied him the supreme quality of greatness, calling him 'an English gentleman of genius', who, although reviled and isolated in his lifetime for his antiimperialism, might one day 'be voted a statue for his attempts to make the world a more just place for all'.[3]

As an old man, with a spreading beard and eagle nose, he was extremely dignified and theatrical. He would be clad in Arab robes and surrounded at Newbuildings by things kept for their associations: beaded camel charms, ostrich eggs and other mementoes he had acquired from his pioneering journeys in Arabia and the Middle East. And this included his mission to save the thoroughbred Arabian horse from extinction, which took him and his wife across the Nefud Desert in Egypt, Lady Anne being the first European woman to do so (Plate 15). This led, after repeated journeys to Cairo and beyond, to his respect for desert Arabs and others, who he claimed had not been corrupted by the false values of Western industrial society. Elizabeth Longford, his biographer, has remarked that he seemed like a prince from the *Arabian Nights*, whose long life was, in every sense, 'A Pilgrimage of Passion'.[4]

Opposite: Fig. 17: Wilfrid Scawen Blunt and Anne Blunt (née Noel), from a report of his life at the time of his imprisonment in Ireland. (*Illustrated London News*, Saturday, 3rd March 1888, p. 224)

It is said that he had thirty-eight lovers in the forty-eight years from 1862 to 1910.[5] The eldest daughter of the Hon. Percy Scawen Wyndham MP (1835–1911) was Mary Constance (1862–1937), married as Lady Elcho from 1883 to 1914 to Hugo Charteris, later becoming 11th Earl of Wemyss and 7th Earl of March. She was a founder member of the social and intellectual coterie 'The Souls'. In early 1895, she travelled to Egypt and there met her father's first cousin, Wilfrid Scawen Blunt, who had seduced her mother, Madeline (Mrs Percy Wyndham), thirty years before.

Mary and Blunt lived in a tent and Blunt called her 'my true Bedouin wife'. The result of this passion in the desert was Lady Mary Charteris (1895–1991), who, nevertheless, in keeping with aristocratic mores, grew up as Lord Wemyss' second daughter, with her three brothers and two sisters, and later married John Lyon, related to Queen Elizabeth, the Queen Mother. She shared Blunt's passion for fox hunting but was sensitive of the trouble her birth had brought to Blunt's legitimate daughter Judith (later Lady Wentworth) and refused Blunt's bequest of his house in the New Forest.

Blunt's Sussex Weald

Despite Blunt's strong empathy with the Middle East and his interests in international affairs, no writer has expressed more passionately his patriotism for Sussex and a love of the Sussex Weald, its country lore, people and their traditions. As he put it, 'my clouted shoon must still stick in the Sussex clay'.[6]

Born at Petworth House, his roots were there, but he was so immensely proud to have Weald clay in his blood and bones that he resented with a sickening sense of intrusion those newcomers alien to the traditions of the county. These included new writers from outside, whom he thought disconcertingly threatened his most private and intimate world as 'sole king', as had been his forebears. E.V. Lucas remarked that the 'whole duty' of squires had never been determined, but very high – next to continuing to keep horses – should come the provision of trustworthy histories of their estates.

Blunt was the perfect squire on both counts for he was a keen sportsman and compiler of the history of Crabbet Park, as well as a staunch defender of all things Wealden. With Anne, he had established the Crabbet Park Arabian stud farm in 1877–78, with the business spreading to Newbuildings Place and to Sheik O'Beyd in Egypt. But in 1906, Wilfrid and Anne separated, and the stud was the subject of a deed of partition between them, subsequently becoming a large element in hostilities between Blunt and his daughter, Judith.[7]

In verse, his fierce possessiveness is brought out in 'The Old Squire':

The lags, the gills, the forest ways,
The hedgerows one and all,
These are the kingdoms of my chase,
And bounded by my wall;[8]

'Blunt country' can be thought of as encompassing the view from the hill Blunt knew as Stammerham Hill, known now more familiarly as Sharpenhurst Hill, south of Broadbridge Heath. Wooded hills rise mistily to the north towards the Surrey Hills with not a dwelling in sight. Southwards is the clay vale of the Low Weald in which Newbuildings lies, with its little woods, clearings and similar sparse settlement, backed by the steep wall of the Downs surmounted by the beech clump on Chanctonbury Ring. Nearby are the former quarries of Horsham Stone around Christ's Hospital School, an alma mater for, among others, Lamb, Coleridge and Edmund Blunden.

In the distance lie the bounds of Worth Forest bordered by Crabbet Park. Soon after the declaration of war in 1914, Blunt drove to the top of Stammerham Hill to take his mind off the awful prospects ahead. In his opinion, it was the finest lookout over rural England of any – even in Sussex, 'No more perfect picture of peace could be imagined, nothing more absolutely beautiful'. To him, the scene was an archetypal embodiment of deep primordial peace, homely, kindly and soothing, and preserving the visible characteristics of an older England. Thanks largely to him and to the difficult farming on the clay, the characteristic features of the Sussex Weald he knew still substantially survive today.

Newbuildings Place is a stone-built house with brick quoins in the Artisan Mannerist style, built by 1677. Ian Nairn described the parish of Shipley as a part of the Weald 'where the whole countryside looks like a tidy landscaped park'.[9] Blunt put beauty ahead of utility and dispensed with a landscape park. Instead, he expended his wealth and affection on his fields and woods, farm buildings and roadsides. He planted up hedgerows with a variety of native trees, built up the wider belts of woodland separating fields, locally called shaws, rounded off sharp angles, removed ugly fences, tidied up verges and conserved the tenanted farmhouses and other graceful effects. Everything was done to please the eye artistically and to make it beautiful rather than fully productive.

He also took care to retain and enhance the historical character of his countryside, notably the numerous ancient sub-parallel droveways, 30–40ft wide or more, that thread the estate in a north–south direction, immemorially woven by men and animals travelling to and from the Downs to woodland pastures in the deep Weald from at least the Saxon period (Plate 16). Churches and farmsteads were built along these droves, for example, Shipley Church and Crookhorn Farm, and the now obsolete ways have shaped boundaries and fields. These broad, grassy ways are ribbons of wildlife and are charming landscape features, and in walking them in summer, often sunk below the fields in hollow-ways and fringed with trees and field banks, one can still feel a real sense of history.

Blunt was so proud of his handiwork and the historical landscape he was sustaining (though some thought his woods and pastures unkempt and not in the interests of good husbandry) that he showed it to William Morris, who was himself haunted by the Middle Ages and a lover of a country wholly and exquisitely fitted for the gentler uses of life. Altogether, this and Crabbet Park with its holdings in Worth Forest was a perfect setting for Blunt the pastoral poet, who fell under its spell. To this day, large traces of this man's personality remain on the landscape and after more than seventy-five years of intensive post-war agriculture, the visitor still senses a mildly implausible working landscape. A place like that, intimately associated with Sussex's literature and landscape history, has an individuality worth conserving for posterity, a countryside in which everything, natural and man-made, is small and of its kind in a distinctive landscape that should be considered a national treasure.[10]

To Blunt, the Weald's 'green oak woods, its deep brown clay fallows, its sheltering hedgerows, the ancient forest wastes and that chain of majestic mountains, the South Downs' formed a sanctuary invoking the 'still small voice of calm':

Naught here may harm or hurt.
This is a sanctuary
For the world's weak, hedged in with love and fenced
and sealed.[11]

Blunt perceives the peace and 'immemorial silence' of Worth Forest as a heritage and a sanctuary from the modern world outside, although once it was a busy centre of the iron industry. Most explicitly, the theme of the Weald as a private hideaway is expressed in his 'Sonnet of Assonance':

A thousand bluebells blossom in the wood,
Shut in a tangled brake of briar roses,

And guarded well from every wanton foot,
A treasure by no eye of man beholden,
No eye but mine. No other tongue hath spoken
Out to the joyless world …
    … There hadst thou found a beauty and a silence,
Such as nor tongue can tell or fancy dream.[12]

This was contrasted with the city:

… You cannot know,
In your bald cities, where no cowslips blow,
How dear life is to us …[13]

Here, he could find physical beauty and ways of life that suited his temperament. His sonnet 'A Day in Sussex' tells how he 'fled away from the loud
world/ which long had troubled me' and found 'peace, music, twilight' that
would 'lull a heart to peace'.[14] The same theme arises again in 'Chanclebury
Ring' (Chanctonbury):

Say what you will, there is not in the world
A nobler sight than from this upper Down.

… Dear checker-work of woods, the Sussex Weald!
If a name thrills me yet of things of earth,
That name is thine. How often I have fled
To thy deep hedgerows and embraced each field,
Each lag, each pasture -fields which gave me birth
And saw my youth, and which must hold me dead.[15]

The above last six lines of this sonnet relating to Blunt's love of the beauty
of the Sussex Weald are carved on his tombstone in a ride through a yew
grove on his estate at Newbuildings (Plate 17). In later years, 'lichens have
overgrown the stone; rabbits dart and play about it; birds sing in the nearby
trees; time has brought Blunt's grave into harmony with the Sussex Weald'.[16]
He died leaving effects worth over £78,000.

Blunt's love of the Wealden landscape is also declared in his long poem
'Worth Forest'. On the edge of modern Crawley, now facing across the M23
towards Maidenbower, the forest inspires the poem, revealing what it meant
to him as a place, and includes its description and history, striking a tragic

note with the death of his infant heir (Plate 18). Standing on the high ground of the watershed of south-east England, his eye roves down to the South Downs, 'which look like mountains when the sea-mist crowns/ their tops in autumn' across the wooded Weald and then northwards over the vale of the Medway to the Surrey hills and North Downs. He fondly writes of tickling trout as a boy in the infant River Mole, which rises in the forest and of his devotion to its ragged lands:

> ... this path shall lead us to the gill,
> Where you shall see the Mole in her first rill,
> Ere she leaves the Forest, and her bed
> Is still of iron-stone, which stains her red.[17]

Plainly, Blunt gained something of great value from making the Weald his own. From it came the impulse to write his Sussex sonnets, lyrics and longer poems, and to defend in verse and prose his beloved homeland from what he regarded as adverse change. Furthermore, it can be argued that his grounding and fondness for his native Weald over a lifetime was to profoundly and irrevocably influence the ideals of this strange man and to influence his whole being and attitude to the world. The harmony that he saw existing between people and nature there for centuries shaped his own tastes, feelings and beliefs on things political and cultural, and led him towards long-held values that were at odds with the modern capitalistic and imperialist world.

It is in 'Sed nos qui vivimus', apparently also set in Worth Forest, that Blunt's character and philosophy of life shine out most clearly. Here, he reveals his intuitive understanding of the Weald and its traditional ways of life as a still-living presence, together with his views on civilisation more generally. Walking over his estate at Crabbet Park, he mused on the generations who had passed the very spot where he stood. The questions that came to his mind were: what was the history of the land, what old deeds survive about it and who were the people who made the estate of which he was so proud? Blunt had become aware of the remarkable continuity of thought and feeling that had gone into the shaping of the landscape, its buildings and the lives of the people.

In a reverie unique in Sussex literature, Blunt shows as close an affinity to the Weald as his near contemporary Thomas Hardy demonstrates in his Dorset novel *The Woodlanders* (1887). Musing at his sense of pride in the landscape, he went down towards the trees and fields, following the paths he knew as a child. He thought of the invisible people of the past who had laid out the fields and had turned the sods, planted the trees and tended the gardens, people who had loved them then as he loved them now. He did not mourn them, for although they had physically vanished, he sensed that they still had a presence, for he was doing and cherishing what they had done, gathering from the trees they had planted and enjoying the gardens they had fashioned in a landscape that was a living thing after layer upon layer of Sussex life.

'Who were they all?' he muses, thinking first of boxes of yellow parchments and bundles of old letters. But these were not his goal. He focused his thoughts on past people, who, like himself, 'a clod of Sussex earth more kindly kneaded', also had a passionate love of home, now his but once theirs. He attempts to recall the pioneer, 'unknown to all, untamed, unlorded', who lived on a plot of upturned earth his spade had made amid a vast sea of surrounding woodland:

> I see him stand beneath these pollard oaks, the same, hard handed,
> With hook, and axe, and bill, a wrestler with the forest's green,
> A man grave-featured, dull of thought and wit, slow-paced, unyielding,
> Stern in his toil and niggard still of smile and sign and speech ...

That man, 'this silent first forefather of the paternal woods reclaimed', lived deep in Blunt's soul, for he believed that there was in himself something of that man's hardy sinew and how, like Blunt, he had looked askance at 'foreign' men. In his thoughts too, were the successive 'penurious crews', careful tillers in their stubbornness, who added their store of cultural value to the ancestral fields, men who had lived with woodlands and who were woodmen to the very core of their beings and who practised woodcrafts with small-scale farming. Turning the latch of a cowshed, he contrasts the simple Wealden life in harmony with nature with the prince who slaughtered thousands, the statesman who aims to lie entombed with kings, and the schemes of impossible good for man, made naught by human fraud and greed.

To a surprising degree, Blunt's homeland is still occupied by numerous rooted families bearing such names as Rapley and Laker, whose forebears have lived in the district for generations, and although Blunt died 100 years ago, memories of him are still passed downwards from parents to their children. With these verses in mind, one can fully understand why in old age he wrote possessively:

A love of English country things and more especially of the actual clay soil of Sussex, with its deep hedgerows and its deeper oak woods, is still with me the most permanent instinct of my heart. I can hardly imagine happiness now in my old age without some such local anchorage, and I find it difficult to recognize as beautiful any scenery not that of our weald. So far indeed do I carry the feeling that I resent the intrusion of outside praisers of its loveliness, men who have come to it as strangers and have dared to sing of it as though it were their own.[18]

At times, indeed, Blunt's love of the Sussex Weald bordered on the obsessional, even irrational, something that led him into skirmishes with local authorities who were extending their powers over privately run estates. And in local politics, as in national, he acted as he felt and was never ashamed at his inconsistencies. At the outbreak of the Great War, many felt that Blunt was unpatriotic, a feeling engendered by his anti-imperialism. True or not, his feelings about the Sussex Weald coloured his views quite vehemently. He refused to sign warlike manifestoes; he refused to contribute war poems to the many anthologies that were being compiled. And in answer to a proposed scheme for turning Woodgaters at Shipley – a farm on his beloved Newbuildings estate – into an agricultural school for ex-soldiers, he replied that he was not interested in soldiers being brought to settle on the land in Sussex unless they had been farm labourers there before the war. He did not want, he said, foreigners from the north of England upsetting native Sussex ways and introducing intensive cultivation.[19]

Blunt was angered at the steady loss of Wealden cottagers and smallholders and was frustrated at his attempt to revive their prosperity by the decline in oak felling and coppicing that had supplemented the incomes of the poor, but which was being superseded by imports generated by the principle of free trade. It was these circumstances that put him in favour of land reform, especially for peasant ownership. He started from the conviction that the Weald's character and tradition made it an ideal country for peasant ownership and small tenant holdings, then still familiar in France, when the 'age of gold for our peasantry might come again'. He therefore supported the subdivision of large estates, if only to increase the voting power of the country against the town. He calculated that a family could live by 'plain, unaided agriculture' on a holding of less than 20 acres, especially with milk and chicken interests, but felt that one of the main obstacles to reform were the wrong views of rural needs as seen from the towns.[20]

Blunt's Poetry

Blunt is a most underestimated poet; perhaps he overshadowed his own poetry. But his verse appealed to those lovers of the outdoor world who enjoyed his strong, virile style. He wrote sincerely and frankly, and unusually for his time, threw restraint to the winds in straining after originality. He is also one of the few Sussex poets to express his feelings of romantic love. Like Byron, Blunt wrote verse for men and women very much alive.

He modestly described his poetry as being 'slightly in advance' of the Victorian. As W.E. Henley remarked, he 'put more of himself and his sole experience into his verse than any writer of his time'.[21]

This is very evident in Blunt's 'The Love Sonnets of Proteus' which, as his 1880 preface states, 'lays bare what was once his heart, to the public'. On this account, the England of his day did not acclaim him, but his star may yet reappear in this age of changed fashions. At age 35 these poems marked the end of his youth, and he did not intend to write like them again. His gods drew him into the pleasures and disappointments of love affairs with women, frankly recorded with varying feelings of tenderness, sorrow and despair, to an appreciation of natural and other beauty, and to enlightenment from travels to places such as Florence and his early experiences with people and places in the Near East.

His remarkable sonnet sequence, 'Esther', recounting a youthful love affair that left its scar upon his heart, is one of the most notable of its kind in English literature. His usual mood is one of uninhibited sensuous enjoyment pursued with fury into whatever he was doing, and these were not matters commonly discussed openly by late Victorians. Blunt's verse, dealing with the errors and exaggerations of his youth, conveys a special freshness and frankness about himself, another quality rare in Sussex verse. It is also marked, as Blunt himself stated, by a sincerity that was never written for art's sake but only for matters about which he felt deeply and strongly.

His later work is also characterised by an astonishing versatility of metrical composition and of subjects ranging from the Sussex Weald to Arabia, Egypt, where he wintered, Italy and other places he visited, together with aspects of love and feeling, natural beauty, history, religion, politics and his sports and philosophy of living. His mood and poetical subject matter changed with age, corresponding to his own view of a life that had been lived – 'youth in feeling – manhood in battle – and old age in meditation'. The young Blunt was a great horseman and his 'Golden Odes of Pre-Islamic Arabia' (1903) have a splendid galloping rhythm expressive of his joy in women, hunting and horsemanship. His *A New Pilgrimage* (1889) is a book of poems of the outdoor world that was well regarded by the naturalist W.H. Hudson, who admired and respected the underrated Blunt as a good companion during his rambles in the open Down country.[22]

Blunt was so carried away in his youthful joy of life that he hated growing old, and felt resentful at being robbed by time:

> If I could live without the thought of death,
> Forgetful of time's waste, the soul's decay,
> I would not ask for other joy than breath
> With light and sound of birds and the sun's ray
> [...]
> I must be up and doing – ay, each minute.
> The grave gives time for rest when we are in it.[23]

A number of the sonnets are cameos of his well-loved Sussex Downs and woods, such as 'St Valentine's Day', beginning 'To-day, all day, I rode upon the Down,/ With hounds and horsemen, a brave company', or 'A Day in Sussex', 'I left the dusty high road, and my way/ Was through deep meadows, shut with copses fair'.

Bitter antipathy to modern civilisation and 'Londonisation' is also frequently to be found, as in 'Worth Forest':

> [...] And, when the wind blows north, the London smoke
> Comes down upon us, and the grey crows croak,
> For the great city seem to reach about
> With its dark arms, and grip them by the throat.
> Time yet may prove them right. The wilderness
> May be disforested, and Nature's face
> Stamped out of beauty by the heel of Man,
> Who has no room for beauty in his plan [...]

Anti-Imperialism

Blunt founded the Crabbet Club, whose literary members included Cabinet ministers George Wyndham and Lord Curzon as well as Oscar Wilde and Lord Alfred Douglas. His letter to Lord Curzon on his appointment as Viceroy of India (1899–1905) read with characteristic irony:

> I write to console with you on the appointment which I grieve to think severs you long as member of the Crabbet Club. I hope you will be the best, the most frivolous and the last of our Viceroys.

For this kind of sentiment Gladstone thought him charming, but politically mad. His daughter Judith, with whom he had quarrelled, thought 'he was completely at the mercy of oriental deceit and Irish blarney, believing every tale of oppression by the British government, however fantastic'. Further- more, 'His house soon became famous as a hot-bed of conspiracy for the scum of every nation'.[24] On the other hand, few tributes would have pleased him more than that by a former Indian Minister of External Affairs, who said, 'Blunt was a true interpreter of the deepest and wisest instincts of the Anglo-Saxon race. England's greatness will be hereafter remembered through Blunt's ideas and writings rather than through Balfour and Curzon.'[25]

Blunt's foray into Middle Eastern and Egyptian affairs began with the visit in 1875–76 with Lady Anne, following a somewhat desultory career in the Diplomatic Service, and then again when he met Lady Gregory and her husband in Egypt. Thereafter, he firmly took the side of Arabs and the cause of Egyptian nationalism for more than twenty years, to the fury of the English Establishment. Disliking Disraeli's 'imperial spangles', and summon- ing up his Byronic associations, he wrote 'The Wind and the Whirlwind' (1883), one of his most savage denunciations of British Empire policy:

> I have a thing to say, but how to say it?
> [...]
> How shall I speak of them, the priests of Baal,
>   The men who sowed the wind for their ill ends!
> The reapers of the whirlwind in that harvest
>   Were all my countrymen, were some my friends.
> [...]
> Alas for Liberty, alas for Egypt!
>   What chance was yours in this ignoble strife?

Scorned and betrayed, dishonoured and rejected,
    What was there left you but to fight for life?
[...]
The nations of the East have left their childhood.
    Thou are grown old. Their manhood is to come;
And they shall carry on Earth's high tradition
    Through the long ages when thy lips are dumb.[26]

Following a meeting with Lord Lytton, Viceroy of India (1876–80), he wrote in his diary, 'We both agreed that the day of England's empire is fast fading – for my own part I do not care how soon'.[27]

With Lady Augusta Gregory, one of his many lovers from 1881, early in his time in Egypt he also worked for Irish freedom from British imperial rule and the literary revival in Ireland with writers such as W.B. Yeats and George Moore. Indeed, he was imprisoned in Galway jail for sedition after speaking openly about the freedom of Ireland and taunting the police to arrest him. He sent Lady Gregory a length of oakum his jailers required him to untangle and she used it as a bookmark for the rest of her life. In jail he wrote several poems, including the sonnet 'Dream of Good', which throws light on his formidable political purpose, symbolised at his Sussex home by yearly observing the anniversary of the British bombardment of Alexandria:

To do some little good before I die;
To wake some echoes to a loftier theme;
To spend my life's last store of industry
On thoughts less vain than Youth's discordant dream;
To endow the world's grief with some counter-scheme
Of logical hope which through all time should lighten
The burden of men's sorrow and redeem
Their faces' paleness from the tears that whiten.[28]

Years later, he relished informing the authorities who had invited him to be a Sussex magistrate that he was ineligible, being a convicted felon.

Jack Rapley, a gardener-handyman who was employed by Blunt, recalled that he had helped Blunt work his private printing press. This was almost entirely made of wood and had wooden characters. Blunt used it to publish amateurishly his accounts of imperial events that he considered the Establishment wanted to conceal. In 1961, it lay rotting in a shed, as did invalid carriages, together with papers strewn about in a basement that have never been recovered.[29]

Blunt's Diaries

Of Blunt's diaries, E.M. Forster has written:

> Never was such a delightful book. One doesn't know where to begin. So much humour, a charming good-temper, such opportunities of seeing them, such powers of describing them, including Oscar Wilde ('I never walk'). It is a wonderful gift this writing of one's fellow creatures as if they were alive. He leaves a portrait gallery, invaluable for students, and delightful to all.[30]

These diaries, which convey aspects of his many-sided personality, are still largely unpublished, apart from his own edited version in two parts covering the years 1888 to 1914. Since then, Lady Longford has concluded that while there is room for differences of opinion about Blunt as poet and politician, as a social diarist he is on a par with Charles Greville. A sample of entries, beginning with Sunday, 4 October 1896, reads:

> Morris is dead. I got a letter telling it from Lady Burne-Jones this morning. She says, 'Our dear friend Morris died at twenty minutes past eleven this morning, as quietly as ever a babe went to sleep in its mother's arms'.
>
> It has come sooner than I expected, though I knew his case was hopeless. It is better as it is. He is the most wonderful man I have known, unique in this, that he had no thought for anything or person including himself, but only for the work he had in hand. He was not selfish in the sense of seeking his own advantage or pleasure or comfort, but he was too absorbed in his own thoughts to be either openly affectionate or actively kind. […] He liked to talk to me because I knew how to talk to him, and our fence of words furbished his wit, but I doubt if he would have crossed the street to speak with me […] It will be a great grief for Jenny, a great break-up for Janey, and a great loss for the world at large, for he was really our greatest man.

When compiling his diary in 1911, Blunt thought that he should have softened the above remarks about Morris' lack of tenderness but decided to let the original text stand.

31st December 1900:

I bid good-bye to the old century, may it rest in peace as it has lived in war. Of the new century I prophecy nothing except that it will see the decline of the British Empire. Other worse Empires will rise perhaps in its place, but I shall not live to see the day. It all seems a very little matter here in Egypt, with the Pyramids watching us as they watched Joseph, when, as a young man four thousand years ago, perhaps in this very garden, he walked and gazed at the sunset behind them, wondering about the future as I did this evening. And so, poor wicked nineteenth century, farewell![31]

'I was Lord There of My Own Manor'[32]

The descendants of Blunt's tenants, servants and neighbours still living in his 'kingdom' have the fondest memories of his courtesy and kindness towards them, where the old world of the Sussex Weald 'plodded the rut of centuries'. Blunt was happy, 'for his rule was that of the feudal lord of ancient times, he had only to speak and his wishes were carried out'.[33] In old age he toured his estate in a carriage behind his Arab horses, to ensure that all was in order. Newbuildings Place had a character that was:

> ... highly civilized and a little wild; its English homeliness in a region of small oaks, combined with far-fetched attar roses from Damascus and Arab horses in the paddock; peacocks strutting or perched on wood-stacks [...] and a squire clothed in a Bedouin robe.[34]

But as we have seen, Blunt walked on a wider stage, bringing an exotic coterie to Crabbet and Newbuildings, deep in the Weald. He was, for example, as we have seen, unfailingly kind to the poet Francis Thompson, who spent some of his dying weeks as his guest, and to the retired architect Philip Webb, co-founder with William Morris of the Society for the Protection of Ancient Buildings, who, as we have seen, was provided with Caxtons, a cottage on the estate. Blunt shared with Morris a love of landscape and natural beauty and Morris published a Kelmscott edition of Blunt's best poems.[35] A younger generation of poets, including Ezra Pound and John Masefield, organised a 'Peacock Dinner' in his honour (not entirely appreciated), while young enthusiasts for the East including T.E. Lawrence and St John Philby revered him for his Middle Eastern journeys.

Nevertheless, as Blunt aged he felt his efforts to reform the world had failed and he became depressed at what he sensed to be the culture of human-kind changing in ways to which he could not adapt. He surmised, largely correctly, that 'The people who are growing up now will not care for our art and literature, they will not understand our thoughts or read our poetry'.

E.M. Forster remarked that:

Perhaps only for an Englishman, and only in the nineteenth century, was such a career possible. The chivalrous free-lance, who loves justice and beauty, and is drawn to a distant quest, will doubtless be born in the future, but he will not have enough money to effectuate himself.[36]

Forster thought that the time had not yet come to sum up Blunt's career, which was of one 'whose birth and education destined him to be a high official but who spent all this life tilting against officialdom'. Blunt's friend, Wilfrid Meynell, told him over dinner in 1911 that the world would eventually come round to his opinions.

This may well be prophetic. Hitherto, Blunt has not had the recognition that is his due, either literary, politically, or in his attitudes to the land and its management. Reviled and isolated in his lifetime as a standard bearer of lost causes, most of his causes have now been won and his moral courage is an example of what is needed more than ever in the present day in the fight against deprivation and injustice.

RICHARD JEFFERIES (1848–87): 'THE INFLUENCE OF NATURAL OBJECTS UPON THE HUMAN MIND'[1]

Where man and nature have dwelt side by side time out of mind there is a presence, a genius of the spot, a haunting sweetness and loveliness not elsewhere to be found.[2]

John Richard Jefferies (always known as Richard) is not always to the forefront of modern literary knowledge, and in his lifetime his work yielded little by way of income. Yet, he was one of the greatest writers on the landscapes, agriculture and natural history of southern England. Prominent literary figures such as Edward Thomas, W.H. Hudson and Henry Williamson have acknowledged their debt to him, as have Julian Bell and Arthur Beckett. He has been compared to his near contemporary Henry David Thoreau in his lifestyle and writing.[3] In a short life, his output was prodigious (Plate 19).

His father James was a not too successful farmer and dairyman at Coates Farm near Swindon and the Jefferies family came from a long line of farming forebears based around Gloucestershire and Wiltshire. Although his mother's health caused him to be fostered by relatives in Sydenham when young, he returned to the countryside around the farm and began to write.

Through his mother, the family had relatives who were printers, including friends at Lewes, the Baxters, the well-known local printers, and in 1866 Richard became a reporter on a local newspaper, the *North Wilts Herald*. He was a voracious reader, first coming to wider attention aged 24 with his letters to *The Times* in 1872 on the condition of tenant farmers. These received great publicity, coming at the time of Joseph Arch's formation of the National Agricultural Labourers Union. He gradually found openings for agricultural articles, but until he moved to Tolworth early in 1877, then still largely rural, near Surbiton, to write on natural history, rural life and agriculture for the London villa readership, he did not secure success as a writer. However, by the later 1870s he was seen as a leading authority on English rural life, drawing on memories of his Wiltshire childhood.[4]

Jefferies and Sussex

Tall and thin, Jefferies was far from robust in health and by the late 1860s he was already experiencing the early symptoms of tuberculosis. He was reserved and sensitive, and spent his last years in Sussex searching for a congenial climate from which to recover from the illnesses, which became increasingly serious. He had often visited the Sussex coast in childhood, but his last few years were peripatetic. He was living at Long Ditton on the outskirts of London in 1881 but moved during 1882 to an address at No. 8 (now No. 27) Lorna Road, Hove, an area near Hove station then being sought 'principally for rest and quiet'.[5] He enjoyed living by the sea, which became hugely important in his writing, enjoyed the sights of fashionable Brighton life and rambled the South Downs. 'There is always hope in the hills,' he wrote. 'This is the land of health.'[6]

By September 1884, he had moved to Eltham in Kent, but returned to Sussex by June 1885, renting Rehoboth Villa (now Brook View House), at Jarvis Brook for a short time while a search was made for a villa in Tunbridge Wells. However, he was very soon residing for the sake of his health at a stone cottage called The Downs, Crowborough, with fine views over Ashdown Forest (Plate 20).

His son, the late Richard Harold Jefferies, wrote, 'The Crowborough district was ideal for a wanderer like my father – a rather wild rolling hilly country, well wooded and with small streams. Ferns were very plentiful and father loved bracken with its peculiar odour when crushed.'[7] But Jefferies was so ill there, 'mind alive but body dead', that most of his work was dictated to his wife Jessie, whom he had married in 1874.[8] The last essay he wrote himself was 'Hours of Spring', from his Crowborough cottage:

> But today I have to listen to the lark's song – not out of doors with him, but through the windowpane – and the bullfinch carried the rootlet fibre to his nest without me. They manage without me very well [...] The earth is all in all to me, but I am nothing to the earth: it is bitter to know this before you are dead.

He was wheeled about in a bath chair to his favourite spot, an ancient oak at Cook's Corner, from which he enjoyed the extensive view of wooded Kent. Boys Firmin's *Illustrated Guide to Crowborough* (1900) gives a brief account of his life in the district and in the 1905 edition he gives a list of the essays Jefferies wrote there. But he moved from Crowborough, where he described the air in the harsh winter of 1885–86 as 'sharp as a knife and the wind a rude barbarian giant knocking at the house with a giant club', to Sea View at Goring-by-Sea in 1886. There was then a good stretch of country road between Goring and Worthing and southwards down the track of Sea Lane was the open beach backed by cornfields. From the breakfast room window, coasters and luggers could be seen reaching for the shore where today twentieth-century housing blocks the view.

He died at Sea View in August 1887 aged 38, but his final years had been dogged by what he called 'the giants of Disease, Despair and Poverty'.[9] He is buried in Broadwater and Worthing Cemetery. On his grave is inscribed 'Prose poet of England's fields and woodlands'. His cottage at Goring in Cat Alley (now Jefferies House in Jefferies Lane) bears a plaque, as do his homes in Hove and Crowborough (Plate 21).

When still relatively healthy and 'strong of foot', Jefferies strode rapidly over the chalk landscape of the South Downs alone, enjoying the springy turf and seeking some form of solitary communion with nature, but in illness he became inevitably more sedentary and meditative. However, his remarkable mental acuteness heightened and rarefied as his physical strength waned. He had the gift of making readers see what he himself saw and, as with the freshness of Gilbert White of Selborne, he never failed to see something new in nature. He developed a heightened vision that may have originated in disease, as in Keats. This was marked by his intense joy of life and deep absorption, which could lead to rapture and ecstasy as well as the emotional exaltation of a manic depressive. He is still often referred to as a 'mystic', and as a follower of Walt Whitman, he might even be called an early hippy.

Jefferies' communion with nature had no peer in England in his own time, save the priest and poet Gerard Manley Hopkins, although something of his passionate love for landscape and natural beauty is also to be met with in William Morris. His fervour was also to enthuse succeeding Sussex writers, many young poets taking him for a mentor. Yet, Jefferies was also a down-to-earth man, bitterly resenting the misery of workers in both town and countryside.

By his death from tuberculosis at 38 he had produced twenty-two books, many written while he was very ill. There are five containing Sussex material: the last three essays in *Nature Near London* (1883); his outpouring of nature-mysticism *The Story of my Heart* (1883), finished while living at Lorna Road; *The Life of the Fields* (1884, mostly written in Hove); *The Open Air* (1885); and *Field and Hedgerow* (published posthumously in 1889). But little, overall, of his writing was inspired by Sussex, and some of these books included material describing other locations. Even obvious Sussex themes are sometimes difficult to locate precisely, but the above books certainly included some of his best and most characteristic work.[10] In particular, he was prolific in his writing when living in Hove.

He was many sided and wrote of Brighton and its beach as readily as farming and nature. Unlike the contemporary naturalist W.H. Hudson, Jefferies was concerned with the interaction between humans and nature. He enthused on the prehistoric tumuli and field systems then imprinted on the higher slopes of the Wiltshire and South Downs and was the earliest writer to perceive them as a sequent evolution of settlement and farming that has underpinned prehistoric archaeology to the present day, thereby anticipating W.G. Hoskins' concept of the landscape as a palimpsest of human decisions over millennia. He loved locality and serves today to remind us of its importance.

Possibly no one has absorbed the South Downs more into his very being, although Virginia Woolf would also come to mind in this respect. There are hints of this in some of his best essays in *The Open Air*, when he was still at the height of his powers, such as that on the Downs at Wolstonbury Hill. He noted that there was a 'double England' there, 'two countries side by side', because the Downs shut off the sea like a wall with a different climate on either side. Coming over the range from the coast, he passed the one 'hard, harsh, flowerless, almost grassless, bitter, and cold', while the sheltered part was 'warm, soft, with primroses and fern, willows budding and birds already busy', a contrast reminding him of the experience of travellers coming over the Alps into Italy.

He writes of the most delicate 'Grecian air, pellucid' and of his sensation of being alone and isolated with only butterflies and bees in the thyme 'amongst endless masses of hills on three sides, endless Weald or valley on the fourth [...] deep under liquid sunshine', with no harshness of man-made sound. It was such a beautiful and peaceful place that he mused on how an adult man or woman would react to it who had never looked upon the earth. He concluded that the hues and shapes and songs of birds in the sunlight under the breadth of heaven would be like a radiant vision.[11]

As a superb naturalist, he was particularly sensitive to changes in the air, feeling and tone of a place, although it might be only half a mile distant.

In discovering these differences, often minute but significant to plant and animal life, he was inspired by the Chinese concept of Feng-shui, 'casting the horoscope of an acre'. He cited an example of what made one locality healthy and the other less so, by remarking that bird's-foot trefoil marked a fortunate site – dry, warm in soil – where one could safely build a hut ('a kibitka' or yurt). He was humbled to find the orange-red plant for the first time that very morning, a pictured flowerbook, just purchased, to hand. After so many years of wildflower hunting, he felt only at the beginning of the beginning. The bird's-foot trefoil was pictured in his mind as summer and sunshine, but of the summers known in youth when not alone, and he was dismayed at his inability to fix it adequately for the reader, 'It is like a story that cannot be told because he who knows it is tongue-tied and dumb.'[12]

Even so, Jefferies had great facility in conveying the immensity and silence of the downland to a walker. Grasping tough grass and climbing up the first ridge, he was at once out of civilisation. There, the long slopes, the endless ridges, the gaps between, hazy and indistinct, were absolutely without noise. The only sounds were soothing: bees buzzing, birds singing and the beating of their wings. Looking over the silent earth, his first impression was of an immense void like the sea. By walking a mile, he might meet one or two people and realise, now not in the best of health, the hopelessness of getting over the hills to the hazy horizon where the ridges crowded on each other in a wide expanse, 'Like rowing at sea, you row and row and row, and seem where you started – waves in front and waves behind. In the largeness and freedom thoughts could roam broad as the down itself and free as the wind.'[13]

For Jefferies, the view could never be wide or large enough, and as the air of the hills enriched his blood, so did beautiful things enrich his inner sense, his heart was lifted, and he was transported into ecstasy. As for the turf, the plough had nibbled at it and gnawed away great slices, but it still extended mile after mile in grass, furze, heath and bramble.

He touched on the downland winter, noting that those living in isolated farmsteads laid in a good store of fuel and provisions and as many books as they could to their bookshelf because they might be practically imprisoned for weeks together, as in the snow tempest of 1880–81.

As a naturalist the potency of new growth in spring had a special power. He never failed to ponder on the mysteries of life and its colour and beauty and would note, year by year, the dates when he first heard the cawing of rooks in February, the thawing of a frozen stream, when fish came into sight, when green corn shot up and buds burst again, and when the first flowers came before they were hidden among grass in May.

'Sun Life' and Sussex Diary Entries

Jefferies' most rapturous feelings for the South Downs are reserved for his extraordinary *The Story of My Heart*, which Ronald Blythe has called 'a remarkable part-psychological, part-dream confession' containing a vision of his inner life and his deepest feelings.[14] It is certainly not a conventional autobiography, although it commences at length with his boyhood experiences on the Wiltshire Downs and on this account, it has not been usually considered a Sussex work. Yet it concludes with Jefferies throbbing with life at the Devil's Dyke in the Downs above Brighton and Hove, where the book was written (Plate 22). Up there, he found himself in the presence of the immensity of the inexpressibly beautiful countryside. There was, too, the pure air, the feeling of ancientness and continuity and the mystery of the mighty geological forces that had shaped this paradise. And there was the sea and its sunshine that always left Jefferies rapt and carried into ecstasy. In these presences he was intoxicated with visual emotions and his mind went into mystical exaltation while plumbing the depths of the universe.

His diary reveals that it was on the Dyke one evening in the dusk that he shaped more clearly for himself, for the first time, his mysticism of exalting the individual's soul and perfecting human life. The entry for 27 April 1883, written after an excursion to the Brighton Downs, suggests the germ of the book '… Sun Life [the working title he gave to *The Story of My Heart*] […] superabundance for all – these are but the beginning of an idea, merest beginning', and on 6 May, again after a day on the downs, he writes, 'Sun Life … ingrained selfishness of 12,000 years', another theme of his book. Up there, he meditated on his bafflement at the 'madness' that after 'twelve thousand written years' the human race could still live hand to mouth like domestic animals and wildlife, and with a utopian vision that anticipates Wells, he envisaged endless scientific developments that would remove man from drudgery and hard manual work.[15] The book was a failure on publication, but is now regarded as a classic account of English nature mysticism.

These diary entries for 1883, when he was living in Brighton, reveal his wide range of interests, his keen eyesight and acute observation on the South Downs, and the inspiration he received for his books, all of which were stored up in his consciousness. His essay 'Clematis Lane' in *The Life of the Fields* is one example. He writes of scenes observed on the South Downs and of his delight at his never-ending discoveries of nature: the commonplace and rarer wildflowers, such as the light-blue petals of the grey field veronica, which he hunted in the stubbles, and the wildlife that went unobserved by most people while the 'grasshoppers sang, the wind swept through the grass and swung the harebells, the "drowsy hum" of the threshing machine rose up from the plain, the slow, slumberous melody of harvest time floated in the air'.[16]

Of the Devil's Dyke, just to the north of Brighton on the downland, 'I have found a grooved valley, deep, climbing to whose lip the sea is visible. Here I see (on the turf) how little is the highest thought to the thoughts that must be.' And in *The Story of My Heart*, he writes, 'I found a deep hollow on the side of a great hill … Yonder lay the immense plain of the sea … Silence and sunshine, sea and hill, gradually brought my mind into the condition of immense prayer.'[17]

In his diary for 10 May 1883, 'The roar of the sea, largeness of the tide, the blue horizon, the sun burning'. Jefferies refers constantly to this experience as 'Sun Life', his shorthand reference to the feelings he would encapsulate in *The Story of My Heart*.

On 19 July:

Goat's Beard out. 10 o'clock Dyke Road, not so broad nor thick as dandelion. Black marks in centre, really the black stems of stamens, sepals beyond flowers. Milk in stalk. Like parasol turned inside out. Flower more like hawkweed. Stained skin.

In the diary, there then followed three pencil sketches of flowers. On 21 August:

Harvest red cap reaper – red handkerchief on head. Grey veronica flowering amongst the stubble as in February […] Mist, threshing engine hum. Yuckyuckle in the beeches, behind the whiz-rr of pigeon's wings. Red reapers glad to be allowed to work like this. You can see assemble all his energy and moil.[18]

The continuation of the above can be found in *Nature Near London*:

Red spots, like larger poppies, now appear above and now dive down again beneath the golden surface. These are the red caps worn by some of the reapers; some of the girls, too, have a scarf across the shoulder or around the waist. By instinctive sympathy the heat of summer requires the contrast of brilliant hues, of scarlet and gold, of poppy and wheat.[19]

W.H. Hudson considered that Jefferies' book had been powerfully influenced by his stay in Sussex, and he was undoubtedly correct. There, he was gaining in self-assurance and maturity of thought, despite the handicap of carrying much more in his imagination than he could express in words, and he tells us that the inspiration to write it was his visit to the ancientness of Pevensey Castle in 1880:

> At last, in 1880, in the old castle of Pevensey, under happy circumstances, once more I resolved, and actually did write down a few notes. Even then I could not go on, but I kept the notes, and in the end, two years afterwards, began this book.

And in the book, he writes:

> It happened just afterwards that I went to Pevensey, and immediately the ancient wall swept my mind back seventeen hundred years ... the grey stones, the thin red bricks laid by those who had seen Caesar's Rome, lifted me out of the grasp of house-life, of modern civilization, of those minutiae which occupy the moment ... The marvel of existence, almost the terror of it, was flung on me with crushing force by the sea, the sun shining, the distant hills.[20]

The Sea and the Fields

The invalid Jefferies paid a memorable tribute to breezy Beachy Head:

> But the glory of these glorious Downs is the breeze. The air in the valleys immediately beneath them is pure and pleasant; but the least climb, even a hundred feet, puts you on a plane with the atmosphere itself, uninterrupted by so much as the tree-tops. It is air without admixture ... The sun searches out every crevice amongst the grass, nor is there the smallest fragment of surface which is not sweetened by air and light ... Lands of gold have been found, and lands of spices and precious merchandise; but this is the land of health.[21]

In the Weald Jefferies rests in the delicious air under the oaks and admires the autumn colours. Straying into a well-to-do place with villas inhabited by wealthy people, he was struck by the absence of men actually paid and employed in the countryside and how very few seemed to have appreciated its quiet beauty, 'Somehow, they never seem to see it – to look over it; there is no excitement in it, for one thing. They can see a great deal in Paris, but nothing in an English meadow.' But Jefferies did not forget that if something was pointed out to them or described, they took an interest, an anomaly that later Sussex writers attempted to counteract with possibly as little success.[22]

Jefferies' 'idea of nature' became expanded into a deliberate personal faith and this is apparent from his account in *The Story of My Heart* of an experience by the sea that can be linked to his diary entry for 10 May 1883. This is how he greeted the Sussex seashore:

I was weary for the pure, fresh springs of thought. Some instinctive feeling uncontrollable drove me to the sea ... I found the sea at last; I walked beside it in a trance away from the houses out into the wheat. The ripe corn stood up to the beach, the waves on one side of the shingle, and the yellow wheat on the other.

There, alone, I went down to the sea. I stood where the foam came to my feet, and looked out over the sunlit waters. The great earth bearing the richness of the harvest, and its hills golden with corn, was at my back; its strength and firmness under me. The great sun shone above, the wide sea was before me, the wind came sweet and strong from the waves. The life of the earth and the sea, the glow of the sun filled me; I touched the surge with my hand, I lifted my face to the sun, I opened my lips to the wind. I prayed aloud in the roar of the waves – my soul was strong as the sea and prayed with the sea's might. 'Give me fulness of life like to the sea and the sun, to the earth and the air; give me fulness of physical life, mind equal and beyond their fulness; give me a greatness and perfection of soul higher than all things; give me my inexpressible desire which swells in me like a tide – give it to me with all the force of the sea' ... Once more I went down to the sea, touched it, and said farewell. So deep was the inhalation of this life that day, that it seemed to remain in me for years. This was a real pilgrimage.[23]

Jefferies was not only a naturalist, which is usually considered his proper field, but he dealt insightfully with the farm labourer. In the essay 'One of the New Voters', he has Roger the reaper, a single man, rising from his 'bed' on a raised platform in the cowhouse. He had shared his abode with cows, which wandered in and out at night, and bats which had wearied at moth catching. He had not taken off his boots, but flung himself on the boards and slept deeply, curling himself up hedgehog fashion with some old sacks and instantly began to breathe heavily under the impact of muscles tried to the utmost and at least a gallon of harvest beer, 'the very smallest and poorest wishywashy beer'. In his own words, it 'blowed him up till he very nigh bust'. Jefferies claimed it was the vilest drink in the world, and yet 'upon this abominable mess the golden harvest of English fields is gathered in'.[24]

Typical of his writing is his account of threshing in Sussex in *Field and Hedgerow*. It shows his acute observation and his intense interest in rural life, including both agricultural operations and people, which appealed to urbanites and suburbanites subscribing to the new enthusiasm for the open air:

> ... Laughing the children romped round the ricks. They love the threshing and flock to it, they watch the fly-wheel rotating, they look in at the furnace door when the engine-driver stokes his fire, they gaze wonderingly at the gauge, and long to turn the brass taps; then with a shout they run to chase the unhappy mice dislodged from the corn. The mice hide themselves in the petticoats of the women working at the 'sheening', and the cottager, when she goes home in the evening, calls her cat and shakes them out of her skirts. By a blue wagon the farmer stands leaning on his staff ... [Meanwhile 'hopping' is going on at the kiln] ... Up comes a carter to see how the hops 'be getting on'. In five minutes another waggoner looks in, then a couple of ploughboys, next a higgler passing by; no one walks or rides or drives past the hopkiln without calling to see how things are going on ... Round and round in the pocket brings out the perspiration [on the 'drier'] and the dust of the hops gets into the air passages and thickens on the skin of his face.[25]

And in *Nature Near London* there is a superb description of the old Sussex ox-drawn plough on the Downs and the ploughman on Ditchling Beacon (Figure 18). 'The ploughs are at work, travelling slowly at the ox's pace up and down the hillside':

> [The plough] is made of many pieces, chiefly wood, fitted and shaped and worked, as it were, together, well seasoned first, built up, like a ship, by cunning of hand.
>
> None of these were struck out—a hundred a minute—by irresistible machinery ponderously impressing its will on iron as a seal on wax—a hundred a minute, and all exactly alike. These separate pieces which compose the plough were cut, chosen, and shaped in the wheelwright's

workshop, chosen by the eye, guided in its turn by long knowledge of wood, and shaped by the living though hardened hand of man. So complicated a structure could no more have been struck out on paper in a deliberate and single plan than those separate pieces could have been produced by a single blow ...

The thing has been put together bit by bit: how many thousand, thousand clods must have been turned in the furrows before the idea arose, and the curve to be given to this or that part grew upon the mind as the branch grows on the tree! ... the various makers, who gradually put it together, had many things to consider. The fields where it had to work were, for the most part, on a slope, often thickly strewn with stones which jar and fracture iron.

The soil was thin, scarce enough on the upper part to turn a furrow, deepening to nine inches or so at the bottom. So quickly does the rain sink in, and so quickly does it dry, that the teams work in almost every weather, while those in the vale are enforced to idleness. Drain furrows were not needed, nor was it desirable that the ground should be thrown up in 'lands', rising in the centre. Oxen were the draught animals, patient enough, but certainly not nimble. The share had to be set for various depths of soil. ...

Fig. 18: The old Sussex Plough in use in the Cuckmere Valley (postcard).

Jefferies then illustrates the plough's components. The framework, on wheels in front, was called collectively 'tacks' and the shafts of the plough rested on it loosely, so that they swung almost independently. The ploughshare could be raised or lowered at will, so that it could dig deep or shallow, according to the varying depth of soil in a field. Other components included a 'cock-pin', the 'road-bat', the 'shervewright', the 'rist' and spindle. When the oxen reached the top of a field they stopped and the ploughman moved the iron rist and the spindle, which held it to the other side, and moved the roadbat, a piece of wood, so that it pushed the coulter aside. This operation took about a minute, the object being that the plough would now turn soil in the furrow in the opposite way, leaving the surface of the field perfectly level and not ridged. The ploughman then leaned heavily on the plough, which lifted easily on its pivot in readiness for the next furrow. Altogether, Jefferies' account is a glorious word-painting of the old Sussex agriculture and a reverence for the skills of its wheelwrights and ploughmen that no other writer has surpassed.[26]

Jefferies: The Material and the Spiritual

Jefferies was not deceived in his rural investigations by any idyllicism. In his essay 'One of the New Voters', he concluded, 'The wheat is beautiful, but human life is labour'.[27] Degradation and hardship was observed – but to what extent might the grim work in the fields be alleviated by mechanisation? If he looked back to an earlier age, fifty or 100 years before, he was also something of a predecessor of the more modernist, internalised writing characterised by Edward Thomas or Henry Williamson. But it would be fair to conclude that, like Blunt, who he otherwise resembled not at all, his was not the spirit of modernity. He was many things, from amateur archaeologist to rural sociologist, but above all, he walked, observed, thought and wrote for a living. And what he wrote sprang materially or spiritually from his natural surroundings. Walter Besant wrote in 1905, 'In a hundred years he will be only more truly appreciated than at present.'[28]

As noted at the beginning of this chapter, Jefferies exerted a profound influence on others who aspired to explore and communicate their feelings about the natural world they saw around them. One acquaintance called him 'a shy, proud recluse' with few literary friends, and he himself wrote in his diary, 'There is nothing so repulsive as one's own species', but even so, many were entranced.[29] It is fitting, therefore, that W.H. Hudson was buried

nearby in the same cemetery as Jefferies, at Broadwater, and that Edward
Thomas' biography of Jefferies was dedicated to Hudson.

Although there has been some debate about his religious beliefs, a fitting
end might be to quote from the fine memorial to Jefferies in Salisbury
Cathedral, unveiled in March 1892:

> To the memory of Richard Jefferies
> … who observing the works of almighty God,
> With a poet's eye has
> Enriched the literature of his country
> And
> Won for himself a place amongst
> Those
> Who have made men happier,
> And wiser.

IN HILAIRE BELLOC'S COUNTRY: 'THIS EDEN THAT IS SUSSEX STILL'

I will gather and carefully make my friends
Of the men of the Sussex Weald,
They watch the stars from silent folds,
They stiffly plough the field.
By them and the God of the South Country
My poor soul shall be healed.[1]

The Complexity of Belloc

No modern writer of corresponding stature has been repudiated so fiercely by an immediately succeeding generation than Joseph Hilaire Pierre René Belloc (1870–1953). Never counting self-effacement a literary virtue, and once enjoyed in bulk by readers under the sway of his brilliant and masterful pen, this many-sided man of continuous and enormous creative energy, who 'shovelled out work by the ton', is now hardly read at all. One biographer referred to him as 'out of fashion, out of print, in most cases out of mind'.[2] His all-consuming militancy as a flaming radical, shared with G.K. Chesterton, for a Catholic solution to Britain's economic and social ills led him into polemical extremes, close to antisemitism and a willingness to sanction fascist remedies, which has had a hugely deleterious effect on his reputation.[3] Yet, the modern reader will always find something irresistible in Belloc's John Bullishness writing, with its strong sense of the majesty and music of words (Figure 19).

On his death, a lengthy estimate of his character and achievements that appeared in *The Times* made no reference to his connection with Sussex, which, despite his many other activities, played a most important part in his life and writings.[4] It had nourished his boyhood, became the centre of his universe, healed his soul, was celebrated in fertile verse and prose, and was

Fig. 19: Joseph Hilaire Pierre René Belloc (1870–1953) in his boat, probably *The Nona*. (Alamy.com)

agonised over and unambiguously propagandised all his life. His somewhat dank and inconvenient home and windmill at King's Land, Shipley, dependent financially solely on his writing, was the core of his being.

Writing Belloc's life without placing him in Sussex would leave a great part of his life unexplained, rather like attempting Wordsworth without 'The Lakes'. Indeed, one wonders whether any author loved his adopted county more, created verse so resounding to the Sussex mind and served it so ardently, evoking its spirit more evocatively?

This preternaturally vital man of great wit, versatility, vivacity, tremendous gusto and huge physical energy – a far more interesting personality than the noisy, gusty, bullying, roistering and beer-swilling man he is often thought to be – was born in 1870 at La Celle-Saint-Cloud, west of Paris, of one French and one English parent. He was legally a French citizen until his naturalisation in 1902. G.K. Chesterton amusingly contrasted Francis Yvon Eccles, Belloc's friend and a distinguished French scholar, who had an English surname but looked like the Frenchman he was, with Belloc, who had a French surname but an Englishman's appearance (although he spoke with French 'rs').

His mother was Elizabeth Parkes, who converted to Catholicism in 1864 and married Louis, son of the celebrated French painter Jean-Hilaire Belloc. His maternal grandfather was Joseph Parkes, known as 'the last of the English radicals' for his prominent part at the time of the Reform Bill, and Belloc, the social reformer strong in him, was determined to follow him politically with his ideas for a property-owning democracy. In 1896, he married Elodie Hogan (1868–1914), of Irish American ancestry, following a seven-year engagement, during which he completed military service in France and his time at Oxford. They were married in Napa, California.

Belloc, in fact, although inspired by French culture and republicanism, matured into an old-fashioned Englishman of bluff demeanour. Some thought he resembled the personality of Sussex itself – Saxon in build, bruff, hearty and seemingly as English as the South Downs themselves. His prose style also recalls at times the old country writers and squires who spoke and wrote with relish, caring more to express themselves heartily than with scientific or historical accuracy.

The Inspirational Centre of his Universe

It is significant that, for all his overbrimming vitality, restless travel and writing about many places in western Europe, his exploration of the history of France and his engagement in national politics and religious issues, Sussex remained the inspirational centre of his universe. Here he had been brought up and lived all his life, clinging tenaciously to the childhood memories of a well-remembered countryside. With wondering childish eyes from 8 years old and as a youth, he experienced moments, even hours, of intense exhilaration on the South Downs.

Like a refreshing breeze, those boyish fancies never left him, so that recollections of this little corner were the spring that fed his mind and spirit and nurtured his body and imagination, and the longing for them was one of the key influences on him throughout the years that followed. The sight and recollection of the long line of the hanging woods of the western Downs was immured in him, and he had a lifelong hunger for Sussex landscapes, which helped make him a poet and writer seeking to reproduce the homeliness and graciousness of his 'noble' hills and their ancient traditions. In some subtle way, the Downs became a symbolic part of Belloc's emotions and depth of feeling, an alter ego, as other writers have consistently used a persona as a mouthpiece for their philosophy.

In his passion for walking, he was to discover landscapes that captured his fancy all over Europe, but none filled the springs of his soul as had those of his childhood. To the end of his life, as J.B. Morton has remarked, Belloc never failed to exclaim pleasure when travelling in Sussex, at the sight of each homely and well-remembered object in the lines of his childhood Downs.

This exceptionally intense patriotic feeling for Sussex is possibly due to having been born in France and settled in England among different sounds and sights, feeling like an exile or a displaced person and needing to identify with another place he could call home. Kipling went through the same sentiments as a stranger in somewhat similar circumstances (page 139). His objections to later landscape and social changes in Sussex largely arose from a strong sense that every corner of the lanes and fields of his boyhood was vanishing and being forever lost except as poignant memories. This Belloc called the 'loss of place' and no Sussex author had a deeper sense of that loss or worried more over the placeless future, still a contemporary dread, so that reading him is a reminder of the Sussex that has largely disappeared.[5]

Sussex came to be conceived by him as 'Not London' and the 'most English England', her blessed Eden, a refuge from the pursuit of men and a creative civilising heart that he hoped might yet reform the whole nation. It was also to be an emblem of innocent solidity, of the permanence that forever eluded his restless spirit. With what friends called his 'glorious arrogance', he elevated Sussex to such heights of hyperbole, as in 'The South Country', that it was an irritation to those whose loyalties were to other counties. But he must have been responsible for the immigration of very many urban dwellers seeking to savour the joys he was himself experiencing.

At Home in Sussex

The core of Sussex, geographically as well as spiritually, in Belloc's mind, was that of the South Downs near Slindon where his mind was shaped in boyhood. He writes in *The Four Men*, 'My part of Sussex is all that part from the valley of the Arun, and up the Western Rother too, and so over the steep of the Downs to the Norewood, and the lonely place called No Man's Land [near the summit of the Downs].'[6] This was of intense significance to him because it was from there that he first caught a distant view of the sea. He considered his Arun Valley the antechamber to paradise and the jewel of which Sussex was made (Plate 23).

In the essay 'The Mowing of a Field' in *Hills and the Sea* (1906), he told of the moment in boyhood when he first discovered his idyllic countryside, the remote, semi-wild downland. It was that discovery of Gumber and its surrounds in an incident in his youth that promoted scores of responses in his verse and prose through his lifetime:

There is a valley in South England remote from ambition and from fear …
In this place, when I was a boy, I pushed through a fringe of beeches that
made a complete screen between me and the world, and I came to a glade
called No Man's Land. I climbed beyond it, and I was surprised and glad,
because from the ridge of that glade I saw the sea.[7]

This is in the heart of still lovely and lonely downs. Belloc would presumably have ridden up Mill Lane and followed the track, now popular with
walkers, up to Northwood and Great Down to reach this isolated spot with
distant views to Chichester Cathedral and the sea. From Gumber Corner,
also known as Coldharbour Hill, is a spot where so many of the special
features that make up Sussex may be seized in one view. The views from
the Trundle and Chanctonbury, as well as the Caburn, have already been
mentioned, but for Belloc there was no other place in the county where the
landscape was as full of early history, and at the same time so diverse and so
characteristic.

Poised high and looking down commandingly, to the south is the closely
patterned coastal plain and the sea with the Owers lightship flashing at night.
Selsey Bill, the Isle of Wight and the creeks of the Hampshire–Sussex border
extend westwards, dominated by the spire of Chichester Cathedral. The
coastal resorts lie eastwards to Worthing. Northward lies the stretch of the
Weald to the Surrey Hills, to the elevated Hindhead and Blackdown and
across to Ashdown Forest. At one's feet is the best-preserved section of the
Roman Stane Street. Gumber remains a lonely place amid woods on the high
downs, of which Belloc wrote, 'Here am I homeward and my heart is healed'
and so 'Lift up your hearts in Gumber, laugh the Weald/ And you my mother
the Valley of Arun sing'.[8]

Four of Belloc's homes were in the village of Slindon near Gumber, a
delightful village now largely owned by the National Trust on the edge
of the Downs and near views of the Weald and the sea. His mother had
moved the family here to his first Sussex home, Slindon Cottage (now
called Dower House), when he was 8, after losing £12,000 through a
financial advisor on the Stock Market. It was from here, and at their second
house, the Grange, near the charming village pond, that he explored his
boyhood surroundings on foot and horseback on the high downs overlooking the Arun Valley, the Western Rother and the Weald. Here were the
'great hills of the South Country', which imbued him with his passionate
love of Sussex.

His first married home was Bleak House, also in the village street, and in 1905, on leaving the more expensive Cheyne Walk in London, he rented Court Hill Farm House on the edge of the village (Plate 24). Here, he wrote his essays, collected in *The Hills and the Sea*, amid 'great forests of wonderful beeches and firs and beyond the blue line of the Downs'. Halnaker Mill was visible from his home and its decline was the subject of his famous poem 'Ha'naker Mill' (1913) symbolising to him England's rural decline and corruption:

Ha'nacker's down and England's done.
Wind and thistle for pipe and dancers
And never a ploughman under the Sun.
Never a ploughman. Never a one.[9]

Moving again, from 1906 Belloc lived at King's Land at Shipley, near Horsham in the Sussex Weald, and resided there until his death more than forty years later (Plate 25). From his adjacent early nineteenth-century smock mill (later restored in his memory), he had magnificent views southwards to Chanctonbury Ring and northwards to Leith Hill and the line of the North Downs. Here, he was thoroughly at home in a Catholic countryside that had secretly remained loyal to the faith after the Reformation and among small farmers who symbolised for him the Old England he cherished as much as had William Cobbett, untainted by the industrialist, capitalist society he saw as anti-human to the core.

King's Land offered the remoteness from modern life and the complete silence that his soul required when he dashed back sweating from the London train. But his biographer, A.N. Wilson noted that, paradoxically, until his old age this 'opinionated supertramp' was so restless and active that for long periods he rarely lived in Sussex.[10]

This is the clue to the complex genius of the young Belloc. He combined this love with a historical fascination, acquiring sensuous stimulation from suggestion, associations, legends, religion. Edward Thomas remarked of him that he was 'such a geographer as I wish many historians were, such a poet as all geographers ought to be, and hardly any other has been'.[11] This was very true.

Belloc developed a topographical-historical approach to a living landscape because, for him, to belong to a place meant to know its history and geographical setting. As a consequence, one room at King's Land was overflowing with maps. In his essay on 'The Weald' (1909), he writes in memorable phrases, such as 'Economics break against the Weald as water breaks against a stone.'[12]

His writing is imbued with an exceptional sensitivity to the *genius loci*, the spirit of place, and he tried to show how a particular place was special and different from elsewhere to its inhabitants, the importance its people attached to living there, and ways in which it was changing. Accordingly, he wrote of a place not simply in terms of landscape or architecture, language or customs, but of the little differences that made a place distinctive. He was curious to know the history of every such place that he grew to love 'as a platform upon which can be constructed some little of the future' – a principle even more worthy in the threatened Sussex of today. He despaired at reports of people driven out of their homes all over Europe and the growing tendency for sprawls of housing in parts of Sussex to blur the boundaries of traditional communities, thereby losing their local identity in the process.

Wistfully, he wondered whether the little differences between places would survive. He would have been horrified at the trends over the past seventy years or more since his death, where now hardly anyone belongs anywhere any longer, and with a catastrophic loss of the sense of place with alien and insensitive building styles. Yet, he would be delighted to know that his cause has been taken up enthusiastically by such organisations as Common Ground and increasingly by planners wherever possible.

Belloc's idea of landscape was under the spell of running water. In the Poet's words in *The Four Men*, 'There is always some holiness in the rising of rivers, and a great attachment to their springs.'[13] Despite his Catholicism, there was a pagan interest in springs and he would walk miles to trace the source of a river with which he had a special relationship. In particular, the Arun had a special sanctity for him, together with the Western Rother, not as inanimate but as living beings that had been his companions. Of the Western Rother, he wrote, 'If ever again we have a religion in the South Country we will have a temple to my darling valley … and there I will hang a wreath in thanksgiving for having known the river.'[14] Conceivably, Belloc regarded the course of a river from spring to brook and tidal flood as analogous to the stages in human life.

The Four Men and 'This Eden that is Sussex Still'

The Four Men, his best-known work, is based on a walk across Sussex that he probably did solitarily ten years earlier on a journey of self-discovery of the county, although in its published form he ('Myself') is accompanied by three companions ('Grizzlebeard', the Sailor and the Poet). It is his greatest

Sussex work and one of the most remarkable books on Sussex ever written. It is redolent of the young Belloc: a hearty, athletic, out-of-doors man, companionable, digressive, religious, pessimistic and high-spirited in turns.

The vision of 'This Eden that is Sussex Still' has a profound, tender and disquieting originality. The book's main purpose, as he explained in his preface, was to put down in writing his own horizon and his fields 'before they were forgotten and had become a different thing'. For this reason, the book has exquisite descriptions of landscape, the 'graven images' he wanted posterity to recall after he was buried in Sussex soil. He considered that with decay and change Sussex was approaching its doom, 'For I know very well in my mind that a day will come when the holy place shall perish and all the people of it, and never more be what they were'.[15]

This eulogy of Sussex is ostensibly the story of a walk with the three companions, starting from The George at Robertsbridge and ending on Barlavington Down above Petworth in twilight (Figure 20). It took him five years to write and was originally called 'The County of Sussex'. In 1909, he told his friend Maurice Baring that he would describe 'Myself and three

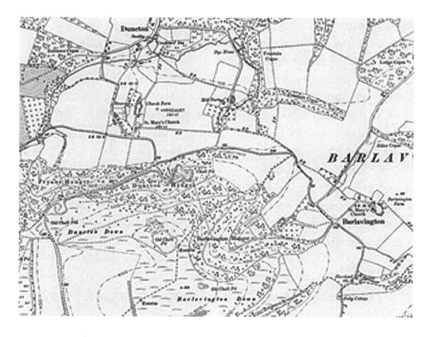

Fig. 20: Barlavington Down and Duncton Hill. (National Library of Scotland, Ordnance Survey, County Edition Scale: 1:10560, 1898)

characters walking through the country; the other characters which are really supernatural beings'. This became *The Four Men*. It had been ordered by Scribner, the American publisher, but then rejected on account of its 'religious tone'. Nelson published it in 1912. Belloc drew his own illustrations and composed the tunes for the Sailor's songs, which he would often sing for friends. It has been generally agreed that each of the three characters that accompany 'Myself' are aspects of the author's own personality: the philosopher Grizzlebeard, the Poet and the Sailor.

In this extraordinary book, we learn how St Germanus of Auxerre defeated the heretic and St Dunstan destroyed the Devil; how Adam established place names in the county, the first place to be created and therefore exempted from the Day of Judgement; and how the King of Sussex took the east bank of Rye Harbour from Kent. With all this and much else hurled at us, we are entertained throughout (or wearied, according to taste), not least by the walkers' inebriated celebration of 'Hog and Ale' at various inns, since immortalised.

For all its high spirits and playful fantasies, the book is tinged with the autumnal melancholy of All Saints' Day, the November Day of the Dead, the day the walk ends, and of the foreboding Belloc had for Sussex's future. It is a book for the outdoors man and woman who likes to be refreshed by draughts of good drink and conversation, or is so in spirit, and are imbued with the love of Sussex running through their veins. No one else is qualified to read it.

In November 1951, Lord Duncannon's dramatic version of *The Four Men* was broadcast by the BBC on the *Third Programme* and then performed throughout Sussex in connection with the Festival of Britain. Belloc's biographer, Robert Speaight, performed the part of Belloc himself with insight and Ian Wallace, of Glyndebourne and Drury Lane, was a success as the Sailor, bringing the house down with such famous Belloc songs as 'In Sussex Hills Where I was Bred'. Belloc's daughter, Elizabeth, said at that time, 'Long ago, I heard my father say "I put my whole heart into that book, but no one cares about it". How delightful for him to know how many people care for it and how much.'

The modern reader finds tedious passages in it, and its religious tone makes it unfashionable, but Ann Feloy has revived the book as a play at the Chichester Festival and in a more extended form at the Brighton Festival in 2010 and 2017.[16] Patrick Garland, a former director of the Chichester Festival Theatre, has remarked that 'The Boy that Sings on Duncton Hill' should be regarded as the anthem of Sussex, and Richard Ingrams applied it more widely when he selected it as the epilogue for his anthology of the nation, *England* (1989).

Belloc is the Sussex poet of autumn. Like Tennyson, his delight in natural beauty and his sad awareness of its transience were both peculiarly acute: not the still and early autumn days that Tennyson loved but autumn in glorious days of wind, rain and sun with great clouds over the Downs. His ear was attuned to noises in the high woods, his senses to sunsets beautified through a waning sun, clouds of leaves stirred up by the foot and waves leaping on the surf, and he enjoyed intense physical exhilaration amid great trees bowed against the wind. He could then feel Sussex, smell it, taste it, hear its voices of sea, river and woods, and experience the greatest joy of life.

Belloc should also be nominated the Prince of Sussex Walkers, not only for his pioneer walk of four to five days along the South Downs Way in 1897 and his other great walks in the county, but for the long walk recorded in *The Path to Rome* and *The Four Men*. Sidgwick remarked that Belloc 'not only records walks, but writes in the true walking mood, with plenty of irrelevancy, plenty of dogmatism, and thorough conviction on the matter of eating and drinking'.[17] Belloc imbues this atmosphere in his long introduction to the anthology for walkers, *The Footpath Way* (1911).[18]

He was also a keen yachtsman and one of the few Sussex writers who have written about sailing the English Channel. In his 'Stanzas Written on Battersea Bridge During a South-Westerly Gale', he expresses his sadness that although the little seas are leaping and he would sail his little boat 'roaring hard a' weather', he is restrained by business drudgery in London and the necessity to write incessantly to earn a living on land:

> The woods and downs have caught the mid-December
> The noisy woods and high sea-downs of home;
> The wind has found me and I do remember
> The strong scent of the foam.
>
> The wind is shouting from the hills of morning
> I do remember and I will not stay,
> I'll take the Hampton road without a warning
> And get me clean away.

Furthermore:

> The channel is up, the little seas are leaping,
> The tide is making over Arun Bar,
> And there's my boat, where all the rest are sleeping
> And my companions are.[19]

The Cruise of the Nona (1925), an account of his voyage from Wales down the Irish Sea and up the English Channel to his home port of Shoreham is a sea classic. Few have described so well the silences of the sea and its solitudes, the calms and rolling breakers, and the sunsets, tidal races and dangerously narrow harbour entrances of the Sussex coast. One shares his battles with the wind, the strain of the timbers, the anxious piloting and the laying-up in some little port. He was fond of Shoreham, warts and all, and thought it a proud day when *The Nona* returned to her old moorings in 'Stinking Shoreham', which she had not seen for two years.

Belloc's Rise and Fall

Posterity has given Belloc little reward. It is difficult since the fall in Belloc's esteem as a writer, which took place before his death in 1953 and has never recovered, to give any idea of the extent and intensity of his former fame and immense popularity. His lecture in Hove Town Hall in 1906 was eloquent in a quite spontaneous manner, racy, intoxicating and unforgettable. As an MP, he had already published some of his underrated Sussex poems, one of his best Sussex books, *The Hills and the Sea* (reaching its sixteenth edition in 1927), some children's verse and *The Path to Rome*, one of his best-known books. A local newspaper reported that a crowded audience, curious to meet this famous figure, had 'a rare intellectual treat' given by 'one of the cleverest men we have in England'.[20]

When Belloc's reputation was at its zenith in the 1920s, the novelist Ernest Raymond thought, 'Surely, surely, in a century's time there will loll on all shelves by the side of *The Compleat Angler* Hilaire Belloc's *The Four Men*.' Similarly, in 1936 Esther Meynell wrote of this book that it 'holds a place held by no other, as it is the most perfect book that has ever been written on Sussex'. Others have remarked on a similar enchantment, and in the same year as Meynell's comments, excerpts from the book appeared on pioneer television. In 1940, John Buchan considered that 'no man has written purer and nobler prose in the great tradition'.[21]

G.M. Young had earlier noted that 'the younger generation found his little ways tiresome', but nevertheless treated him gently and kindly; Edward Marsh complained of his 'crankiness' and Virginia Woolf of his mannerisms, affectations and his voice, which sounded as if he was speaking through a megaphone to a crowd on a windy day. In several respects, Belloc resembled William Cobbett in heartiness of manner, style of writing, wild prejudices and blunders. But listeners reported being spellbound by the sheer brilliance of his conversation. His was an intoxicating presence.

But examined today in his bodily absence he is less riveting. As a historian, he is now seen as a polemicist rather than an objective scholar, placing more faith in legends than in archival sources, scorning footnotes and serious research. One learns a lot that has later to be discarded. His mannered, belligerent prose, the embodiment of eighteenth-century bombast, now tends to grate on modern readers 'like a squeaky pencil on a slate', so that much of it is untransmissible to posterity. His writing is also very uneven and some in later life carelessly written, the result of having to write continuously on anything for a precarious living. Someone asked him why he wrote so much and he replied, 'Because my children are howling for pearls and caviar', and although it was said in jest there was a ring of truth in it. But he could write lightheartedly of his plight:

Would that I had 300,000 (Pounds)
Invested in some strong security;
A Midland Country House with formal grounds,
A Town House, and a House beside the sea,
And one in Spain, and one in Normandy,
And Friends innumerable at my call
And youth serene – and underneath it all
One steadfast, passionate flame to nurture me.

Then would I chuck for good my stinking trade
Of writing tosh at 1s. 6d. a quire!
And soar like young Bellerophon arrayed
High to the filmy Heavens of my desire ...
But that's all over. Here's the world again.
Bring me the Blotter. Fill the fountain-pen.[22]

Belloc's children's verse was an immense success in its day. His light verse was unmatched for vitality and tends to the satiric rather than the humorous, being much concerned with class and politics. *The Four Men* was a landmark in his career. Hitherto, as his sister, Marie Belloc Lowndes, remarked, he had enjoyed a glorious life, and he was widely read and loved, 'Nothing like him had been seen in the high little world in which he lived'. Sadly, after the death of his wife Elodie in early 1914 and the advent of the Great War, he never really ever again came to terms with contemporary life. In fact, his muse began to dry up soon after he became an MP in 1906, a masterpiece, 'Heroic Poem in Praise of Wine' being an exception. His lack of inspiration from Sussex in later life is illustrated by the fact that despite living in the Weald for nearly forty years he had little to say about it, in contrast to Kipling, who reinvented himself in it.

The explanation is that Belloc, after failing as an MP to reform Britain's economic and social ills through Parliament, became a courageous reformer, ferociously unleashing his radical crusade against international capitalism, imperialism, political corruption and social ills. In this, his debt to Anthony Trollope, who he greatly admired, is immense. A sign of this influence is Maurice Baring's complaint that he could not borrow books on Trollope from the London Library because Belloc had preempted them. Like Trollope, Belloc never tired of preaching the gospel that things were getting worse with 'progress', and he was a great mocker of follies, serving up lashings of satire as Trollope had done in the 1870s.

This trenchant criticism came to centre on 'Distributism', a word invented by Belloc. In conjunction with G.K. Chesterton and the latter's brother, Cecil, this advocated a rural-oriented, property-owning democracy that owed much to William Morris but was a particular Roman Catholic approach, looking back to the teachings of St Thomas Aquinas. This had been foreshadowed in Belloc's *The Servile State* (1912), which exposed government corruption, the growing influence of plutocrats on British domestic and foreign policy, and the advance of the centralised, bureaucratic state. There were also several satirical novels such as *Emmanuel Burden* (1904). As George Orwell pointed out, this book, then recently republished, was a prophetic insight into the modern world of mega-corporations and mega-governments.[23]

The anti-industrial, anti-urban and anti-capitalist Distributism, based on the individual ownership of land enough to make every man morally and financially independent as an alternative to Fabian, Liberal, Conservative and communist policies, failed to gain ground in the 1920s but involved Belloc and Chesterton ('Chesterbelloc') in savage invective against the Establishment. It is usually suggested that Belloc gained much of his inspiration for peasant proprietorship from his deep knowledge of the French peasant, but equally his deep knowledge of the Sussex Weald would also have given him an example of a similar community.[24] Although a forlorn failure after gaining some initial intellectual traction, Distributism is perhaps not totally dead. The love of the small and ideal community was similar to that advocated by Kropotkin and idealists for the back-to-the-land movement of the 1930s.[25] In fact, it can be argued that Distributism has applications to issues raised by present day post-industrial society.

Belloc's *The County of Sussex* (1936), his saddest book, is despairing of the future.[26] It reads like his last testament, following the anguish of bleak despair that had overtaken him for more than forty years. He had written of Sussex's 'approaching doom' in *The Four Men* years before, predicting that the county must, like all created things, decay.[27] His idea of Sussex was of a stable Victorian and Edwardian England and in his brief essay, indicative of his declining powers in saying little new, he assumed the role of Deplore-Laureate of Sussex with a sense of longing for the landscape of his youth, now seemingly lost forever with changes brought about by the railway and the internal combustion engine. Among his lamentations were the penetration of towns, the fate of the Wealden peasantry and the break-up of great landed estates with successors who use it 'only as a sort of park for their momentary pleasure'. He considered that Sussex, apart from the metropolitan counties, had sustained more damage than any other and that already 'the Weald had lost half its nature'. At the end, he raised anxiously the question, 'Can Sussex endure?' He reckoned the odds were against it, and submissively thought that the point of surrender had come and resistance should be abandoned.

Two poets, Wordsworth and Belloc, have both famously defended their respective homelands 'against assault'. Both were worried about adverse change and both had a very penetrating eye for landscape, allied to a fervent imagination. Both deplored current trends and castigated those offenders whose arrogance violated the natural order. Wordsworth's *Guide to the Lakes* (1810) has a brilliant introduction, one of the most memorable in English topographical writing, and Belloc similarly wrote of Sussex with distinction all his life.

There the similarities end, for whereas Wordsworth suggested at length measures of protection against disfigurement, Belloc prescribed nothing that would have made a positive contribution to the conservation of Sussex, despite what, to him, was an ongoing catastrophe, and neither did he engage in active environmental conservation, as did Arthur Beckett and his followers. It is as if reason and discretion deserted him. He wished to put back too many clocks in his environmentally precarious world. The sense that landscapes must change as we ourselves change eluded him, and he apparently did not realise that he was asking for people to live embalmed lives in a frozen landscape they would not have chosen themselves. In short, Belloc was always the boy that sings on Duncton Hill.

When friend and fire and home are lost
And even children drawn away –
The passer-by shall hear me still,
A boy that sings on Duncton Hill.[28]

Belloc had a slight stroke in 1942 and wrote no more. In 1943, the prime minister, Winston Churchill (Belloc had predicted as far back as 1921 that he would eventually become prime minister), wrote to ask if he would accept the Companion of Honour. He refused, although literature was his life and blood.

Robert Speaight reported that in old age Belloc was 'like a great wind that had blown itself out into the calm of a summer evening'.[29] In his prime, he would meander in blustering ups and downs, with rumbustious twists and turns, perhaps for an hour and in a loud voice, accompanied by steady draughts of wine or beer, food and laughter, a gusto of good spirits and assertiveness, but which did not command the admiration of everyone. But now all that was over and in old age he tended to become a reactionary with nothing more to say, and like a child, he surrendered to his daughter's and son-in-law's care.

For all his compulsive gregariousness, Belloc was melancholy by temperament and, at times, felt a sense of intellectual loneliness. And so in 'The South Country':

... A lost thing could I never find
Nor broken thing mend
And I fear I shall be all alone
When I get towards the end.
Who will be there to comfort me
Or who will be my friend?

He died in July 1953, after falling and burning himself on the fire at King's Land, an unhappy and disappointed man who thought (wrongly), that he had outlived his time. Belloc reckoned up his debt to the county that was so very dear to him. It had done a very great deal for him, 'had nourished him and given him his being' and it had brought him much happiness:

The Southern Hills and the South Sea
They blow such gladness into me
That when I get to Burton Sands
And smell the smell of the home lands,

My heart is all renewed, and fills
With the Southern Sea and the South Hills.[30]

It was his image of a perfect England, a place without disharmony or injustice and a place where he applied the balm of landscape to his heart to heal wounds suffered in the city. He seems to have asked himself in an act of piety and patriotic duty what he should do for the hills that had folded and fed him and he concluded that he should, as a moral obligation, 'lend Sussex glory and do it service':

> In this love he remains content until, perhaps, some sort of warning reaches him, that even his own County is approaching its doom. Then, believe me Sussex, he is anxious in a very different way; he would, if he could, preserve his land in the flesh, and keep it there as it is forever. But since he knows he cannot do that, 'at least' he says, 'I will keep her image, and that shall remain'.[31]

As a writer, he thought that if he could convey to his readers a fraction of the pleasure that the Sussex landscape gave him, he would not have lived in vain and as a beneficent champion of the county against adverse change he would be regarded as father to his people. And summoning up all his creative powers, he developed one of the most beautiful lyrics in the English language, 'The Boy that Sings on Duncton Hill', which dramatically closes *The Four Men*, and is, in effect, his own epitaph:

> He does not die … that can bequeath
> Some influence to the land he knows,
> Or dares, persistent, interwreath
> Love permanent with the wild hedgerows;
> He dies not die, but still remains
> Substantiate with his darling plains.[32]

Belloc certainly did not believe in the inevitability of progress, swimming against the tide of popular thought. But he was a radical thinker, passionate about the distribution of land, about the inequities of British politics, and fiercely Catholic. Together with Manning, Chesterton and Waugh, he was a leader in the Catholic literary revival during the early twentieth century in England. He is buried at West Grinstead Catholic Church.

There were many who felt that he was a great character, although others have doubted his literary ability and criticised what they perceived to be his antisemitism. As a sailor, he had a premonition that he would make his last landfall at Hy-Brasil, the legendary Isle of the Blest off the western coast of Ireland, but he never arrived.

A fitting way into the world of Belloc is to take the pretty lane that turns off westwards from below Bury Hill and runs under the wooded Downs to the Cricketer's Inn at the foot of Duncton Hill (Plate 26). This was Belloc's walking route towards the end of *The Four Men*. Over-arched with trees in many places, it winds narrowly up and down in sharp dips through the little sandstone villages of West Burton, Bignor and Sutton, cutting here and there through the Upper and Lower Greensand rocks in deep hollow-ways bordered by myriads of wildflowers in spring. If one pauses at the utterly simple St Mary's Church at Barlavington (Belloc's 'Barl'ton'), the centre of a tiny community grouped round the farm and great barn, there is through the church door one of the finest views of the line of the Downs in Belloc's 'South Country'. Here, with the sight of cattle in the silent, flower-rich meadows, there is still a sense of the ageless quiet that Belloc knew. Such places have a precious ancient feeling about them, which makes them special and remembered for years.

Taking the track uphill from this sheltered place, the walker reaches the semi-wildness of Barlavington Down, which retains, against the odds, an eerie primeval sense as conveyed in *The Four Men*. In the loneliness of the high Downs, where he had passed such memorable hours, occurred his melancholy thoughts on mortality and of a Sussex that was ceasing to be itself. Here was his inspiration for 'The Boy That Sings on Duncton Hill'.

RUDYARD KIPLING AS A SUSSEX WRITER

Here lives a man of world-wide fame,
Who wandered North, South, East and West,
And sampled many lands but came
And found that Sussex is the best!

Charles Dalmon, 'Outside the Gates of Bateman's'[1]

If other writers considered in this volume were strongly anti-imperialist, such as Blunt and Belloc (and Chesterton), we move on here to consider one whose very fame is strongly associated with Empire and jingoism. Kipling (1865–1936) was, like them, a restless soul, who also came to settle down in Sussex. He was born in colonial Bombay, spending many years of his life in India, but was sent to England for his education, as was then normal for Anglo-Indian families.

Becoming an established author in India, he and his American wife Carrie returned to England in 1896, initially to the Torquay area but also visiting London, where he met and was inspired by the arch-imperialist Cecil Rhodes.[2] To avoid the bustle of London's preparations for Victoria's Diamond Jubilee, he and Carrie initially took a temporary home in Rottingdean belonging to his uncle, the distinguished Pre-Raphaelite painter and craftsman, Edward Burne-Jones, and his wife Georgie, who lived at North End House. A group of family and friends welcomed them, including Stanley Baldwin, his cousin. From there, they moved over to The Elms at the northern edge of Pump Green with its pond, Rottingdean's village green, across which he proudly wheeled his infant son John in 1897 (Plate 27).[3]

As his prosperity increased so further plots of local land were acquired, with one facilitating a village rifle club following the Relief of Mafeking. While at Rottingdean too, he helped to raise public enthusiasm for the Boer War, resulting from his overwintering in South Africa on many occasions.

With the ongoing South African War many thought a jingoistic note had crept into his work and he was violently criticised by Max Beerbohm for imperialism and militarism in cartoons entitled the 'Second Childhood of John Bull'. Another critic has noted that he 'vigorously beat the imperial drum'.[4] He was also debunked for these traits by Belloc and G.K. Chesterton, but others were strongly influenced by and supported his standpoint. Despite such controversy, his short stories were immensely popular among Edwardians and he moved in elite circles. A 1908 edition of his enduring novel *Kim* accompanied Scott's ill-fated polar expedition, with an inscription written on the day of the expedition's departure from Cardiff.[5]

Kipling and the Downs

Kipling had occupied a world stage from the age of 24, but lived in Rottingdean between 1897 and 1902, and then Bateman's in Burwash for the remainder of his life. His popularity was at its height in his Rottingdean period when finishing *Kim* (1901, after serialisation) and writing *Stalky and Co.* (1899, again following serialisation), various short stories, 'Recessional' (1897) and the immediately controversial 'The White Man's Burden' (1899).

In Rottingdean, Kipling turned away from his Indian stories that had already brought him celebrity status and he now began to absorb the character of the local South Downs and there wrote 'The Absent-minded Beggar' to raise funds in 1899 for the military and their families in the Boer War, as well as his early Sussex verse – 'Sussex', 'The Run of the Downs' and other poems. He wrote 'The Knife and the Naked Chalk' after moving to Burwash, featuring the protagonists Puck of Pook's Hill, Dan and Una, who hear the story of the flint men who kept their sheep on the Downs 3,000 years ago.[6] The well-known 'A Smuggler's Song' (1906) was also written from Burwash.

In so doing, he wrote himself into the landscape with vivid evocation and imagination, a word-painter who captured the characteristics of the countryside – its unbroken turf on the gleaming cliffs, the long swells and continuous summits, the scooped-out combes and almost foreign sky, and the sense of antiquity that he especially loved. No one has so graphically and succinctly pictured the Downs east of Brighton as well as Kipling.

He was accomplished in the art of conjuring up a landscape at a stroke in a few essential words, such as, from 'Sussex', 'No tender-hearted garden crowns. No bosomed woods adorn, our blunt, bowheaded, whale-backed

Downs, but gnarled and writhen thorn.' In this, he perfectly describes the profiles of Firle Beacon, Kingston Hill, Wolstonbury and other ridges near Lewes, and he had such a power of words that in an instant his picture is drawn (Figure 21). Thus:

We have no waters to delight
Our broad and brookless vales
Only the dewpond on the height
Unfed that never fails.

Fig. 21: Firle Beacon, 'Our blunt, bowheaded, whale-backed Downs'.
(*Britain From the Air: The Weald and its Environs* [Macmillan Education Ltd, 1971])

Or 'Close-bit thyme that smells like dawn in Paradise', 'half wild and wholly tame' and 'wind, heavy-winged with brine', which describe the Downs, and phrases like 'ports of stranded pride' and 'the sheep bells and the ship-bells ring along the hidden beach' to describe the sea. It is said that there are more Kiplingisms in the *Oxford Dictionary of Quotations* than there are words from Shakespeare. And heard sung uproariously at patriotic meetings was the refrain, 'The Downs are sheep, the Weald is corn, You be glad you are Sussex born!'[7]

What is so remarkable about Kipling's authorship at Rottingdean is that he wrote with great familiarity of his patch of the South Downs although he had enjoyed only limited acquaintance with it in his youth before he came to reside there. Almost overnight, he penetrated the very being of the Downs to a greater depth than any previous writer apart from Belloc. Kipling's exceptional sensitivity to environment is the freshness of vision of a stranger but one who sees with both a wider perspective and detail than the one who takes for granted their familiar surroundings. But as T.S. Eliot noted, Kipling's 'foreignness', both in India and Sussex, had 'a remoteness as of an alarmingly intelligent visitor from another planet'.[8]

This appropriately characterises the Rottingdean work. Kipling himself made the point when he said, 'I am slowly discovering England, which is the most foreign land I have been in.' He luxuriated in the strangeness and exoticism of his old, new-found home county of Sussex. He brought an acute eye and an understanding of the distinguishing characteristics that is totally penetrating. These qualities were the same as Belloc's, and arose from similar circumstances of 'foreignness', but whereas the latter is broad-brushed, Kipling is specific about places, although this obsession could too often degenerate into a string of names.

Kipling's Sussex Weald

Kipling sought a haven from the increasing number of trippers at Rottingdean, coming to inspect his house on a Brighton double-decker horse bus, which he and Carrie found unbearable. And with the sorrow of his daughter Josephine's death while on a visit to New York in 1899, they determined to move. It may well be that Kipling longed to be in the Weald rather than on the Downs on the edge of Brighton. And in searching to live elsewhere, they found Bateman's at Burwash, on the banks of the little River Dudwell in the deep, secretive Sussex Weald (Figure 22). They fell in love with it at first sight, even though there was no bathroom and no electricity.

He wrote to a friend, 'I have moved from Rottingdean to an old stone house about 300 years old, in the middle of the most English country that ever you dream of.'[9]

He and Carrie arrived by train to Etchingham and on by horse and fly, not in their steam-car Locomobile, as Kipling described, and which was out of action:

> [I]t was the heartbreaking Locomobile that brought us to the house called 'Bateman's'. We had seen an advertisement of her, and we reached her down an enlarged rabbit-hole of a lane. At very first sight the Committee of Ways and Means [Mrs Kipling and himself] said 'That's her! The only She! Make an honest woman of her – quick!' We entered and felt her Spirit – her Feng Shui – to be good. We went through every room and found no shadow of ancient regrets, stifled miseries, nor any menace though the 'new' end of her was three hundred years old.[10]

After an agonising delay, Kipling was able to move into the 'stuffy little valley' during early September 1902 and thereafter establish himself as a small landowner of little family farms such as the nearby Rye Green Dairy Farm, Little Bateman's, part of Dudwell Farm, and later also further fields and a brickworks nearer to Burwash itself, '[A]t last I'm one of the gentry'. All eventually amounted to about 300 acres.

Fig. 22: The 'very own house', Bateman's, in the Dudwell Valley, 1911. (Judges postcards, courtesy Peter McCleod)

'We learned,' said Kipling, 'that farming the Weald was a mixture of farce, fraud and philanthropy that stole the heart out of the land.' After many, some comic, experiences, he fell back on the Red Sussex breed of cattle. His friend Rider Haggard gave him much advice. 'Put in orchard trees and a goat,' said he, 'and you might as well put in Satan in an orchard as a goat.'

Kipling frequently corresponded with Haggard on farming matters, usually expressing despair at some disaster or another on the miry clays:

Now hear me moan! The land is porridge. We send out whiskey with the drenches to the wretched little calves that are now being born, we litter down twice a day and the wet bog swallows it all: all my winter wheat is dead. No-one has been able to set foot on the land since November and all my sheep have footrot.

His opinion of his tenants could be low. Their abilities might be question-able, to him at least. He thought that they were incapable of sustainable farming, with the land being 'let down year by year'. In 1906, he wrote to Haggard, 'An intelligent tenant of mine has gone and let die 20 good apple trees that I put in for him – through pure asinine neglect.'[11]

Over the next decade, Kipling treated new subjects and was above all inspired by his love of the past Sussex Weald, seen by one biographer as his 'last despairing search for a new country to love [which] was in the world of the past'.[12] No other author has interpreted it at once with both such realism and historical imagination.

The past was written all over the Sussex Weald of his day, inspiring him to aim at a sense of the antiquity of England by drawing on the visible signs of English history in so far as they had pervaded his own surroundings. In doing this, he had flashes of profound insight. All was 'alive with ghosts and shadows'.[13] His description of the Burwash village commemoration service for the death of King Edward VII in May 1910 was exquisite:

Nobody was in the fields; no one was driving sheep or cattle so one did not hear any distant lowing or bleating; nobody was driving a horse or getting a fallow ploughed, or packing pigs into market carts. It was absolute stillness. I listened long and often but except for the bees there was nothing. [...] We went by the fields. There was nobody in sight: one could just hear the bell tolling, muffled [...] through the hot still air. The street was empty; every blind was drawn; all shutters were up.[14]

He created Old Hobden, the poacher-hedger, to symbolise the archetypal Sussex Wealdsman with all his traditions and history. Hobden is the focus in *Puck* and in *Rewards and Fairies* and he is memorably the hero of verses entitled 'The Land':

> When Julius Fabricius, Sub-Prefect of the Weald,
> In the days of Diocletian owned our Lower River-field,
> He called to him Hobdenius—a Briton of the Clay,
> Saying: 'What about that River-piece for layin' in to hay?'
>
> And the aged Hobden answered: 'I remember as a lad
> My father told your father that she wanted dreenin' bad.
> An' the more that you neeglect her the less you'll get her clean.
> Have it jest as you've a mind to, but, if I was you, I'd dreen.'
>
> So they drained it long and crossways in the lavish Roman style —
> Still we find among the river-drift their flakes of ancient tile,
> And in drouthy middle August, when the bones of meadows show,
> We can trace the lines they followed sixteen hundred years ago.
>
> Then Julius Fabricius died as even Prefects do,
> And after certain centuries, Imperial Rome died too.
> Then did robbers enter Britain from across the Northern main
> And our Lower River-field was won by Ogier the Dane.

The poem continues in this manner to give the history of this particular field up to the then Hobden's lifetime. It concludes:

> His dead are in the churchyard—thirty generations laid.
> Their names were old in history when Domesday Book was made;
> And the passion and the piety and prowess of his line
> Have seeded, rooted, fruited in some land the Law calls mine.
>
> Not for any beast that burrows, not for any bird that flies,
> Would I lose his large sound counsel, miss his keen amending eyes.
> He is bailiff, woodman, wheelwright, field-surveyor, engineer,
> And if flagrantly a poacher—'tain't for me to interfere.

'Hob, what about that River-bit?' I turn to him again,
With Fabricius and Ogier and William of Warenne.
'Hev it jest as you've a mind to, but'—and here he takes command.
For whoever pays the taxes old Mus' Hobden owns the land.[15]

By means of Old Hobdens in each generation, Kipling 'gets beneath the skin' of the Sussex Weald and conveys a deep knowledge of country life through his personal observation. He brilliantly conveys the deep-rooted isolation of Wealden folk, and that the Weald responded more slowly and unsteadily to farming than other regions of south-east England. It was, instead, a hard-won battle with repeated setbacks, notably from flooding. In bad times farmers might submit to adversity, reduce expenses and practically withdraw from the fight to win a living from the land.

In a single poem Kipling imaginatively encapsulates the succession of farmers who have repeatedly tried, and failed, to bring the meadows of his local Dudwell Valley into a secure and profitable farming system despite the advice of Old Hobdens. Old Hobden was actually based on William Isted, a local poacher.[16] And while Kipling's real relationship with local people may not have been totally idyllic, but rather patronising and distant, this was undoubtedly a brilliant literary device.[17]

Kipling makes numerous references to floods, perhaps influenced by the great flood of 1909, which he thought the worst since 1852, and the sound of the Dudwell's swollen, thrusting, overflowing water in winter is brilliantly captured in, for example, the short essay 'A Friendly Brook', a wry tribute to his beloved little local river. He renders the farm labourers with the fidelity and empathy of Emile Zola, who greatly influenced the story.[18] They are introduced entirely by means of a dialogue in local dialect. He expresses the speech and interprets the working-class Wealdsman with the same skill as the 'Tommy' in *Barrack Room Ballads*.[19] He puts into their mouths the words they actually used and under their coarseness of speech he shows with insight that, in their way, they were quite near, and like, many of his readers.

The dialogue is interrupted by the flooding of the Dudwell Brook, 'There was a growl in the brook's roar as though she worried something hard' – and we learn that farming in the valley was adapted to nature and not fully commercial. In November, the brook is in flood, a big corner-piece of the bank had slipped into it, water lying in the flats already and backing up to the wheat, with Wickenden, the farmer, helping his labourers fight the rising waters. As the brook came sweeping up, an object thought to be Wickenden's bee skep from his cottage garden floated past in the gathering darkness. It was pulled into the shadows and turned out to be a drowned man, Wickenden's wife's father, who had been repeatedly opportuning her for money. So, the brook was a good friend to Wickenden. All is in serio-comic tone and the story is entirely in dialogue that flows as freely and gently as the 'Friendly Brook' normally flowed itself.

The opening is one of Kipling's most memorable descriptions:

The valley was so choked with fog that one could scarcely see a cows' length across a field. Every blade, twig, bracken-frond, and hoof-print carried water; and the air was filled with the noise of rushing ditches and field-drains, all delivering to the brook below. A week's November rain in water-logged land had gorged her to a full flood, and she proclaimed it loud.[20]

He repeatedly writes about floods, which were inexorably part of his life in the Dudwell valley, as in the short story, 'The Floods':

The floods they shall not be afraid –
Nor the hills above 'em, nor the hills –
Of any fence which man has made
Betwixt him and the hills.
The waters shall not reckon twice
For any work of man's device.

But life is renewed after a flood, as repeatedly it was in the Sussex Weald:

The floods shall sweep corruption clean –
By the hills, the blessing of the hills –
That more the meadows may be green
New-mended from the hills.
The crops and cattle shall increase,
Nor little children shall not cease.
Go – plough the lowlands, lowlands,
Lowlands under the hills![21]

In 'An Habitation Enforced', a sick American is advised by his doctors to rest and heal abroad. He takes one of the numerous semi-derelict Wealden farms and, flushed with the pride of ownership, plots alteration and restoration at every turn. But gradually, the local people induce him to abandon his schemes and he falls into 'the customs of his little kingdom' and, like his tenants, 'moved about the soft-footed ways by woodland, hedgerow and shaw, as freely as the rabbits'. Kipling's description of the site of the farm suggests that he was drawing upon his own story, his first impression of Bateman's when he moved in. As an account of the dereliction spreading across Sussex with free trade, it has not been equalled.[22]

This story can be read with interest and amusement as another example of 'Hobdenism' without considering the deeper implications of Kipling's fundamental principles underlying it. He is firmly putting forward the old Wealden customs and traditions as opposed to modern commercialism and industrialism. He sees the Weald as untamable and only inhabitable by people who adapt themselves to it and live close to nature. This he conceived as the lesson from its history. The newcomer American, George Chapen, even says at one point, 'I give it up. People don't seem to matter in this country compared to the places they live in.'[23]

Kipling was deeply troubled by the recent changes in ownership that were destroying the old regime and he wanted to restore the old values. This is evident in the verses of 'The Recall', which accompany the story, where Kipling himself speaks for the Weald:

I am the land of their fathers.
In me the virtue stays.
I will bring back my children,
After certain days.
...
They shall return as strangers.
They shall remain as sons.

Over their heads in the branches
Of their new-bought, ancient trees,
...
Scent of smoke in the evening,
Smell of rain in the night –
The hours, the days and the seasons
Order their souls aright,

Till I make plain the meaning
Of all my thousand years –
Till I fill their hearts with knowledge,
While I fill their hearts with tears.

Kipling's Wealden Environment and its People

Through Kipling's works, the Dudwell Valley has helped to open up an awareness of the Sussex Weald for the general reader. Kipling found that if one scratched a few inches in the rabbit-shaven turf among the slag heaps of the old ironworks, one discovered the narrow tracks used to take ironwares to market. A 'ghost of a road' climbed up across Kipling's fields and was known as the 'Gun Way':

> See you the dimpled track that runs,
> All hollow through the wheat?
> O that was where they hauled the guns
> That smote King Philip's fleet!

Kipling wrote in his autobiography:

> You see how patiently the cards were stacked and dealt into my hands ...
> The Old Things of our Valley glided into every aspect of our outdoor
> works I saw it at last – in full conspiracy to give me ten times as much as
> I could compass, even if I wrote a complete history of England, as that
> might have touched or reached our Valley ... Parnesius came later, directly
> out of the little wood above the Phoenician forge.[24]

As ideas occurred to him for his stories, he would amuse his family and visitors by hurried returns to his study, writing to uncover the deep roots of Wealden tradition and customs embedded in the landscape, and seeking to arrive at a popular history of the region.

The historian G.M. Trevelyan confessed that Kipling's work he liked best were the children's stories *Puck of Pook's Hill* (1906) and *Rewards and Fairies* (1910). 'Perhaps,' he said, 'It is because I also have never grown up.' Furthermore:

> Puck is naturally beautiful, gentle, and if you like, childlike. In a setting
> of fairyland and childhood the very opposite of brutality, he tells us tales
> of the ancient history of English land as he imagines it, with a marvellous
> historical sense, I think. When he fell under the charm of rural Sussex and
> its folk like Old Hobden and all their traditions, he had a sudden vision of
> the whole length of our island history.[25]

Vaughan Williams included words from Kipling's 'Three Children's Song' from *Puck* in his *Thanksgiving for Victory*, a BBC celebration at the end of the Second World War in 1945.[26]

Kipling succeeded in a reconstruction of the Wealden landscape that enthralled adults as well as children, although the history was largely a fantasy of his own imagination. But *Puck* is interspersed with realistic little details of Wealden life, generally centred round Old Hobden, the hedger. We read of the mill stream flowing along the Old Slip, carrying water to the mill, flowing through the Long Slip, on the banks of which, overgrown with willow, hazel and guelder-rose, was the large old fairy ring that was the stage for the children's theatre, 'Everything else was a sort of thick sleepy stillness smelling of meadow-sweet and dry grass'. A corncrake jarred in a hayfield; the small trout of the brook began to jump; fishing in the brook was under trees closing overhead making long tunnels; tea was at Hobden's Old Forge by the hives; there were hop-pickers, and the 'cramped' country of the pheasant shoot. There was also folklore: the singing of 'Old Mother Laidinwool', a song sung in the Burwash hop gardens in the nineteenth century. The Dudwell Valley on Mid-Summer's Eve is depicted at the opening of *Puck* as an idyllic scene, the setting for the children's acting of *A Midsummer Night's Dream*, and this is contrasted with the change in the stream during winter.[27]

Was Kipling aware that when he came to Bateman's in 1902 the old rural order was about to change and that he was taking part in the very end of a great tradition? Nevertheless, he caught the whole spirit of that tradition in three stories, 'An Habitation Enforced', 'My Son's Wife' and 'A Friendly Brook', composing word-pictures of his Weald as a lost world, but one that was still in full flowering, and with no trace of nostalgia.[28]

But if he was indeed moving into the Weald as the older ways were fast disappearing, his standpoint is gaining ground now that 'greening' has become one of the new ways of modern life. Sustainability in the Weald is as old as the Weald itself, because it was not a land that the farmer could drive hard. Indeed, it could only be worked with an unusual amount of skill and hardship by those who understood its limitations. The outsider has failed to grasp this throughout history and has tended to scorn or mock Wealden agriculture. Kipling, like William Cobbett, came to understand how to live comfortably and happily within its limitations. It is a message of great validity at the present time.

Again, as unelected spokesman for the country, Kipling, wrote outspokenly about the wasted skills and craftsmanship of young men driven off Wealden farms into menial employment in towns:[29]

I have heard as much criticism among hedgers and ditchers and woodmen of a companion's handling of spade, bill-hook, or axe, as would fill a Sunday paper. Carters and cattle-men are even more meticulous, since they must deal with temperaments and seasonable instabilities. We had once on the farms a pair of brothers between ten and twelve. The younger could deal so cunningly with an intractable cart-mare who rushed her gates, and for choice diagonally, that he was called in to take charge of her as a matter of course. The elder, at eleven, could do all that his strength allowed, and the much more that ancestral craft had added, with any edged tool or wood. Modern progress has turned them into meritorious menials.

One of my cattle-men had a son who at eight could appraise the merits and character of any beast in his father's care, and was on terms of terrifying familiarity with the herd-bull, whom he would slap on the nose or make him walk disposedly before us when visitors came. At eighteen he would have been worth two hundred a year to begin with on any ranch in the Dominions. But he was 'good at his books' and is now in a small grocery, but wears a black coat on the Sabbath. Which things are a portent.[30]

Kipling's Motoring Genre

Kipling has been tainted for glorifying the British Empire with militarism and with the reactionary associations that accompanied such sentiments. But in one way, he also embraced material modernity. Always interested in the power of steam and mechanical engineering, from 1899 he was a pioneer motorist (with chauffeur), whose passion to experience the joys of the open road was not only the love of his life but was the inspiration for a new genre of motoring adventures that were later imitated by other fanatics behind the wheel, such as Dornford Yates and Ian Fleming.[31] Virginia Woolf was also to find pleasure in observing her surroundings from inside a moving car. The chief end of this, Kipling remarked, was the discovery of England:

To me it is a land full of stupefying marvels and mysteries; and a day in a car in an English county is a day in some fairy museum where all the exhibits are alive and real and yet none the less delightfully mixed up with books. For instance, in six hours, I can go from the land of the 'Ingoldsby Legends' by way of the Norman Conquest and the Baron's War into Richard Jefferies' country, and so through the Regency, one of Arthur Young's less known tours, and Celia's Arbour, into Gilbert White's territory. Horses, after all, are only horses; the car is a time-machine on which one can slide from one century to another at no more than the pushing forward of a lever [...] To me it is still miraculous that if I want petrol in a hurry I must either pass the place where Sir John Lade lived [Warbleton], or the garden where Jack Cade was killed [Old Heathfield, 1454] [...] In England the dead, twelve coffins deep, clutch hold of my wheels at every turn, till I sometimes wonder that the very road does not bleed. That is the real joy of motoring – the exploration of this amazing England.[32]

Kipling's experiences with a succession of cars at this early stage in their evolution were not always happy. Upsetting other road users was normal; running out of petrol on Brighton seafront amid hordes of 'trippers' was embarrassing; the abandonment of a car at Rye while attempting to visit his friend Henry James was another, much to the latter's wry amusement.[33] There were many such motoring stories, including 'Steam Tactics' in *They* (*Traffics and Discoveries*), 'The Village that Voted the Earth was Flat', 'The Horse Marines' and 'The Vortex' (in *A Diversity of Creatures*), and a delightful pastiche of other writers published as *The Muse Among the Motors*. In *They*, a description of a journey through Sussex, his words recapture the essence of the beauty of the countryside as it was a century ago:

One view called me to another; one hilltop to its fellow, half across the county, and since I could answer at no more trouble than the snapping forward of a lever, I let the country flow under my wheels. The orchid-studded flats of the East gave way to the thyme, ilex and grey grass of the Downs; these again to the rich cornland and fig-trees of the lower coast, where you carry the beat of the tide on your left hand for fifteen level miles; and when at last I turned inland through a huddle of rounded hills and woods I had run myself clean out of my known marks. Beyond that precise hamlet which stands godmother to the capital of the United States [Washington], I found hidden villages, where bees, the only things awake, boomed in eighty-foot lindens that overhung grey Norman churches [possibly Burpham]; miraculous brooks diving under stone bridges [Stopham Bridge?] built for heavier traffic than would ever vex them again; tithe-barns larger than their churches [probably Sullington], and an old smithy that cried aloud how it had once been a hall of the Knights of the Temple [presumably Shipley]. Gipsies I met on a common where the gorse, brackens, and heath fought it out together up a mile of Roman road [Greensand Way]; and a little farther on I disturbed a red fox rolling dog-fashion in the naked sunlight.[34]

As the wooded hills closed about me I stood up in the car to take the bearings of that great Down whose ringed head is a landmark for fifty miles across the low countries [Chanctonbury]. I judged that the lie of the country would bring me across some westward-running road that went to his feet, but I did not allow for the confusing veils of the woods. A quick turn plunged me first into a cutting brim-full of liquid sunshine; next into a gloomy tunnel where last year's dead leaves whispered and scuffled about my tyres. The strong hazel stuff meeting overhead had not been cut for a couple of generations as least, nor had any axe helped the moss-cankered oak and beech to spring above them. [...] As the slope favoured I shut off the power and slid over the whirled leaves, expecting every moment to meet a keeper; but I only heard a jay, far off, arguing against the silence under the twilight of the trees.[35]

His attitudes to modernity were complex. He was fascinated by the deep-sea cables ('There is no sound, no echo of sound, in the deserts of the deep,/ Or the great grey level plains of ooze where the shell-burred cables creep...') and had electricity installed at Bateman's driven by a water turbine and generator in the old adjacent mill. We have already seen his enthusiasm for the motor car but he never took to the typewriter, writing out everything stylishly in longhand with his much-polished pen dipped in densely black ink.[36] Doubtless, his remarkable craftsmanship was in part inherited: his father was gifted artistically as, of course, was his uncle, Sir Edward Burne-Jones.

Kipling Country

To visit the beautiful dwelling and ancient landscape that sustained Kipling for more than thirty years and shaped his imagination for original literature is a rewarding experience. There is an excellent *Guide to Bateman's* by Adam Nicolson but unfortunately it does not cover the numerous features on Kipling's Park Mill Farm and its surroundings in Burwash on which he set his mark and mentions in his writings.[37]

Bateman's, the 'Very Own House', stands solitarily with no noise of traffic in one of the loveliest of landscapes, and its remoteness only adds to its appeal, as it did to Kipling himself. Entering from Burwash, the narrow Bateman's Lane drops down into the little secret valley of the Dudwell Brook, and with one of the almost theatrical surprises of which the High Weald is capable, a view suddenly appears of a solitary seventeenth-century stone house framed in hanging woods with pastures muffling the slopes and still exuding the image of peace and character of a visible older England that Kipling had found.

There have been many critics of Kipling's writing, even of *Puck* and *Rewards and Fairies*, but as Seymour-Smith writes:

> [W]here the books succeed is in their evocation of English – and of course in particular, East Sussex landscape. You don't have to have lived in that part of the world to feel this, for it is based upon a love that is never gloating, but truly grateful.[38]

Amid historical memories, the water mill that Kipling imaginatively thought was clacking at Domesday has now been restored, more than once, and National Trust visitors can see it working. A mill dam marks the location of Old Hobden's cottage and forge. A very fine greenway leads off for a mile from the pond through green fields to the site of Burwash Forge, mentioned several times by Kipling and now a secluded site covered in dense bracken with a few visible traces of the forge house and garden and spoilbanks by fields and woods bearing the name 'Forge'. This was owned by the Collins family in the fifteenth and sixteenth centuries and was seen working by the poet and Burwash cleric James Hurdis at the end of the eighteenth century. A memorial cast-iron tomb slab to a sixteenth-century John Collins (Jhone Coline) is in the south aisle of Burwash Church.

Also in the Dudwell Valley, redolent of Kipling, is the hollow-way from Dudwell Bridge, which runs eastwards past Minepit Shaw and Nepland's Pit (Figure 23). The latter, now disused, is mentioned by Kipling in his correspondence with Rider Haggard as a 'newly opened quarry'.[39] The former is the subject of 'The Ballad of Minepit Shaw', being a classic example of a site of iron-ore extraction, with a surface riddled with water-filled pits and spoil banks. The hollows mark partially infilled bell-pits from which ore was winched into carts that travelled over the adjacent greenway (now stopped up) to Brickhouse Farm and Etchingham, where there was a forge. A brick and stone bridge over a stream here indicates that the way was still used for traffic in relatively recent times. It might be 'The Way Through the Woods', the subject of Kipling's mysterious lyric and which was closed at the time of his writing:

They shut the road through the woods
Seventy years ago.
Weather and rain have undone it again,
And now you would never know
There was once a road through the woods.[40]

The parish church stands magnificently on its ridge on the edge of the village. Scenes of medieval human workmanship are displayed on the slopes of the Dudwell Valley, where a series of slightly S-shaped fields of medieval origin (the curving sides are due to the use of plough oxen, which had to be

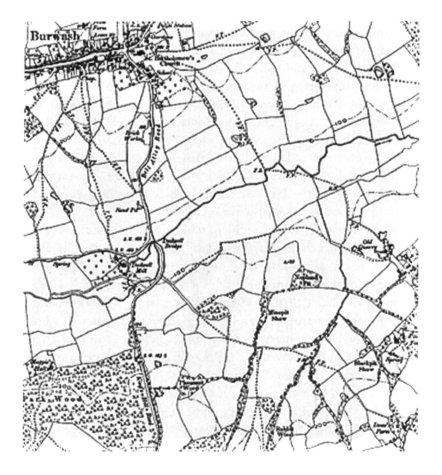

Fig. 23: Kipling's Minepit Shaw, the Dudwell Bridge and the village of Burwash. (National Library of Scotland: Ordnance Survey, Sussex XXX. SW, 1899)

turned in towards a near side before they could be swung round at a headland for the return) lie on the grassy slopes below the village and are visible from Minepit Shaw. Glimpses of a chequerwork of fields some 700–800 years old are to be seen on the way up to Brightling Down.

Kipling's biographer, Angus Wilson wrote, 'His Sussex was so evidently disappearing rapidly under his eyes with the invasion of commuterdom and growing towns. It simply could not function even in his imagination as a world on its own.' And so, by 1926:

> Farewell to the Downs and the Marshes
> And the Weald and the forest known
> Before there were Very Many People
> And the Old Gods had gone![41]

In fact, Kipling's life after the First World War became increasingly circumscribed. The loss of his young daughter in America and his son, John, at Loos in 1916 was a terrible blow to him. His health, and that of Carrie, declined and they maintained a privacy at Bateman's that few, other than close friends, could permeate, although the extent of his search for privacy should not be overstressed.[42] There were still many visits, and short stories were written (although none touching Sussex), and he developed a liking for France, which he toured by car and where he was bound, via London, when he died in January 1936. Carrie died at Bateman's in 1939, leaving the house to the National Trust. Kipling's papers were placed by his surviving daughter Elsie with the Trust and are now in the Special Collections of the University of Sussex.

In the early interwar years, he was a poet and patriot who almost all held in honour, affection and gratitude. Thinking only of his Sussex work, 'If', 'the greatest poem that ran round the world from the Dudwell valley' and the 'Children's Song of England' from *Puck*, come readily to mind.

Yet, once a literary star, he burned out. Kipling's reputation has come under fierce attack in more recent years as an anti-imperialist, anti-racist mode of thought has come to dominate much of modern consciousness. It would not be too strong, indeed, to say that in some quarters he was hated. In fact, neither he nor Carrie were particularly likeable people, indeed, they were disliked by local tradesmen and workers, and they often offended by treasuring their privacy at Bateman's, only welcoming the wealthy or influential. The work of Edward Said, in particular, has revealed how such Western representations of Eastern cultures have created an 'orientalism' of which Kipling's emphasis on 'the White Man's Burden' was an early and popular example.[43] And he was, as we have seen, also criticised during his lifetime for his conservative, indeed strongly reactionary views. He was casually anti-Semitic.[44] News of his death was met with indifference by many.

Through his friend Robert Baden-Powell, his influence on the Scouting movement was profound, with wolf-cub packs and Akelas. His *Jungle Book* stories and characters have become so well known through film and television adaptations. But children no longer read his books. Nevertheless, in 1996 a BBC poll voted 'If' the nation's favourite poem, he is constantly quoted in popular speech, and even cited by such politicians as Margaret Thatcher and Aung San Suu Kyi.[45] During his lifetime, a large proportion of the general reading public took his work to heart, but:

> There can have been few great writers whose personality had so little to do with his reputation. For every hundred people who could quote from his prose or poetry, there is only one who could tell you much about his life.[46]

A Three-Part Song
I'm just in love with all these three,
The Weald an' the Marsh an' the Down countrie;
Nor I don't know which I love the most,
The Weald or the Marsh or the white chalk coast!

I've buried my heart in a ferny hill,
Twix' a liddle low shaw an' a great high gill.
Oh, hop-bine yaller an' wood-smoke blue,
I reckon you'll keep her middling true!

I've loosed my mind for to out an' run
On a Marsh that was old when Kings begun:
Oh, Romney level an' Brenzett reeds,
I reckon you know what my mind needs!

I've given my soul to the Southdown grass,
An' sheep-bells tinkled where you pass.
Oh, Firle an' Ditchling an' sails at sea,
I reckon you keep my soul for me!

Thus it was, as R. Thurston Hopkins concluded, that Kipling gave his heart to the Weald, his mind to the Marsh and his soul to the Downs.[47]

HABBERTON LULHAM

Give praise for wheat-fields and their golden prime,
And bless the workers that about them go;
But if thy dreamings from the bare Downs flow,
Up, then, brave heart! – up where the harebells chime
Sing in the light air, breathe the scented thyme;
And waste no longings on the corn below.[1]

Another man rejuvenated in Sussex was one of the most representative of the Sussex poets of the early 1900s, Habberton Lulham (1865–1940), who explored the idea of escape from towns within a never-never land of his imagination before finding a real country place at Ditchling and latterly Hurstpierpoint. Although a qualified doctor in south London, he had connections with Sussex, and his distaste for the city and the endless allure of the South Downs made him their foremost poet, a craft he learned, among other ways, by tending sheep and consorting with shepherds (Plate 28).

If Lulham is remembered at all nowadays, it is for his photographs of sheep and shepherds on the South Downs.[2] But he was popular among sophisticated readers in his day, his verse running into several editions and being reviewed in national and provincial presses. As Alice Meynell perceptively remarked, his verse is different from any other Sussex poet or writer of his time. Three of his photographs illustrate Esther Meynell's *Sussex Cottage*. When leading poets and authors read his poems they were struck by vivid actuality (as with Thomas Hardy), beauty in a bold new way (as with Edward Thomas) and sincerity of feeling and originality of expression (as with Percy White, novelist). A.E. Houseman, E.V. Lucas, Rudyard Kipling and others, expressed their appreciation of numerous of his poems. Clearly, Lulham's expressions of humanity, often profound and moving, were read with the greatest of pleasure for his richly varied language and the flowing musical lines of his verse. Although his work was predominantly serious in nature, his last volume was of light verse. His writing, above all, shows a passionate love of Sussex.

Lulham stands out in another respect. Despite his passion for Sussex, he moves on from the local or regional context of landscape to the national stage in pursuance of the contemporary problems of social injustice and deprivation. He also explores, like Blunt, the entanglements of love and personal tragedy, all with an extraordinary insight that must have been derived from personal experience and close involvement, as a medical man, with his patients. A number of his poems drew special praise, such as 'Red Dawn', 'On the Downs', 'The Weed Burner', or 'The Old Doctor'. Edward Thomas thought that there was a special personal freshness in Lulham's details of the Downs.[3] Such high esteem was evidently widely shared for he was shortlisted as Poet Laureate when Masefield was appointed in 1930, even though he was not by then writing poetry.

Towards a Fragment of Biography

There is a remarkable lack of biographical information about Percy Edwin Habberton Lulham, so a little more might be appropriate here. He identified himself so thoroughly with Sussex that it was assumed that he was Sussex born and bred, but his birth in April 1865 was actually at Heigham, near Norwich, where his father Edwin (1832–1921), a leather merchant and boot and shoe manufacturer, had married Elizabeth Habberton (1839–1901), a daughter of the owner of a shoe factory. The eldest child, he was eventually joined by a brother and six sisters.

By 1870, the family had moved to Brighton, the town of Edwin's birth, and in 1871 Lulham was living with his father, who was by now a freemason, and his mother at No. 17 Grand Parade, Brighton. But by 1878, the family had moved to Abbotsford House, Burgess Hill (then in the parish of Clayton), a country house in sight of the Downs, and his father was by now a Brighton town councillor and successful businessman, with a full retinue of household servants.

Abbotsford held affectionate memories for him.[4] But Percy (as he was called) was now away at the University School in Hastings, and by 1886 he was sufficiently attracted to the medical profession for him to be 'dressing' for Dr N.P. Blaker, a senior surgeon at the Sussex County Hospital. Between 1887 and 1896, when he qualified as a doctor at Guy's Medical School, Lulham resided as a student with his family at No. 4 Hill Crest Road, Sydenham. Blaker, also a student at Guy's and presumably the subject of his poem 'The Old Doctor', had previously lodged at Sydenham with the station master.

Plate 1: Peter Brandon following the award of a PhD degree, University of London, 1963. For many in Sussex, he was known simply as 'Dr Brandon'. (Family photograph collection, by permission of Mrs Gill Hooker, née Brandon)

Plate 2: Looking south-south-west from St Roche's Hill. (© Barry Shimmon, cc-by-sa/2.0)

Plate 3: View northwards from Firle Beacon. (Editor's collection)

Top left: Plate 4: Hurdis country – the footpath off Spring Lane, Burwash. (© N. Chadwick, cc-by-sa/2.0)

Left: Plate 5: Memorial to James Hurdis, Bishopstone Church. (www. sussexrecordsociety.org/dbs/esm/church/310)

Top right: Plate 6: Woolbeding House, the home of Charlotte Smith in the 1780s. (© Stephen Richards, cc-by-sa/2.0)

Below: Plate 7: The joy of the open air in Alfriston. (Gravelroots.net)

Plate 8: Eric Ravilious, 'Chalk Paths' watercolour, 1935. (Private collection)

Plate 9: Sussex shepherd. (Gravelroots.net)

Top left: Plate 10: A fifteenth-century hall house and its garden – the Priest House, West Hoathly. (By kind permission Sussex Archaeological Society)

Top right: Plate 11: Caxtons, the Grade II-listed home of Philip Webb, now in Pound Hill, Crawley. (Editor's collection)

Left: Plate 12: Humphrey's Homestead, home of the Meynells, with the converted farm building to the left where D.H. Lawrence and Frieda stayed. (Editor's collection)

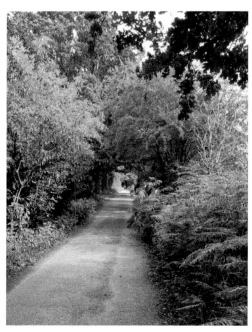

Plate 13: Stella Bowen, *c.* 1920. (Ford Madox Ford Collection, #4605, Division of Rare and Manuscript Collections, Cornell University Library, New York)

Plate 14: The track to Red Ford Cottage – isolated and 'just country'. (Editor's collection)

Clockwise from top left: Plate 15: 'Wilfrid Scawen Blunt in Arab Costume', etching for *albumen carte-de-visite*, 1883. (NPG D1079)
Plate 16: Two-Mile Ash Road, one of the sub-parallel old droveways, formerly much wider, near Blunt's Newbuildings estate. (© Ian Cunliffe, cc-by-sa/2.0)
Plate 17: W.S. Blunt's table tomb at Newbuildings Place. (Editor's collection)

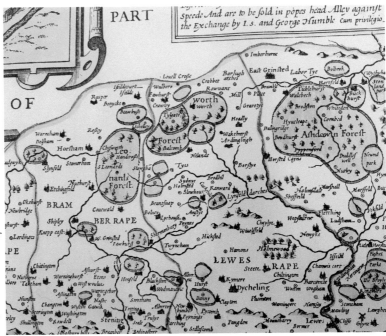

Plate 18: Worth Forest and Crabbet from Morden's *Map of Sussex*, 1695. (www.envf.port.ac.uk/geo/research/historical/webmap/sussexmap/morden106large.htm)

Plate 19: Richard Jefferies.
(NPG x18860)

Plate 20: Richard Jefferies'
Down Cottage, Crowborough.
(Cyril Wright (1909–95),
Jefferies House and Museum)

Above and right: Plates 21a and b: Sea View, now Jefferies House, off Sea Lane, Goring, and his grave in Broadwater Cemetery. (Editor's collection)

Plate 22: The Devil's Dyke, north of Brighton, where Jefferies roamed in the early 1880s. (Courtesy of Alan Grey)

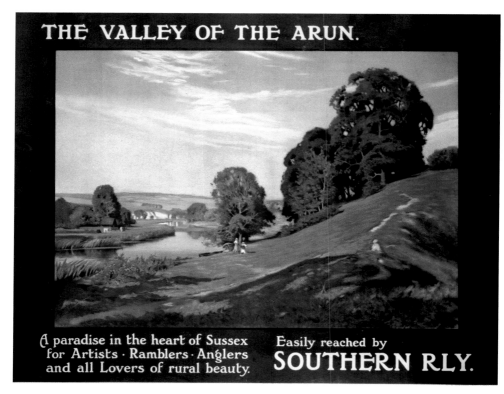

THE VALLEY OF THE ARUN.

A paradise in the heart of Sussex
for Artists · Ramblers · Anglers
and all Lovers of rural beauty.

Easily reached by

SOUTHERN RLY.

Plate 23: The valley of the Arun, Sussex. A Southern Railways vintage travel poster by Albert George Petherbridge. The antechamber to Paradise, but 'easily reached by Southern Railway'. (© National Railway Museum/Science & Society Picture Library)

Plate 24: Court Hill Farmhouse, Slindon, rented by Belloc in 1905. (Historic England, IOE01/13955/22)

Clockwise from right: Plate 25: Belloc's mill at Shipley with his final home, King's Land, just behind the nearest cottage. (Editor's collection)
Plate 26: The Cricketers at Duncton. Originally The Swan, it was renamed in 1867 after landlord John Wisden's interest in cricket, a name forever associated with the eponymous cricket annual. (Courtesy of The Cricketers pub)
Plate 27: The Elms, Rottingdean, on the north side of the village pond. (© Peter Whitcomb, cc-by-sa/2.0)

Left: Plate 28: Dr Habberton Lulham. (*SCM* 4 [1930], p. 543)

Above: Plate 29: Habberton Lulham and the Sussex travellers. It was in the possession of Habberton Lulham but was taken earlier. (East Sussex County Council Schools, Library and Museums' collection of magic lantern slides, courtesy of East Sussex County Council Library & Information Service)

SUSSEX SHEPHERD
(*Photo : Dr. Habberton Lulham*)

Plate 30: 'Sussex Shepherd' by Dr Habberton Lulham. (N.P. Blaker, *Sussex in Bygone Days*, 1919)

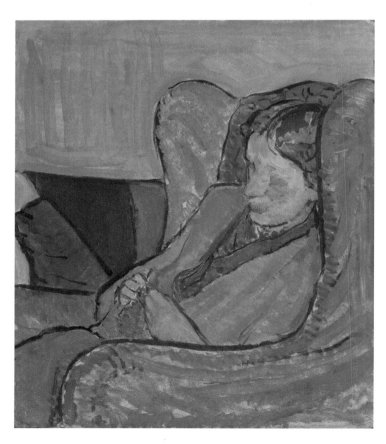

Plate 31: 'Virginia Woolf' by Vanessa Bell, oil on board, 1912. (NPG 5933)

Plate 32: Façade of Asheham House, with Itford Hill, July 1914. (Harvard University, Houghton Library, htc_ms_thr_557_photo_0191)

Plate 33: Monk's House in Rodmell High Street. (Editor's collection)

Plate 34: Frank Wootton, 'Windover in Winter, Alciston', January 1945, oil on canvas. (Courtesy of the Towner Collection, Image Towner, Eastbourne)

Plate 35: Virginia and Leonard memorials in the garden at Rodmell. Their ashes were buried beneath two intertwined elm trees here, which sadly are now gone. (Editor's collection)

Plate 36: Sheila Kaye-Smith – her popularity is reflected in this cigarette card of 1937. (NPG D42404)

Plate 37: Bridge over the River Tillingham, near Conster Manor, the countryside setting for *The End of the House of Alard* (© Janet Richardson, cc-by-sa/2.0)

Plate 38: Eleanor Farjeon. (www.findagrave.com/memorial/6531735/eleanor-farjeon)

Plate 39: 'Amy Sawyer' by Rose Cobban. (Courtesy of Ditchling Museum of Art & Craft)

Plate 40: The Hall at Southwick, facing the green – the home of S.P.B. Mais. (Editor's collection)

Plate 41: Ernest Raymond from the front cover of *SCM* (January 1930).

Plate 42: Newtimber Lane.
(Courtesy of Alan Grey)

Plate 43: The horizontal grave
slab of Arthur Bell, by Eric
Gill (1919), in Storrington
Churchyard. Surrounded by
bushes, he lies between Father
George Tyrell and Maude Petre.
(Editor's collection)

Plate 44: Lady Dorothy Wellesley's garden at Penns-in-the-Rocks, Withyham.
(© Oast House Archive, cc-by-sa/2.0)

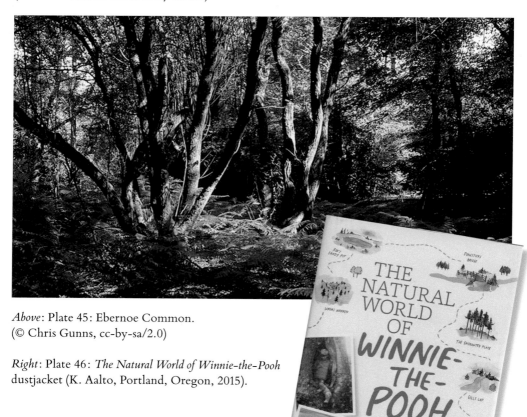

Above: Plate 45: Ebernoe Common.
(© Chris Gunns, cc-by-sa/2.0)

Right: Plate 46: *The Natural World of Winnie-the-Pooh*
dustjacket (K. Aalto, Portland, Oregon, 2015).

Here, Lulham played cricket for the Crystal Palace Club and then London County Cricket Club at the Crystal Palace ground, going on later to play his one match for Sussex as a fast bowler against Yorkshire in 1894, picking up three wickets but making few runs.[5] In 1900–01 he was at Sutton, Surrey, but had later returned to Sydenham when he published his first volume of poems, *Devices and Desires* in 1904.[6] His mother Elizabeth had died in 1901 and his father was to die in November 1906.

Blaker was the author of *Sussex in Bygone Days,* to which Lulham contributed an admiring foreword to the second edition in 1919, describing Blaker as:

> ... an admirable combination of the practical man of Science and the constant lover of Nature's ways and beauty, with the affectionate remembrancer of ancient customs and old sterling characters and the surgeon who for so many years fought successfully in the front ranks of a steadily advancing profession.[7]

This testimony to Blaker and his reference to the friendship of a 'medical man' who frequently accompanied him on the Downs, as Lulham mentioned in Barclay Wills' *Shepherds of Sussex*, together with contact with Lulham's life at various points, suggests that Blaker was strongly influential in Lulham's own medical and literary career. Clearly, Blaker also strongly influenced his interests in the Sussex past and its people, which became the theme of his verse and the subjects of his popular 'laugh and learn' lectures.[8]

These were reported in many places. In February 1933, for example, he lectured to the pupils of Rendcomb College, near Cirencester, illustrated with lantern slides and including an exhibition of sheep bells, shepherds' crooks and horse brasses: 'Dr. Haberton Lulham, probably one of the most popular of our regular lecturers, gave a talk on "Downland Ways." Starting with stories of the Sussex shepherds, some of which he told in his own verse.'

And in 1934:

> Dr. Habberton Lulham gave us another sample of his own species of diverting humour, blended with serious nature study. He brought, as usual, a fine collection of slides, some being of outstanding merit. By a number of sketches and anecdotes at the beginning, he established the rural atmosphere in which he prefers to move.[9]

Again, at Lewes County School for Boys in February 1935, he spoke on 'Rustic life and Humour', which was seen as 'in many people's opinion, the best that has yet been given in the School'.[10] Or at Cranleigh School in November 1938, apparently surprising his audience:

LECTURE: ROLLING STONES. As Dr. Habberton Lulham is now an old friend of ours, it was with an air of expectancy that we filed into the Speech Hall in our usual orderly fashion to hear his lecture, which bore the slightly unpromising title of 'Rolling Stones'. The astonishing collection of poachers' firearms, which we were shown at the outset, indicated at once that the lecturer was in form. Of the slides, we found that many depicted some of the less savoury types of humanity (which does not, of course, include the delightful pictures of the lecturer as a small boy), the tramps, the gipsies, the vagrants of this land, instead of the very beautiful pictures of the countryside which are the usual fare offered to us by Dr. Lulham.

[But] after a lecture by Dr. Lulham one thing stands out above all others: that this popular lecturer has that real love of the countryside which fully understands not only the country itself, but also, infinitely more difficult, the people who live in it.[11]

Similarly, there were talks to the local divisions of the British Medical Association in the 1920s and 1930s, such as 'Human nature through a doctor's eyes'. He seems to have been a popular speaker, with requests for repeat lectures. His poetry too, was popular and was printed in publications not only in Britain but in Canada and New Zealand. He seems to have been determined to combine the roles of poet and physician in tandem, and for this he was exactly prepared. He looked upon his medical career as a means by which to live in the workaday world he detested and thought of his life's real work as that of a poet-humanist and physician offering healing to all men through his medical skills and verse.

In later life, Lulham was familiar to readers of the *Sussex County Magazine*, edited by Arthur Beckett, for his verses and articles on the Downs, such as 'Downland Destiny' in 1928, for his photographs of sheep and shepherds, and for reports of his lectures.[12] He contributed to *Punch*, and was a founder member of the Society of Sussex Downsmen, now the South Downs Society, and one of its vice presidents. A collection of his photographs of the Sussex Downs was presented by the Society to Queen Mary, the wife of King George V. In 'A Downland Thought' he had asked that:

... What, though that the old beliefs be riven?
A hill-top still seems nearer heaven

...

O strong hills of your strength still lend
That I may seek you till life's end.[13]

Of his personal life, his passions or literary aspirations, we know next to nothing on account of the lack of any known family papers. Fortunately, his verse remains as a monument, a distillation of his personality, and tantalisingly intertwined with lovers and friends. He remains solitary and apart, unlike, say, Ford Madox Ford or Virginia Woolf. It is evident from his remarks in later life that visits to persons now unknown in the village of Amberley had also greatly inspired his verse.

He had led a somewhat migratory life. In 1911, he was enumerated at No. 38 Sweyn Road, Margate, the home of Dr Thompson, for whom he may have been acting as a locum, while his own home was apparently rented by the proprietor of a nursing home. About 1913, when he had published his third volume of poems, *The Other Side of Silence*, Lulham returned to Brighton to Prince Albert Street, evidently to take up an appointment as consultant to the Royal County Hospital.

He was married late in life in 1921 to Christine Phyllis Emma Morris (1894–1982), the novelist Ernest Raymond officiating as clergyman. She was 27, Lulham was 57. There were no children, and the marriage may not have been entirely happy, since although their initial residence was at the Garden House, Upper Drive, Hove, by 1924 she is returned as living in Great Ormond Street, London, and by 1939 they were listed as living apart, she as an actress at the Three Arts Club in London, and now also using her maiden name, Phyllis Morris, he with Rose Smallman, a domestic nurse from a Shropshire farming family, at Haven in Hurstpierpoint. Probably not coincidentally, Hurstpierpoint was also Blaker's own choice for retirement, a village with which he had longstanding family connections. Haven had its front, not on its residential road but at the back, facing onto fine views over meadows towards the South Downs including Wolstonbury and the Devil's Dyke.

During their marriage, Phyllis was arguably better known than Habberton Lulham, and she went on after his death to appear in several postwar films including *The Secret of St Ives* (1949), *That Forsyte Woman* (1949) and *The Devil's Disciple* (1959). She died in February 1982 at Denville Hall, Northwood, a retirement home for professional actors and actresses.

Lulham appears to have been rarely at ease of mind and experienced periods of loneliness and depression. In 1922, he had published his last volume of poems, *Kettle Songs*, on everyday humorous things:

My verses
To them no polished art belongs –
Just cricket-chirps and kettle-songs;
But they would greet you, if they may,
As cheery friends of everyday.

He had a deep love of nature but wrote trenchant, restless pieces about the
sordid life he had left behind in the city, anguished responses to the traumas
of his day. A poetic example is 'A Downland Destiny' (1928), a harrowing
tale of entangled love in which Lulham shares his friend's grief in offering
advice to humanity in general, based on his own personal experiences.

He had retired from medical practice during the 1920s, probably due
to high blood pressure and sciatica. He committed suicide in June 1940 by
injecting himself with an overdose of morphine at Haven, in Hurstpierpoint,
rather than undergo an operation for prostate cancer. His doctor reported
that Lulham had been concerned with his medical condition more than was
justified. He wrote a last note hoping that he would have the courage to
undertake the final task and asking for forgiveness.[14]

Shepherds and the Freedom of the South Downs

The preoccupation with shepherds, which repeatedly entered his verse and
prose, continued to the end ('Ere the Storm Breaks' 1940) and among his
papers intended for publication after his death were pathetic verses entitled
'A Farewell in Downland'. He was also fascinated by other working country
people, by travellers and by gypsy lore, and the photographs that he took of
them remain as a valuable historical record (Plate 29 and Figure 24).[15] There
can be few townsmen who embraced country ways so intensely as Lulham
that they ruled his life, and none who, in so doing, meticulously prepared
himself to be their leading poet. Like other downland poets, his spirit soared
and his soul was calmed by observations of nature and the enjoyment of
wide horizons and salty air, but he is distinguished from other writers by his
yearning for nothing more in life than to be allowed to live in the Downs
among country people and their traditional customs and superstitions.

Lulham had moved to Ditchling, under the Sussex Downs, by the time
Songs from the Downs and Dunes appeared in 1908, living in South Street at
Sundown Cottage at the foot of Ditchling Beacon. From here, he would
have enjoyed the sunsets that figure in his poetry and from where he tells us

Fig. 24: Dr Lulham attending a patient 1920s. It is marked 'Dr Habberton Lulham of Hurstp.Pt Photographer of Gypsies'. (Courtesy of East Sussex Brighton and Hove Record Office, R/L 39)

he assisted Tom Rushbridge, the shepherd of nearby Wick Farm, at lambing time. Such experiences give life to his poetry:

> I linger still about the sleeping farm;
> Here are the lambs, that start up from their straw
> And stare with bright eyes as the lanthorn beams
> Above their wattled walls. How soft the moon
> Shines on their gentle forms, and throws the Shade
> Of each small head upon its neighbour's fleece.[16]

Coming to live so near the Downs was a reintroduction into an old and happy world at variance with the South London from which he exiled himself. Above all, it was the last of the old shepherds and where they lived and worked, that captivated him. He went out at dawn to 'look the hill', helped to drive sheep and assisted at lambing, clipping and dipping. In doing this, he became friends with several shepherds, who admitted him into the secrets of their downland life. His chapter on shepherds contributed to Barclay Wills' *Shepherds of Sussex* (1938) was based, as he explains in the book, on his unusual empathy with shepherds, who were among his most valued friends and who engaged his admiration for 'their whole-hearted, and often selfdenying, devotion to their duties, and their general good sense and intelligence' (Plate 30).[17]

As well as Tom Rushbridge, Lulham got to know Henry Rewell, who succeeded him, Jim Fowler, another Ditchling shepherd, and 'Darkie' Funnell of Wilmington, among others. He clearly derived great satisfaction from learning about an entirely new way of life. And, astonishingly, for a qualified doctor who had been a town dweller, he looked back to nights of great happiness when he left his cottage at the foot of Ditchling Beacon with a thermos of hot chocolate for Rushbridge and helped him on the high downs with the lambing for a few hours. Again, at Amberley, he would arrive on the Downs allowing the exhausted shepherd to instantly fall asleep on the straw of an empty pen and sleep on like a child until Lulham woke him and told him what lambs had been born and what he had done with them. He recalled these 'happy, peaceful hours'.[18] He was as skilled an 'ovine accoucheur' as a doctor at childbirth.

His 'apprenticeship' to sheep inspired his verses to a shepherd in his poem 'On the Downs' and strengthened his literary connection with the Sussex Downs more generally. His contributed photographs to Gosset's *Shepherds of Britain* (1911), including the cover illustration and frontispiece, together with others depicting downland scenes, one of the downland above Fulking, one of Southdown sheep, 'models of what hill sheep should be', and one entitled 'Springtime in the Sussex Weald'.[19] A shepherd lad features in his wartime poem 'His Only Way', published in 1917, where the lad resolves finally to follow his rival in love, now dead in Flanders, to enlist and leave his girl behind him in Sussex.

An Intimacy with Nature Mixed with Humanitarian Concern

Although Lulham had an intense love of nature and Sussex folklore, his writing included a wide range of subjects. Flowing through his verse is a liberal humanitarianism that brought him closely in touch with the joys and sorrows of people of all kinds. To this he brought a tolerance and compassion, a sense of brotherhood, defence of the underdog and an agonised striving to make people happier and more fulfilled. There was also a deep spirituality running through his works, contrasting with the materialism of much contemporary life, and the Sussex Downs were the agent that released it into prominence.

Lulham's longest poem, 'On the Downs' (1908), is the greatest tribute the Sussex Downs have ever received. 'It gave a glow of joy as I read it and lifted me up,' said one of Lulham's correspondents. Apart from two editions, the poem was also published separately with pictures of downland by Sussex artists and a dedication of the poem to Rudyard Kipling. The poet climbs up his 'long-beloved hills', apparently up Clayton Bostal, and looks across to his boyhood home of Abbotsford House in the Weald below. In the little farm in the hollow, noise is conveyed by the chink of milk pails, the jingle of a jolting wagon ringing up from lichened tiles and mossy thatch and the cheery voices and laughter of the waggoner's and maid's 'jolly rustic burr'. He continues, noting cows sauntering to the milking shed and the plodding black oxen.[20] He then climbs higher, blessing the 'perdurable hills' for their rooted changelessness and draws near the crest to the place he knew in boyhood and loves best:

> Ah! … once again I stand upon thy brow,
> O blessed hill, my Hesperid, the home,
> My heart loves best on earth Green headland-isle,
> Set all about with blue.

And he invokes their power over man with their space, height and freedom:

> Dear Downs! That lead the feet not over high
> Above the homes and humble ways of men,
> Yet lift the soul to visionings beyond;
> …
> … How rich ye make
> Your lover! – as a king that dips his hand
> Idly within a casket of rare gems,
> So he who loves you draws forth when he will
> And lingers over jewel-memories.

The action in the poem then moves away and the reader would reasonably assume that it is within the vicinity of Ditchling Beacon. Yet more than thirty years after writing the poem, Lulham explained that his inspiration had been mainly derived from Amberley in the Arun Valley, and this actually appears to have been the part of the Downs that captivated his fancy after leaving Burgess Hill.

The quiet hour before the dawn, which shepherds knew more than anyone else, specially captivated him:

> How oft have I climbed eastward ere the dawn,
> My foot prints dark upon your grey, wet grass,
> And seen the sunrise crown the dewy crest
> Above me with an irised coronet;
> Or marked the rising tide of golden light
> Flood up the sunward slopes, and overflow
> The rims of purple hollows, those great cups
> That every morn await the glorious wine
> That sets them brimming.

This scene would appear to have been experienced by Lulham from Amberley Mount.

Here, too, apparently was his first love-making as a 'lightfoot lad who climbed here long ago/ With one he loved', weaving a little song as the happy couple roamed the hill. From Lulham's later evidence, his encounter with the shepherd also seems to have happened at Amberley. From this began his interest in Sussex folklore, figuring in the poem as a melodious fairies' song of their dainty daily activities for humans. Then, when evening approaches, he paints the lovely moment when the sun sinks through clouds and purple mist behind the western hills, the last reds glowing for a moment 'like a watchman's fire'. By darkening lanes, Lulham walks behind the pattering feet and tinkling sheep bells of the flock that the shepherd's dog brings down towards the fold. As he re-enters the village, he is again entranced by the transience of beauty flooding away before him, for it is the time when light and dark filter together to make the wondrous blue that 'old painters used to drape about their stately dreams of God'.

Then, looking upwards in the moonlight to the shoulders of the hills, he visualises Pan, the goat-foot god, drawn out from his hillside cave and imagines he hears the ghostly music from his shrunken pipes. His final description of the area at night is poetically exquisite: as he passes down the village street there is occasionally a light from an open lattice and as a shadow on the lamp-lit blind, a mother rocks her child to and fro, singing a lullaby. This is Amberley, the village in which Lulham stayed, and he tells us that as late as

Fig. 25: 'Back to Work from the Wild Brooks Meadows' by Habberton Lulham, from *Amberley and Her Wild Brooks* (*SCM* 13, 1939, pp. 598–603)

1939 cottagers would come to their windows to see the train of farm horses, tied one behind the other, with a boy astride the leading horse, making their way to the lush grass of the Wild Brooks in the evening (Figure 25).[21]

In this poem, Lulham provides the best description of the musical effects of sheep bells. He wrote elsewhere of when standing alone on one of the downland 'beacons' he caught far off the deep dong-dong of one of the old 'canister' bells. Then he heard another and others of varying pitch, 'but all low-toned and sweet'. Then the music-makers appeared over the crest and 'the hill seemed peopled, purposeful and charged with its true life and significance', and when the flock passed on down to the next valley that held their fold, 'the soft mellow clangour of the bells – many hand-wrought in Sussex forges' – welled out over the landscape.[22]

This long poem in blank verse has not been excelled in its word painting, passion, imaginative strength, variety of ideas and depth of feeling, by any of the myriad of downland poets who came before or after Lulham. The bold and beautiful imagery, the loftiness of the ideal and his infectious enthusiasm for the Downs, rises to a special height. With this poem he staked out the Sussex Downs as his kingdom so successfully that Lulham should be put with Belloc and Kipling at the top of the Sussex pantheon.

In his verse, the need to escape from the city into the country, the conventional theme of the Sussex poet, is persistent. In 'Escape' (1908) he pleads with his lover to leave with him the 'reeking' streets for 'wave and star and heather'. In 1912, he returns to this and cries (to another lover?):

> We were not made for cities, you and I,
> And in their reek lies poison for our souls,
> Their riches but impoverish our hearts,
> Make but a wedge to rive us from our best.
> Escape, true heart, escape!
> Break free to me,
> And with me, bare your tired brow to the breeze …
> (Come)

And although he and his lover are always on breezy sea cliffs or in the unspoilt countryside, he personally feels disadvantaged:

> How dare I dream to wind our woodland grace
> With this poor city soul, and form and face?
> And he speaks directly to the hills themselves:
> What do we ask of you, and asking, find?
> That which the glittering cities may not give,
> What in the fields of flowers can never live,
> Nor all the hurrying seasons leave behind
> Unchanging shelter from the blast unkind,
> …
> Refuge and solace for the unquiet mind.[23]

Clearly, Lulham enjoyed an intimacy with nature. He is observant of bird life and song and an intensely felt experience of nature suffuses much of his poetry, as in 'May Dawn' where he lovingly depicts nature in the 'waiting hush that preludes dawn'. He observes everything, from tiniest blades of grass to the topmost bough of a tree and has several poems on birds and bird music. But he does not always see nature in a kindly mood: indeed, also as the ceaseless rivalry between bird, animal and tree, 'the trampling-under and the thrusting-by' which was all too evident in the rasping human world he hated, and from which he had escaped. Instead, he hopes for unity between plants, animals and man.

Another striking characteristic of his verse is its humanitarianism. Lulham is splendidly eloquent on behalf of the downtrodden and oppressed, the sick and poor, as was Michael Fairless (*nom de plume* of Margaret Fairless Barber) in her 'The Roadmender', taking on the role of a humble roadmender in the Adur Valley but with glimpses of the essential unity of people with nature.[24] Lulham has tender utterances of pity and sympathy for all his fellow men who are underdogs, especially hapless city-dwellers.

He does not denounce or condemn but poignantly touches on their limited opportunities, suffering, their struggle against poverty, and the sorrow and misfortune of the 'voiceless' urban masses, 'moiling and toiling in their sweat of tears'. His contemplative poem, 'The Meeting', is an exceptional expression in Victorian and Edwardian England of a sense of 'brotherhood' with all mankind, the failed and thriven, the rich and poor. Lulham's phrase for life's losers is 'mates of my own mind', comrades, brothers and sisters and 'spirit-kith and kin', implying a comradeship and a sense of human equality that has undertones of Walt Whitman, a consciousness of the unity of life which is, in a sense, religious and certainly egalitarian.

An article in *The Downland Post* in 1924 also exemplified his concern for the poor and disregarded in rural Sussex, as 'Granny Coombe' is allowed to return to the cottage of her younger days by the author purchasing it for her, the article being illustrated by a photo of the elderly woman at the door of her thatched cottage.[25]

In a real sense, his putting a hero's laurel crown on the 'common' man was an indictment of the nineteenth-century England that had done so little that was worthwhile for them and of contemporary England in which most upper-middle-class people rather regarded others as a slave class of half-witted troglodytes. Yet, he expresses his deprecation with humility and wisdom:

Friend, dost thou wake while still 'tis early night,
Stung by injustice, or some maddening wrong,
And do the swift night-thoughts come raging, strong
With all the indignant strength of truth and right?
Then stay thy pen, or seal thy strained lips tight,
Stand fast and hold the leaping wrath in throng –
Thou'rt one, a million such wronged souls among,
For their sake spur thy heart up to the height

Of a supreme forbearance; store the strength
Thy words had wasted; so thy life at length
Working with Time and that hid spark of good
In every hostile breast – shall win to peace,
With skill to furnish, and thine own pangs cease,
Solace for all thy heart-sore brotherhood.
('Forbear!')[26]

The human side of life is a theme well developed in *The Other Side of Silence* (1913), where in 'Muted Strings' he is anguished by the 'sudden troubled line of brows', 'the sombre-droop of longing-laden eyes', by people 'oft dim and misty with unfallen tears', 'town-weary children with town-tired eyes', the 'poor still doomed to marred and sunless lives' and readily stung by injustice or some maddening wrong.

Among other humanitarian causes, he writes, for example, of 'Daft Dick' – 'Daily I met him, toiling towards the Downs' – who goes to pray for release into heaven; of a boyhood playmate now 'locked from the world … in mad-house walls'; he heartens a lad who found that no one wanted to hear him singing; cheers a blind man tapping the pavement in a dense fog, and with difficulty, attends a funeral in the mud of London streets.[27]

Love and a Sussex Retirement

Yet another strand in Lulham's verse is that of fervent love poems, spontane-ously written without affectation, in which he throws light on his own love of women and his complex and agonisingly frustrated lovelife, which may have involved a clandestine, guilt-ridden relationship earlier in life. Rather like Wilfrid Blunt of an earlier generation (see pages 99–102), he put more of himself into his poetry than any of his contemporaries. He wrote a moving elegy to his mother, and more than a dozen poems were inspired by his love of women. He evidently remembered his younger life and vexed relation-ships experienced by people in love. In 'Through the Borderlands' he advises on wooing, telling of the happy hours of longing of the man who 'hastens never'. Unrequited love is the subject of 'Once', and other poems deal with inconstancy, being accused of infidelity, his unbridled joy at being in love and his difficulties in loving a woman of complex personality.

In Lulham's *Devices and Desires* (1905) there are several charming love sonnets and other short pieces addressed presumably to the same woman.

This lovemaking apparently resulted in climactic sexual moments. The sonnet 'Heart-Husbandry', charmingly addressed to the 'mother that shall be', alludes to his heartfelt wish that a child shall, in its hour, be beautifully born and 'A Birth' tells of the birth of a male child. Bereavement is reported too, for 'A Smiling Picture of One Dead' (in *The Other Side of Silence*) is a poignant epitaph to a lover. His last major poem, 'A Downland Destiny', is an elegy with a great flood of grief and an insatiable sympathy for his friend harrowingly entangled in the mesh of love. Lulham is not depressed by the horror and despair but uses it optimistically to offer strength to those similarly afflicted with the knowledge and wisdom stored in his heart from his own bitter experiences:

O listen, listen lovers all,
Whom love hath made to agonise,
One who has known the cup of gall,
Seen Hope lie cold beneath her pall,
And thereby grown a little wise –
A very little wise.

He is for forgiving not for anger, for giving more and more of love was his way of healing aching wounds. These outpourings, sometimes heartbroken, about his personal relationships contrasts with the simple description of 'bachelor aged 57' on Lulham's marriage certificate of 1921.

In his final years as a writer, he was a different person from the absorbed young poet of his younger days. He had written almost all his best work and was coasting downhill at the end of his poetic career. He was in retirement, and his mission for his fellow men slipped out of the picture and he has nothing more to say. In his valedictory volume, *Kettle Songs*, his style and thought changed completely. His world got smaller; gone is the profound philosophising, the stoic defence of the underdog and his disappointments and explorations of nature.

He retired to his cottage home at the foot of the Downs with his new wife and companions. We can imagine him serenely telling 'pot-calling-kettle' tales by the fireside in a deep hearth of the inglenook with that pleasant noise of water boiling in a kettle among the warmth and laughter of cheerful and good-natured people who gossip humorously and light-heartedly about their memories and the little happenings in the village. As pipe smoke dreamily wreathes upwards, and with the curtains drawn and the sofa drawn up, we hear, in the manner of a modern version of Cowper's 'The Task', of the abortive attempts to tame part of Ditchling Beacon, a disappointed gardener, the rescued cuckoo chick that unfortunately was choked with a chocolate cream, of various animals and birds that came into the house or garden, and of the cock that beat a fox. When the fire burnt low upon the hearth and the shadows of the room were deepening, it was time for bed.

It was at this period that Lulham wrote. 'Afternoon in a Downland Village' (presumably Amberley), recounting its sleepy life on a quiet afternoon when the only noises are those of children passing to and from the village school and 'of the clank and rusty creak and wheeze/ of handle, pail and chain that / tell folk draw from nigh a garden well' that denoted the filling of kettles for cottage teas. Nothing more disturbs the somnolence until sundown when Mus' Wersfold brings his team clattering down the lane, drinking first at a wayside spring, and then 'kicking like Maytime colts' through the field gate and roll to rub their smoking backs to cool.

Summing him up, he was a man of many parts, with an unusual range of talents, devoted not for his own benefit but for the sake of others. But his beautiful verse seemingly disappeared along with himself. Now almost totally forgotten, he richly deserves rehabilitation as one of the 'greats' in the Sussex literary canon. This does not give, however, a full indication of the man he was: an extremely sensitive person, subject to disappointment, periods of troubling depression and loneliness, and vexed by the modern world. He held strong and unconventional views and was not afraid to speak his mind. Sadly, Lulham at the end was neither poet nor physician-healer, but a cancer sufferer who, in a suicidal state of mind, took his illness to be his death warrant. He had worked honestly in literature, photography and medicine and given to the best of his power until he had no more to give. But his poems are his greatest monument. They paint his portrait in his own words.

John Betjeman shall have the last word. Writing to the poet Edmund Blunden in 1942, he asked, 'Do you know Dr Habberton Lulham of Brighton (dc 1939)? He is up to Hurdis at his best and in the Hurdis manner. I wish I knew something about him.'[28]

VIRGINIA WOOLF AT RODMELL

The view across the meadows to Caburn is before me now.[1]

If other authors have been more characterised by their wish to find a retreat from London, from modernity, from the increasing pace of nineteenth-century life, we now turn to one who was fascinated with explorations of modernism, with observation and inward processes of self-discovery and experimental writing. And yet, Virginia Woolf also longed for the peace and benefits of a quieter rural existence, while also – and almost simultaneously – wanting the stimulus of the London streets and society.[2]

Adeline Virginia Woolf née Stephen (1882–1941) loved the vast agglomeration of London as few writers have done, and her explorations of its upper-middle-class life have won her worldwide renown. Yet no author has written of the South Downs with greater perspicacity or discovered in them more inexhaustible interest. As her father, Leslie Stephen, editor of the *Dictionary of National Biography* between 1882 and 1891, had discovered before her, standing alone, like a 'desolate sea-bird' before an immense view, one could be oneself with one's thoughts (Plate 31).

Early Days in Sussex

There had been early visits to Bognor ('muddy misty flat utterly stupid') and Hove, and in 1900 she went with her sister Vanessa and uncle George Duckworth to the sale at Crabbetts of Wilfrid Scawen Blunt's horses. There had also been the summer of 1907 spent at Playden near Rye, from where she explored the surrounding countryside and Romney Marsh, took tea with Henry James and even flirted with the idea of taking a cottage at Peasmarsh among its apple orchards.

But Virginia Stephen first really encountered the Downs from December 1910 when staying for a week at the Pelham Arms in Lewes, househunting with her brother Adrian. In January 1911, she rented an 'inconceivably ugly'

Edwardian villa in Firle village, with useful access to London via the station at nearby Glynde. And soon Leonard Woolf and other guests were being welcomed to her 'hideous suburban villa'.[3]

However, later that year, as she and Leonard went on long downland walks, they developed plans to rent Asheham House, Beddingham, to the east of Lewes, and duly moved there in February 1912 (Plate 32). In August, she and Leonard were married at St Pancras Registry Office, and spent their wedding night at Asheham, continuing to use the house as a holiday and weekend home, but otherwise living at No. 38 Brunswick Square, Bloomsbury. Thereafter, as and when Virginia's delicate health allowed, there were guests at Asheham, such as Lytton Strachey and Katherine Mansfield, and visits to the Gills at Ditchling, and to Sidney and Beatrice Webb. Of Asheham, Leonard wrote in his autobiography, 'I have never known a house which had such a strong character, a personality of its own — romantic, gentle, melancholy, lovely.'[4] They both adored the house.

There was also a move to the smart Georgian Hogarth House at Richmond (1913), where the Hogarth Press was later initiated, while sister Vanessa came down to Charleston in 1916 with her husband, Clive Bell, and Duncan Grant, a fellow painter. Later, Maynard Keynes and Lydia Lopokova (who, to general astonishment, he married in 1925) moved to nearby Tilton.

Asheham was initially merely a brief refuge from the uproar of London, where Virginia could write in peace, catch ideas for her books in her walks, be spared travelling and avoid the constant intrusion of self-invited friends. Her experience of Sussex was the fulfilment of her dream of periodically escaping from London. Her diary for 17 December 1918 sets the tone, 'At Asheham for a week [...] Will write here in some form a new book. We shall have one week entirely alone at Asheham, the greatest and most unmixed pleasure this world affords.'[5] Her first novels, *The Voyage Out* (1915) and *Night and Day* (1919), were conceived here.

But soon after this, and upon receiving notice to quit Asheham, they again began house hunting in April 1919. They now felt committed to the Sussex downland, and in June, Virginia impulsively purchased the brick-and-flint base of a converted windmill, the Round House, in Pipe Passage, Lewes. But then, at an auction at the White Hart Hotel, just a month later, she bought Monk's House, Rodmell, for £700, across the River Ouse from Asheham. The Round House was sold two weeks later for £20 profit.[6] The 'unpretending' Monk's House was old-fashioned and inconvenient, with few concessions to the twentieth century but with a garden that delighted Leonard.

Virginia proudly boasted of her garden at Rodmell as the 'finest in Sussex' and its remarkable beauty was largely owed to Leonard, a fanatical gardener. Here they lived from September 1919, alternating with No. 52 Tavistock Square, Bloomsbury (purchased in 1924), until her suicide on 28 March 1941.

In 1927, Virginia thought briefly about buying Laughton Place, the Tudor moated house, but decided that it was too dreary.[7] Instead, in 1928, the adjoining field to Monk's House was purchased, as was another cottage, and successively more weekends, holidays and summers were spent at Rodmell. Leonard continued here until his own death in August 1969.

Seeing and Visiting the Sussex Landscape

Virginia always had passionate things to say about the Downs. Indeed, in the last weeks of her life the curves and deep hollows of the Downs were among her few consolations. Between 1915 and 1941, her diary, regarded as one of the most important in English literature, contains voluminous reflections written up during stays in Rodmell, throwing light on her reactions to Sussex, her state of mind and ideas and images that she later incorporated into her works.[8]

The mainspring of her intense emotion for the Downs arose from her hypersensitive keenness of the senses. She would sit and look intensely at the Downs in all seasons and weathers until, in her own words, 'one becomes an opium eater in one's eye'. Her challenge to herself was to represent in a new way the aesthetics of the downland landscape: how to translate the beauty into words on a page with all their slipperiness and malleability.

She had a painter's way of looking at landscape, painting in words. She said she felt the beauty of landscape, especially its colour, subtly and changeably flowing over her pen. She wrote, for example, of 'the willows ruby red, no rust red', Downs stretching 'like the outstretched wings of grey birds' and colour over Asheham Hill 'like the green backgrounds of Vermeer'.[9] Despite her constant investigations into human character and the reactions of one upon another, her people on the Downs are almost incidental to the grandeur of the world around them because while there she wanted to avoid them.

Her diary and letters are peppered with excited observations of natural phenomena, colour and the countryside, just as she had shown beauty everywhere in *Mrs Dalloway*'s London streets. As Virginia maundered over the Downs, she would compose words, phrases and sentences and collect ideas for future novels, catching them 'hot and sudden' while walking over Asheham Hill or to her favourite farm outside Telscombe.

These daily solitary walks fed her imagination, which her nephew Quentin Bell described as being 'furnished with an accelerator but no brakes'.[10] Such regular afternoon walks enabled her to generalise boldly about the landscape from different places and in different seasons and conditions of light and shadow. Sights towards nightfall belied what they showed in the morning, and, as we have seen, she was irritably conscious that, try as she could, she was able to get so little of it down onto paper.

She noticed how smoke issued from a steam train under Mount Caburn like the ears of a rabbit; how rooks beat up against the wind; and the wooden way sheep walk, one stiff foot after another, which appeared in *The Waves* (1931).[11] One of the passages in her diary describing 'the extraordinary primeval appearance of the farm wagons' at Rodmell in August 1928, so laden with hay that they looked 'like some vast shaggy animal moving on very short legs', is transferred almost word for word in *The Waves* (see further on page 184).[12] It may be presumed that the inspiration for the vivid descriptive passages of changing light and shade between the various episodes in *The Waves* were drawn principally from observations while at Rodmell. On 31 August 1927, she wrote:

> This is the last day of August and like almost all of them of extraordinary beauty. Each day is fine enough and hot enough for sitting out; but also full of wandering clouds; and that fading and rising of the light which so enraptures me in the downs; which I am always comparing to the light beneath an alabaster bowl.[13]

The exceptional importance of solitary walking to her is evident from the fact that when foot and mouth disease struck her part of the Downs, and she was temporarily unable to walk there, she felt bereft. She wrote to Ethel Smyth, the composer, from Monk's House on Boxing Day 1937:

> We're entirely marooned here. Foot and mouth to right of us, to left of us, foot and mouth all around us, so that if we want to step off the road we have to drive 5 miles. A murrain be on all farmers who cut me off my one wildest and purest pleasure! There are the marshes and I cant walk there. So I cant think, cant read, cant write.[14]

Sounds, too, set her vivid imagination and powers of description to work. On hearing the far-off guns from France on the Downs in 1916, it sounded at a distance like:

… the beating of gigantic carpets by gigantic women. You may almost see them holding the carpets in their strong arms by the four corners, tossing them into the air, and bringing them down with a thud while the dust rises in a cloud about their heads.[15]

Although she found London gave her a story without any trouble, she often felt badgered by Leonard's political work and their social engagements and was unable to write in the city. She longed for respite in the countryside where only Mr Botten might deliver the milk or the postman call.[16] So she expressed, when writing *To the Lighthouse* in 1926, 'To write a novel in the heart of London is next to an impossibility. I feel as if l were nailing a flag to the top of a mast in a raging gale'.[17]

In the same year, she wrote of Rodmell, 'I think I shall retire there next year and write innumerable books'. Although this did not happen for more than ten years (from October 1939), there were successive improvements to her writing room in the garden at Monk's House, with its view of Mount Caburn, which was the studio from which so much of her incredibly prolific literary achievement came. Her stays in Sussex became longer. In the beginning, Virginia noted that there were 'no buses, no water, no gas or electricity'. But the Woolfs improved the house: there were two water closets, one paid for from *Mrs Dalloway*, the other from *The Common Reader*. She was happy and productive in the seclusion there, released from the London scrimmage. To her lover, Vita Sackville-West, she wrote in August 1931, 'One walk here fills my poor old head with a sense of such natural happiness as I never get a whole summer in London.'[18]

Rodmell

Reached along the narrow and winding road between Lewes and Newhaven, Rodmell lies in the lower Ouse Valley within a wide, flat-floored vale, on the water meadows known locally as Brooks, and almost enclosed by Kipling's 'whale-backed Downs'. It still retains some of its rural simplicity and seclusion in an exceptionally tranquil countryside (Figure 26).

From the Monk's House National Trust car park, on part of the field Leonard bought to prevent house building, is the fine view eastwards across the Brooks to Itford Hill and Asheham, their former summer home, but also to the hated but short-lived cement works. At the other end of the field, Mount Caburn rises above the valley and a short walk northwards leads

Fig. 26: Rodmell – Monk's House is west of St Peter's Church on the main village street. The River Ouse is to the east. (National Library of Scotland: Ordnance Survey, Sussex LXVII.NW, 1911)

to another superb view of Kingston Hill and Lewes Castle, the latter now dwarfed by the modern monstrosity of County Hall, but backed by Mount Harry and extending round to more chalk pits.

There were constant anxieties about development of the countryside in the area and the incursions of Londoners (such as themselves!). The Woolfs were involved in helping to save most of the open spaces giving access to these views and this almost complete encirclement by unspoilt downs gives a feeling of being fenced off from the outside world, a feeling that grew in the hearts and minds of the Woolfs. But missing today are the small and medium-sized farms in the village the Woolfs knew, the larger herds of cows that then lowed in the brooks, the horses coming down to the river to drink, the old farm labourers drinking at the local pub and the nearby village school that has now closed.

Virginia's letters and diaries over the period 1919–26 relating to Rodmell reveal an initial urbanite's detachment from the local residents and a perception of the village as a romantic paradise and a delectable spectacle. But the changing relationship of Virginia and Leonard to Rodmell must be one of the best-documented records anywhere in the world. Like any typical Londoner who loved daily life in the city, Virginia often dreamt of such an escape. Among her many inconsistencies was revelling in the hectic rush of town but also dreaming of living down a long lane a mile from a main road in the country. She would complain of distractions and then telephone or write people invitations to visit, and although seeking seclusion, she wrote thousands of letters in anticipation of replies.[19]

The dream of getting away to Sussex is a constant refrain in her diary, writing of London as purgatory, but it was to London that she regularly returned like a moth to the lights of a lamp. She leans to one but would be lost without the other. Her diary entry for 1 March 1930 reads, 'O thank God a thousand times – to Rodmell & there be at rest ... Not an anxiety, not a stir anywhere. No one coming. Nothing to do. All strain ceased ... Everything is shut off.' But then, on another occasion, she returns to London after a long weekend at her Sussex refuge, writing in her diary under 28 June 1937:

Home is the hunter, home from the hill; and the Wolves are back from Monks House. And much refreshed into the bargain. Three solitary nights. Think of that! Was there ever such a miracle? Not a voice, not a telephone. Only the owl calling, perhaps a clap of thunder, the horses going down to the brooks to drink, and Mr. Botten calling with the milk in the morning.

She was writing again before noon, hoping to drive her pen the harder after her restful holiday.[20] Her delight in brief, invigorating release into London's countryside and her relish for her return to the city, expresses the opposed raptures of departure and return. Like many Londoners, she occasionally thought of retirement to the country.

Her state of mind regarding town and country can also be illustrated by her remarks in September 1926 when she wrote in her diary of her extreme happiness when walking on the Downs, 'I like to have space to spread my mind out. I like to breathe in more light and air and see more grey hollows and gold cornfields with their fresh ploughed land showing white, with gulls flickering', but in May 1928 she had remarked, 'London itself perpetually attracts, stimulates, and gives me a play & a story & a poem without any trouble save that of moving my legs through the streets.' Both town and country were, in fact, indispensable to her well-being and writing, and the loss to her of one or the other was to prove disastrous.[21]

The Woolfs' sense of downland beauty led to two quite contradictory thoughts and actions. In her diary, she wrote of the views from her garden, 'As for beauty, as I always say when I walk the terrace after breakfast, too much for one pair of eyes. Enough to float a whole population in happiness if only they would look.' However, the Woolfs did not want to share their contentment with newcomers. In the early years of their stay in Rodmell, they were irritated beyond measure by the incoming Georgian poet Edward Shanks to Sussex, and hated such other 'cronies' of (Sir) John Squire from the world of publishing and advertising, 'the Squirarchy'.

Their sense of proprietorial possession of Rodmell reached extreme lengths: she resented that the Downs should be seen by cultivated eyes, self-conscious eyes, and wished there were nothing but Dedmans, Bottens and Staceys (representative local people), as they alone peopled the graveyards. She was chagrined at living in 'a colony of poets' and found it hard to have young Edward Shanks living next door. By 1930, she was in such despair at landscape deterioration around Rodmell that she enquired of a friend in London about a member of 'some Committee or Council – I cannot remember what' (evidently, her vague recollection of the Council for the Preservation of Rural England, formed in 1926).[22]

Yet, the Woolfs were at their happiest at Rodmell in the 1930s. In her diary for 2 October 1932, Woolf wrote of her pleasure at her free life, coming in when and how they liked from the daily foray into the surrounding countryside. In fact, by September 1927, her interest in Rodmell as a community had grown sufficiently for her to feel that she could be its 'annalist' on the basis of long talks with the rector, her neighbour, but this was to compare the history of the village as an agricultural settlement in contrast to the contemporary speculative 'villains', whom she regarded as spoiling the place.

She learnt that thirty-five years ago there had been 160 families living there but by 1927 there were no more than eighty. It was a decaying village. Not a boy was being taught to plough, while people wanting weekend cottages were buying up the old cottages 'for fabulous sums'. She heard that Monk's House had been offered to the rector for £400, but the Woolfs had paid £700 for it, and she thought they might be able to sell it for £2,000 (Plate 33). Yet, it was only when the Woolfs had purchased land to effectively preserve their downland views that they began consciously to become part of the Rodmell community.[23] 'Owning the field has given a different orient to my feelings about Rodmell. I begin to dig myself in, take part in it, and I shall build another storey to the house if I make money,' she wrote.[24]

From 1928, we can trace the beginnings of Virginia the countrywoman, through her solitary walks and her garden lodge, her working retreat, and a taste that Leonard shared through his passion for gardening. Whereas the Woolfs spent about a fifth of their time annually in the village in the 1920s, this rose to a third or more in the 1930s when they were continually improving Monk's House with the proceeds from their literary successes. And they were totally marooned in Rodmell from September 1940 by the London Blitz, which bombed the Woolfs out of their flat in Mecklenburgh Square. But in reality, the transformation had been more prolonged and complicated.

Virginia had now developed a growing passion, almost obsessive, for rural landscape, with much directed towards Mount Caburn, visible across the Ouse brookland from her garden lodge, with stunning view of the elms and the marshy land fronting its round summit. Furthermore, she rearranged her table in the garden lodge so as to take pleasure in observing the same landscape in the intervals between writing, a source of great delight as she surveyed the view and lit a cigarette 'to tune up', as she put it, before writing until midday.[25] In 1934, her old writing lodge was demolished and a new one built in the orchard with open doors in the front of it to give an even better view towards Caburn.[26]

On a lovely September day in 1930, she wrote of her project of turning her bedroom into a sitting room for the sake of its view, 'To let it waste, day after day, seems a crime elderly eyes cannot waste', which she herself remarked enlarged her garden to the chalk hill by merely opening her garden door.[27] In 1932, when she and Leonard walked over Mount Caburn she thought the downland 'primeval' and Leonard considered the turf as smooth and comfortable as the Heals bed he had recently bought at the Tottenham Court Road store.[28]

Between the Acts

Virginia Woolf's posthumously published novel *Between the Acts* (1941) tells of a pageant of English history performed by villagers and the reactions to it by an upper-middle-class audience in the grounds of a country house, Pointz Hall, which Wolf set in deep Middle England. That such a 'country book' should be written by a now-famous interpreter of the contemporary London scene and its sophisticated society in *Mrs Dalloway* and who had previously found the capital city so perpetually attracting and stimulating, is at first surprising. But, as we have seen, Virginia had turned into a countrywoman.

After several years of continuous improvements to Monk's House, her diary entry for 16 September 1938 records that at dinner at Charleston all seemed agreed that country life was best, and with the uncertainty of the future of Tavistock Square, she first contemplated in writing the possibility of living permanently at Monk's House. On 8 October, in a typewritten letter to Vanessa, she renewed this proposal, despite all their London connections, allowing her to enjoy the peaceful routine of writing, reading, walking and music, 'this immortal rhythm, in which both eyes and soul are at rest'.[29] Vanessa, as early as 1928, had dreaded returning to London on account of the distractions and thought that some day she would act on her feelings.

All these incidents have an important bearing on the new book, eventually entitled *Between the Acts*, and on the state of Virginia's mind when she began to write it. But her diaries become increasingly despondent from anxieties arising from the near certainty of war. Indeed, in February 1937, Julian Bell, Vanessa's son, had said that 'if only the world weren't so demented', he would also readily and contentedly settle down to country life. But the Woolfs spent much of that summer and autumn at Monk's House consoling Vanessa for his death in the Spanish Civil War (see page 225).

In the following year, they were back in Sussex and anxious at the time of the Munich Agreement. And it was at Monk's House that they heard Chamberlain declaring war on Germany on 3 September 1939. As Quentin Bell noted of both the Woolfs and the Bells of Charleston there was, just before the war, 'a general atmosphere of retreat and fortification in the country, of making all secure and shipshape before the coming of the storm'.[30] This involved the Woolfs moving from their house in Tavistock Square, which was to be pulled down, and Vanessa and Duncan Grant making further additions at Charleston, which were so valued when their studios at Fitzroy Square were bombed in September 1940.

The Woolfs also now experienced increasing anxieties about the Hogarth Press and the constant demands in London on two people getting older and not enjoying the best of health. In short, both had been thinking of leaving town as a form of retirement. Virginia's recurrent bouts of depression such as her 'horrid state of misery' in the summer of 1936, Leonard's own health problems and the growing distractions arising from Leonard's political activities, prompted them to consider living at Rodmell for longer periods and more frequently. This was Virginia's sentiment in October and November 1938 when she said that she aimed to be free of London by planning to retire to Rodmell forever, even asserting that 'the country is better than London with raids or without'.[31]

In January 1941, after the loss of her London home, Virginia again wrote that she found in old age that she really preferred country life, even if there was no war, unsociable though it sounded. And she reported that Leonard adored country life and that Clive Bell had reverted to being a country gentleman. Thus, although Hitler was the immediate cause of turning the 'Bloomsburies' into Sussex country people, there had been some years earlier a growing predilection among them for the comfort of rural life.

Compounding such thoughts, there were other considerations bearing on the theme of Virginia's last book. She recalled to her friend Ethel Smyth in early 1941 that, seven years earlier in 1934, travelling through Warwickshire, the sight of 'a stallion being led, under the may and the beeches, along a grass ride' inspired her 'patriotism' by leading her to think, 'that is England'.[32] And ten years earlier, she and Leonard had looked over their wall into the churchyard at the wedding of a village woman dressed in white and wearing a wreath, who was to be married to an unemployed carter from the next village. He arrived fifteen minutes late for the ceremony and they were to spend their honeymoon in Pevensey. Virginia reflected as she waited outside the church:

> I felt this is the heart of England – this wedding in the country … Mr and Mrs Jarrad seem more the descendants than I am: as if they represented the unconscious breathing of England and L. and I, leaning over the wall, were detached, unconnected.[33]

It appears that this represented to Virginia the truth of English history rather than the imaginary lives in Mrs Dalloway's or Orlando's London. She similarly caught a sense of old England in 1936 when old Mrs Mockford, a Rodmell villager, was buried in February among the snowdrops and a raging wind.[34] Whether as the uncertain insider or a parvenue outsider, Virginia certainly felt her Englishness.

So, by early 1940, the Woolfs were becoming complete villagers, except perhaps that they had considered how they would commit suicide at Monk's House in the event of a Nazi invasion and, until towards the end of the year, they still had the flat in Mecklenburgh Square to which they had moved to avoid building work in Tavistock Square and lived partly there until it was bombed.[35] But in helping with a village play, she learnt more of village affairs, violent quarrels and incessant intrigues, a theme introduced to *Between the Acts*. Furthermore, she was now an active member of the community, especially the Women's Institute. She was elected treasurer, lectured to them and got Vita Sackville-West and other eminent speakers down to talk. Leonard joined the Home Guard.[36]

Meanwhile, she was also becoming fascinated with the past and evolution arising from Darwin's writings.[37] As early as 1916, when at Asheham, she had noted the curious ridges or shelves on the hillsides that 'local antiquaries variously declare to have been caused by ice pressure or by the pickaxes of prehistoric man'.[38] Increasingly, like so many of her generation, she became interested in the discoveries of ancient downland settlement and particularly the exciting new ways of seeing that had been introduced by aerial photography, popularised by O.G.S. Crawford, and by Brighton bookseller George Holleyman's article in *Antiquity* (1935) on downland discoveries.[39] Thus, we find early in *Between the Acts* the remark of Mr Oliver:

> From an aeroplane ... you could still see, plainly marked, the scars made by the
> Britons; by the Romans; by the Elizabethan manor house; and by the plough,
> when they ploughed the hill to grow wheat in the Napoleonic Wars.[40]

Virginia doubtless found intellectually satisfying the notion that a maze of
disconnected objects and apparently trivial detail on the ground could be seen
from the air as a meaningful pattern throwing light on the sequence of human
occupation.

Virginia also became interested in local archaeological excavations. In 1937,
she promised to help Hogarth author John Graham to disinter the remains of
the Iron Age hillfort on the summit of Mount Caburn and she also invited
her sister to volunteer. In fact, none are mentioned as volunteers on the
Curwen's 1937–38 excavations. But what remained of the library of Virginia
and Leonard, when catalogued by Holleyman, included four volumes of
the *Sussex Archaeological Collections*, two of which, for 1931 and 1939, contain
articles on excavations on Mount Caburn. The Woolf library also included
Massingham's *Pre-Roman Britain* (1927) and Holmes' *The Age of the Earth* (1927).
Clearly, archaeology had become some source of stimulus to Virginia's literary
imagination.

Then, too, there are hints that she was becoming interested in the evolution
of English history, which was the theme of the pageant in the book. She was
sufficiently inspired, for example, to write about Gibbon and visit his mauso-
leum in Fletching Church.[41] In *Between the Acts*, Lucy Swithin's avid reading
of Trevelyan's *Outline of History* set her mind racing on 'rhododendrons in the
Strand and mammoths in Piccadilly'. Clearly, she was startled as a general reader
by such novel ideas.[42]

This gives some indication of Virginia's interests and state of mind when she
made the first allusion to the new book on 12 April 1938, and she wrote in her
diary on 26 April a sketch of it intended as a relaxation from her biography of
Roger Fry, which she was finding frustrating to complete. She was sketching
out a new book on 'English country', the country house and English literature,
just when builders were 'exploring the attics' of Monk's House, for a new
room that would give her an even better view of Mount Caburn:

> Why not Poyntzet Hall: a centre; all lit[erature] ... anything that comes
> into my head; ... we all life, all art, all waifs & strays — a rambling, capricious
> but somehow unified whole — the present state of my mind? And English
> country; & a scenic old house — & a terrace where nursemaids walk.

This became a remarkably accurate account of the shape and theme the book eventually took.[43]

Although superficially *Between the Acts* appears not to deal with anything in Sussex, of the only two place names mentioned in it, both are from the county – Pyecombe and Bolney. Her former home at Asheham may have also been in her thoughts because this was set in a hollow in a rim of high ground, which is also the setting of Pointz Hall. Indeed, she had previously used Asheham as the setting of her short story, 'The Haunted House'.

But another strong impression stayed with her. Several of her diary entries between 5 January 1939 and January 1941, when she was absorbed in writing the book, provide clues as to another source of inspiration. These relate to a Sussex farmhouse, Court House Farm, in the downland village of Alciston, a few miles east from Rodmell. On 5 January 1939, they visited and admired the farmhouse and envied the view from the garden, although Leonard preferred Monk's House to live in. On Christmas Eve 1940, she and Leonard lunched there with the tenant, Helen Anrep, who had been Roger Fry's mistress before his death in 1934, and Virginia again remarked that she fancied living at the place. The 1940 visit, following the Battle of Britain and the threat of Leonard's certain proscription on account of his Jewishness in the event of a German invasion, gave rise to one of her deepest appreciations of the place:

An incredible loveliness. The downs breaking their wave, yet one pale quarry; & all the barns & stacks either a broken pink, or a verdurous green; & then the walk by the wall; & the church; & the great tithe barn. How England consoles & warms one, in these deep hollows, where the past stands almost stagnant. And the little spire across the fields ... So back through Lewes. And I worshipped the beauty of the country, now scraped, but with old colours showing.[44]

Although the household at Pointz Hall bore no relation to that at the farm, several of its interior and exterior features are realistically portrayed in the story. Court House Farm is a former medieval hall house that, uniquely, contains the fourteenth-century masonry remains of arched windows that, before bedrooms were inserted, extended the full height of the walls. It has additions from later periods and a surviving massive crown-post roof. Inside, the 'chapel' can be identified with the room with stone arches and 'the big room with its windows open to the garden' can be identified with the apartment described in Virginia's diary in which the Woolfs lunched with Helen Anrep.

The garden is as 'flat as the floor of a theatre', as in the novel, though formerly rose beds and flower borders marked it as the home of a gentleman farmer.[45] The wall running down from the house mentioned in the novel is intact but the 'walk by the wall', which Virginia mentions in her diary for Christmas Eve 1940, and which would have been used by the audience to reach their seats at the pageant, is now totally overgrown and unused. This led down to the ha-ha, separating the garden from fields and known as the 'moat'. This was barred by bushes and trees where the actors changed, a feature mentioned in the novel. Apparently, here was the terrace where the nursemaids trundled their perambulators in the novel and where the family could rest in deckchairs.

The beautiful view from this spot was of the sweep of downland, together with the spire of Berwick Church (called Bolney Minster in the novel), backed by the rising bare ridge of Windover Hill beyond the Cuckmere valley, later painted by Frank Wootton in 1945 (Plate 34). The view is now much obscured by the subsequent growth of trees on the garden boundaries and Berwick Church is now also almost buried in trees. The similar entrancing view from the church-yard has also been obscured by the planting of trees and shrubs.

The house lies adjacent to the little parish church with its weather-boarded bell turret, adjacent ruined dovecote and a huddle of other outbuildings. One or two buildings have been lost since the 1930s, such as the ox stall in which were kept plough beasts, but the farmstead remains one of the most historic and loveliest places in the Sussex Downs.

Outside is the impressive aisled barn which features prominently in the novel. 'The mere ladder at the back for the servants' still exists, originally intended for temporary labourers living on the farm at harvest time in the nineteenth century. This immense barn, on thirteenth-century foundations but mostly sixteenth century in date, and one of the largest in southern England, is mistakenly called a tithe barn but was built by the Battle Abbey monks for storing their prodigious harvests of wool, corn and hay. And unlike most old barns, it is still fully functional.

> The barn to which Lucy had nailed her placard was a great building in the farmyard. It was as old as the church and built of the same stone, but it had no steeple. It was raised on cones of grey stone at the corners to protect it from rats and damp. Those who had been to Greece always said it reminded them of a temple. Those who had never been to Greece – the majority – admired it all the same. The roof was weathered red-orange and inside it was a hollow hall, sun-shafted, brown, smelling of corn and dark when the doors were shut, but splendidly illuminated when the doors at the end stood open, as they did to let the wagons in – the long, low wagons, like ships of the sea, breasting the corn, not the sea, returning in the evening shagged with hay.[46]

A Sussex Ending

Little more than a month after the completion of the manuscript for *Between the Acts* Virginia committed suicide. The reasons why she killed herself are still discussed, but her fragility of mind, susceptibility to mood swings and inconsistency is demonstrable. She would say, at one moment, 'It is a perfect life but for the war, ever so much nicer than London', and in another, 'country life is so odd'. In a letter to Edward Sackville-West of 1 December 1940:

> Sometimes the country is so heavenly and reading and writing become so absorbing I'm very happy; then all at sea. It's like living on an island. Rodmell of course pulls us in to various societies; all very simple; I've not seen a clever person this six months, save the family over the way [at Charleston]. I daresay it's good for one; but oh lord – how bare and barren in many ways.[47]

She continued to switch from depression to cheerful ideas for future work. She had in mind a book showing how the English landscape changed and shaped the literature that was both read in it and written about it – the view from writers' windows as they worked.[48]

On an occasion of one of Hitler's broadcasts in the late summer of 1939, Leonard refused to stop planting iris in the orchard to hear his ravings:

> One afternoon I was planting in the orchard under an apple tree Iris reticulata, those lovely flowers … Suddenly I heard Virginia's voice calling to me from the sitting-room window 'Hitler is making a speech'. I shouted back 'I shan't come. I'm planting Iris and they will be flowering long after he is dead.'

And indeed many years later, long after Hitler was dead, the iris were still flowering.[49] 'L. is doing the rhododendrons,' was Virginia Woolf's last entry in her diary in 1941 before walking to her death in the nearby River Ouse.[50] Leonard believed that it was the strain of finishing her final book and anxieties about the war, especially perhaps the mess and cost created by salvaging the remains of their possessions from their bombed-out London house and finding room for them in Rodmell. Nigel Nicolson thought that she felt that she was about to go so mad that she would never be able to write again, and writing was her life.

So ended the career of a literary genius. Her ashes were buried in the garden at Monk's House (Plate 35).

11

A SHEAF OF
TWENTIETH-CENTURY WRITERS

They're changing all the names ... I biked by Medersham yesterday and it
had Mandalay painted up on the gate.[1]

From what has gone before, it will be appreciated that there was no shortage
of writers and poets working in Sussex before 1939. In this chapter, we place
the work of six more writers in their landscapes, and in the next chapter, we
do the same for six poets.

Sheila Kaye-Smith

There has been no more prolific Sussex novelist than (Emily) Sheila Kaye-
Smith (1887–1956). Indeed, she was referred to in her lifetime as 'the Sussex
novelist' (Plate 36). Her fiction evokes the Sussex Weald, its life, farms
and fields, showing how land and people took their character from each
other, though she perhaps overstates and overemphasises her characters and
landscapes.

Her father, Edward, was a doctor practising in and around St Leonards
on the Sussex coast but including the rural Wealden hinterland. Nearly all
her novels are indigenous and rooted in the soils of the beloved countryside
she knew best and loved from her earliest childhood: the Kent and Sussex
countryside, especially that little corner of Sussex – the valleys of the Eastern
Rother and Tillingham, and including the parishes of Brede and Ewhurst.
She claimed that the first twelve years there made her a novelist.

In a sense, every farm she wrote about is Platnix Farm, near Westfield,
where she spent several summers with her sister while her parents took European holidays, and was the one that most powerfully captured her young
imagination:

There was never a time when I did not know and love the countryside outside Hastings - Platnix and the primrose lane by Ireland Farm, where father used to drive us as tiny children to fill our hands with flowers.[2]

In 1924, Kaye-Smith married Penrose Fry, an ordained Anglican in St Leonards, but by 1929 they had converted to Catholicism. And in that year, they settled at Little Doucegrove, near Broad Oak, a place that thereafter provided inspiration for her writing in the district around the house and little oratory they had inaugurated. By 1935 the chapel was proving inadequate and they founded the new Catholic Church of St Teresa of Lisieux at the nearby hamlet of Horns Cross, Northiam, where both Sheila and Penrose are buried.[3]

In depicting the life of the small farmer in her stark visual sketches, the Sussex Weald is projected not as a yielding and ever-fruitful earth, but as a protagonist with a grudge against him, and its hungry and obstinate soil is constantly revenging itself against his cultivation. As with Hardy, her landscapes were themselves positive characters. One commentator has suggested of her early work:

The earth of Sussex might be called the chief of her *dramatis personae*. The affection of her heroes is really reserved for the land. No more is it accidental that Miss Kaye-Smith grows impassioned only when she describes a landscape, analyzing her characters as coldly as if they were mathematical theorems.[4]

But she successfully portrays the Weald as the cradle of an enduring way of life, with a community wresting a livelihood from its curmudgeonly soils that turn health into sickness and youth into age. Her farms, though small, had never really been cultivated, being no more than scratched, and the soil was still almost virgin clay, and yet deeply loved by generations of family farmers. But the farmers remained silent after a thousand batterings and patiently accepted the fact that they would always struggle and always be beaten.[5] A persistent fatalism and endurance is the response she evokes. She has few illusions about the bitterness of the struggle and many of her books have a sombre mournfulness lacking any gleam of humour, befitting a rural society deeply rooted in mud and clods.

Take young Reuben Backfield in *Sussex Gorse*, a successful, realistic novel that just falls short of outstanding. He is a plain Sussex farmer, 'as hard as iron and as brown as a nut, and there was a warm red glowing through the swarthiness of his cheeks like the bloom on a russet pear'.[6] Here is the obstinate, resolute, ruthless, inflexible Wealdsman, who lives close to the earth and 'won't be druv'. The men seemed part of the clay.

Then there is Joanna Godden, who is thought of as 'a great big strapping wench, the kind this marsh [Romney] breeds twelve to the acre like the sheep', and then Kaye-Smith adds, 'the same as the Kent sheep in comparison with the Southdowns – admirably hardy and suited to the district and all that, but a bit rough and coarse-flavoured?'[7]

Sussex Gorse (1916) was the first novel to make a favourable impression on the reading public, but in August 1921 her most successful novel, *Joanna Godden*, was published and sold 10,000 copies. This novel enhanced her literary reputation and was later filmed as *The Loves of Joanna Godden*, starring Googie Withers and Michael Dennison.

The theme of *Sussex Gorse*, set 5 miles north of Rye, is the story of a tough farmer's fight with Boarzell Common, whose stubborn soil he is determined to bring under his plough. This epitomises the history of the Weald, the obsession with one idea for generations, that of the reclamation of uncultivated land, although it might bring a hundred disappointments. Backfield's stubbornness brought him a farming triumph, but he paid a terrible price for it, the loss of his mother, brother, his wife and eight children, his second wife and the one woman who might have brought some beauty into his life. At the end he is old, white-haired and utterly alone, but the Common is covered in corn, and he closes the book with the words, 'Boarzell's mine – and when I die ... well, I've lived so close to the earth all my days that I reckon I shan't be afraid to lie in it at last.'[8]

Another success came with *The End of the House of Alard* (1923), set on the estate of Conster Manor, a house that can be identified with the former medieval hall house lying in a wooded valley within walking distance of the author's home at Little Doucegrove. The tenanted farms that form the background to the story, Dinglesden, Starvecrow, Conster, Doucegrove, Winterland, Ellenwhorne and Spelland, are actual places, as Thurston Hopkins pointed out in his book *Sheila Kaye-Smith*, but lie, in the main, off principal roads and earlier could only be visited on horseback or on foot.[9]

The trail of the book takes one down little lanes like that from Pett village to Icklesham to Winchelsea, hollowed in places and single track behind high hedges, or the byway that leads to Tillingham Bridge that, in Hopkins' day, was constructed to prevent cattle crossing it and only allowed one person to pass over it conveniently at a time (Plate 37). Characteristically of the author, the estate is not just the background to the drama but the leading character in it, influencing the course of events.

Kaye-Smith's story epitomises the great transformation, physically, economically and socially, which took place all over Sussex as a consequence of the massive sales of landed property following Lloyd George's attempts to tax land values, and the declining role of forestry and agriculture following the end of the Great War. She records the demise of a great landed estate as members of the Alard family vainly struggle to retain their accustomed lifestyle in the face of falling land and produce prices, declining rentals, encumbered mortgages and heavy taxation. She sketches the emotions of the whole family as they go under with the estate's ruin, conveying how an ancestral estate worked itself into a person's system and could not fail to be part of them, whether or not they were happy there. Ultimately, following various family tragedies, the estate is sold and the family disperses.

In *Little England* Kaye-Smith writes of Dallington, again using real local place names and real family names, and of the short-lived 'Golden Age' of rising wages for farm labourers during the First World War before farm prices collapsed. The beat of heavy guns heard from Flanders signified the corner of England for which local boys were fighting and dying:

> Before their dying eyes had risen not the vision of England's glory, but just these fields ... with the ponds and the woods, and the red roofs ... and the women and children and old people who lived among them.[10]

The Village Doctor (1929) is set in the 1840s when farming was reasonably prosperous and farmers led fairly comfortable lives, but their labourers were not so fortunate.[11] *The Ploughman's Progress* (1933) is mainly concerned with the struggles of family farmers in Wealden Sussex during the depressed interwar years and follows the life struggle of the sterling ploughman Fred Sinden, and his courage and resource when his job disappears. The real crisis in East Sussex farming at the time is portrayed, and Kaye-Smith shows herself to be one of the very few Sussex authors of her day who gave a thought to agricultural problems, other than living and writing in an illusory Arcadia.

To some extent this novel takes up the story left unfinished by the sale of the Alard estate. Small farmers who took on the farms of these estates often struggled in the unfavourable conditions for farming in the 1920s and 1930s, struggled in the interwar depression, and this is brilliantly encapsulated:

> Fred Sinden's job had been the occupation of mankind for hundreds and thousands of years ever since the dawn of the world some scientist had invented the first plough. But now it was a job that mankind no longer

wanted ... In the small, hilly, countryside of East Sussex, civilisation was abandoning the idea of self-contained, self-supporting communities ... As methods of production changed and transport facilities grew, men would no longer argue whether the High Field or the Low Field bore the better crop, but whether to sow in Russia or in Canada or in Rumania [*sic*].[12]

Newcomers might move in, find the farming conditions tough and go under. Alternatively, some smaller farms might be purchased by 'retired townsmen and colonials' or by opportunistic builders and gentry weekenders.

Moving on in time, the themes of Kaye-Smith's late novel, *The Valiant Woman* (1939), are the issues facing landowners on the eve of the Second World War. The central focus is on two established families, the Challens and Sadgroves, at the village of Cowplain, one or the other of which had owned the Trulilows Estate for 300 years. When it was put up for sale, a land agency acquired it but had torn it to pieces and sold it off in building plots.

As the seller looked over his lovely landscape, 'a chequer broken only by soft woods and little reddish farms that seemed as much a part of the growth and nature as the woods', he felt enraged and humiliated now that 'Birmingham vulgarians' had come to live in the farmhouse, guessing that he will see bungalows like hen houses, villas like matchboxes on end, broken chicken coops, collapsing goat sheds, stinking pig styes – a rural slum, in fact. But it turns out that the 'Birminghams' were more cultured than expected; they became inextricably intertwined with the established families, and the Challens eventually acquired the estate and saved it from major disfiguration.[13]

In *The Treasures of the Snow* (1950), the great snowfall, gales and floods of 1947 form the foreground and in the background are the changes in farming during the Second World War:

The old slow, comfortable ways of farming were over. Pastures had to be turned into ploughs, bad lands had to be broken in – for the first time wheat was grown in the Turzel field and the Star – new crops such as flax and new ideas such as autumn calving had to be tried in the teeth of opposition from every farmer over forty. At the same time farming was made almost a schoolmaster's job with forms to be filled in and letters to be written to a newly created enemy called the War Agricultural Committee known locally as the War Ag.[14]

Kaye-Smith was adept at describing localities and embedding them in her readers' minds. In *Challenge to Sirius* (1917), she writes of the Isle of Oxney, all the real names of which she again preserved in her book:

> … a little pip of a county wedged between Sussex and Kent. It belonged properly to Kent but held itself aloof. Bounded on the west and north by the Reading Sewer, on the south by the Rother and Kent Ditch, on the east by the Military Canal, it was a separate land with old Wittersham for its London.[15]

Similarly, her short stories had their own special locales figuring as a major aspect of the tale. In *Joanna Godden Married and Other Stories* (1926), besides the main Joanna Godden story (abnormally set in the Selsey area of West Sussex), we have 'Mrs Adis', which is about a fatal poaching accident in the woods near Scotney Castle; 'A Working Man's wife', whose husband was drunk on a day's outing and presumed drowned in a charabanc in the Medway, but who walked home when everyone thought him dead; and 'A Day in a Woman's Life', set around Hawkhurst and Rye. All these are superb examples of the genre, crisply and movingly related from a woman's point of view.

Her novels drew increasing sales and favourable reviews but were not a complete success. Fastidious critics who were put off by the uncomfortable, disturbing factors in 'the still, sad music of humanity' nevertheless found abundant life and compassion, although always hand in hand with trouble.[16]

There were biographies as well, together with topography and later autobiographies and more religious publications. Although in her Sussex novels she did her best to see life honestly, her view was mediated through the enlarging spectacles of romance and the indirect experience of childhood rather than actual knowledge, experience and intuition. This made her easy prey, as we shall see, for the venomous satire of Stella Gibbons. Nevertheless, we can appreciate her ability to use fiction to illustrate and provoke readers into thinking more deeply about change in the countryside.[17]

Eleanor Farjeon

By 1911, Eleanor Farjeon (1881–1965) (Plate 38) was 'an author and poetess' and living with her American mother in Lancaster Road, Hampstead, with a highly artistic and creative family, although her father, himself an author, had died in 1903. During the Great War, the family moved to Sussex, and in 1921, her extraordinary *Martin Pippin in the Apple Orchard* was published, setting her on a successful literary career. Nothing like it had appeared before or since. Its essence was her inspiration derived from the Weald and South Downs where the wildflowers, woods and delightful place names had become personal to her.

But this was not a conventional natural history or topographical description. Instead, she created a curiously individual caprice of Arcadian innocence in which she inserted whimsical pastoral, dovetailed with songs improvised by a minstrel hero (Martin) and written, to the disappointment of D.H. Lawrence, in an affected, antique mannerism of language.

An old cottage in the Meynell's complex at Greatham afforded the basis for one such in *Martin Pippin*.[18] Alice Meynell was also a friend of Sheila Kaye-Smith, and the Meynells were very important in Eleanor's life from 1913. In 1920, she wrote from the cottage of having collected material for her book for eighteen months, waiting for a shape to present itself 'when the thing happened like a gift from heaven in one instant, and after that I was a lost woman, a hopeless inebriate ... [with] Sir John Mandeville waiting for me'.[19]

In this spirited manner, the book's hero hails a youth who explains that he loves Gillian, who is locked up in Old Gillman's well-house, where she weeps beside the well. Six milkmaids, all sworn virgins and man-haters, keep the six keys of the gate and live in the orchard outside. Martin finds the orchard, tells the girls love stories and, overcoming their prudishness, wheedles and tricks the keys from them. Finally, Gillian goes off, not with her tearful lover but with the minstrel himself. Martin's lilting roundelays are wrapped round the names of wildflowers and there is wit and wrangling in the coy conversations. Finally, the converted milkmaids climb down the apple-picking ladder and over the hawthorn hedge with some last-minute lovers.

Martin's Arcadia for his new lover is in a Sussex meadow carpeted with wildflowers, seen with a childlike wonder:

Beyond Hardham is the sunken bed of the old canal that is a secret not known to everybody; all flowering reeds and plants that love water grow there, and you have to push your way between water-loving trees under which grass and nettles in their season grow taller than children; but at other times, when the pussy-willows bloom with grey and golden bees, the way is clear. Beyond this presently is a little glade, the loveliest in Sussex; in spring it is patterned with primroses, and windflowers shake their fragile bells and show their silver stars above them. Some are pure and colourless, like maidens who know nothing of love, and others are faintly stained with streaks of purple-rose. So exquisite is the beauty of these earthly flowers that it is like a heavenly dream, but it is a dream come true; and you will never pass it in April without longing to turn aside and, kneeling among all that pallid gold and silver, offer up a prayer to the fairies.

This is merely an antechamber:

And though you and I may never know why this lane is called Shelley's, to us both it will always be the greenest lane in Sussex, because it leads to the special secret I spoke of. At the end of it is an old gate, clambered with blue periwinkle, and the gate opens into a garden in the midst of the forest, a garden so gay and so scented, so full of butterflies and bees and flower-borders and grass-plots with fruit-trees on them, that it might be Eden grown tiny. The garden runs down a slope, and is divided from a wild meadow by a brook crossed by a plank, fringed with young hazel and alder and, at the right time, thick-set with primroses. Behind the meadow, in a glimpse of the distance full of soft blue shadows and pale yellow lights, lie the lovely sides of the Downs, rounded and dimpled like human beings, dimpled like babies, rounded like women. The flow of their lines is like the breathing of a sleeper; you can almost see the tranquil heaving of a bosom.[20]

Farjeon began writing her book in Billingshurst, where she had a room in Gillman's Cottage, her brother Joe's rented accommodation of wattle and daub and oak beams set among apple orchard and corn fields. Here, she heard the news of Edward Thomas' death in April 1917. But in 1924, in a letter to admirers of her book, she stated that most of *Martin Pippin* had been written at The End Cottage, a thatched cottage at the bottom of what was known originally as Cow Sh★t (then Mucky, now South) Lane in Houghton, 'in the very cream of the Downs'.[21] She stayed there alone for almost two years, still in mourning and with her unrequited love for Thomas, her great friend and rambling companion. But it was here, as her niece Annabel Farjeon wrote, that she learnt not to be afraid:

As a child, she had feared almost everything ... now she taught herself to be alone. She walked the Downs at all hours of the day and night ... here she wrote and went to bed, leaving doors and windows open. It seemed to her an almost perfect way of living, filled with natural and necessary things, like collecting wood, picking flowers and mushrooms from the fields, watching the seasons change.[22]

Farjeon thought that the nearly two years she lived alone in Mucky Lane were the most important in her life. She walked the Downs at all hours, day and night. She lived by no timetable, eating, writing, walking as the mood took her. She wore the coarse woollen dress of a Russian peasant, bought before the Great War at the height of the ballet craze.

Eleanor wrote:

> Follow the path to the right, with the river on your left, in five or six minutes you come to the loveliest quarry in the world – but there. [...] Hidden in it is the hollow where Rosamund hid with the Hart. But the place is so beautiful that if you don't know it, it takes your breath away at the first look. Southwoods, it's known as, and when you've seen it you can – if you're lucky – go in and in, and discover it.

She had found happy children playing in the lane outside her window or in the meadow at old games that were part of their local heritage and singing the same songs as their forebears had done for generations. The singing game of the 'Spring-Green Lady', which she had first heard at Adversane (near Billingshurst), runs through her book as a connecting theme. Furthermore, the place name Adversane was particularly fascinating to her, as we shall see. It was here, in what might be called 'Eleanor Farjeon country' – the sweep from Adversane, over the Wild Brooks and up the steep chalk scarp to Amberley Mount – that she wrote *Martin Pippin*, set in an orchard in Adversane, together with the much-loved and republished *Elsie Piddock Skips in Her Sleep*, which features Mount Caburn.

And in due course, many more Sussex villages and landmarks came to feature in her work. Anne Harvey has explained that when Farjeon wrote the follow-up to *Martin Pippin*, the later *Martin Pippin in the Daisy Field*, the story that was her favourite, this was begun in her mind when the children skipped outside her Mucky Lane Cottage. *Elsie Piddock skips in her Sleep*, one of Farjeon's best fairy tales, was based on this incident and on a real child, Elsie Puttick, the most deft of the skippers, who was traced later by Eleanor's last partner, Denys Blakelock.[23]

Place names had a fascination:

> Adversane! I was already fascinated by the place-names on the Ordnance maps as I walked by, names of pure nursery skimble-skamble, like Hawking Sopers, Open Winkins and the Pillygreen Lodges. But Adversane was a name out of Morris or Mallory, evocative of the troubadour world in which, ten years ago, I had conceived a Minstrel Knight who sailed to a gold isle on a sapphire sea in Brittany and sang Aubades and Serenas to a captive Princess. What should I find in Adversane?

There she actually found Billy Hoad 'with his jolly rubicund face and hearty manner as good as home-baked bread and home-spun wool' and puckish Lewis Townsend, a dentist but a poet at heart, of whom she wrote that 'There was never a rounder peg in a squarer hole … a light burns in him in talk.'

She also met Victor Haslam there, another friend of Edward Thomas, to whom she dedicated and sent *Martin Pippin* in instalments. Farjeon later explained that in 1920, J.D. Beresford, reader for Collins, accepted the fantasy of *Martin Pippin* based on one of the stories sent to Haslam at the Front, but it was written to amuse an officer of 30, serving in France. She was surprised that her book came to be regarded as one for children.[24]

An important clue to what she found particularly appealing in the Sussex landscape is her repeated use of the world 'tiny'. She discovered a landscape of miniatures, intimacies and unsullied humanisation, the kind of charm she imagined Sussex had centuries back and still retained in 'secret' patches. In this, she was drawing attention to the essence of the Low Weald of Sussex, deemed 'ordinary' by many planners but still a relatively unspoilt landscape in which everything is small – streams, woods, fields, lanes and farmhouses. Appropriately, while her last home with her English teacher partner of thirty years, George Earle, was in Hampstead, they also lived at Hammond's, a cottage on the outskirts of Laughton in the Low Weald of East Sussex.[25]

Farjeon clearly loved Sussex. She lived long in the county and many of her stories are set there, not only *Martin Pippin*, but also *All the Way to Alfriston*, *Martin Pippin in the Daisy Field* (1937) and her *Sussex Alphabet* (1939). Eleanor would herself describe how deeply affecting those landscapes had been in a letter to George Earle:

> They are so much beyond human beings to me that I can almost not talk of it – I don't mean I love them more, and yet in a sense I think perhaps I do … They've healed me more, and given me more strength and certainty and peace, than any other living thing.[26]

She loved walking and talking in the South Downs. She recollected watching young horse riders laughing as they rode on Amberley Mount. She decided, on a spring day in 1915, to walk from Greatham, where she had been staying with Alice and Wilfrid Meynell, to Chichester, and thence on to Steep (Hampshire) to visit Edward and Helen Thomas. She was accompanied as far as Chichester by D.H. Lawrence, setting out early in 'one of those white Sussex mists which muffle the meadows before sunrise', and drinking shandy at the inn at East Dean. Lawrence then caught the train back to Pulborough from Chichester. Thereafter, they exchanged views on each other's work.[27]

Before he was killed in action, Edward Thomas suggested that Farjeon should visit his great friend James Guthrie (1874–1952), artist, typographer and printer, who had set up his Pear Tree Press at the White House, Flansham, near Bognor in 1907, which now therefore seethed with artistic activity, including hand-printing. Guthrie vividly reveals her character in 1915, much changed, apparently, from the shy, somewhat withdrawn and self-contained days of her girlhood:

> Miss Farjeon turned up and spent the night and the gist of a day ... Miss Farjeon is great fun. She stumps along with her knapsack on her back and her chalala [shillelagh?] in her hand, looking for all the world like a pilgrim. And in she comes, straightway, and goes into the pantry, and eats a pancake and a little pastry off a tart and lights a cigarette – she lights a pipe sometimes and talks and shouts and laughs and turns the place into the very merriment. She is one of the most marvellous personalities that I know.[28]

Farjeon's *All the Way to Alfriston*, with drawings by James' son, Robin Guthrie (1902–71), was published by Robin when in his teens at the Greenleaf Press, an offshoot of the Pear Tree Press, in 1918. *A Sussex Alphabet* was published by Guthrie's Pear Tree Press at Flansham in 1939, with a collection of characters, folklore and landscape emphasising the particularities of the Sussex dialect.[29]

Other incidents in her life reveal her abounding energy, passionate interest in people, a love of words, food, music, theatre and, above all, books. 'It would seem more natural to live without clothes than without books,' she wrote of her childhood when her father, a novelist himself, had 8,000 books filling every room. Although London-born and living in later life in Hampstead, where she was returned in the 1921 census, she ensured that the pastoral tradition that had been so intense before and during the First World War did not dim thereafter. For her, 'disenchantment never came. Summer pervades her books: milkmaids, pedlars, elves and shepherd boys people her [Sussex] countryside'.[30]

Making a little pilgrimage today takes one to South Lane, Houghton, and its attractive old houses, presumably once farmhouses and their cottages. Farjeon's cottage has been demolished and replaced by a larger modern house. It would have overlooked the Arun Brooks across to North Stoke Church, on the opposite side of the valley. A footpath runs along the banks of the Arun, in spring covered with kingcups, lady's smocks and overarching willows; and with brimstone, tortoiseshell and other butterflies basking in the warmth; and with swans gliding by. It remains as Arcadian as when Farjeon loved it, but the quarry, beside a magnificent beech clinging to the valley side, has been abandoned and is so overgrown that it is mostly only accessible in the winter.

Amy Sawyer

Amy Sawyer (1863–1945) was born the daughter of a grocer and draper of East Grinstead, and was proud to have been descended from the Sawyer family of West Hoathly. She remained true to her roots, relishing at a time of mass immigration the fact that she was a 'true rural Sussexer, and not one of those Dagoes who pretend to be'. Sawyer trained as an artist at Herkomer's art school at Bushey from 1885, where she developed her love of folklore, fairies and witches. She was living at Bushey as an art student with her mother and sister, Mabel, in 1891. Prolific exhibiting including at the Royal Academy initially followed.

Her parents, Charles and Eliza, had moved to Ditchling in 1897 and Amy followed, the first arrival in this artist's colony. She bought Russell House in North End in 1904 and renamed it The Blue House, so called because she painted it a striking blue – remembered by her admirer and artistic helper, Joanna Bourne, then a young girl, as 'Reckitt's Blue'. She also decorated the fireplace surrounds in the house in ceramic and the lavatory with a mosaic. She had a first-floor studio built onto the house.

Eric Gill's friendship with her led to the 'Gladys Panel', incised in Hopton-wood stone, which is still located in this room. She also laid out a garden with great artistry, though this was sacrificed to vegetables during the last war.[31] The friendship with Gill cooled, however, after he moved to Ditchling Common in 1913. He later, in 1936, wrote, 'We were not the first of the horrid Arts and Crafts people to corrupt the ancient village – it was Amy Sawyer who lived there first.'[32]

Unfortunately, her career as a watercolourist had been cut short when paint in the nails of her right hand turned septic with lead poisoning. By 1939, she was living at the Blue House with her widowed sister Mabel, a wood carver.

Instead of pursuing her painting career, she used her talents as a play-wright, specialising in plays for village halls – writing, producing, designing costumes and rehearsing performers from Ditchling. The first play, 'Love is Blind' was produced in her garden, in keeping with Herkomer's ideas, in 1922, there then being no village hall. From this evolved the modern Ditchling (Village) Players. Her plays were natively rustic, with performers speaking mostly genuine Sussex dialect and wearing old Sussex clothing.

Apart from her plays, she initiated the Ditchling Handworkers Guild, which held annual exhibitions of handicrafts in the village from the 1920s and was a notable pioneer exploring the English folk song revival.

Arthur Beckett, who thought that Amy Sawyer was the only Sussex author to devote her talents chiefly to the writing of local drama in the interwar years, edited twenty-four of her plays in *Sussex Village Plays* (1934), dedicated to the Ditchling Village Players.[33] They are invaluable now because they preserve vestiges of dialect, idiom and customs that have since vanished. She wrote for village drama societies, the WI and the Boy Scouts and Girl Guides organisations. They were seen in many towns and villages of Sussex, and several were performed in London under the aegis of the British Drama League, an association formed in 1919 to promote the interests of both amateur and professional drama. Those performed locally were often advertised by hand-printed posters from Hilary Pepler's Ditchling Press.

'The Brown Pot' was one of her most notable plays. Okah Tester, an elderly farmer dressed in smock frock, leather leggings, a straw hat and carrying a crook, is poisoned in his farmhouse kitchen after eating a meal prepared by his wife. It was performed at London's Century Theatre and received a review in *The Times*. But some Ditchling residents criticised the play's lack of social responsibility.

Amy Sawyer was a loveable, somewhat reclusive, eccentric, mercurial and humorous woman with an arresting personality enhanced by flamboyant clothes (Plate 39). In a photograph, she is wearing a leopard skin she made herself and a scarf woven by Ethel Mairet, the Ditchling hand-weaver. The quicksilver in her was said to have gypsy origins. She shunned modern inventions, would cook with a haybox and was dismissive of doctors, preferring the old country remedies.

She died following the end of the war in late 1945, and at her funeral, a particular Ditchling tradition was adopted – a famous white mare called Blossom drew her coffin on a farm cart to the parish church. In Ditchling churchyard is a small plaque, now partly sunken, 'In memory of Amy Sawyer, Artist and Playwright 1885–1945', a mystery, given that her real birth date was 1863. In her obituary, it was remarked that Ditchling was indebted to her more than could be repaid. For over half a century, no one had done more to encourage art and beauty. The affectionate tribute to her from Joy Sinden, sister of the actor Donald Sinden, who had both lived in Ditchling as children, is appropriately in dialect:

Well, Amy, so 'ee've gorn 'n jined un,
They Pharisees 'n elves o' yourn:
And now I recollects our village
Baint quite the same now you be gorn.

S.P.B. Mais

Stuart Petre Brodie Mais (1885–1975), the Southwick novelist, writer and broadcaster, always referred to as S.P.B. Mais, was a prolific Sussex writer of the interwar years. His family home was in Derbyshire, where his father was a rector, but he was largely brought up in Devon before going to Oxford, where he began working after graduation for the *Oxford Times*. He was also a schoolteacher at Fleetwood and then Sherborne between 1913 and 1917. As a former pupil, the novelist Alec Waugh remembered him arriving at the school in 1913, 'He talked at the top of his voice. He was breathlessly alive. He hit Sherborne like a whirlwind … Poetry and literature were taught with great gusto.'[34]

He later taught at Tonbridge School (1917–20) and was styled a Professor of English at RAF Cranwell. From 1918 to 1930, he worked as a journalist on several papers, including the *Daily Telegraph*, where he was a leader writer and book reviewer. From 1927 to 1934, he and his second partner, Gillian Doughty, lived in a large eighteenth-century house, the Hall, at Southwick, where he became president and fierce champion of the local cricket team, and although not an altogether wonderful player himself, he succeeded at great personal cost in combatting the local council and ensuring the team continued to play on Southwick Green, which they still do today (Plate 40).[35] He later lived in Buckingham Road, Southwick, but was widely travelled.

His forte, however, was writing – travel books, topography, history, school textbooks or magazine articles. He had been made redundant from the *Daily Telegraph* in 1930, and thereafter went freelance. Several of his novels are set in Sussex: *Caged Birds* (1922) and *Quest Sinister* (1922) around Brighton; some of *Eclipse* (1925) and *Orange Street* (1926) around Angmering; *First Quarter* (1929) in Southwick and *Frolic Lady* (1930) on the coast and downland between Brighton and Goring.[36]

In 1932, he was commissioned by the BBC to travel through England, Scotland and Wales to provide material for seventeen talks. They were published as *This Unknown Island* (1932) and quickly reprinted. Other books followed, opening up the British countryside for the townsperson, and his output became even more prodigious after the Second World War when his travel writing expanded to foreign holidays, written up in all manner of literature. There were also lightweight novels and some books of literary appreciation.

His precept was that without at least intermittent contact with nature, townspeople would suffer, hence his remarkably popular travel books on various parts of rural Britain. During the Second World War, he was a regular broadcaster to huge audiences listening to his *Kitchen Front* and *Microphone at Large* programmes. And his series *This Unknown Island*, introducing listeners to the British landscape, led to his being acclaimed 'Ambassador of the Countryside', typified by the radio script for *Sussex by the Sea: A Walk down the Adur Valley with S.P.B. Mais*.[37]

His knowledge was achieved through his own solitary country walking and his organised walks into London's countryside for Londoners. He wrote of walking as 'the healthiest and cheapest as well as one of the greatest human pleasures. Few things have added so much to human happiness'.[38] He published his pocket book of country walks, *Southern Rambles for Londoners* (1947), attempting in his schoolmasterly vein to educate the urban population in understanding natural surroundings:

> Your object is to achieve as complete a change as possible from your ordinary life in office or street, to let your eyes roam at one moment over wide horizons with an unbroken vista of blue sky overhead and at another moment to concentrate on the myriad colours interwoven in the carpet at your feet. Your object is to regain your lost senses, the sense of hearing that has been dulled by traffic and by bombs, the sense of sight that has been obscured by poring over ledgers, the sense of smell which has been vitiated by living too much indoors … There is a healing power in nature … 'I have two doctors,' said Sir George Trevelyan, 'My left leg and my right'. So set out on foot.

Mais was clearly strongly influenced by Trevelyan, the foremost historian of his day, who was himself an admirer of George Meredith, poet and novelist, and like him, a passionate walker. Mais felt that, whether we like it or not, we are children of the earth and quotes Trevelyan's remark that 'removed from her our spirit withers and runs to various forms of insanity'.[39]

With an extraordinary total of over 200 books listed in the British Library catalogue, Mais never ceased to lament the deprivation Londoners suffered as a result of the loss of countryside. His notable account of the reaction of

Londoners on organised walks in the Sussex countryside in the mid-1930s remains fascinating:

> The scene is Victoria Station on a rather cold, grey arch Sunday morning. The London streets are deserted.
>
> The platforms of the station are crowded with an eager chattering mob of some six hundred ramblers as gay as they are diverse in their clothes ... Most of them carry haversacks on their backs containing mackintoshes, maps, sandwiches, a change of socks, a flask, and perhaps a book of poems or a pack of cards. The excursion this Sunday is southward to the long range of smooth, free chalk downs that rise above the Sussex coast ... The distances to be covered on foot are not large. The shortest is ten, the longest, twenty miles.
>
> The time is 10.59. The train pulls up at the little country station of Hassocks and everybody jumps out, gesticulating, laughing, on to the platform and into the station yard ... The clouds are dispersing, the sun is shining brightly as we of number eight group under our leader set off over meadows for the green, bare knoll of Wolstonbury Hill, rising some six hundred feet above the Weald about a couple of miles away ... It is very gentle walking, this South of England walking, very like the people who live here, who are sunny-tempered, great lovers of quietude, slow in movement, unchanging in outlook, and very friendly.
>
> After a few fields we begin to climb up the sides of the free chalk downs. There are no paths. You just walk or ride wherever you like ... Everybody stops to breathe in the pure air coming up from the sea, to gaze over the scores of miles of open country, to stretch their arms as symbol of the scene of perfect freedom in a scene of pure loveliness.
>
> It is difficult not to give vent in some way to ecstasy that suffuses us.
>
> Hazlitt used to leap and sing. Some of our number lie down and hug the sun-warmed mossy earth for sheer joy ... We wonder, as we wander along in this warm, bracing air, over these pleasant ridges, how we can ever bring ourselves to go back to the cramped greyness of the towns. This is obviously the right life to live, unhurried, slow, deliberate, with time to absorb beauty, and beauty at every turn waiting to be absorbed.[40]

On an abortive night-time walk to Chanctonbury to see the sunrise, Mais wrote candidly in his autobiography *All the Days of My Life* (1937) of the disaster which overcame him and his group of 'lunatics' on a special railway excursion to Steyning (Figure 27). Asked how it panned out, he replied:

We expected at the outside, forty. One thousand, four hundred and forty turned up. It took four trains. It was a tribute to the Southern Railway's power of persuasion, for the moon had sunk below the horizon long before our arrival and the sun refused to rise to order. It was a very startling occasion, for I was called up at four in the morning on the top of Chanctonbury to explain the absence of sun and moon; I felt like Bottom. Still, it was a memorable experience. I've never been allowed to forget it.[41]

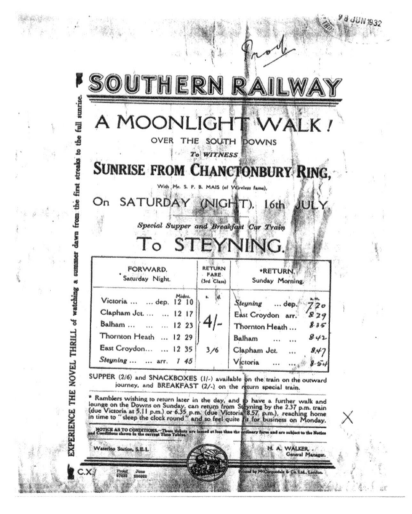

Fig. 27: The moonlight walk for sunrise over Chanctonbury Ring, originally from S.P.B. Mais, *All the Days of My Life* (Hutchinson, 1937), pp. 182–83. (Courtesy Dr Geoffrey Mead)

Mais was also an ardent campaigner for the countryside. As he moved to Southwick, so did his *Sussex* (1929) appear. And in the same year, worrying about the looming presence of Brighton's suburbs to the east, he also published a hymn of praise for his new home:

> The hills, the village green and the sea combine to make Southwick an ideal home for those who love natural beauty, but it is the people even more than the place who contribute so largely to the happiness of those who adopt it as their home.[42]

Was this written tongue in cheek? It was certainly somewhat over the top! He died in April 1975 at a nursing home in Lindfield.

Ernest Raymond

Ernest Raymond (1888–1974) was a child in an unconventional ménage. He was known as the son of William and Florence Bell Raymond of Paris, a fiction, since his true father was George Frederick Blake, who became a major general in the Royal Marines. He was supposedly born in Argentière, near Chamonix Haute-Savoie, on the last day of 1888, although details of his early family are conflicting, and it is possible that he was born in Montreux, Switzerland, as returned in the 1901 census. But he arrived in England in 1891, where he was strictly brought up by his aunt, Emily Calder, the younger sister of his real mother Ida, and the general, known to Raymond affectionately as 'Dum'. In 1901, he was in the care of Emily and living at Barons Court, Fulham. With them lived Raymond's half-sister, Dorothy, who, though not acknowledged as such, was the daughter of the general and Raymond's aunt.[43]

From 1908–11 he taught at a prep school in Eastbourne and later in Bath, but proceeded to Chichester Theological College in 1912 and then to Durham University. He entered Holy Orders in 1915 and served as a chaplain in the Great War, including a posting to Gallipoli. In the first of his two-book autobiographies, he writes of his time after demobilisation in 1919 as a curate on the staff of the Parish Church of Brighton (then St Nicholas) before he relinquished his Holy Orders in 1923, unable any longer to accept Christian dogma.

He was in Brighton when his spectacularly successful first novel, *Tell England* (1922), was being turned down by publishers, a tense episode that

he assuaged by visits to Hove Cricket ground.[44] He lived in Sussex for more
than twenty years, residing, for example, at Muster Green, Haywards Heath
(1930) and in 1939, returned in the National Registration Survey as 'novelist
and author' living with Zoé (née Doucett), his wife since 1922, in Heath
Road, Haywards Heath (Plate 41). But he moved to Hampstead in 1940 on
the breakdown of his marriage to Zoé and early remarriage to Diana, née
Young, in 1941.[45]

Although many of his novels were based in London, by the time of his
death he had also written ten novels set in Sussex.[46] They also included
characters and places drawn from his past life there. Writing to G. and R.
Thurston Hopkins, the collaborators in *Literary Originals of Sussex* (1936),
Raymond listed his Sussex novels at that point as following the line of the
Downs from east to west:

> 1922 *Rossenal* (Eastbourne)
> 1925 *Daphne Bruno* (Ditchling Common and neighbourhood)
> 1926 *The Fulfilment of Daphne Bruno* (ditto)
> 1927 *Morris in the Dance* (Brighton – called Temple Gowring)
> 1929 *A Family That Was* (Hurstpierpoint and Twineham)
> 1931 *Mary Leith* (ditto and Wolstonbury)
> 1933 *Newtimber Lane* (Newtimber, Poynings, Fulking and Edburton)[47]

He might also have included *Wanderlight* (1924), which has its hero attending
the theological college at 'Widdering' (Chichester) to be trained as a priest.
At his Haywards Heath home, he would pace the long drive of the little
cottage he built while musing over a new novel. He felt that his fiction that
followed *Tell England* lacked the central inspiration that had made the first
novel such a success. Nevertheless, he began work on another successful
book, *We, the Accused* in 1932, but temporarily abandoned the huge task of
research and said, 'I ran away again, I ran into the lanes and fields of Sussex
and wrote a book which ran easily from my pen' – *Newtimber Lane*, named
after a much-loved byway below Newtimber Hill, a spur on the Downs
escarpment near the Devil's Dyke. The novel contains many descriptions of
rural Sussex and begins, 'Last night was a night of great beauty; and in my
garden under Fulking Down I thought for a little of committing suicide.' [48]

Newtimber Lane is a sustained prose rhapsody on a Sussex landscape (Plate 42).
Raymond takes the reader in spirit on a walk in the 1860s through Newtimber, Poynings, Fulking and Edburton – villages strung out along that beloved
road running along the foot of the Downs. The lane began at a battlemented

church, a gentleman's house and a cottage and then tilted upwards and broke through the magical beechwood which climbed Newtimber Hill, the trees including mighty trunks of fairytale shapes. Then the lane dived down into charming Poynings:

> God! This is a mountain we are facing now. Ay, and with a steeper side than many of your Alpine hills … Not mountains, you say? Look again. We are walking under their flanks and looking in the same direction as their march, and we see the shoulder lines, one behind the other, falling in the steepest curves to the earth. … They are as a herd of gargantuan beasts marching in Indian file towards the West.

Pursuing the sinuous road, Fulking is reached, flint and stone cottages, thatched cottages and barns smelling richly of manure, 'There is something Alpine about this village; you feel the mountain close to your side, the manure smells Swiss and there's the prattle of a rivulet.' This served as a sheepwash and travellers had to wait patiently to continue until the farm workers corralled the sheep safely and reopened the lane to its scarce traffic. Finally, under the brooding Downs, Edburton was reached, a little round garden with a church in its midst, a rectory, a cottage or two and little else. It was here that the novelist wanted to be buried if he was living at Fulking, as he asked his God that he may. He added that the lane was so narrow that passing places had been provided for wheel traffic to pass one another and that bells round the necks of the leading wagon horses warned of their progress. The lane, and the bordering Downs, have hardly altered since Raymond wrote and the Preston Nomads' cricket ground must have been one of the loveliest rural settings in England.

He now felt ready to complete *We, the Accused* (1935), about a man accused of a premeditated murder, and which contained informed criticism of the English legal system. Raymond had loved the Downs and Weald of Sussex since childhood, along with the Surrey Hills, North Downs and the Lake District. In the 1935 novel, his murderer was actually a struggling schoolmaster in a suburb of London but in the novel, the murderer flees in terror to the Wealden villages and Sussex Downs Raymond had known as a boy. We follow the criminal's flight, manhunt, capture, trial, conviction and execution. Bloodhounds chase the criminal over the Downs and when the hunt presses close, it is on the woody slopes of the greensand hills of the western Weald that he is run to earth, but then escapes to a lonely fellside in the Lake District.[49]

Not one of his many books had meant so much or cost so much in the research needed to uncover every detail, including the complicated legal proceedings. He was rewarded with a generous review from Compton Mackenzie and wide acclaim, together with the award of the Gold Medal by the Book Guild for the best novel in 1935. It was translated into many languages. The Committee of the Book Guild stated, 'We have one of the most intimate and most brilliant character studies that have ever been etched by the master-craftsman ... only a very great novelist could have turned out a masterpiece.' Norman Birkett, later Lord Birkett, said that it was the only 'criminal' novel he had read without finding in it a legal or technical error.[50]

In the tragi-comedy *Don John's Mountain Home* (1936), Raymond deals belligerently with the new ways of life that were clashing with the old traditions. Here was a new Sussex of housing estates at 'Avonsmead', apparently a composite of the Haywards Heath, Hassocks, Three Bridges and Burgess Hill townships created by the railway and now sprawling with the impact of the motor car. Before the railway, Raymond pictured 'Avonsmead' as a farmhouse or two with adjacent fields, but now he saw a jostle of haphazard houses, within which no one knew his neighbour ... If the father of Avonsmead was the Iron River [the railway], its mother is the Age of Bewilderment.'

Raymond's attack on the townsman's defilement of the countryside was hot and strong:

No tradesman in Seabourne [Brighton] so money-grubbing and tight-fisted, no professional man so cumbered with material cares, but longed at times for the quiet of country things; and here were the homes of those who had undone their purses, packed their traps, and come out to find the spinneys and the meads ... and the Little Avon [the Ouse] winding near, and the bird chorus at dawn. Their stucco mansions might be pompous and dull, but they were their poetry; they were the palaces of children, the poems of the immature. And the gabled houses of after years and cheaper men, with their tiles and white paint, were at least an attempt at escape from the dust-grey stucco and the pool-grey slate into something like laughter and coloured living. And as for the mock-Tudor cottages, the homes of the very little men, they were fairy tales written in timber and brick. Their litter out here on the fields was the litter of a Sunday School treat. All pathos is tinged with beauty; and the pathos of Avonsmead, a town built, like the whole of our Western world, by men economically adult, but mentally adolescent and spiritually infantile, was the pathos of the nursery.

In all this, 'Don John', a former public school teacher, is the iconoclast who sees nothing but sham and humbug in this way of living, and his vituperative attacks on his self-satisfied neighbours and their violent reactions to him are the theme of the novel. One memorable passage in the book describes the construction of a new road for its attendant housing estate, an almost universal incident in coastal and mid-Sussex in the 1930s, made all the more startling by what was then the novel use of mechanical appliances:

Like the advance of a slayer who leaves a ribbon of destruction in its wake, The New Road marched towards Avonsmead. [It] took the course of an ancient lane, and laid about it with a will, throwing hedges, felling trees, levelling banks, uprooting fences, and tearing up the grass. Leaving this lane, it advanced across the green acres, a long white wound. It reached the fringes of Avonsmead and the tarmac road that would lead it to Vagabond's Lane. It tore up the tarmac between the pavements and ploughed on, with its workmen and wagons and baggage train in tow.

And so it came to the foot of Vagabond's Lane. Now in the upper parts of this lane it would have to cut away and disperse high curving banks covered with brambles and bracken, ivy, hazel and thorn. And for this purpose [was] the most monstrous machine of all. This was a giant excavator, and it was like some huge dockyard crane which had broke loose from the quay-side and come lumbering into the country for a sight of trees and a view over garden walls. Above its crunching caterpillar belts it had a humble cab for its driver, and in front of this a mighty girder, maybe twenty-five foot long, up and down which the huge excavating shovel could run like the car of an aerial railway.

Its entry upon Vagabond's Lane was an Oriental triumph. The noise of its approach was not unlike the beating of drums and cymbals. And added to this was the noise of voices, for the children ran beside it, shouting their hosannas, … The Advance of the Machine, … Padding along on its caterpillar feet, rolling and pitching, grunting and spitting, its long neck stretching before it almost into the next parish, it advanced to its task of demolition, removal and change. We have likened it to a giant crane on a country ramble; we might have likened it to an old reptilian monster, to Diplodocus wallowing in a track in the swampy primeval forest.[51]

Ernest Raymond, awarded an OBE in 1972, had authored more than fifty books. He died, not at Fulking, but in Hampstead, in May 1974.

Stella Gibbons

Finally, we turn to a quite different evocation of Sussex, and one that fed off much of the literature we have so far discussed. Stella Dorothea Gibbons (1902–89), like Winifred Holtby or Vera Brittain, was a woman writer by trade. She grew up in Kentish Town, London, where her father was a doctor, but her parents were depressive and oppressive, relishing melodramatic scenes that apparently influenced her characterisation of the unpleasant, indeed, almost bestial Starkadders in her famous comic fantasy *Cold Comfort Farm* (1932). In 1923, she obtained a Diploma in Journalism and worked successively for *The Evening Standard* and *The Lady*, where she reviewed books on the countryside, which she reckoned second-rate to the point of absurdity and which she mocked in her inspired novel.

Following the success of *Cold Comfort Farm*, she gave up her post at *The Lady* and in April 1933 married Allan Webb, an actor and minor operatic singer, setting up home in Belsize Park, and then from 1936, near her beloved Hampstead Heath. She continued to produce novels and poetry and during the 1950s she became a regular contributor to *Punch*. She never relished literary fame, nor sought the company of those within the literary culture of the time. Even so, her novel did win the Prix Etranger of the Fémina-Vie Heureuse Prize in 1934.[52]

In contrast to other writers dealt with in this volume, Stella Gibbons never lived in Sussex but will forever be associated with the downland through the pages of her most famous novel. In fact, she wrote more than twenty novels. Three of these, including her first novel and its two sequels, the short story collection *Christmas at Cold Comfort Farm* and *Conference at Cold Comfort Farm* are set in Sussex. A fourth, *The Matchmaker*, is set in Sussex in the immediate post-war years.[53]

Inevitably, her later work did not attract the same interest, nor could she aspire to the same heights. Her second novel, *Enbury Heath* (1935), was thinly based on her own childhood, but by 1936 a stage play based on *Cold Comfort Farm* appeared in London, the first of several other adaptations for radio and film. The true sequel to *Cold Comfort Farm* is the satirical *Conference at Cold Comfort Farm* (1949), set again at the awful Starkadders' farm, but now, with the male Starkadders in South Africa, the farm is an American conference centre and hosting 'the International Thinkers' Group'. Upon the men's return, chaos again ensues and the farm sinks once again into its primitive state.[54]

Her fictional neurotic and uncouth Starkadders at Cold Comfort Farm, high on the Sussex Downs, remain memorable and humorous. The phrase,

'Something nasty in the woodshed' has become well known. Her nephew Reggie Oliver reveals that Stella Gibbons went for a few days to Alfriston in 1931, where she hoped to write a lot of her book. She recited the latest chapters at a badly run bed-and-breakfast establishment run, by curious coincidence, by a Mrs Comfort, to the great joy of fellow guests. The result was a complex and sophisticated parody.

Oliver lists the targets in her satirical novel as the fads and fancies of the period, including Freudian psychology, avant-garde foreign films, Holly-wood (affectionate mockery), D.H. Lawrence, the Powys brothers and Thomas Hardy's earnest and earthy novels, county society, the Arts and Crafts movement and the 1930s equivalent to Fringe Theatre, as well as her main objects, the contemporary overdramatised rural novel typified by Mary Webb on Shropshire and Sheila Kaye-Smith on Sussex. Taking it a stage further, Evelyn Waugh and Cyril Connolly were among those who loved the natural beauty of the Downs but despised the 'awfulness' of the people who wrote about it.[55]

However, one significant target seems to have been omitted by Oliver – Sussex literature extolling the praises of the county in general. Although, early in the book, the heroine Flora Poste tells her friend of her plans to visit her relations in Sussex:

'Sussex ...' mused Mrs Smiling, 'I don't much like the sound of that. Do they live on a decaying farm?'

'I'm afraid they do,' confessed Flora reluctantly.[56]

In her literary journalism, Stella Gibbons would have been familiar with this avalanche of Sussex material and Flora's remark, 'that Sussex, when all was said and done, was not quite like other counties', prepares us for the deli-cious mockery to come. She would have felt the need to debunk the constant 'Sussex worship' from writers. It is ironic that the novel was drawn to the attention of the English committee for the Femina Prize by none other than Sheila Kaye-Smith.[57] The timing of publication was important: many avid readers were by now replete with what the *Times Literary Supplement* called 'the earthy and passionate novel', or else referred to as 'the loam and love-child school' (Figure 28).

So, instead she painted an exaggerated pastiche of primitive life on a decay-ing, bathless Sussex farm amid masses of mud a mile from Howling village and 7 miles from Beersholm, probably Lewes. She has delicious purple patches of deadly satire of this appalling but interesting place, marked in the text by

Baedeker stars, to help those ordinary individuals 'who are not always sure whether a sentence is Literature or whether it is just sheer flapdoodle ... It ought to help the reviewers, too'.[58]

One such passage tells of the farm, in bad repair, 'crouched on a bleak hillside', its fields 'fanged with flints', within earshot of the 'solemn, tortured-snake voice of the sea, two miles away'.[59] Another compares the rounded rim of the Downs to 'a vast inverted pot-de-chambre' and 'the frosted roofs of Howling, crisp and purple as broccoli leaves, were like beasts about to spring'.[60] The countryside was perceived to be in 'its annual tortured ferment of spring growth; worm jarred with worm and seed with seed. Frond leapt on root and hare on hare'.[61]

Extracts give a flavour of her descriptions. The first one is well known, and both are prefaced with the Baedeker stars to emphasise their importance. They also serve to illustrate and parody the distance between 'fine literature' and the rural speech of the Starkadders, something found in so many rural novels:[62]

AUTHOR OF " COLD COMFORT FARM ":
MISS STELLA GIBBONS.

Miss Stella Gibbons's novel has been most favourably reviewed. It is a well-sustained parody of the Loam-and-Love-child school of fiction.

Fig. 28: Stella Gibbons (from an NPG portrait). Note the reference to the 'Loam-and-love child' school of fiction, originally from *The Sketch* (London), 21 September 1932, and reproduced in wordhistories. net/2017/08/17/something-nasty-woodshed-origin (Available under Creative Commons Licence)

★★Dawn crept over the Downs like a sinister white animal, followed by the snarling cries of a wind eating its way between the black boughs of the thorns. The wind was the furious voice of this sluggish animal light that was baring the dormers and mullions and scullions of Cold Comfort Farm.

★★...All the surrounding surface of the countryside – the huddled Downs lost in rain, the wet fields fanged abruptly with flints, the leafless thorns thrust sideways by the eternal pawing of the wind, the lush breeding miles of meadow through which the lifeless river wandered – seemed to be folding inwards upon themselves. Their dumbness said: 'Give up'. There is no answer to the riddle; only that bodies return exhausted, hour by hour, minute by minute, the all-forgiving and uncomprehending primeval slime.[63]

The unpleasant Starkadders, ripe for rows and mischief, comprised an elderly widow who kept to her bed and her daughter and son in-law, who ran the farm with numerous children and relatives, but who failed to make it productive:

> The seeds wither as they fall into the ground, and the earth will not nourish 'em. The cows are barren and the sows are farren and the King's Evil and the Queen's Bane and the Prince's Heritage ravages our crops. 'Cos why? 'Cos there's a curse on us.[64]

A memorable scene is in the great kitchen where the porridge is 'leering' in the snood, while Adam Lambsbreath is 'clettering' the dirty dishes; another is of the packed congregation in the tiny church of the Quivering Brethren (possibly either the Eastgate or the Jirah Chapel in Lewes), led by Amos dressed in black fustian and accompanied by an old man who conducted the music with a poker when the sect quivered at the mention of burning by hell-fire. There is the shocking, noisy scene in the dimly lit kitchen when more than a dozen of the Starkadders argued together with the head of the family, the batty Aunt Doom, until the small hours of the morning.

Cold Comfort Farm is a difficult work to pin down, moving between rural reality, urban modernism, landscape description and the analysis of family despair. Raymond Williams described it as an 'odd work', exhibiting a 'tension of attraction and repulsion' towards the countryside in the interwar period.[65] It remains a fascinating book, although Stella Gibbons herself thought in later life that its fame had been detrimental to her overall career as a writer and poet. Her poetry, which has a great feeling for nature, is neglected, as are her opinions on ecological and animal rights issues, which were in advance of her time.

AMONG TWENTIETH-CENTURY POETS

Oh, land that holds my heart in fee,
Where'er my feet may roam,
Dear land of down and weald and sea,
I hear you call me home.
Never the south wind sings and sighs,
But the voice of your woods will fill
The mean and empty leagues between,
And my heart grows fain for the things unseen,
For combe and hurst and Sussex skies
And the breast of a Sussex hill.[1]

Speak to the earth, and it shall teach thee.[2]

Arthur Stanley Cooke

Few writers loved the Sussex Downs more truly or knew them more intimately than Arthur Stanley Cooke (1852–1919) who, for over fifty years,
dedicated himself to describing them in prose, verse, sketching and painting.
He was also a good musician. He felt that the Downs, where he had walked
since childhood, were largely unknown to most visitors.

He was born into a Brighton family, his father Matthew being a Post Office
clerk. He married Eliza Hunt in 1877 (who ultimately predeceased him by a few
months), and he worked as a gas inspector. He had various addresses in Brighton,
including No. 7 Dorset Gardens, No. 25 Eaton Place and No. 77 West Street.
He was a Freemason from 1885 until shortly before his death, resigning in 1917.
In 1911, he published *Off the Beaten Track in Sussex* with thirty-seven different
rambles described, and with 160 sketches provided by members of the Brighton
Arts Club and by Cooke himself (Figure 29). His friend and executor, H.M.
Wallbrook, referred to it as 'one of the best books in existence on the South
Downs' and one of the 'golden lights' of the terrible war years.[3]

POYNINGS POST OFFICE IN 1897.
(*By A. S. C.*)

Fig. 29: Poynings Post Office – the 'rooms were low pitched, small and not too pretty'. (A.S. Cooke, *Off the Beaten Track in Sussex*, 1911, pp. 57–58)

There were other publications too: his *Southdown Songs and Idylls* had been published in 1909, a miscellany of stories, sketches and narrative poems about the South Downs; and the posthumously and privately printed *Songs of the Sussex Downs* (1920). They might not contain 'great' poetry but they certainly express a deep tenderness for the Downs, with the latter written partially in their honour as a refuge from pain, illness, bereavement and anxiety during the First World War. His only son, Arthur, was killed in April 1917, aged 26, at Gavrelle while serving in the Royal Navy Volunteer Reserve. Arthur Senior was also an organist and his son had developed a career in organ building after graduating with a BSc from Kings College London.

The majority of his poems in *Songs of the Sussex Downs* were written in 1917 and 1918 when he was too ill to walk the Downs, but through their composition he was able to assuage his grief in the remembrance of their peace and beauty. We have the sonnet on 'The Coombe':

The solitude and silence are as balm,
The turmoil of the world seems very far;
Sweet Peace dwells here, and with the breeze is blent
A kindred sound – her sigh of deep content

This was almost Cooke's sole theme. His world is the nodding necks of sheep and their ringing bells, the rippling undulations of harebells in the wind, dew ponds, the purple Rampion – and he loved buildings such as Ashcombe Mill, Eastwick Barn, the ruined Balsdean Chapel and the little downland churches.

Arthur Bell

Another contemporary, like-minded Sussex poet, though more poetically distinguished, was Arthur Francis Bell of Storrington (1875–1918), who was disabled resulting from an accident to his legs in infancy. He was born in Titchfield, Hampshire, into the comfortable household of William Warden Bell, an East India Company civil servant. By 1901, he was living with his widowed mother in Compton Avenue, Brighton, and by 1911, he was returned in the census as a visitor at York Road, Hove, as a gentleman of private means. By this time, however, he had come to know Storrington, where he was living by 1913, having made the acquaintance of Father George Tyrrell there.[4]

His *The Dear Land of the Heart* was published in 1913, containing lyrics based on the memories of places he had visited on his walks, such as Bury Hill, the Pulborough Brooks, Church Norton and Sidlesham Mill in the Selsey peninsula. Many were addressed to his lovers, friends and companions, including one to Hilaire Belloc in praise of Storrington and one to Belloc's daughters, Elodie, Eleanor and Elizabeth. Although once a lover of London, he expresses, too, his longing for Sussex while in exile in London:

My ghost shall go on a North wind
To the combe of a Sussex down,
And hover about a homestead
Where the thatch is old and brown,
And hear the creaking waggons
Set off, ere dawn, to town.[5]

The poem was reproduced in C.F. Cook's *The Book of Sussex Verse*, to which Bell also contributed a foreword, sent from 'The Studio' at Storrington in November 1914, beginning 'Dear land of the heart …' and effectively a hymn of praise to the 'grave and gracious beauty' of rural Sussex. Like Arthur Stanley Cooke, Bell loved the Downs, to him a 'Hidden City …, God's own town'. One of his memories resounds in the lyric he composed at Old Shoreham Church:

Under Shoreham church that stands by Adur river
Watching over Lancing down the cloud-shade shiver blue,
Where swift spread wings of gulls ever flash and sweep and quiver
Under Shoreham church I made a song of you.

Love was in that song, the love of earth for heaven,
Earth a bride unrobing to the kisses of the sun,
Love of buds that drink the light, their close sheaths riven,
Love of all things moving to the spell that knits them one.

March winds stole the song from my lips by Adur river,
Bore it high, and tossed it to the foaming white and blue,
Leaving us a memory that moves to music ever
Of joy and love and faith in spring and you.

Bell's 'Song of the Sussex coast' conveys the romanticism of the days of sail in the busy English Channel:

For every craft that the waves race after,
Lashed by the wind and rain and foam,
From fading twilight to first grey morning
Searches somewhere a light of home
Northward or south, or west or eastward,
Somewhere's a haven where each would be;
So spread my sails to the hoarse sou-wester,
For the lights of Shoreham call to me.
Shoreham town by the changing river,
Wet, waste flats where the gulls fly free,
And the lights of Shoreham low on the land-line,
Dancing, flashing, across the sea.

Liners hull-down, with the world before you,
Colliers nearing your journey's end,

Grim destroyers and stately cruisers,
Seek ye the harbours that hail you friend,
I will go home where the wide-winged sunset
Hovers in flame o'er a racing sea,
To the square church tower and the red roofs clust'ring
To Shoreham haven where I would be,
Shoreham town in the long blue twilight,
Grave and dreaming you call to me;
Oh, lights of Shoreham, waxing, waning,
Lights of Shoreham across the sea![6]

Bell died on 26 November 1918, just after the conclusion of the Great War. He lies buried in St Mary's Churchyard in Storrington (Plate 43). His circle of friends in the village included the Catholic modernist, Maude Dominica Petre (1863–1942), ex-member of the Daughters of Mary and noted writer on religion, and the brilliant ex-Jesuit priest, Father George Tyrrell (1861–1909), who were both living at the Square at Petre's large eighteenth-century Mulberry House. Maude Petre arranged for all three to be buried side by side, and Bell left his meagre effects to her on his death. Petre's Storrington home became a meeting place for many Catholics involved in thinking through relations with modernism in religion.

Letters from Bell, such as one from No. 58 York Road, Hove, to K.M. Clutton in 1909, dealt with the death of Tyrrell, who had attempted to reconcile traditional Catholic teaching with scientific Modernity but had been excommunicated in 1908 shortly before his death. He also lamented his own lack of belief, the unreality of academic life at Hertford College, Oxford, where he went late in life, and his dreading a biography of Tyrrell to be written by Maude Petre.[7] His own 'Memorial to George Tyrrell' is included in his *Dear Land of the Heart*. Petre, his executor, did in fact produce a memorial volume, *The Happy Phantom*, to Bell's memory:

With none but the moon to mock me,
    High up on the hills alone,
I will run with the flickering shadows
    By racing cloud-wisps thrown,
And laugh to think of my body
    That lies 'neath the church-yard stone.[8]

Charles Dalmon

The poetry of Charles William Dalmon (1862–1938), was probably enjoyed by Sussex readers more than that of T.S. Eliot or W.H. Auden. He was a contributor to *The Yellow Book*, the leading *fin de siècle* literary journal of the 1890s, and published his first poetry collection in 1892.[9] He continued to be appreciated by a small group, including his Pimlico neighbour, Noel Coward, and Siegfried Sassoon (Figure 30).

The poet's own moving epitaph is revealing of his character and personal disappointments:

> Men scarcely saw him as he passed along;
> And few were there who listened to his song;
> He laboured with the lowliest; and gave
> His love to Sussex till he reached his grave.[10]

He was a somewhat elusive character. Indeed, Edward Thomas wrote in 1914 in a foreword to Dalmon's *Poor Man's Riches*, later published in 1922, that 'It is rumoured that Mr Charles Dalmon is still alive.'[11]

He was born in Shoreham in 1862, the son of a farm labourer and coachman.[12] His parents William and Sarah moved to Washington, where Dalmon attended the village school and grew up with a love and deep knowledge of nature, folklore and legend, which he later felt only someone 'Sussex born and bred' could possess. His work was Arcadian, but placed in England, and Sussex in particular. Nymphs and fairies inhabited his Sussex countrysides alongside humans, such as the Wealden milkmaid, Phyllis, who was late for her milking duties:

> Come pretty Phyllis you are late!
> The cows are crowding at the gate:
> […]
> Now Faeries, fays, elves, goblins go
> And find out where she lingers so.[13]

He was also proud to proclaim some Romany blood, and was certainly an inveterate traveller who would disappear and reappear seemingly at random:

> From far-off hills and far-off plains
> A wild cry comes to me:
> *'The blood of Kings is in your veins –*
> *The Kings of Romany!'*[14]

He began working for the London and Brighton Railway company at the age of 14 but was dismissed for 'incompetence' in 1876. By 1881, aged 19, he was a footman in the household of John Whalley, a clergyman 'without cure of souls' in South Bersted.[15]

As an aspiring but struggling young poet, he lived and worked in London for a while, often going hungry, and then sailed to New Jersey as a steward on SS *City of Berlin* in September 1888 to visit Walt Whitman. He wrote a pleading letter:

> Today I was coming to Camden full of hope that I might see you but I have not enough money to pay my railway fare to and from Camden. I am only a steward on the City of Berlin—you will see me? Yes—you are good—may I come to see you when my ship returns in about a month? The City of Berlin sails early on Saturday the 29th—may I hope for a few words from you before she sails—I cannot write the things I would write to you—I could not speak the words I would wish to speak—but if I could see your face—if I could hear your voice! I hope—Will you accept my 'Minutiae'? Will you—if you are able—write to me.[16]

The ailing Whitman remained a mentor to him until his death in 1892, sharing his unecclesiastical approach to religion, his unworldliness and love of freedom in the open air.

We thereafter only catch glimpses of Dalmon: by 1891 he was living in Piccadilly as a valet for a senior army officer, and by 1901 he was a librarian (in fact, for the Post Office), living in South Square, Gray's Inn.[17] And continuing this peripatetic life, by 1903 he was living in Wimbledon and joining the Freemasons there by 1904, but their register covering 1906 unusually has no occupation listed for him. Then we find him back at Shoreham, working at a printing press in Brighton, where he was discovered by Roden Noel, the father of Conrad Noel, the controversial Rector of Thaxted in Essex from 1910. Dalmon chose to live at Thaxted during Noel's incumbency and was prominent in the prevailing Socialist and Anglo-Catholic atmosphere.[18] His words, to be sung at May Day to the tune of 'We plough the fields and scatter', include the refrain:

Lift up the people's banner
And let the ancient cry
For justice and for freedom
Re-echo to the sky.[19]

This varied life continued: he even became an art director in early British films, such as *The Garden of Resurrection* (1919) or *The Blue Peter* (1930), and with the new Langham Productions in the early 1930s, although he found that the British film art director was 'a despised creature'.[20] Another surprise came in 1934 when Dalmon joined the British Union of Fascists.

But throughout all this, his love of Sussex inspired poems on Rye and Winchelsea, Thakeham pinewoods, Muntham Wood, Steyning, Southwick and Birling Gap, among other places. But Chanctonbury Ring, above Washington, was his inspiration, which he missed greatly when away. He dedicated his poems in *A Poor Man's Riches* to it, 'With the love of a lifetime I dedicate my poems to Chanctonbury Ring, the most beautiful of all the Downs.'[21]

Dalmon seemingly enjoyed a carefree existence. He sang of the old-time simple, rustic, honest life of West Sussex and its rooted communities, often drawing upon happy memories of that vanished landscape in his poems – wild thyme, the harebells, 'the ferny brakes' of Parham, the heathy commons of West Chiltington and the cherry orchards of Thakeham. And he artlessly recalls no fewer than twenty-five of 'the merry crew of boys and girls who were his childhood friends, names matching exactly those in the school register of the period'.[22]

He chose a homely Sussex garden in Washington, riotous with sweet-smelling flowers in the evening dusk to acknowledge the inspiration he derived from the Sussex landscape and the pioneer Sussex poets. Crouching among the quince and medlar trees and spellbound with deepening quietness, he told of his enjoyment of the garden and in the loving detail of flower after flower, when hearing voices that made him a poet:

... where verbena, night-stock, herb-o'-th'-sun,
Balm, sweetbrier, lad's-love, rosemary and musk
Diffused their mingled fragrance all around,
A holy presence came into the dusk
And hushed to breathless silence every sound
In deference to one
Who held an old-world lute, and, for myself
Alone, against the sundial leaned and played
The inspiring tunes of Sussex she had made
For Fletcher, Otway, Collins, Shelley, Realf.[23]

He loved music, his collection *Song Favours* being published in 1895. The sound of children dancing and singing, the gurgle of brooks, the jingling of horse bells, the tinkling of sheep bells, the hum of bees and the fluting of birds burned into his memory. Men drink and sing cheerily at village inns and in 'Autumn Allegory', we find people living with the rhythms of nature, the welcome is 'come our old mate' to a table bedecked with country food, sweets and drink, a freshly tapped cask of cider, William pears, plums, grapes, medlars, bottled gooseberries, various nuts, damson cheese and frumenty.

More than any of the minor poets, Dalmon captured the spirit of Sussex wanted by the reading public at the turn of the twentieth century. And of course, his example of 'living deliberately' with locally sourced food and drink is certainly catching on again.

The title of his last volume of verse, *Singing as I Go* (1927), is indicative of his inclination to instinctively break into song, as did seventeenth-century Herrick, a favourite of Dalmon's. His drinking songs were thought by his friend Edward Thomas the best of their kind.[24] He also seemed to know the farm labourer in ways that few other Sussex writers ever tried. In one of his last poems, 'The Old Gaffer', he quoted H.J. Massingham's remark that the agricultural labourer, 'landless, powerless, and culturally limited as he is, is yet the salt of the English earth'.

The cottage gardens are not as fruitful in Washington as they were in Dalmon's childhood, and the orchards are thinner, but in every respect, Washington remains a poet's village, with its own identity, strong sense of community and an exquisitely beautiful landscape. Dalmon, the fascinating wanderer, finally found rest and happiness in retirement as a Brother at the Charterhouse in London, a 'refuge for indigent gentlemen', where he died in 1938.

Canon Andrew Young

Andrew Young (1885–1971) shared with Gerard Manley Hopkins a combination of religious intensity with a surprising preponderance of nature in his prose and poetry. He also shared Hopkins' intensity of observation and literary isolation, evidently in agreement with Andrew Marvell's sentiment in 'The Garden' in wishing for seclusion and privacy in communion with nature:

But 'twas beyond a mortal's share
To wander solitary there:
Two paradises 'twere in one
To live in Paradise alone.[25]

Unlike Hopkins, however, Andrew Young has never achieved universal respect, with many originally dismissing him as 'yet another "nature" poet of the Georgian ilk', outside the changing times of his day and against change in general. A reassessment was long overdue and has been provided by Richard Ormrod.[26]

A Scottish-born poet and clergyman, he spent most of his long adult life in Sussex. Following seminary studies, in 1914 (the year he married Janet Green), he was elected Minister of the Temple United Free Church in Midlothian. Throughout the First and Second World Wars, he maintained a somewhat ambivalent pacifist stance, but served in the former as the superintendent of a YMCA rest-camp in France. After the war, he became Minister of the Presbyterian Church of St Cuthbert in Holland Road, Hove, of which he later said, 'Although I was not attracted to the place, Hove was where I lived.'[27]

And it was from here that small books of poetry were published between 1920 and 1931. They attracted the attention of Viola and Francis Meynell, whose Nonesuch Press published his *Winter Harvest* in 1933 (Figure 31). In 1939, following a meeting with Bishop George Bell of Chichester at the unveiling of the Edward Thomas memorial in Petersfield,

Fig. 31: Canon Andrew Young in 1937. (NPG x81717)

he was ordained into the Anglican Church, becoming successively Curate of Plaistow Chapel and then, in 1941, Vicar of St Peter's Stonegate near Wadhurst in East Sussex, where a stone memorial plaque to him 'priest, poet and naturalist' was installed in 1976.

John Arlott, in a radio broadcast, declared him to be the finest pastoral poet since Clare and Roger Sell described him as 'one of the greatest sons of Hardy at Hardy's greatest'.[28] Young first met John Arlott in 1943, when Arlott requested permission to use some of his poems in his anthology *First Time in America*, eventually published in 1948. Arlott became a firm family friend and frequently visited Stonegate, commenting that 'he dislikes the values of London'.[29] He commented on Young's manuscripts and proofs, enthusiastically reviewed his works, conducted negotiations with publishers and arranged for Young to give talks on both literary and botanical topics for the BBC. Arlott himself gave two BBC talks on Young's poetry in 1946 and 1947. Mutual friends mentioned in letters between the two included John Betjeman, Richard Church and Viola Meynell.[30]

Young was a reticent, humble, meditative and unassuming man. He was described in his near neighbour Ted Walker's anecdotal elegy as a 'close, remote, loved, unknowable companion and he did not write until some brooding thought forced itself into the world'.[31]

His earlier poems are primarily seized with the beauty of earth and natural things, loveliness for its own sake and deeply moving. He was a true countryman and representative of Sussex poets as a naturalist out of key with modernity and civilisation. His visits to London were brief, mainly to the London Library, and he deliberately refrained from joining literary circles and avoided publicity. Although awarded the Queen's Gold Medal for Poetry in 1952 and receiving a later tribute from fourteen writers, the freshness of his poetry, its high distinction and his extraordinary knowledge of plants has been insufficiently recognised.[32] He was a naturalist who wrote poetry, a wild plant expert in the English tradition of botanising country parsons, but with a special involvement with Christianity, all resulting in a special contribution to literature.

His passionate devotion to wild flowers resulted in two prose books while he was at Stonegate: *A Prospect of Flowers* (1945) and *A Retrospect of Flowers* (1950), in which he identified with them in such a personal way, writing, 'I have seen flowers look at me as I have looked at them, with the light and speech of living eyes.'[33] Robin Tanner thought that in Young's rare power of almost becoming the things and creatures that moved him, he also had a kinship with Thomas Bewick, the engraver. He had the same kind of receptiveness to trees, wild birds and animals and an almost childlike sense of awe and wonder.

Poetry was his real medium, however, dealing with hills and valleys, trees, woods, rocks and, like Richard Jefferies, in his later verse he had a mystical relation with nature that recalls the seventeenth-century Metaphysicals. He loved old lanes, little churches and prehistoric burial mounds but his vision was often focused reflectively on some small object at his feet rather than on the broad horizons that so generally inspired the Sussex poet. Missing, too, are the stock raptures, the ready-made responses and the sentimentalism that so often mars Sussex poetry. But characteristic of old-fashioned Sussex literature is Young's sense of wonder at the comparatively unchanging natural world, giving a timelessness to his work that Norman Nicholson calls 'an essentially contemporary view of an essentially non-contemporary scene'.

Notable in his work is his skill with words. 'You catch words as a cat watches a mouse,' said Walter de la Mare. Hassall has remarked that he 'makes silences in the Downs more silent by an uncanny choice of vowels and consonants and by an intricate system of well-placed cadences'.[34]

And untypically among modern poets, Young, the parish priest, is also an intuitive witness of Christianity and man's relationship with his God. To him, commonplace natural objects were sacred and to share his vision means participating in an act of praise. This perhaps makes him the most oblique religious poet in the language, represented, for example, in *Nicodemus*, a mystery play broadcast in 1937 with incidental music by Imogen Holst.[35]

A specimen of his fascination with small things, with an eye trained to extraordinary exactness is:

I went down on my hands and knees
Looking for trees,
Twin leaves that, spring from seeds,
Were now too big
For stems much thinner than a twig.
These soon with chamomile and clover
And other fallow weeds
Would be turned over;
And I was thinking how
It was a pity someone should not know
That a great forest fell before the plough.[36]

In 'The Flood', Young demonstrates a masterly compression of language with striking images of naturalism combined with his deep grief at the death of his mother, expressed in long, flowing lines:

> The winter flood is out, dully glazing the Weald,
> The Adur, a drowned river, lies in its bed concealed;
> Fishes flowing through fences explore paddock and field.
> Bushes waist deep in water, stand sprinkled here and there;
> A solitary gate, as though hung in mid-air,
> Waits idly open, leading from nowhere to nowhere.
> These bushes at nightfall will have strange fish for guests,
> That wagtail, tit and warbler darkened with their nests,
> Where flood strays now, light-headed lapwings lifted crests.
> But soon comes spring again; the hazel-boughs will angle
> With bait of yellow catkins that in the loose winds dangle
> And starry scarlet blossoms that blind buds bespangle;
> Dog's mercury from the earth unfold seed-clasping fists
> And green-leaved honeysuckle roll in tumbling twists
> And dreams of spring shake all the seeds that sleep in cists.
> O blue-eyed one, too well I know you will not awake,
> Who waked or lay awake so often for my sake,
> Nor would I ask our last leavetaking to retake.
> If lesser love of flower or bird waken my song,
> It is that greater love, too full to flow along,
> Falls like that Adur back, flood-like, silent and strong.

Paradoxically, and like Edward Thomas, Young's personal qualities were not detectable in his poetry. He tended to be somewhat patriarchal, reflecting his own upbringing with a stern father, but one would not know this from his verse. His wife Janet acted as a personal servant and to his children he could be overbearing or distant, often craving solitude.[37] His poetry was brilliantly perceptive about nature, but rarely did it include much depth about his fellow humans.

He retired to Yapton in 1959, where he became a canon of Chichester Cathedral, and died in a Bognor Regis nursing home in 1971, crippled by arthritis.[38] His brilliant last book, *The Poet and the Landscape* (1962), which included material on pastoral poets in the rural places in which they lived, was one of the inspirations behind this present work.[39]

Julian Heward Bell

Julian Bell (1908–37), son of the painter Vanessa Bell and the art critic Clive Heward Bell and beloved nephew of Virginia Woolf, was born in Bloomsbury but spent much of his short life at Charleston. He was educated at Leighton Park School, a Quaker institution, and at King's College Cambridge (1927–34). He felt that his own early discovery of Richard Jefferies was a turning point. His first volume of poetry, *Winter Movement*, was published in 1930, and in 1932 the Woolfs included his poetry, along with that of W.H. Auden, Cecil Day-Lewis and Stephen Spender, in a collection entitled *New Signatures*. In 1936, he published a second volume of poetry, *Work for the Winter*.

He wrote frankly and despairingly in the troubled 1930s of his past joys and present sadness. With some early minor success as a poet and writer, and following nearly two years teaching English at Wuhan National University in China, the outbreak of the civil war in Spain, with its political and moral implications, drew him to join the Republican side as an ambulance driver for the British Medical Aid Unit in June 1937. But he was killed near Madrid just over a month later under heavy Luftwaffe bombing in the Battle of Brunete. He was just 29.[40]

In many ways, Bell's early life was an easy one. Born into a relatively wealthy upper-middle-class intellectual family, he nevertheless struggled to

find his own voice, different from that of the Bloomsbury set from which he sprang. In his 'autobiography' poem, he recalled boyhood holiday joys at Wissett Lodge in Suffolk in 1916:

Fig. 32: Julian Heward Bell and 'Clinker' the dog, *c.* 1927. (NPG x136464)

Orchard trees run wild,
West wind and rain, winters of holding mud,
Wood fires in blue-bright frost and tingling blood,
All brought to the sharp senses of a child.

His love for the countryside continued, and after the family move to Charleston in 1916, he would later, in 'Pantheistic Metaphysical', sensuously compare the curves and mould of the Sussex Downs to his girlfriend's figure. Charleston became his most treasured boyhood memory. He wrote to his girlfriend, 'quite frankly I don't want a mistress who's a nervous wreck, but someone healthy and strong and fresh ... who will walk over the downs all day, and make love half the night, so cheer up sweetheart ...'.[41]

In 1926–27, Bell lived in Paris as a preliminary to Cambridge but here his thoughts still ran to his beloved South Downs. In 'Brumaire', we hear of sheep breaking out from their hurdles, the cry of hounds, 'As, from the coast, the geese/ Sweep inland, clamorous'. And in 'Frimaire', there is a description of an autumnal pheasant shoot.[42] He was even to be described as one who 'infuses a new vigour into English pastoral poetry'.[43]

Contrastingly, in 'London I', he wrote of the 'wringing horror' of incarceration in the city:

I have always thought of you with birds and wind
As a match to your rapid beauty and distant mind,
As I have always loved the plough and down.
Now we must lead the long lives of this town,
Daily work for daily bread
Until we win fame or an old age pension
Or get shot down in a revolution:
I prefer absence and trees
To the choice I make of these.
No help now: this town could do
With some poison gas and a bomb or two.[44]

But Bell did get back. He would 'swing and stride and march again' over the Downs and triumphantly resurrect his intellect and senses (Figure 32).[45] John Maynard Keynes, living nearby, recalled Bell living for weeks on the Downs, observing nature and then returning to 'boisterous Bohemian parties'. He wrote of:

Bare ploughland ridges sweeping from the down;
Black hedges berryless; dead grass turned brown,
   And brown-tipped rushes on each field,
   And bare woods. Mists across the Weald,
      While the night soon
      Blurs afternoon.[46]

The poets lived in literary England, not in agriculture. The passion for the soil as seen by Richard Jefferies and John Halsham was not carried forward by later writers. We would never have known in the interwar years that their Downs were undergoing a disastrous recession, that sheep and shepherds were fast declining, scrub overtaking fields and farmers and labourers struggling to earn a living. In fact, soil as a factor in production or any knowledge of Sussex farming as a way of making a living was paradoxically utterly lost under a welter of sentiment for 'country life'. There is little of the realism of Hardy or Zola, since it was a utopian England that townspeople yearned to recapture, but which even they must have suspected never existed.

But Julian Bell was an exception, writing from Charleston in a way that was neither jingoistic nor sentimental, but with a deep feeling for farmers and the land itself amid economic depression. By 1931, he was absorbed in socialist politics, chaired the Glynde branch of the Labour Party and crossed swords with the landowner Lord Gage, who was in fact his mother's landlord at Charleston. However, he was temperamentally unsuited to the tasks of local politics and soon reverted to his writing, although retaining a passionate interest in wider political issues. In 'Arms and the Man' he wrote a brilliant but scathing description of the interwar Sussex farming landscape:

As one by one, the farmers break and fail,
And barns are emptied at the bankrupt's sale,
Mark from some hill, across the fertile Weald,
The arable retreating field by field,
The waste advancing as the corn recedes
Where the lean bullocks chew the fallow weeds,
See rotting gates hang by the rusted catch,
The unstopped hedges and the mouldering thatch,
The mildewed hay beneath the August rain
The fly-pock'd turnips and the shredded grain,
Thistles and brambles choke the sinking tracks
And deep corruption rots the tumbling stacks.

Here, in a language all can understand,
See plainly told the history of our land.[47]

It is significant that this was published in *New Signatures*, edited by Michael Roberts, because the editor specifically writes that he was giving 'voice to those whose instincts in a time of economic depression and political reaction turned them away from an earlier, now seemingly elitist modernism'. A new generation of writers now reacted to the world they saw around them and were generally depressed. Roberts saw this collection as '[A] clear reaction against esoteric poetry in which in it is necessary for the reader to catch each recondite allusion'. For long, even as an undergraduate, Bell rebelled against the modernism espoused by many in the Bloomsbury set, and he continued to hold such opinions until his untimely death in Spain.

Lady Dorothy Wellesley

Dorothy Ashton (1889–1956) was the much-travelled daughter of a wealthy cotton spinner and stepdaughter of the Earl of Scarborough. In April 1914, she married Gerald, Lord Wellesley (1885–1972), from 1943 the 7th Duke of Wellington, but they separated in 1922 after the birth of two children, although because they remained married, she technically became the Duchess of Wellington (Figure 33). She thereafter briefly fell in love with Vita Sackville-West, who dedicated *The Land* (1926), with its realistic depictions of the Kentish countryside, to her with what Edith Sitwell called 'poetry in gumboots'.[48]

Her poems are examples of deep observation of nature, explored in minute detail, and with a curiosity for the picturesque in shells, flowers, fish, animals and trees. She also conveyed her childhood with descriptive flair and W.B. Yeats thought her work had an accomplished skill with passages of grandeur and dignity, in a powerful onrushing masculine rhythm.[49] She also sponsored and edited the Hogarth Press' *Hogarth Living Poets* series.

In 1928, she moved to Penns-in-the-Rocks, near Withyham, one-time home of the Quaker William Penn, which became her home until her death and was both refuge and inspiration for much of her poetry. It faces huge rocks with deeply fissured crags carved into blocks with crevices. These sandstone rock outcrops bring a flavour of Exmoor or even Wales to a district within 30 miles of Piccadilly. The encompassing woods contain several ancient species of vascular plants, which have remained relatively undisturbed for millennia on account of their inaccessibility.

Fig. 33: 'Lady Dorothy Wellesley' by Lady Ottoline Morell, 1935. (NPG Ax143879)

In *The Land*, she apparently appears in the well-known lines:

She walked among the loveliness she made,
Between the apple-blossom and the water-
She walks among the patterned pied brocade,
Each flower her son, and every tree her daughter.[50]

She built up the walls and laid out planted avenues of flowering trees set in acres of spreading daffodils, which are still a magnificent sight in spring (Plate 44). And she applies much creative imagination in her own poem, the 'Walled Garden', Virginia Woolf, never far from criticising 'Dottie', noted archly, following a visit in August 1928:

She has brought for ever & ever all these couchant rocks; rocks like kneeling elephants; agonized writhing rocks elongated rocks, rocks with grotesque roots grown into them, & Japanese trees on top.

Despite the 'wildness' and mystery, Virginia was unimpressed with her rocks 'grey as elephant backs', and the trees 'liked by some people, but [Dorothy] is too anxious for people to praise it':

After that country, though, how I adore the emptiness, bareness, air & colour of this! Really, I would not give this view for Dottie's rocks. A relic I think of my fathers feeling for the Alps. – this ecstasy of mine over the bare slope of Asheham hill.[51]

Wellesley remembered her first visit to Penns, when she lost her heart to it and had run straight for the rocks, bounding from boulder to boulder, shouting, 'I must have it.' Vita, who found Penns for Dorothy, described the scene as 'absolutely fantastic – a mixture of the most absurdly romantic age, and Shakespeare scenery, especially a Midsummer Night's Dream, and Walter de la Mare and Piranesi and Mrs. Anne Radcliffe'.[52] In Dorothy's 'Lost Forest', she goes deeper into the trackless rocky wood, passing boulders in a great depth of moss from which beech trees and yews 'like pythons' intertwine, the sense of wildness enhanced by the sound of snuffling, half-wild pigs rooting amongst the bracken. Beyond still, were bilberries in the dampness of a patch of peat, smelling of the musk of Pan. As for the trees whose seed has been spilt on rock, she imagines that at twilight in the shelving glade they try to fly 'Straining away from the boulders like great birds/With pinioned wings'.

The house and its surroundings could cast a spell on visitors. A long, winding drive through bluebell woods and great trees revealed a small, dignified early Georgian manor in rose-coloured brick with careful early Victorian additions giving a larger dwelling concealed beneath William Penn's frontage. The dining room was designed by Vanessa Bell and Duncan Grant. Sloping lawns lead onto the rocks, Ashdown Forest lies beyond, and her 'The Forest in October' includes vivid detail of observed nature. And in 'Lost Lane', dedicated to her children and grandchildren, there is no conventional description of an old track but a soaring imagination.[53]

Wellesley strove to make Penns a haven for poets and other writers and her Temple of the Muses, erected in full view of the house and dedicated to 'the muses and gods of the countryside', bears the names of her friends and visitors. Chief of these was W.B. Yeats, who appears to have been smitten by Dorothy in his old age on his several visits between 1935 and his death, two years later. When making a selection of poems for his Oxford Book of Modern Verse, he came across Wellesley's poems, no fewer than eight of which he included in his anthology, while others were published in a new selection of her poems which he encouraged.[54]

Yeats' inordinate exposure of Wellesley in his idiosyncratic anthology did not go unnoticed in the press but even Virginia Woolf in her diary grudgingly admitted that 'with all her faults, she has scope, proportion'. Yeats' visits were greatly welcomed by Dorothy and his verse and favourable comments on her poems inspired her adoration and awe, resulting in the publication of her strange book of her letters to Yeats and the letters on poetry she had received before he died. According to Kathleen Raine, Yeats had also found his relationship with Dorothy rewarding, 'the beauty of a woman, the charm of her house and her companionship, friendship, dreams and kindness, these nourished immortal poetry'.[55] In her last days, and following the death of her long-time lover, the pioneering BBC radio producer Hilda Matheson in 1940, who had lived at Rocks Farm in the grounds of Penns, Dorothy gradually fell prey to depression and alcoholism, dying at Withyham in July 1956.

13

THE LAND OF FAERY[1]

She is not any common Earth,
Water or wood or air,
But Merlin's Isle of Gramarye,
Where you and I will fare![2]

Fantastic forms, wither are ye fled? ...
Ye inexplicable half-understood appearances.[3]

Sussex Pharisees

Fairy poetry has been a central element in British writing since at least the sixteenth century and has continued to the present day. Certainly, in the time period under consideration here, and in Sussex, which is rich in folk narratives, the genre is worthy of study, although among literary circles it has become decidedly niche as an interest.[4]

Perhaps it comes hard on poets that we seem no longer able to people our world with nymphs and fauns, elves and witches, and other fantastic forms. As late as 1884, country people in Sussex reportedly still held to superstition, including their belief in the existence of 'pharisees' (fairies).[5] Moreover, families who had been in their home districts for two, three or more centuries, were imbued with legendary folklore, local customs and tradition, which were kept alive in churches, village inns and local festivals. Shepherds, who tended to follow the same family calling for generations, habitually passed down great stores of fantasy. Habberton Lulham, for example, learned from an old shepherd on the Downs near Amberley:

And he can tell how down the midnight coombe's
Green, winding hollows, still the little folk
Go dancing 'neath the moon, and round their rings
Sit in applauding circles while their queen,

Light-poised upon a mushroom's milky crest,
Lilts the old fairy laws and spells once more.
Then speeds their quivering wings upon her quests.[6]

Lulham's Amberley and Ditchling shepherds incorrigibly peopled their
world with nymphs and fauns, as did their forefathers, and thus it was that
he recreated in his poetry the land of faery as if time had been suspended
in downland. In 'On the Downs', fairies tell melodiously of their activities
on behalf of humans. The lovemaking scene of a young couple on the dark
Downs, at first mistaken for Pan and his Dryad in 'Love's Neophyte', and the
faery in several other poems reveal his fascination with downland folklore.
His poem 'Will there soon be Nine?' tells of a little girl 'straight from the
reeking slums' of London on an organised outing to Ditchling who left her
group, returning to the railway station to seek, at Lulham's suggestion, fairy
rings and elfin foxgloves in the evening light. But an angry voice 'from the
land of every day' summoned her to rejoin the homeward group and she
left without knowing whether the sky would soon show nine 'fairy stars
ashine'. But, 'Seek still for the rings of faëry,/ Count the stars your whole
life through.'[7]

Arthur Bell's 'Shepherd's Song' (1913) has a fairy maid at the feet of a
slumbering shepherd at Sullington:

She paused, and she gave me fairy bread,
A draught of fairy wine,
She clasped her lithe hands about my head
And pressed her lips on mine.[8]

Yet, with accelerating modernity, poets had stoutly to refute growing doubts
that fairyland existed. One such was Maurice Hewlett (1861–1923), in 'The
Open Country' (1909):

Who said Pan is dead? He is not dead, and will never die. Wherever there's
a noonday hush over the Weald, wherever there's mystery in the forest,
there is Pan. Every far-sighted unblinking old shepherd up here afield with
his dog [at Chanctonbury] knows all about him, though he'll never tell
you anything of what he knows.[9]

And Arthur Stanley Cooke, to whom the Land of Faery was an escape from
the anxiety of modern life, sang:

When first upon the green the fairies danced,
...
O wordlings, sick at heart, and dull of mind!
That ye might hear the singing –
See the fairies – hear the ringing –
The ringing of the harebells in the wind![10]

But it is Charles Dalmon, of all the Sussex poets, who most gave his heart to Faeryland. In the section 'The Sylvan Way' in *Flower and Leaf* (1900), his lyrics are awash with dryads, naiads, elves, satyrs, fays, goblins and wood nymphs, who spoke to him from every greenwood tree as he walked through the woods and orchards. And not only there. He found them where the 'yellow poppies bloom' and 'where pink salt-roses blossom along the Sussex shore'. They even pinched the nose, chin and ears of the dairymaid.[11] Such lyrics appear to have given Dalmon repose from his personal life of struggle and frustration:

... O Leave me, leave me, Sorrow!
O leave me, weeping Sorrow,
Leave me for evermore!
I hear the golden harpers
The olden faery harpers
Playing their dancing tunes
Singing their dancing tunes,
Behind the Secret Door.[12]

And Dalmon never doubted that the 'over wise' Sussex man of his day could be reintroduced to faery lore:

O, never say that Pan is dead
And every nymph and satyr fled,
Though, grown too wise, men seek no more
The presences of country lore,
Nor go on pilgrimage to find
The magic pipes Pan leaves behind![13]

Around Chanctonbury Ring, fairies were always present for Dalmon (Figure 34), although he also claimed that the 'sound of faery dancing could be heard along the Sussex shore'. It is in connection with them that he tells us how and when he became a poet. He writes of seeing a vision one summer evening when the Muse appeared to him, when from a barn, 'Black flitter-mice fly round her head, and mine/ As if they would discover who we are' and in 'breathless silence', he heard the inspiring tunes played on the lute for Fletcher, Otway, Collins, Shelley and Richard Realf, a Framfield poet who emigrated to the USA.[14] When the moon arose, the faery voice spoke of the times Dalmon had called to her at sunrise from Chanctonbury Ring, 'Out from the northern pastures of the Weald,/ Or southward from the slopes toward the sea', and that he would have her blessing to be a poet if he could show that he had a voice to tell what Barnes in Dorset had told so well. The Muse faded away as 'Up in the churchyard yews/ The parson's owls begin to hoot'.[15]

The Weald readily lent itself to faery: Kipling found it famously on Pook's Hill above the Dudwell in 1906; Eleanor Farjeon at Adversane in 1922; Graham Robertson at Ebernoe and Lurgashall, near Petworth in 1927; and in 1932, Edmund Blunden recalled it from his childish imagination at Christ's Hospital near Horsham. But it was on the Downs the 'little people' swarmed at dusk and sunrise. Belloc's *The Four Men* has them out on Barlavington Down on the eve of All Souls' Day and George Gissing discovered them on the Pevensey Levels at the end of the nineteenth century.[16]

But that was before the London Electrics came down from Victoria Station.

Fig. 34: Chanctonbury Ring, before the 1987 hurricane that decimated the tree cover. (E. Meynell, *Sussex*, 1947, facing p. 17)

Conjuring Fairyland in Music, Poetry and Prose

The composer John Ireland (1879–1962) also found his magic at Chancton-bury Ring. He first came to Sussex in the 1920s and found much inspiration from the downland. He retired to live nearby in a converted windmill at Washington from 1953. Earlier, while picnicking at Harrow Hill, he was considerably shaken at a vision of dancing children who had appeared from nowhere and were dancing silently around him. They were children not of this age, but of the 'remote past'. He confided this to only a few of his most intimate friends – 'it could be so easily misunderstood. ... people would not understand'. His friend Arnold Machen simply wrote on a postcard, 'So you've seen them too'. Ireland's 'Legend for Piano and Orchestra', finished in 1933, commemorated this incident.[17] He is buried at Shipley.

Alfred Noyes (1880–1958) was a poet steadfastly clinging to the traditions of Victorian literature. Strongly anti-modernist, he exhibited great interest in the Land of Faery, with dreamlike sequences and inspiration derived from long walks over the springy chalkland turf with its myriads of miniature wildflowers. In his volume of poetry, *The Forest of Wild Thyme* (1905), 'a tale for children under ninety', all the tiny flowers and insects are magni-fied, so when three small children searching for their brother Peterkin enter the wonderful Forest, the Wild Thyme is as towering as trees and ladybirds loom large as dragons. In 1908, he edited *The Magic Casement: An Anthology of Fairy Poetry*, with some 400 pages of fairy poems. And in an original and imaginative poem, he wrote, 'The Tramp Transfigured' in which a tramp, 'Bill the chicken-thief', who gives an old travelling woman pence he had earned by selling nosegays of cornflowers on Brighton sea front for her to get to Piddinghoe to meet her son, last heard of twenty years previously, is transfigured into a butterfly as blue as his cornflowers.[18]

The downland fantasies of Alfred Noyes reach their high point here:

All the way to Fairyland across the thyme and heather
Round a little bank of fern that rustled on the sky,
Me and stick and bundle, sir, we jogged along together, –
(Changeable the weather? Well, it ain't all pie)

Just about the sunset – Won't you listen to my story? –
Look at me! I'm only rags and tatters to your eye!
Sir, that blooming sunset crowned this battered hat with glory!
Me that was a crawling worm became a butterfly –

(Ain't it hot and dry?
Thank you, sir, thank you, sir!) a blooming butterfly.
—

All around me, gliding and gleaming,
Fair as a fallen sunset-sky,
Butterfly wings came drifting, dreaming,
Clouds of the little folk clustered nigh,
    Little white hands like pearls uplifted
    Cords of silk in shimmering skeins,
    Cast them about me and dreamily drifted,
Winding me round with their soft warm chains.

Faeryland often possessed secret places in heavily wooded districts with thick hedgerows, copses and ancient standing trees interspersed with glades and meadows. In the Weald, with the decline of agriculture from the 1870s, woodland and scrub had encroached onto fields in the manner imaginatively described for the North Downs around the Darent Valley by the Irish peer Lord Dunsany in his *The Blessing of Pan* (1927). Here birches slipped every year from the woodland edges to grow at first like fairy children that you barely saw unless you were looking for magic. After a few years, they would be standing where ploughshares had worked, and privet too spread quietly and unostentatiously. Then came more sturdy trees and, wherever a difficult slope appeared, the wild came back, joining bush to bush to form a dense thicket that was loved by the local fauna.

Graham Robertson (1866–1948), painter, illustrator, author and William Blake enthusiast, found such a magic place in the Weald and declared that London had begun to loose its hold upon him:

> … in the remote 'fold' country, whose villages, all ending in 'fold', were once clearings in the huge pre-Saxon forest of Andreadsweald, could be found old people who had seen the 'Pharisees': (the folk of Faerie) and had watched their moonlight dancing.[19]

He was inspired to write the Edwardian Christmas dream play for children, *Pinkie and the Fairies*, which opened at His Majesty's Theatre, London, in 1908 and included the famous actress Ellen Terry in the cast.[20] He also wrote other stories for children.

Walking in the Weald, he recalled:

> Yesterday afternoon Richard [the dog] and I really got as near faeryland as we are likely to do on this side of the moon. He and I and Mrs. Eastwood drove over to a place called Ebernoe – a place that doesn't really exist, as it consists only of one biggish house and two or three farms scattered over miles of wild country. There we got out and strayed over a golden common into a wood threaded with twisting alleyways and full of little glades which seemed each to specialise in one particular flower … like the jewel chamber of Maeterlinck's Adriane.

In April 1927, Robertson returned to Ebnernoe and his hidden valley, 'the secret store of the spring', and it was almost more wonderful that time:

> All was in a golden dream light and the surrounding woods were dark caverns of mystery … I have never seen the place openly confess its unreality. It is a glade in the Forest of Brocceliande, and anything might happen there.[21]

Robertson made an annual pilgrimage to Ebernoe from Sandhills on the Surrey–Sussex border at Witley, which he had rented in 1888 from poet William Allingham and his artist wife, Helen. William himself had written 'The Fairies' and 'The Maids of Elfinmere'. Here, Robertson purchased the local Sandhills Common and sixteen cottages, and hosted actress Ellen Terry. He also founded the Chiddingfold Players, writing *Old Chiddingfold: A Village Pageant-Play* in 1923.

At Sandhills, there was no electric light, running water, telephone or bathroom, nor was there to be talk of war to marr the nostalgic atmosphere. He also discovered the Low Weald around Lurgashall, but each visit to Ebernoe still left him feeling that he must have dreamt it (Plate 45). And picking up the theme, we should note that Robertson refers to Helen Allingham's paintings – in a few years they will be 'visions of a lost fairyland, a dream world fabulous and remote … few painters have ever penetrated so close to the soul of the English country'.[22]

Extinguishing Faeryland

But Sussex faeryland did not survive the Second World War. Did modernity destroy the pre-war poetry of the Sussex countryside? Or was its demise simply one of literary fashion? Within the literary circles of London, the fairy story genre was disregarded. It was marginal, being associated with child audiences and rejecting modernist writing. By its very nature, it also ran counter to ideas of scientific rationality and modern progress. Perhaps should we instead say that, in our hearts, Sussex was not really like the image they painted?

Poets were shaken by their wartime experiences – how to reconcile the gentle concept of 'faery', and indeed the pre-war pastoral idyll in general, with the actual horrors of the wartime battlefield? Edmund Blunden was struck by his time at the front in a landscape that reminded him of his own countryside, but which was 'amuck with murder' and laid waste.[23]

One element of modernity entailed the replacement of handmade and horse-ploughed landscapes almost overnight by a more mechanised and industrialised farming that, in the eyes of poets and writers, is a painful landscape, poverty-stricken in terms of beauty and nature. In the emergency plough-up campaign from 1940, the land girls gathered their corn harvest with Fordson tractors from the former sheep-nibbled turf at Falmer, on the Brighton Downs, helping to save a nation from starvation, but it was at the cost of some of our power to breathe imaginative life into our surroundings. Would that we could see Sussex's fantastic forms through the eyes of its early twentieth-century writers, as children can still do!

The Land of Faery had existed before the fairies were driven away by the trains, motor car and charabanc, symbols of mass tourism and modernity. There were also the profusions of hillside villas and the rows of bungalows. Faery in the erstwhile land of wonder also elude us in the present day, with unending noise and light pollution. And without the wonder, it is not easy to be a poet, for delighted wonder is the basis of all the arts.

And Blunden, survivor of the Great War, a doughty champion of an Arcadian pastoralism and heavily influenced by the Romantic poets, had sensed the loss of the elusive magic of Wealden countrysides while still a schoolboy at Christ's Hospital School, Horsham:

There is in much of Sussex a fairy wildness which may be perceived very readily as one travels into the county from the plantations and hop-gardens of Kent. The romantic secrecy, or truest green thought in a green shade, I know above all at Denne. If the improvements of society which we are enduring have spared that nook, it is a happy exception. It can scarcely be that the 'economic factor' has left those antlered oaks, those rushy pools, those deer in the bracken. Along the slopes, I first caught the meaning of the Sussex poet [Collins] who wrote of 'many a Nymph that wreathes her brows with sedge'. The avenue of limes with the grey sleepy face of the mansion at the far, the sacred, end, was like some half-real vision of eighteenth-century France. Beyond, and approached by circuits, there was a region of twilight thickets … It was to be expected that here the wood-gods would pop up suddenly from the foot of the year, or be caught cupping the water of some pebbly brook, while the maid from Denne went unsuspecting on to her mother's house among the twisted apple-trees. It was possible to imagine a grand loneliness in the country with its 'easy access' of London, when one was driving along the bridleways or footways under a white force of cold brown rain towards some world's-end to a place with a name not to be forgotten, Little Locketts![24]

Perhaps the last poem suggesting that elves could be met in the Sussex Weald was in Blunden's tribute to Andrew Young:

Looking on Sussex from afar I find
Much still that stood
In my grandparents' time, though much declined –
Weald still and wood
Yield to their proper travellers mysteries yet,
In shaws and delves
Behind rose-cottages are sometimes met
(They tell me) elves.[25]

Puck certainly entered into people's imaginations (Figure 35). One story of an encounter near a chalk pit at Steyning, recounted in *Sussex County Magazine*, demonstrated this:

There were four of us, and we were sitting in the warmth and stillness wishing with all our hearts that we could see a fairy. Absurd wasn't it? and yet – perhaps we believed very firmly, perhaps our imaginations played us tricks. But we all saw him – 'a little brown pointy-eared person' though he wasn't as big as Puck. He lay under the shadow of a gorse-bush, not ten feet away. His chin was propped on his hands, his legs were kicking behind him, and he was grinning from ear to ear under the shadow of a tall pointed greeny-brown cap. We stared open-eyed with wonder for quite a minute, then with one accord we crept slowly towards him. Of course he went – how, I don't know. He was there one minute, gone the next. […] we carefully searched that gorse-bush for a leaf, a stone, a twig, anything

Fig. 35: 'They saw a small brown ... pointy-eared person ... step quietly into the Ring'. (R. Kipling, *Puck of Pook's Hill*, p. 6)

that might have looked like an elusive, high-capped brown elf. There was literally nothing that could have resembled him in the least.[26]

However, the fairy story genre did idealise middle-class domesticity and drew on materials that would have been very well known to a wide spectrum of British culture. Fairytales were ubiquitous in poetry: Barry's *Peter Pan* or Kipling's *Puck* were popular among a receptive audience that were, it should be remembered, also in thrall to the spiritualism of Conan Doyle (at his home on the edge of Ashdown Forest), and the faked photographs of the 'Cottingley Fairies', supposedly caught on camera in 1917 and 1921. Writing of fantasy worlds for children, but appealing to adults, was a hugely popular undertaking. The anthropomorphised animals, friends of Winnie-the-Pooh, should also be remembered, being created for children by Conan Doyle's near neighbour, A.A. Milne, also living on the edge of Ashdown Forest (Plate 46).

Undoubtedly, the Sussex of the early twenty-first century has provided a less natural and congenial element in which countryside poets can live. However, as we have seen for the 1920s, this may not be the end of this story. In parts of the Weald, the wilderness is perceptively returning with the decline in farming. Little-used bridleways and footpaths are being encroached upon by bracken, nettles and other wild plants like comfrey and thickets are growing thicker, dells deeper in lush vegetation, trees again slipping out of woods on to bordering fields, which are increasingly deserted and dotted with thorns and thistles. The current 'rewilding' projects, such as that at the Knepp Estate in the Low Weald clays near Horsham, may not return fairy hiding places, but all this and more is currently happening. Lovers of imaginative literature may even hope that the naiads and hamadryads will soon return and be rediscovered in their old Sussex haunts.[27]

THE PLACE OF SUSSEX LITERATURE IN THE EARLY TWENTIETH CENTURY

We can never have enough of Nature [...]. We need to witness our own
limits transgressed, and some life pasturing freely where we never wander.[1]

William, you vary greatly in your verse;
Some's none too good, but all the rest is worse.[2]

Brimming with Delight

In literature, a most remarkable change came with the rejection of the
Romantic tradition in verse. Established by Wordsworth, Coleridge, Shelley
and Keats, and running through much of the nineteenth century, the rejec-
tion was emphasised by the appearance of disillusion and dereliction in
T.S. Eliot's 'The Waste Land' (1922) and the publication in 1930 of W.H.
Auden's first *Poems*.[3]

The verbal ingenuities and metrical innovations of this new literary mode
predominating in England in the interwar years were led by a young generation of avant-garde writers, often politically committed, almost exclusively,
to the Left. As well as Eliot and Auden, these included Ezra Pound, Edith
Sitwell, Wyndham Lewis, Christopher Isherwood, Louis McNeice, Stephen
Spender and Aldous Huxley. However, their ultra-modern rhythms,
language, subject matter and modes of expression were those of writers with
a consistent urban outlook. Thus, 'The Waste Land':

Unreal City,
Under the brown fog of a winter dawn,
A crowd flowed over London Bridge, so many,
I had not thought death had undone so many.
Sighs, short and infrequent, were exhaled,

And each man fixed his eyes before his feet.
Flowed up the hill and down King William Street,
To where Saint Mary Woolnoth kept the hours
With a dead sound on the final stroke of nine.[4]

By contrast, Sussex writers were traditionalists in metre and subject matter and were largely uninfluenced between 1850 and 1939 by these prevailing tendencies in English verse and writing. Indeed, most Sussex writers seemed hardly aware of them, and those who were certainly did not approve. With customary Sussex obstinacy, they stood quite apart, threw a wall around their own garden and cultivated it with English lyrics in a traditional pastoralism that owed much to Homer, Virgil, Shakespeare and Milton, as well as Wordsworth and Keats. Running through their early twentieth-century verse is the myth of a rural Arcadia that might still be dreamt, bathed in the calm light of Turner's 'The Vale of Heathfield' and agreeably 'merrie'.

A decade before the 'Waste Land', the first of Edward Marsh's extremely popular *Georgian Poetry* (1911–21), anthologies appeared, setting a fashion for bucolic poems celebrating subjects such as downs, birds and village cricket.[5] Sussex poets basked in these innocent sources of delight, essentially continuing a long tradition in Sussex verse, and the vast army of young, incoming poets tended to conform to the prevailing form of expression rather than become ambitious metropolitans.

Indeed, in late Victorian Sussex, it seemed almost as if every educated man and woman had written verse. This might remain unpublished but by the early 1900s it was being turned out by the wagon-load in lesser magazines and local newspapers. And then came the point, reached before 1914, when metropolitan eyes were regaled with a steadily rising flood of country verse coming even from the national press and high-brow journals. The poet William Arthur Dunkerley, pen name John Oxenham (1852–1941), who had moved from Ealing to live in Worthing by 1930, wrote consoling and healing verse, hymns and novels, that were much published during the bleak years of the Great War and were consumed avidly. Arthur Beckett's *Sussex County Magazine*, started in December 1926, contained large amounts of such poetry. Literary critics might find an occasional 'good' piece hidden away in all this, and pronounce with boredom the rest 'bad', wondering how such stuff could be tolerated.

For eschewing the London and Oxbridge literary establishment, the Sussex writers were severely slated for having either little good verse or none. Their literature was judged to have grown vapid, repetitive, within a narrow range of subjects and diluted with sentimentality. It was much mocked as stereotyped 'tweedy' raptures, and surely on its last legs and about to die. It gave the impression to critics that Sussex was inhabited by jolly farmers whose wives served sixpenny teas.

Robert Graves, an exiled Georgian, thought its later verse feeble and dull and Andrew Young, also formerly of the same label, mocked their facile and cheerful optimism and poked good-natured fun. Both evidently heeded W.H. Auden's warning that 'the danger of English landscape as a poetic ingredient is that its gentleness can tempt those who love it to write genteely'.[6] Furthermore, 'It had to be pleasant, dignified, moral not difficult or introspective, and based on the pretense that the rhythms of suburban life were still those of the old England of the feudal countryside.'[7]

A Sussex poet who was famed in his day and would doubtless not have objected to the label 'Georgian' was Gerald D. Martineau, a descendant from the same family as Harriet Martineau, the prison reformer and author. He was brought up at Fairlight Lodge, near Hastings, and much of his poetry relates to his childhood homeland and the Sussex Weald. As a young man, five volumes of his verse were published on outdoor life, much in Sussex, on cricket and other sports, as well as a history of the Royal Sussex Regiment. The Leavis school of criticism would probably have disregarded his poems, but they were much loved by Sussex people because he expressed with feeling and in a natural style what they themselves felt about Sussex. In a modest way, he fulfilled, in short, the true function of a poet. In the first edition of the new *Sussex County Magazine* there were five of his poems, with titles such as 'The Downland Freed', 'Daft Squire's Song' or 'A Sussex Man in Kent'.[8] Reprinted from *The Downsman*, we have a lament for unsightly development in 'Out! Out! A Sussex Tocsin':

> The world is fair in Sussex hills:
> The wind-lashed turf, the stark old mills,
> The dewpond on the verdant lea,
> The murmur of the distant sea,
> The Weald, the Marsh, the magic ring,
> And all that real poets sing.

But:

> What mean those markings, sharp and square
> Upon the Downs so broad and bare?

And who do notice-boards oppress
The hills that should be masterless.[9]

In such manner, he delivered what was needed at the time, but presumably literary critics were also mortified at the publication of two volumes of his verse on good-quality paper at the hand-press of the poet Victor Neuberg, whose tiny Vines Press works were adjacent to his cottage in Church Street, Steyning. Here, over seventy blocks were made by three brothers West, also of a local Steyning family. Arthur Beckett thought these volumes 'a credit to the county' for the way the skills of poet and painter, artist and craftsmen had combined to make so beautiful a production.

In the light of the public's response to such poets as Martineau, Victor Neuburg and Vera Arlett, the severe criticisms from literary critics to this particular form of literature evidently do not appear to be any guide to the reading habits of the public of the time. Always among the poetry-reading audience were those who preferred minor poems to major ones; lighter to more sophisticated ones; poems with more emotional intensity than thought; and of course, there was the Sussex man or woman who most wanted to read about Sussex. In fact, the more undemanding reading public preferred to read Sussex lyrics rather than discuss the new 'progressive' versifying they often found impenetrable. Instead, Sussex verse gave pleasure, and was read.

We can now also see that critics of the literary aspects of Sussex verse did not take into account the cultural circumstances in which it was written. We need to examine the historical context of the production of this literature, which also brings in relevant cultural issues. Indeed, F.R. Leavis wrote pertinently, 'The possible uses of literature to the historian and the sociologist are many in kind [...] On the other hand the understanding of literature stands to gain much from sociological interests and knowledge of social history.'[10]

Leavis claimed that the new mode of verse associated with Eliot and Auden was needed because the old literary forms had run their course. In discussing the purpose of present-day poetry, Peter Abbs has suggested that its primary task is to 'burn, blow and make us new. But also, at times, to perplex and unsettle us, to keep us unstable and open to change.'[11]

Abbs' preferred qualities in verse might find general acceptance in the context of the present time, yet there have been times and situations in the past when these suggestions would have seemed totally misplaced. During the international crises and galloping urbanisation of the interwar years, and with the manic pursuit of 'progress', a healing word or an expression of delight would have sowed consolation and other benefits on a demoralised and anxious populist urban readership. In helping such readers, the Sussex writers established a niche in English literature that has not been properly recognised.

There was also a more general and deeper cultural need. Stanley Baldwin famously and certainly realised the power of nostalgia for the sights and sounds of a peaceful and homely countryside that had taken hold on many in the 1920s:

> The sounds of England, the tinkle of the hammer on the anvil in the country smithy, the corncrake on a dewy morning, the sound of the scythe against the whetstone, and the sight of a plough team coming over the brow of a hill, the sight that has been England since England was a land.[12]

To many, such 'Georgian' themes were diverting. But very differently, and as a counterpoint, it might be noted that the idyllic past conveyed in Edmund Blunden's and Siegfried Sassoon's reminiscences of the First World War had the same appeal, but with English pastoral visions set alongside the indescribable horrors of industrialised killing.[13] In attacking the 'Georgians', literary critics also failed to consider the rich qualities of some of the Sussex verse.

Not all Sussex poets and writers were tarred with the same brush. Indeed, some of them also doubtless found 'feeble' writers more than trying at times. Major Sussex writers spoke, not to the intellect, as did ultra-modern writers, but to the heart and feelings. Instead of having compelling urges to demonstrate their intellectual dexterity, they imparted a love of countryside by seeing with their keener eyes, hearing with acute ears and feeling with a large heart the Sussex landscape they reverenced. To an urban readership that had ceased to use its own eyes this was of inestimable benefit.

In fact, the greater Sussex writers are not really classifiable at all. Hilaire Belloc's traditional metres and themes resulted from a mastery of classic forms. His serious verse is immensely varied in range and was slowly and repeatedly reworked to his own ultimate satisfaction and not simply dashed off. Speaight has argued that if Romanticism is defined as the escape from reality into dream and the blurring of form by feeling then Belloc is not a Romantic. And yet, if we understand Romanticism as a capacity for wonder and surprise, a refusal of sophistication and a reverence for the unspoilt feelings of the heart, then equally certainly he was.[14]

There were others whose relationship to landscape and nature was more complex. Andrew Young's later work looks for sights and happenings beyond the normal range of human experience, revealing contradictions, alert to the harsh ugly and cruel, and being far more than a 'nature poet', always seeing the 'macrocosm within the microcosm' and 'heaven in a grain of sand'.[15]

There is undoubtedly a greater variety of response to landscape in Sussex poets and writers than might be imagined from the literary criticism. William Harrison Ainsworth could suggest in his novel *Ovingdean Grange: A Tale of the South Downs* (1860) that the Downs soothed rather than excited and induced feelings of placid enjoyment, but others found the bald Downs ugly, even horrible, as in Blunden's and Orwell's experiences of the Downs during the First World War, or Edward Carpenter's account of monotonous, colourless and sad Brighton Downs in winter – although at least the Downs were an antidote to the horrid Brighton, where his family lived in Brunswick Square.[16] But there again, G.D. Martineau found consolation in a Sussex winter, while others, such as D.H. Lawrence and Richard Jefferies earlier, were sent into transcendental attitudes on the Downs.

And yet it must be admitted that there was a great deal of truth in the charge brought by literary critics of banality and dullness in Sussex verse. One cause can be readily identified. Quite simply there was an inadequacy among many of the incoming young poets before 1939. They encountered countryside that still retained abundant traces of its past and found themselves in a foreign country. The traditional culture around them was strange, torn from any country roots as they were, and they were unable to acquire the insight from years of dedication the naturalists put into their chosen patch.

Neither could they emulate the deep roots acquired by more 'native' writers such as Blunt, or as Belloc, Kipling and Halsham had learned over some thirty years of creativity. They tended to remain merely onlookers over the countryside they had discovered, and although writing as if every bush was a burning bush, fleeting experiences were not fully absorbed. The deep roots of the native writer were difficult for incomers to tap into and their past urban life served them badly in their new rural ventures.

The young incomer lacked the language of the fields, woods and people. As Thoreau remarked:

> [A] man's relation to Nature must come very near to a personal one; he must be conscious of a friendliness in her; when human friends fail or die, she must stand in the gap to him. I cannot conceive of any life which deserves the name, unless there is a certain tender relation to Nature [...] It is in vain to write of the seasons unless you have the seasons in you.[17]

Thoreau was, after all, a son of the earth, had paced it as a surveyor, and knew it as a naturalist before he loved it as a poet.

Building on a Heritage: English Neo-Romanticism

The bad press that Sussex verse received from early twentieth-century literary critics has left the impression that Sussex was a cultural backwater out of touch with contemporary developments in the arts. But an alternative cultural history can demonstrate how this is totally misleading. Although the Sussex pastoral tradition was generally moribund at the hands of run-of-the-mill poets, the major writers still preserved the values of an inheritance and this inspired a counter-culture in a resurgence of the related arts of landscape painting, music, architecture, landscape gardening and various crafts in the interwar years. Art, in its widest sense, had now caught up with literature and the two movements converged.

The foremost Sussex poets and writers in the interwar years should therefore be associated, closely or loosely, with creative artists such as John Piper, John Betjeman, Graham Sutherland and Eric Ravilious, who, in turn, engaged in a great national movement of self-discovery by looking at their own country. An outcome of this was the emergence of neo-Romanticism, which flourished in the English countryside alongside the modernism led by Roger Fry and refugees fleeing to Britain from fascist dictators. Alexandra Harris calls these homegrown artists who were determined to work in a particularly English brand of modernism, 'Romantic Moderns'. These Neo-Romantics shared the Sussex writers' love of locality, their desire to dig down roots into the country, their passion for tradition and, like them, found the forms derived from nature the most satisfying. Harris does not read this as a sign of retreat but 'as an expression of responsibility – towards places, people and histories too valuable and too vulnerable to go missing from art'.[18]

Sussex was indeed one of the major English arenas of Neo-Romantic modernism. For at least 200 years it has functioned as a kind of undeclared national park, furnishing an abundance of material and inspiration to the geologist, botanist, ecologist and geographer, the poet and writer, the artist, architect, landscape gardener and composer. Thereby, Sussex in the nineteenth century became one of the cradles of a neo-Georgian renaissance, flowering in the early twentieth century and gaining a permanent place in English culture.

The music of those who lived in Sussex, such as John Ireland (Washington) and Arnold Bax (Storrington), together with Vaughan Williams, is now performed again among a nostalgic reach for the 1930s. Avril Taylor-Coleridge's haunting tone poem 'Sussex Landscape' was composed in 1939 and has more recently received acclaim.[19]

Notable too was the English watercolour tradition followed by such painters as Albert Goodwin, Arthur Rackham, Graham Sutherland, John Piper with his collages, and the quintessential English artist Eric Ravilious. The latter's landscapes from Peggy Angus' cottage near Firle are splendid examples of such a movement, as also are the paintings of Vanessa Bell and Duncan Grant at Charleston Farmhouse, and Stanley Badmin's miniature observations at Bignor of archaic barns and tumbling cottages he could see from his Sussex garden. These and many other artists are enjoying a wide-spread revival of interest at the present time.[20]

The interconnections between the various visual and other arts were conveyed by Lewis Lusk in his novel *Sussex Oak* (1912). Moved by the beauty of a Sussex ghyll below the Forest Ridge near Crowborough, a musician recalls Meredith's poem, 'The Woods of Westermain', then noble passages of Beethoven, and finally echoes of Mendelsson's 'Forester's Farewell' over the landscape.[21] The integration of the arts was intriguing, although a brief review in *The Atheneum* noted the novel as 'over-long and ill-constructed' with a 'neurotic family [...] unconvincing and disagreeable'.[22]

Nevertheless, overall, the Sussex contribution to English literature, both in a literary and cultural sense, was a greater source of happiness and comfort than over-intellectualised works aimed mainly at fellow professionals, 'Poets arguing about modern poetry: jackals snarling over a dried-up well', as Cyril Connolly termed it.[23] Scorned as commonplace, some lesser Sussex literature may have been mediocre, but it had the unusual gift of being able to communicate countryside interests and enthusiasms to the 'ordinary' reader. This poetry and 'country writing' was loved and collected and is still being read, for its quiet voices are timeless in their appeal. Richard Church, in discussing the poetry of Andrew Young, thought that people would go on enjoying what was written outside literary circles 'like apples from an old tree, the age of the tree increasing what might be called the vintage-flavour of the fruit'. And this has actually happened.[24]

Anti-Modernism

Arguably, there is yet another matter that is overlooked by literary critics condemning Sussex verse and prose. A distinctive characteristic of Sussex literature for more than 200 years has been the explicit or implied antipathy to the city, to the emergent capitalist industrial system and all the economically driven life it stood for, coupled with a vigorous defence of rural values. Its particular concern was the progressive severance of man from nature.

Urban malediction first appears in Hurdis' *The Village Curate* (1788). He compares the beauty of the Burwash hop gardens with the 'people pent up in city stench, and smoke and filth', implying that urban living diminished the intensity of one's life, whereas a life spent among nature increased it. An aversion to city life is also strong in Charlotte Smith's verse of the same period. She preferred the unsullied country around her native Bignor Park to 'polluted, smoky atmosphere and dark and stuffy streets', yearning for the western downland, 'unspoil'd by man' and an escape from oppression, injustice and folly. These grievances culminated in political denunciation in some of the most diehard language in English literature.

In seeking radical new ways of life during the later nineteenth century, many were resolutely opposed to the modernism involving an industrial technological society that, by the growth of towns, had fuelled a disconnection with nature. The most explicit utopian alternative was that of visionary Richard Jefferies, to whom happiness was the essence of country living but who sought equality and fundamental changes in human life and society as the real solution for the future contentment of the human race. He thought it extraordinary that after a civilisation of 'twelve thousand written years', the world did not enjoy freedom from useless labour and still lived from hand to mouth in obtaining mere subsistence. He thought the vilest crime in British society was the two thirds of the nation who lived with the threat of the poor house. His aim was to do something that would render future generations happier, envisaging future scientific discoveries that would eliminate much human labour and set men free in idleness that he thought a great good. Jefferies' strongest supporter in more recent times was Henry Williamson, who hoped that Jefferies would be brought to the many minds who needed to know his way of life.

Jefferies' *After London, Or, Wild England* (1885) is a most original book on the decline of English civilisation.[25] Praised by William Morris, it depicts a post-apocalyptic, ruined London stagnating in barbarism and with a dispeopled southern England that has become a world of lake and forest. It is a bitter book, sombrely depicting the ruins of a defunct civilisation and written with Jefferies' conviction that civilisation was doomed to destruction.

His experience of the Sussex Weald had a strong influence on the book. He tells us in his autobiography that he had visited Pevensey Castle in 1880 and he refers to the Roman eagle.[26] It is hardly a coincidence that the central figure in his story, Felix Aquila, bears a form of this name, also held by the medieval holders of Pevensey Rape. Moreover, there was probably no place better than Crowborough, where he was writing his book, for witnessing trees and scrub invading former cultivated fields, the process of natural succession overtaking civilisation, which he so graphically describes. The closing – with a lake athwart southern England from the Severn to the Thames – is thought to have been inspired from his childhood at the margin of a lake at his native home near Swindon. It is conceivable, however, that it is based on the vast delta that Gideon Mantell had described in *The Geology of the South East of England* (1833) and which by Jefferies' time, had entered into a well-read person's consciousness.

Another author reacting against commercial civilisation, as portrayed in Brighton, was the socialist, anarchist and bohemian Edward Carpenter, who reported his 'savage glee as I sought to tear the whole sickly web to pieces', despairing of the 'idiotic life of the place' when writing *Desirable Mansions* (1883).[27] He maintained the optimistic view that:

> Possibly some day we shall again build our houses or dwelling places so simple and elemental in character that they will fit in the nooks of the hills or along the banks of the streams or by the edges of the woods without disturbing the harmony of the landscape or the songs of the birds.[28]

And, as we have seen, a similar aversion to modernisation – indeed, to any external influences – sustained much of the Wealden poetry and prose of Wilfrid Scawen Blunt. His attempts at political and humanitarian reform and battles against deprivation and injustice were also global in scale. It would seem that always at the back of his mind was the age-old harmony he discerned in his homeland in the Sussex Weald, which ever remained in his thoughts as an exemplar of a landscape and society free of the world's ills. Thinking, like Carpenter, that Brighton was 'an excrescence of West End London', he asked himself, in his Sussex home, 'Why was I born in this degenerate age?'[29]

Moving into the twentieth century, a similar antagonism to urban influences culminated in Hilaire Belloc's ferocious attack on privilege and corruption in his penetrating *The Servile State* (1912).[30] A student of Sussex dialect, he always wrote naggingly as if every new, incoming resident to Haywards Heath and anyone who mispronounced the name of the country town of Hors-ham as Horsham or Sea-ford as Seaford was another nail in the coffin of Sussex's identity. The drift of the indigenous population to cities and their replacement by urbanised newcomers were processes changing Sussex landscapes, ways of life, speech and attitudes more than any other southern county apart from Surrey. Many believed that the polyglot Sussex people were psychologically becoming almost as cockney as Londoners themselves. John Halsham believed that 'London has brimmed over ... We are all Londoners now in our cradles, from Bow Bells to Berwick'.[31]

Broadly speaking, the county's poets and writers of the interwar years appear to have agreed with T.S. Eliot that for a long time, society had believed in nothing but the values arising from the machine, driven by wealth creation and material self-interest. In the insecurity of the time, they began to consider the disconnection with nature, what had gone wrong with the way people lived, what were the permanent things that made life worthwhile and how any reform could go forward.

The economist John Maynard Keynes, whose outburst against the Versailles Treaty and other works were concerned with the diseases of modern capitalism and remedies for them, worked at Charleston Farmhouse and his later home at nearby Tilton House. He raised the questions: if growth is a means to an end, what is the end? How much growth is 'enough', and what other valuable human purposes may be pre-empted by a single-minded concentration on economic growth?

In the interwar years, many Sussex writers were also prominently engaged in their defence of the county against the intrusion of 'Londonisation', which, in changing speech, habits and attitudes to life was altering it even faster than bricks and mortar. Fresh from the Front, Ford Madox Ford was vitriolic about London, which he thought had little sense of the values of life. He had long felt London to be soulless, although its immensity made it impossible to grasp its essential qualities. Chesterton thought the capital's future was bound up with returning London to a collection of medieval townships, wrapping this in with his critique of modernity and imperialism.[32]

Changes were coming fast: it seemed that from the end of the nineteenth century, Sussex was being remade by tourism and leisure with roadhouses and petrol filling stations, advertising hoardings and invitations to take tea. Stark rows of naked houses and bungalows, shiny and new, studded much

Fig. 36: The early beginnings of Peacehaven. (University of Sussex: Rendel Williams Collection)

of the Channel coast and ribbon development ate up the countryside. And in the process, a deadening uniformity was threatening the identity of the county as a distinctive place.

Those who hated towns, modern civilisation and all they stood for considered this a wrong too great to be left untold. Some led a campaign for the physical rescue of the past and its landscape from the destruction of progressive modernity. Halsham was so distressed at the steady and irrevocable housing development of the mid-Sussex district around Haywards Heath that in 1898 he was the first to propose a form of national park status for the district to arrest the creeping urbanisation. His favourite view from the Forest Ridge extended across fold after wooded fold to the blue line of the Downs.

One of the angriest of writers on the subject was C.E.M. Joad, who wrote that London had burst like a bomb and scattered its debris far and wide over southern England. Clough Williams-Ellis confessed his love of the elegant Brighton Regency stucco but was distressed at its replacement by 'rubbishy romanticism or halfwitted, half-timber or any other pretentious shame or heavy-handed stupidity'. He considered Brighton 'a dropsical old slattern' and difficult to love, 'still less her little dogs – those obscene mongrels called Peacehaven, Saltdean, Shoreham and Portslade. Sussex is to be left free to maul itself to death'.[33]

Virginia and Leonard Woolf rattled their sabres in an extraordinary diatribe against 'the blasphemy of Peacehaven' and its residents (Figure 36). Virginia thought that nothing more 'cheap and greedy and meretricious' could have been placed against such a lovely background of nature, compared with which Wembley was beautiful and the Mile End Road respectable. She yearned for some really statesmanlike mind to take stock of all that human activity and 'direct and weld it together'. Leonard Woolf confessed that he preferred the civilisation of the sheep and 'the simplest of shepherds' to Peacehaven:

> Would it much affect us, we ask ourselves, if a sea monster erected his horrid head off the coast of Sussex and licked up the entire population of Peacehaven and then sank to the bottom of the sea? [It] lies like a sore, expressed in gimcrack red houses and raw roads ... we did not know we had such evil in us ... Human beings bask inside them, dipping alternately into paper bags for peppermints and into newspapers for comic cuts, while the sea and the downs perform for them the same function that the band performs when they eat ices at Lyon's.[34]

Modernity or Post-Modernity in the Post-Industrial Age?

In the interwar years, the campaign against the fundamental disconnection with nature was kept alive by Sussex writers who advocated more enduring values beneficial to well-being than those held generally. Their central message was that an urban population needs accessible quiet and open spaces for self-fulfilment of life, and that when, through disconnecting people and nature, there is no longer a countryside there would be no city worth living in either.

Their attempt to demonstrate this through their own assorted escapes into the countryside proved unrealistic, but the basic truth it embodied is still as valid today. Criticism of the worship of economic growth for its own sake is now seen in the twenty-first century as an acceptable view, as is the current discussion of ways to achieve a more harmonious lifestyle in keeping with the sustainability of the planet. The destruction of nature in the interests of international capitalist commerce has recently come to the fore in very many ways. Environmental resilience is sought, together with the need to move towards a low-carbon existence. This will entail changes in human behaviour and a balance being maintained between economic growth and nature's wellbeing.[35]

The concerns of Sussex writers on these matters in the years before the Second World War can now be seen as anticipating issues that have since become of universal significance with technology's ravaging of the earth's finite resources. They temporarily died away during the immediate post-war years of austerity and man's painful spiritual recovery but were resurrected from the 1970s with growing anxiety at unregulated economic and financial markets, terrorism, social inequality, the unsustainability of resource depletion and environmental well-being generally, which has been accompanied by a surge of interest in what constitutes human happiness, rural self-sufficiency and simple-lifery. Yesterday's wrongs are still being fought.

But these viewpoints of the interwar years that gnawed at Sussex writers should be regarded as among the earliest major begetters of English environmentalism. Their views have now found a greater acceptability and should be considered, because they clearly have a relevance for the present-day conservationist living in what is becoming a post-industrial age.

Sussex pastoralism can, therefore, be regarded in two distinctly different ways: from a purely literary perspective, it is a late manifestation of English literature, criticised by contemporaries as one of deliberate and cowardly escape. Yet, the wheel has turned, and the writers' visual and moral engagement with their landscape in the 1930s is now important once again. We neglect at our peril the concerns they raised and the reasons they gave for their resolve not to live in the contemporary world of 'progress', money-making and worldly success. They did not find the right answers, but they asked the right questions.

In recent years there has been a great surge of interest in the relations between literature and nature. We have eco-criticism and eco-poetics, for example, the latter advocated by Jonathan Bate, who has stated in his study of Romanticism that poetry continues to matter: indeed, his concluding sentence runs, 'Poetry is the place where we save the earth.' Poetry dissolves the boundaries between the human mind and nature and concentrates on the literature of regions, locales and ecosystems, even the interweaving of deep geological time and the lived-in present. If this is acted upon, we can judge that the Sussex writer did not write in vain.[36]

It is perhaps even conceivable that future inhabitants of Sussex will have a lifestyle somewhat like that envisaged by R.S. Thomas:

The dinosaurs have gone their way
into the dark. The time-span

of their human counterparts
is shortened; everything
on this shrinking planet favours the survival
of the small people, whose horizons
are large only because they are content to look at them
from their own hills.[37]

All who are anxious to avoid a lessening of the values of life for us, now and
for generations to come, in one of the loveliest and lovable lands in England,
should heed this verse.

FINAL THOUGHTS: LITERATURE, PLACE AND ENVIRONMENT AND THE ROAD NOT TAKEN

Brian Short

Two roads diverged in a wood, and I –
I took the one less traveled by,
And that has made all the difference.[1]

The interweaving of the work, thoughts and lives of writers with their Sussex surroundings has never been attempted in this detail and on this scale before. The text above surely demonstrates how Peter Brandon's profound knowledge of the Sussex rural landscape is transmitted not only in his own words, but in those of the writers to whom he has turned. They perceived a 'brute reality' in the countrysides around them but reacted differently according to so many different factors within their own lives. This book focuses on the point where an independent reality meets creative construction.

The Choices Made

Robert Frost's well-known poem 'The Road Not Taken' reminds us that there are choices we make in our lives, sometimes with clarity of purpose, sometimes not. Peter Brandon's subjective choices within the cultural formation that was literary ruralism are shown in this book: which authors and poets to include or exclude; the beginning and ending years of his survey; the spatial concentration emphasising some parts of Sussex but not others; upon which aspects of the writers' lives to concentrate, and so on. The psychological, emotional and indeed spiritual relationships between the writers and their environments form the essence of this book. But no one sees the whole picture, no one hears the whole story. In what follows, we can explore some of these elements, certainly not to detract from the foregoing text, but to contextualise it.

Enough has been written in the chapters above to explain why Sussex was so favoured and why it is the subject of this book. Yes, there were artists' groups in the Cotswolds, Suffolk coast and Cornwall, as well as the more plebeian interwar plotlands, for example, in the middle Thames, Essex and along the North Downs in Kent and Surrey.[2] But from 1850 to 1939, Sussex seemed to be a veritable magnet for artists of all types. As such, it became a constituent part of that over-concentration on the 'South Country' that was held to be emblematic of 'Englishness' and which has latterly been subjected to a more intense academic scrutiny.[3] Much has been written on this, and Sussex was easy prey for what R.G. Collingwood called 'sentimental topography: books about the charm of Sussex ... [intended] to call fools into a circle'. But the concept is worthy of further dissection, since few of the more recent writers have attempted such a depth of treatment as Peter Brandon has afforded here.[4]

So, to begin, who exactly was to be chosen for inclusion in this book? As well as highlighting those who he deemed to be forerunners of Sussex writers prior to around 1850, such as James Hurdis or Charlotte Smith, he devotes whole chapters to others, mostly well-enough known, such as Jefferies, Belloc and the canonical Kipling and Woolf. Blunt was perhaps less so, but the name of Habberton Lulham comes as something of a surprise, as must some of his twentieth-century writers and poets. One issue, of course, despite his disavowal, is that most of the writers he includes were from an articulate, avantgarde sector of society and writing for an elite 'high brow' audience. Most, but not all, by any means, for the writings of Kipling and Belloc, for example, were avidly consumed by all and even incorporated into modern culture. Kipling's *Sussex* (1902) with its last stanza 'Sussex by the Sea', is familiar via a later 1907 song to supporters of Brighton and Hove Albion.

One obvious issue here is how to define a Sussex writer. Is such a person necessarily engaged in writing about Sussex? Or living in Sussex but not necessarily writing much about the county? Or more strictly, both living in Sussex and writing about it? Peter Brandon has taken the stricter last definition, or at least allowing that such an inclusion was on the basis of having lived in Sussex for an appreciable majority of their lives.

This has, for example, excluded Arthur Conan Doyle, living in Crowborough from 1907 to his death in 1930, but writing little about the county or its environment. The same could be said for John Galsworthy, living and dying at the imposing Bury House, north of Arundel. Tom Paine lived in Lewes only from 1768 to 1774, when he left for America. But John Cowper Powys is omitted, although he first came to Sussex in 1893, initially to Southwick, and the connection with his family only ended when his wife sold their house in Burpham in 1928. His novel *After My Fashion* and his *Autobiography* are well endowed with Sussex detail, much drawn from the area between Chichester and Arundel.[5]

Similarly, there is no Tennyson, except for a brief mention of him at Blackdown from 1868. A.A. Milne features only marginally. He was an expatriate Londoner, and this chimes with one of the key themes of the book. There is no Horace Smith, who wrote romantically of Brambletye House and Brighton – 'Farewell old Ocean's bauble, glittering Brighton'. Or Ezra Pound, who had many connections with Sussex, with Stone Cottage abutting Ashdown Forest, Penns-in-the-Rocks at Withyham, or Steyning, but his writing was certainly not to be included within the group of Sussex nature writers.

So, choices were made, indeed had to be made about who to include. What about the time span chosen? In the post-enlightenment period of literature, the Romantics brought a hugely influential discernment to the experiences of people and nature. Here is a clue to the approximate starting point adopted within this book, as the writings of Wordsworth, Byron and Coleridge, together with Keats and Shelley (whose early years were spent at Warnham), had become so well known by about 1850. So, the starting date stands but here was one theme – a continuation of Romanticism's concern with environmental perceptions and the beauty, or sublimity, of one's surroundings. Here was the fertile soil into which Sussex writers could drill.

Of course, the tenets of Romanticism have been assiduously criticised, not least by those who deplore the elision of myriad human rural working lives into the later archetypal 'folk' forms of Edward Thomas's 'Lob' of Pewsey Vale or Kipling's 'Hobden' of the Weald. Instead, they would attempt to understand the social and economic complexities of country living as, for example, in the writing of Raymond Williams. Landscapes incorporate the social relations that have gone into their making, but they can also mask those relations behind a seemingly unchanging and benign view. And what we see is what we bring to it ourselves, with our own cultural backgrounds. The landscapes described by the writers in this book were forged from a politics of seeing, since nature outside of human experience is inarticulate.

More broadly, one allied intervention usefully advocated by Martin Ryle was to see an approach comprising three distinct levels: at the base there is material nature, then come cultural discourses and interventions, and finally the social relations that partly determine these cultural forms. Looked at in this way, we can see that Peter Brandon was certainly interested in the first two of these and less so in the third.[6]

More prosaically, there were other themes developing. By 1850, the rail network was beginning to infiltrate the Sussex countryside, allowing an unparalleled ease of access between London and the coast and placing Sussex firmly 'in the shadow of the metropolis'. London had become a booming global mega-city and by 1900, 80 per cent of the British population lived in urban areas. Furthermore, by the 1870s, the beginnings of an agricultural depression had threatened farm livelihoods, which would imbue much of Sussex's countryside with a more unkempt atmosphere but also make available more cottages as many working families turned their backs on their villages and moved to the jobs that might present themselves in the growing towns on the coast.

Small farms might also become available that might be transformed into *fermes orneés*. This trend was seen by some as a problem for Sussex farming. Kipling, disturbed at the dereliction he saw about him in the Weald, sought to bring back the small farmers who had left for towns and lavished scorn on motorised trippers invading the Downs, yet ironically, by his own verse and motoring stories, he was attracting them. Ernest Raymond's denunciation of the advance of the machine, as we have seen, took the form of an actual new road-making monster around Haywards Heath, 'a slayer who leaves a ribbon of destruction in its wake'.[7] A report to Parliament following the end of the Great War agreed:

> For agricultural purposes Sussex is, or has been, too much in possession of rich people who do not depend on the cultivation of the land for their livelihood. This tendency has, of late years, been increased by a fashion with a group of literary men who have come to live in Sussex, of extolling this county in verse and prose, thus attracting other invaders ... the fact remains that we are too near London.[8]

In the later years of the First World War, the Sussex countryside had taken on a brief air of productivity as the nation sought food from its own soil. But from about 1920, the grim cycle of depression began again and continued, more or less, through to 1939, although hitting some agricultural sectors harder than others. Much of the rural landscape again reverted to a more overgrown and thus wildly romantic but still accessible air. Nothing here to match the picturesque landscapes beloved of the Romantics, of course, but as writers, poets and painters moved in, by a process of cumulative causation, so did others follow. Peter Mandler has it that:

> The country[side] acquired a talismanic significance as everything that contemporary, urban England was not but yet might be. Of course this polar opposition required a sleight of hand, as the real countryside of the present – depopulated, plantation-like, increasingly subject to speculative development – was not suited to a rural idyll.[9]

Sussex was Never a Wessex

The fact that the intimate connection between the metropolis and the Sussex countryside developed very strongly at this time may have been a factor in ensuring that no writer could satisfactorily develop and sustain a local world, a region within which to unfold timeless characters, cultures and themes. Mrs Henry [Alice] Dudeney, the prolific Lewes novelist, was invited to address the Hastings Literary Society in November 1924 as 'leader of the Sussex movement in novel writing', with Rider Haggard in the chair. But despite her wide circle of friends, some influential, she was an isolated writer with few other like-minded Sussex authors.[10]

Edward Thomas might embrace the 'South Country' more broadly and Sheila Kaye-Smith's work did attempt this for the far stretches of the eastern Weald and marshland edges, but in Sussex more generally, there was no part-real/part-fiction 'Hardy's Wessex', no 'Wordsworthshire' or 'Brontë Country', no single dominating authorial figure or any specific regional culture to draw upon. Instead, it was already London's countryside. This lack is all the more striking when one realises that the period 1850–1939 is generally considered as the veritable heyday of the regional novel and a time when literary tourism was fast developing as people flocked to see for themselves the countrysides about which they had been reading.

Of course, this Sussex countryside remained a hardworking reality for many poor villagers but equally now became a literary and artistic creation – a representation of reality seen through the cultural power of artists' eyes and pens. 'What constitutes a life of toil for the field-worker is culturally transformed into a site of leisure for more privileged groups.' The awful destabilising jolt of war only served to heighten the perception of a countryside that was now to be fought for and brought out in the writings of Wilfred Owen or Siegfried Sassoon, draped emblematically with jingoism and seen nostalgically from Flanders. And it was in aid of the Sussex County Prisoners of War Fund that Lady Violet Leconfield arranged a fete in Petworth Park on 5 August 1918 and assembled previously written poetry from the major poets, including Kipling, Blunt, Belloc, Alice Meynell and one written in July 1918 from E.V. Lucas, for her 'Petworth Posie' ('price, one florin net').

The time span covered by Peter Brandon in this volume is difficult to defend in absolute terms of literary development. He posits instead something of a 'bubble' into which writers and poets might fall and work their magic against their surrounding environment. This took precedence over the literary canon. Thus, we have the representational nature writing of Richard Jefferies, but this realism then also includes the more mystically informed writing of Belloc or Kipling's later work, until giving way to the literary modernism of Virginia Woolf with interior monologue and introspection. Much of this was self-referential and elitist, a reaction to the realism inherent in the nineteenth-century novel, for example. But the same could be said for much other poetry, such as that of the Georgian poets.

The emphasis of modernist writers on reactions to the city, industry, technology, mass communication, internationalism and alienation from the 'masses' with their penchant for tinned food, was precisely the kind of project against which Sussex writers were recoiling, looking instead to reveal rural truths, traditions and landscape aesthetics.[11] In this, the closer analogy was the writing of Thomas Hardy, who himself railed, through the medium of Angel Clare, against 'feelings which might almost have been called those of the age – the ache of Modernism' as a rootless industrial strength threatened rural traditions.[12]

But whatever might be the genre, Romanticism, Nature Realism or modernism, all wrote with depth and insight about their Sussex surroundings, although doing so in ways that became increasingly different as the twentieth century moved along. For F.R. Leavis, it was clear by 1933 that mass culture was killing the older rural way of life by its machine-age leisure, hence the subtitle, 'Self-fulfilment in the Age of the Machine' of this present book.[13] So, 1939 was Peter Brandon's chosen ending, but by then the Sussex 'bubble' had run its course. For H.E. Bates, the war was a decisive ending for the rural novel as a literary form, 'portions of a world that has vanished as surely as the world of my boyhood street games has vanished'.[14] Although immediately following the war there was initially another resurgence in nature writing and a neo-Romantic search for nostalgic and peaceful publications, this was a quite different genre, not to be confused in any way with the pre-war writings, and it was soon swamped by rightful concerns for social issues of class, post-colonialism and gender.

The Varieties of Sussex

This, then, was the background to the development of the writers' Sussex. But Sussex is a county greatly elongated east–west and with a highly variable environment, so what parts of the county were favoured, and what neglected? Here, Peter Brandon was, to a large degree, needing to follow the writers themselves – where did they live, and why there? Of course, there are a multitude of contingent reasons leading to a choice of a home: a birthplace, family association, the serendipity of finding a house for sale or at an affordable rent, searching for a healthy spot, an accessible location, and so on.

But when all these are taken into account, there was a clear spatial pattern to the Sussex writers. A crude textual analysis of this book reveals that there are twice as many mentions of Downs/downland/chalk as of Weald/wealden/sandstone or sea/coast/beach. Apart from London, the town most mentioned is Chichester; the writer most mentioned is Hilaire Belloc.

Overall, the pattern can best be described as a generalised inverted T-shape (see Figure 3, page 21), with a great concentration in and around the coastal towns and South Downs, from Chichester in the west to Hastings in the east, together with a lesser north–south axis following the coaching routes, roads and railways from Horsham, through Haywards Heath to Lewes and Brighton. Predominently, writers were attracted to write about the downland, the scarpfoot zone and the seashore. Far fewer found attraction in the Weald to either side of that Horsham–Brighton axis. Of course, there were notable exceptions: Kipling found inspiration from his surroundings at Burwash, as did A.A. Milne on the fringes of Ashdown Forest, or Belloc at Shipley. But generally the far eastern and western edges of Sussex attracted fewer such people.

One exception lay to the east of Hastings, where Rye greatly appealed. Here was to be found Henry James, regarded as a key transitional figure between literary realism and modernism. E.F. Benson took over Lamb House after James and many were seduced by the old town's history, mild climate and proximity to the strange landscape of Romney Marsh. James, together with Joseph Conrad, Stephen Crane and W.H. Hudson, savoured the joys of Rye and nearby Winchelsea. Indeed, it is said, 'The marsh flowed with manuscripts, at the turn of the century, and as one flood ceased another gushed forth a few years later,' now from the brothers E.F. and A.C. Benson, together with the American Conrad Aiken in Mermaid Street.[15] Henry James, in a letter to his sister-in-law, had written of Rye:

> But the great charm is the simply being here, and in particular the beginning of day no longer with the London blackness and foulness, the curtain of fog and smoke that one has each morning muscularly to lift and fasten back, but with the pleasant, sunny garden outlook, the grass all haunted with starlings and chaffinches ... This indeed – with work, and a few, a very few people – is the *all*.[16]

Radclyffe Hall (1880–1943) certainly saw Rye as an escape from the world of London. Recovering from the controversies surrounding her novel *The Well of Loneliness* (1928), she lived with Lady Una Troubridge in a cottage off Church Square, with wonderful views towards Romney Marsh, before moving to other properties in the town. Her later novel *The Sixth Beatitude* (1936) was set in Rye (called Rother), and she continued to find solace and some friendship until 1940 when the couple moved to the West Country.[17]

At the far western extremity of Sussex a similar story was to be had. Here was H.G. Wells at Uppark and Midhurst, 'three hours sturdy walking' apart, with the former, where his mother was a housekeeper, appearing as 'Bladesover House' in his *Tono-Bungay* (1909) and repositioned on the Kentish Downs, and Midhurst disguised as 'Wimblehurst'. The latter was an 'exceptionally quiet and gray Sussex town, rare among south of England towns in being largely built of stone ... agreeable and picturesque'.[18] This was, in fact, the ochre and brown Hythe and Bargate sandstones of the Lower Greensand group. There are also more fleeting associations: Charlotte Smith was briefly at Woolbeding and John Keats was at Chichester and attended the consecration of the chapel at Stansted in 1819, where the windows found their way into his 'Eve of St Agnes' and 'Eve of St Mark' (both 1819) – this right against the Hampshire border.

Cancellation: Reading the Work, Endorsing the Character?

Finally, we might notice one further element in Peter Brandon's text, and indeed, in much else of his writing. His concern was to unravel the importance of the writers' interpretations of their surroundings and the role that those surroundings played in their lives. In so doing, he was not attempting to set out miniature biographies, and their personal lives feature little, if at all, except to give context and in strict relevance to the influence of their surroundings.

So, how should we deal with the recurring problem that subsequent revelations show that some of the writers included in this book were flawed, and would not necessarily be seen in such a good light in the twenty-first century? And does this matter?

These were writers of their own generation and times, not ours, but their texts remain today and are open to posthumous criticism of their attitudes and values. Whether this is 'fair', to wrench a writer from their own contemporary social and cultural norms, is now hotly debated. Rudyard Kipling is a good example. In a long and successful writing career, which brought him popular and critical success, he nevertheless found himself campaigning for the British Empire as a kind of unofficial spokesman but increasingly at odds with social and political opinion. David Cody has written:

> The White Man's Burden was, so far as (culturally patronising) Imperialists of Kipling's stripe were concerned, a genuine burden – Kipling viewed his Imperialism, predicated on deeply-held political, racial, moral, and religious beliefs which sustained a feeling of innate British superiority, as being primarily a moral responsibility: it might also be profitable … but it had itself to be maintained, defended, and protected – from rival world powers and from the rebellious governed, although ideally these last would recognize their inferiority and freely obey their superiors.[19]

But should these aspects of Kipling's ideology matter to our present purposes? He was probably not the most blatant of imperialists during his lifetime and so did such thoughts impact on his feelings for, and writings about, the deep time of his Sussex surroundings? Perhaps only, as we have seen, in that, for him, Sussex emerges through history as possessing a 'supercharged national identity', which tips over into jingoism. His 'casual antisemitism' has also been remarked upon, and in this he is also joined by Hilaire Belloc. Anathema to most right-minded people today, it was far more common among the literati of the early twentieth century.

Belloc's views were strongly influenced by his friendship with Cecil Chesterton, such that his hostility was 'mirrored, distorted and magnified to an almost grotesque degree'.[20] The complexities of Belloc's character were explored earlier in this book and have fascinated many, but the extent to which his darker views permeated his writings on Sussex have yet to be revealed, if indeed they existed at all.

So, does a lively and relevant modern stance help us here? Reflections of the social attitudes of their time are more available for some authors and poets than for others. Morality evolves. Attitudes have changed markedly, especially since the Second World War, and each generation reads or views art mostly in the light of current perspectives.

Should our appreciation of these writers, or indeed the very questionable Eric Gill, be more nuanced? Should we stop reading the authors? If so, where would the moral line be drawn? Charles Dalmon joined the British Union of Fascists, Andrew Young was patriarchal and overbearing, Virginia Woolf's sexuality might not raise as many eyebrows today, but her snobbishness certainly did permeate her writings about Peacehaven, for example, and the 'trippers' were in part responsible for Kipling deserting Rottingdean for the Weald, although with hugely positive literary results.

Clearly, this is a complex issue: sometimes the underlying character of the author seems irrelevant, but sometimes it colours their perception of Sussex. The toxicity or otherwise of artists' and other prominent people's personal views has lately come strikingly to the fore as statues have become the focus of protests and history is reinterpreted once again. This is an age of 'cancel culture'. At the time of writing, Kipling's statue in Burwash High Street, unveiled in 2019, is still standing.[21] Heritage, as we are still seeing, is contentious and a pressing and political issue demanding individual judgement and a sense of proportion. In *To the Lighthouse*, Virginia Woolf has Lily Briscoe musing, 'But the dead ... one pitied them, one brushed them aside, one had even a little contempt for them. They are at our mercy.'[22]

But one thing is certain: all the writers and poets represented within this book derived benefit of some kind from their location within Sussex and from their writings about the Sussex countryside. For some, it was frankly financial, writing for a living and largely for an urban readership, but for most it offered a sense of peace, relaxation, even recuperation. The result was a brand of nature/society/psychological release writing linked to the beautifully differentiated countrysides of Sussex. Consider the following passage from Woolf's *Collected Essays*:

Instead of being a book it seemed as if what I read was laid upon the landscape, not printed, bound, or sewn up, but somehow the product of trees and fields and the hot summer sky, like the air which swam, on fine mornings, round the outlines of things.[23]

The landscape, then, is part of our heritage, a text to be read and, in post-modern parlance, there is an intertextuality between landscape and literature. Of course, as with any text, its meanings are unstable and open to different interpretations. As Roland Barthes observed in 1968, 'The text floats free.'[24] Different observers see different elements in a landscape, react differently, take in discordant meanings, even react differently to the same landscape depending on their interior states of mind or even the effects of the weather. And after all, what is written can never encompass the totality of what is actually seen; instead, it is filtered through memory and imagination. No words can fully encapsulate a landscape view, so choices are made, emphases given, generalisations made, errors of omission criticised as either essence or detail are sought.

But finally, the release might not be total: a theme running through so much of the foregoing book has been the very coexistence of a metropolitan life and a pastoral retreat, and indeed, surely that was also the essence of much of Peter Brandon's own life, working by day in London but thankfully retreating nightly to the domesticity of his beloved Sussex.

This is Peter's last love song to Sussex. And it is created not from the archive but from the crafted written word, infused by the sense of place that he held so dear.

BIBLIOGRAPHY

Ainsworth, Harrison, *Ovingdean Grange: A Tale of the South Downs* (Routledge, Warne and Routledge, 1860).

Alexander, N., 'On Literary Geography', *Literary Geographies* 1 (2015), pp. 3–6.

Alt, C., *Virginia Woolf and the Study of Nature* (Cambridge University Press, 2010).

Anderson, A.H., 'Richard Jefferies and Sussex', *SCM* 11, No. 8 (1937), pp. 524–30.

Anon., 'Art in Ditchling', *Ditchling Parish Council Magazine* (12 November 2020), p. 16.

Anon. (T.K. Cromwell), *Excursions in the County of Sussex* (Longman, Hurst, Rees, Orme and Brown, 1822).

Anon., '"Slip out of Life" – Sussex Poet's Letter to the Coroner', obituary in *Sussex Express and County Herald* (15 July 1940), p.8.

Anon., 'The Sussex Poetry of Charles Dalmon', *SCM* 1 (2) (1927), pp. 593–97.

Aplin, J., *The Letters of Philip Webb, Vol. 3: 1899–1902* (Routledge, 2016).

Auden, W.H. (ed.), *A Choice of de la Mare's Verse* (Faber, 1963).

Auden, W.H., *Poems* (Faber, 1930).

Barthes. R., 'The Death of the Author' in *Image, Music, Texts/Roland Barthes* (transl. S. Heath, Oxford University Press, 1977).

Bate, J., 'Culture and Environment: From Austen to Hardy', *New Literary History* 30 (1999), pp. 541–42.

Bate, J., *The Song of the Earth* (Picador, 2000).

Beckett, A., 'Song O' the Sussex Men', *SCM* 1 (2) (1927), p. 84.

Beckett, A., *The Wonderful Weald and the Quest of a Crock of Gold* (Mills & Boon, 1911).

Beer, G., 'Virginia Woolf and Pre-History' in E. Warner (ed.), *Virginia Woolf: A Centenary Perspective (Studies in 20th Century Literature)*, (Palgrave Macmillan, 1984), pp. 99–123.

Beerbohm, Max, *Cartoons: the Second Childhood of John Bull* (S. Swift and Co., 1911).

Bell, A., 'A Foreword' in C.F. Cook (ed.), *The Book of Sussex Verse* (Combridges, 1920).

Bell, A., *The Dear Land of the Heart* (Combridges, 1913).

Bell, A., 'The Happy Phantom' in C.F. Cook (ed.), *The Book of Sussex Verse* (Combridges, 1920).

Bell, Julian, 'Arms and the Man' in M. Roberts (ed.), *New Signatures* (Hogarth Living Poets No. 24, 1932).

Bell, Julian, *Work for the Winter and Other Poems* (The Hogarth Press, 1936).

Bell, Quentin, *Virginia Woolf: A Biography*, Vol. 1 (Triad/Granada, 1976).

Belloc, H., *Emmanuel Burden, Merchant of Thames Street in the City of London* (Methuen, 1904).

Belloc, H., *On Everything* (Methuen, 1909).

Belloc, H., *On Sailing the Sea: A Collection of the Seagoing Writings of Hilaire Belloc* (Methuen, 1939).

Belloc, H., *Short Talks with the Dead and Others* (Cayme Press, 1926).

Belloc, H., *Songs of the South Country: Selected from the Poems of H. Belloc* (Duckworth, 1951).

Belloc, H., *Sonnets and Verse* (Duckworth, 1923).

Belloc, H., *The County of Sussex* (Cassell, 1936).

Belloc, H., *The Footpath Way: An Anthology for Walkers* (Sidgwick & Jackson, 1911).

Belloc, H., *The Four Men: A Farrago* (T. Nelson and Sons, 1912).

Belloc, H., *The Hills and the Sea* (Methuen, 1906).

Belloc, H., *The Servile State* (T.N. Foulis, 1912).

Besant, W., *The Eulogy of Richard Jefferies* (Chatto & Windus, 1905).

Betjeman, J., *Coming Home: An Anthology of His Prose 1920–1977* (Vintage, 1998).
Binyon, L., *Selected Poems of Laurence Binyon* (Macmillan, 1922).
Binyon, L., *The Cause: Poems of the War* (Houghton Mifflin, 1917).
Binyon, L., *The Secret: Sixty Poems by Lawrence Binyon* (Elkin Mathews, 1920).
Bishop, E., *A Virginia Woolf Chronology* (Macmillan, 1989).
Blakelock, D., *Eleanor: Portrait of a Farjeon* (Gollancz, 1966).
Blaker, N.P., *Sussex in Bygone Days: Reminiscences of Nathaniel Paine Blaker MRCS* (Combridges, 1919).
Bloomfield, H. (ed.), *The Remains of Robert Bloomfield*, Vol. 1 (Baldwin, Craddock & Joy, 1824).
Blunden, E., *Cricket Country* (Collins, 1944).
Blunden, E., *Edmund Blunden: a Selection of his Poetry and Prose Made by Kenneth Hopkins* (Books for Libraries Press, 1962).
Blunden, E., *Undertones of War* (Richard Cobden-Sanderson, 1928).
Blunt, W.S., *A New Pilgrimage and Other Poems* (Kegan Paul, 1889).
Blunt, W.S., *My Diaries: Part I, Being a Personal Narrative of Events 1888–1900* (Alfred A. Knopf, 1922).
Blunt, W.S., *Poetical Works of Wilfrid Scawen Blunt*, Vols 1 and 2 (Macmillan & Co., 1914).
Blunt, W.S., 'Possibilities of Peasant Ownership in Sussex', *Nineteenth Century and After* 59 (1906), p. 955.
Blunt, W.S., *The Love-Lyrics and Songs of Proteus by Wilfred Scawen Blunt with the Love-Sonnets of Proteus by the same Author now Reprinted in their full text* (Kelmscott Press, 1892).
Blythe, R., 'Foreword' in Peter Tolhurst, *Wessex: A Literary Pilgrimage* (Black Dog Books, 1999), p. 9.
Borrow, George, *Lavengro: The Scholar, the Gypsy, the Priest* (J.M. Dent, 1906 edition, first published in 1851).
Bowen, Stella, *Drawn from Life* (George Mann, 1974, first published by Collins, 1940).
Brandon, P., *A History of Surrey* (Phillimore, 1977).
Brandon, P., '"John Halsham": the Perfect Countryman', *SAC* 148 (2010), pp. 213–24.
Brandon, P., 'Philip Webb, the William Morris Circle, and Sussex' in *Sussex History* 2(1) (1981), pp. 8–14.
Brandon, P., *Sussex* (Robert Hale, 2006).
Brandon, P., 'The Common Lands and Wastes of Sussex' (unpub. PhD thesis, University of London, 1963).
Brandon, P., 'The Diffusion of Designed Landscapes in South-East England', in H.S.A. Fox and R.A. Butlin (eds), *Change in the Countryside, Essays in Rural England, 1500–1900* (Inst. of British Geographers Special Pub. 10, 1979), pp. 165–87.
Brandon, P., *The Discovery of Sussex* (Phillimore, 2010).
Brandon, P., *The Kent and Sussex Weald* (Phillimore, 2003).
Brandon, P., *The North Downs* (Phillimore, 2005).
Brandon, P., *The South Downs* (Phillimore, 1998).
Brandon, P. (ed.), *The South Saxons* (Phillimore, 1978).
Brandon, P., *The Sussex Landscape* (Hodder and Stoughton, 1974).
Brandon, P., 'Wealden Nature and the Role of London in Nineteenth-century Artistic Imagination' in *Journal of Historical Geography* 10 (1984), pp. 53–74.
Brégy, K., *The Poets' Chantry* (Herbert & Daniel, 1912).
Brown, Jane, *Spirits of Place: Five Famous Lives in their English Landscape* (Harmondsworth: Penguin, 2002).
Buchan, J., *Memory Hold the Door* (Hodder & Stoughton, 1940).
Burroughs, John (edited by Charlotte Zoë Walker), *The Art of Seeing Things* (Syracuse University Press, 2001).
Carey, J., *The Intellectuals and the Masses: Pride and Prejudice among the Literary Intelligentsia, 1880–1939* (Faber & Faber, 1992).
Carpenter, Edward, *England's Ideal and Other Papers on Social Subjects* (Swan, Sonnenschein, Lowry, 1887).
Carpenter, Edward, *My Days and Dreams: Being Autobiographical Notes* (George Allen and Unwin, 1916).
Charques, R.D., *This Other Eden* (Peter Davies, 1936).
Chesterton, G.K., 'The Aesthetes in the Kitchen Garden' in Chesterton, *Ultimate Collection* (e-Artnow, 2019).
Chesterton, G.K., *The Napoleon of Notting Hill* (John Lane, 1904).
Church, R., *Speaking Aloud* (Heinemann, 1968).

Clark, Indy, *Thomas Hardy's Pastoral: An Unkindly May* (Palgrave Macmillan, 2015).

Clark, L. (ed.), *Andrew Young. A Prospect of a Poet. Tributes by Fourteen Writers* (R. Hart-Davis, 1957).

Clark, T., *The Cambridge Introduction to Literature and the Environment* (Cambridge University Press, 2011).

Cobbett, W., *Cottage Economy* (J.M. Cobbett, 1823).

Cobbett, W., *Rural Rides* (first published in 1830; Penguin edition, 1967).

Cockman, G., *Charles Dalmon: The Forgotten Poet Laureate of Sussex* (Horsham Museum Society, 2015).

Cockman, G., 'Charles Dalmon' (www.edward-thomas-fellowship.org.uk/Newsletter PDF/Newsletter 45 August 2001.pdf).

Cody, D., 'Kipling's Imperialism', The Victorian Web, (www.victorianweb.org/authors/kipling/rkimperialism.html).

Coffey, H., 'Eleanor Farjeon and the South Downs National Park', (www.southdowns.gov.uk/eleanor-farjeon-and-the-south-downs-national-park).

Cohen, M., *Rudyard Kipling to Rider Haggard: The Record of a Friendship* (Hutchinson, 1965).

Collingwood, R.G., *The Principles of Art* (Oxford University Press, 1938).

Collins, William, 'Ode to Pity: Odes on Several Descriptive and Allegorical Subjects' (1746) from *Collection of Poems in Four Volumes. By several hands. Vol. II* (G. Pearch, 2nd edition, 1770), pp. 17–19.

Colls, R., and P. Dodd, *Englishness: Politics and Culture 1880–1920* (Croom Helm, 1986).

Connolly, Cyril, *The Unquiet Grave: A Word Cycle* (Horizon, 1944).

Cook, C.F. (ed.), *Another Book of Sussex Verse* (Combridges, 1928).

Cook, C.F. (ed.), *The Book of Sussex Verse* (Combridges, 1920).

Cooke, A.S, *Off the Beaten Track in Sussex: Sketches, Literary and Artistic* (Combridges, 1911).

Cooke, A.S., *Songs of the Sussex Downs* (Combridges, 1920).

Cooper, J.A., *The Unpublished Journal of Gideon Mantell: 1819–1852* (https://brightonmuseums.org.uk/discover/wp-content/uploads/sites/7/2014/11/mantell_journal.pdf).

Cooper, S., *The Shining Cord of Sheila Kaye-Smith* (Country Books, 2017).

Copper, Bob, *Across Sussex with Belloc: In the footsteps of the Four Men* (Sutton, 1994).

Corrin, J.P., *G.K. Chesterton and Hilaire Belloc: The Battle Against Modernity* (Ohio University Press, 1981).

Cowley, M., 'The Women of Thornden' in *Dial* 67 (1920), pp. 259–62.

Crawford, O.G.S, and A. Keiller, *Wessex from the Air* (Clarendon Press, 1928).

Crocker, C., *The Vale of Obscurity: Kingley Vale, the Lavant and Other Poems* (William Hayley Mason, 1830).

K. Cuchman, '"I wish that story at the bottom of the sea": The Making and Re-Making of "England, My England"' in *Études Lawrenciennes* 26 (2015) (https://journals.openedition.org/lawrence/235).

Cunningham, P. (ed.), *The Letters of Horace Walpole, 4th Earl of Orford* (J. Grant, 1906).

Dalmon, C., *A Poor Man's Riches: A Bundle of Lyrics* (Methuen, 1922).

Dalmon, C., 'Art Direction in British Film Studios' in *The Bioscope British Films Supplement* (July 1920), p. xv.

Dalmon, C., *Flower and Leaf* (Grant Richards, 1900).

Dalmon, C., 'Parson Herrick's Muse', *The Yellow Book* 3 (1894), pp. 241–42.

Dalmon, C., *Singing as I Go: Poems, Lyrics and Romany Songs* (Constable, 1927).

Dalmon, C., *Song Favours* (John Lane, 1895).

Davies, D., 'The Evocative Symbolism of Trees' in D. Cosgrove and S. Daniels (eds), *The Iconography of Landscape* (Cambridge University Press, 1988), pp.32–42.

Davis, T.C., and P. Holland (eds), *The Performing Century: Nineteenth-Century Theatre's History* (Palgrave, 2007).

de la Mare, Walter, 'Arabia' in *Georgian Poetry* (1911–1912), p. 67.

Delbanco, N., *Group Portrait* (Faber & Faber, 1982).

Dellamora, R., *Radclyffe Hall: A Life in the Writing* (University of Pennsylvania Press, 2011).

Derbyshire, V., *The Picturesque, the Sublime, the Beautiful: Visual Artistry in the Works of Charlotte Smith (1749–1806)* (Vernon Press, 2019).

Douglas, N., *Siren Land* (Dent, 1911).

Drinkwater, John, *Poems 1908–1919* (Houghton Miflin, 1919).

Drinkwater, John, *Swords and Ploughshares* (Sidgewick & Jackson, 1915).

Dudeney, Mrs Henry (ed. Diana Crook), *A Lewes Diary 1916–1944* (Tartarus Press, 1998).

Dudt, C., 'Wilfrid Meynell: Editor, Publisher, & Friend' in *Victorian Periodicals Review* 16 (1983), pp. 104–09.

Ebbatson, R., *An Imaginary England: Nation, Landscape and Literature, 1840–1920* (Ashgate, 2005).

Ebbatson, R., 'Prophecy and Utopia: Richard Jefferies and the Transcendentalists' in *The Glass* 19 (2007) (reprinted in ttp://richardjefferiessociety.co.uk/articles/83_RJ_transandentalists_Ebbatson.pdf).

Eliot, T.S., 'The Waste Land' in *The Criterion* 1 (October 1922).

Erdman, D.V. (ed.), *The Complete Poetry and Prose of William Blake* (Anchor Books, 1988).

Fairless, M., *The Roadmender* (Duckworth, 1911).

Farjeon, Annabel, *Morning Has Broken: A Biography of Eleanor Farjeon* (Julia MacRae, 1986).

Farjeon, Eleanor, *A Sussex Alphabet* (Pear Tree Press, 1939; Snake River Press facsimile, 2017).

Farjeon, Eleanor, *Edward Thomas: The Last Four Years* (Oxford University Press, 1958).

Farjeon, Eleanor, *Magic Casements* (George Allen and Unwin, 1941).

Farjeon, Eleanor, *Martin Pippin in the Apple Orchard* (Wm Collins, 1921).

Farrier, D., *Anthropocene Poetics: Deep Time, Sacrifice Zone, and Extinction* (University of Minnesota Press, 2019).

Finch, E., *Wilfrid Scawen Blunt 1840–1922* (Jonathan Cape, 1938).

Finlayson, I., *Writers in Romney Marsh* (Severn House Publishers, 1986).

Flower, R., *Napoleon to Nasser: The Story of Modern Egypt* (Garrett County Press, 2011).

Ford, Ford Madox, *It was the Nightingale* (Lippincott, 1933).

Ford, Ford Madox, *No Enemy: A Tale of Reconstruction* (The Macaulay Co., 1929).

Ford, Ford Madox, *The Soul of London: A Survey of a Modern City* (Alston Rivers, 1905).

Ford, G.H., *Double Measure: A Study of the Novels and Stories of D.H. Lawrence* (Norton, 1965).

Forster, E.M., *Abinger Harvest* (Edward Arnold, 1936; Harmondsworth Penguin, 1974).

Frost, Robert, 'The Road not Taken' in *Mountain Interval* (Henry Holt & Co., 1916).

Fussell, P., *The Great War and Modern Memory* (Oxford University Press, 1975).

Gammon, V., 'Folk Song Collecting in Sussex and Surrey 1843–1914' in *History Workshop Journal* 10 (1980), pp. 61–89.

Gaskell, Mrs, *Mary Barton: A Tale of Manchester Life* (Chapman & Hall, 1848).

Gibbons, S., *Christmas at Cold Comfort Farm* (Longmans, 1940).

Gibbons, S., *Cold Comfort Farm* (Longmans, 1932).

Gibbons, S., *Conference at Cold Comfort Farm* (Longmans, 1949).

Gibbons, S., *The Matchmaker* (Longmans, 1949).

Gilchrist, A. (ed.), *Life of William Blake*, Vol. 1 (Macmillan & Co., 1880).

Gill, E., *Autobiography* (Jonathan Cape, 1940).

Gosse, E., *Coventry Patmore* (Hodder & Stoughton, 1905).

Gosset, A., *Shepherds of Britain: Scenes from Shepherd Life Past and Present* (Constable and Co., 1911).

Graves, Robert, *Collected Poems* (Doubleday, 1961).

Graves, Robert, *The Complete Poems* (Penguin Books, 2003).

Green, Candida Lycett (ed.), *John Betjeman Letters 1926–1951* (Methuen, 1994).

Green, R.L., 'Kipling' in D.L. Kirkpatrick (ed.), *Twentieth-Century Children's Writers* (Macmillan, 1978), p. 701.

Grigson, G., 'Hills and Poems' in *Geographical Magazine* 29 (1956), pp. 388–96.

Halsham, J. (George Forrester Scott), *Idlehurst: A Journal Kept in the Country* (Smith, Elder & Co., 1898).

Halsham, J., *Lonewood Corner: A Countryman's Horizons* (Smith, Elder & Co., 1907).

Halsham, J., *Old Standards* (Smith, Elder & Co., 1913).

Hammill, F., *Women, Celebrity and Literary Culture Between the Wars* (University of Texas, 2007).

Hancock, N., 'Elusive Encounters: Seeking out Virginia Woolf in Her Commemorative House Museum' in J. Dubino, G. Lowe, V. Neverow, and K. Simpson (eds), *Virginia Woolf: Twenty-First-Century Approaches* (Edinburgh University Press, 2015), pp. 34–50.

Hands, T., *A Hardy Chronology* (Macmillan, 1992).

Hardy, D., and C. Ward, *Arcadia for All: The Legacy of a Makeshift Landscape* (Mansell, 1984).

Hardy, Thomas, *Tess of the d'Urbevilles* (original edition James R. Osgood, McIlvaine & Co., 1891; Macmillan, 1974).

Hare, Chris, *Hilaire Belloc: The Politics of Living* (History People UK, 2022).

Harris, Alexandra, *Romantic Moderns: English Writers, Artists and the Imagination from Virginia Woolf to John Piper* (Thames & Hudson, 2010).

Harris, Alexandra, *Virginia Woolf* (Thames & Hudson, 2013).

Harvey, A., *Like Sorrow or a Tune: A New Selection of Poems by Eleanor Farjeon* (Laurel Books, 2013).

Hay, William, *Mount Caburn: A Poem. Humbly Inscribed to Her Grace the Duchess of Newcastle, by William Hay, Esquire* (British Library, Historical Print Editions, 2011).

Head, D., *Modernity and the English Rural Novel* (Cambridge University Press, 2017).

Heine, H., *The Prose Writings of Heinrich Heine: edited and with an Introduction by Havelock Ellis* (Walter Scott, 1887).

Henley, W.E., and G. Wyndham, *The Poetry of Wilfrid Blunt, Selected and Arranged by W.E. Henley and George Wyndham* (W. Heinemann, 1898).

Hersee, William, *Poems, Rural and Domestic* (Longman & Co., 1810).

Hewlett, M.H., *Open Country: A Comedy with a Sting* (Macmillan, 1909).

Hill-Miller, K.C., *From the Lighthouse to Monk's House: A Guide to Virginia Woolf's Literary Landscapes* (Duckworth, 2001).

Hitchener, Elizabeth, 'The Weald of Sussex: A Poem' (Black & Co., 1822).

Holleyman, G., 'The Celtic Field-System in South Britain' in *Antiquity* 9 (1935), pp. 443–54.

Holliday, P., 'Eric Gill, Amy Sawyer and the "Gladys Panel"' in Holliday (ed.), *Eric Gill in Ditchling: Four Essays* (Oak Knoll Press, 2002), pp. 68–82.

Hopkins, R.T., *Kipling's Sussex Revisited* (Herbert Jenkins Ltd, 1929).

Hopkins, R.T., *Sheila Kaye-Smith and the Weald Country* (Cecil Palmer, 1925).

Hopkins, R.T., *The Lure of Sussex: A Record of Indolent Travel* (Cecil Palmer, 1928).

Houseman, A.E. (ed. A. Burnett), *The Letters of A.E. Houseman* (Clarendon Press, 2007).

Howkins A., 'The Discovery of Rural England' in R. Colls and P. Dodd (eds), *Englishness: Politics and Culture, 1880–1920* (Croom Helm, 1986), pp. 62–88.

Hudson, W.H., *Nature in Downland* (Longman, Green & Co., 1900; J.M. Dent edition, 1925).

Hurdis, James, *The Village Curate and Other Poems* (Sharp, 1809, and Longman et al., 1813).

Jefferies, R., *After London; or, Wild England* (Cassell, 1885).

Jefferies, R., *Field and Hedgerow* (Lutterworth, 1948).

Jefferies, R., *Nature Near London* (Chatto & Windus, 1905).

Jefferies, R., *The Life of the Fields* (original Chatto & Windus, 1884; Oxford University Press, 1983).

Jefferies, R., *The Open Air* (Chatto & Windus, 1885).

Jefferies, R., *The Story of My Heart: My Autobiography* (Penguin, 1938).

Jefferies, R., *Wildlife in a Southern County* (original Smith, Elder & Co., 1879; reprint, 2005).

Joad, C.E.M., *Pieces of Mind* (Faber & Faber, 1942).

Johnson, G.J., 'Ernest Raymond' in G.M. Johnson (ed.), 'British Novelists Between the Wars' in *Dictionary of Literary Biography* 191 (1998), pp. 265–75.

Jones, C., *Virginia Woolf: Ambivalent Activist* (Edinburgh University Press, 2015).

Kaye-Smith, S., *Joanna Godden* (Cassell, 1921).

Kaye-Smith, S., *Joanna Godden Married and Other Stories* (Cassell, 1926).

Kaye-Smith, S., *Little England* (Nisbet & Co., 1918).

Kaye-Smith, S., *Sussex Gorse: The Story of a Fight* (Cassell, 1916).

Kaye-Smith, S., *The Challenge to Sirius* (Cassell, 1901).

Kaye-Smith, S., *The End of the House of Alard* (Cassell, 1923).

Kaye-Smith, S., *The Four Roads* (George H. Doran Co., 1919).

Kaye-Smith, S., *The Ploughman's Progress* (Cassell, 1933).

Kaye-Smith, S., *The Treasures of the Snow* (Cassell, 1950).

Kaye-Smith, S., *The Valiant Woman* (Cassell, 1939).

Kaye-Smith, S., *The Village Doctor* (Cassell, 1929).

Kaye-Smith, S., *Three Ways Home: A Catholic Autobiography* (Cassell, 1937).

Keats, John, *The Complete Poetical Works and Letters of John Keats* (Cambridge edition of the Poets, Houghton and Mifflin, 1899).

Kelvin, N. (ed.), *The Collected Letters of William Morris*, Vol. 2, Part A: 1881–1884 (Princeton University Press, 1987).

Kernahan, C., *Six Famous Living Poets* (Thornton Butterworth Ltd, 1922).

Kettle, A., *Literature and Liberation: Selected Essays* (Manchester University Press, 1988).

Keynes, J.M., 'Foreword' in Quentin Bell (ed.), *Julian Bell: Essays, Poems and Letters* (The Hogarth Press, 1938).

King, Bishop Henry, 'An Exequay to his Matchless never to be Forgotten Friend' (1657) (https://poetryarchive.org/poem/exequy-his-matchless-never-be-forgotten-friend)

Kipling, R., *A Diversity of Creatures* (Macmillan, 1917).

Kipling, R., 'An Habitation Enforced' in *Actions and Reactions* (Doubleday, 1909).

Kipling, R., 'The Deep-sea Cables' in *English Illustrated Magazine* (May 1893).

Kipling, R., *Puck of Pook's Hill* (Macmillan, 1906).

Kipling, R., *Rewards and Fairies* (Macmillan, 1910).

Kipling, R., *Something of Myself and Other Autobiographical Writings* (edited by T. Pinney), (Cambridge University Press, 1990).

Kipling, R., *The Complete Works of Rudyard Kipling* (e-artnow, 2017).

Kipling, R., *Traffics and Discoveries* (Macmillan, 1904).

Knowles, C., and I. Horrocks, *Charlotte Smith: Major Poetic Works* (Broadview Press, 2017).

Labbe, J., *Charlotte Smith: Romanticism, Poetry and the Culture of Gender* (Manchester University Press, 2003).

Lamb, Charles, *The Works of Charles Lamb to Which are Prefixed His Letters and a Sketch of his Life* (Harper and Bros, 1838).

Lawrence, D.H., 'England, My England' in *England, My England and Other Stories* (edited by B. Steele), (Cambridge University Press, 1990).

Lawrence, D.H., *The Rainbow* (Penguin edition, 1949).

Leavis, F.R., *The Common Pursuit* (Chatto & Windus, 1952).

Leavis, F.R., and D. Thompson, *Culture and Environment: The Training of Critical Awareness* (Chatto & Windus, 1933).

Lebeaux, Richard, *Thoreau's Seasons* (University of Massachusetts Press, 1984).

Lee, H., *Virginia Woolf* (Chatto & Windus, 2006).

Lewis, N., 'Introduction' in Lewis (ed.), *The Eleanor Farjeon Book: A Tribute to Her Life and Work 1881–1965* (Hamish Hamilton, 1966), p. 4.

Lidstone, Lydia, 'Habberton Lulham, Sussex Poet' in *SCM* 4 (1930), p. 544.

Longford, Elizabeth, *A Pilgrimage of Passion: The Life of Wilfrid Scawen Blunt* (Weidenfeld & Nicholson, 1979).

Looker, S.J. (ed.), *The Nature Diaries and Note-books of Richard Jefferies* (The Grey Walls Press Ltd, 1948).

Looker, S.J., and C. Porteous, *Richard Jefferies: Man of the Fields* (J. Baker, 1965).

Lower, M.A., *Contributions to Literature: Historical, Antiquarian, and Metrical* (John Russel Smith, 1854).

Llewellyn, N., *East Sussex Church Monuments 1530–1830* (Sussex Record Society 93, 2011).

Ludovici, Anthony Mario, 'The South Downs' in *The Saturday Review* (27 January 1917).

Ludwig, R.M., *Letters of Ford Madox Ford* (Princeton University Press, 1965).

Lulham, Habberton, 'Amberley and her Wild Brooks' in *SCM* 13 (1939), pp. 598–603.

Lulham, Habberton, *Devices and Desires* (R. Brimley Johnson, 1904).

Lulham, Habberton, 'Downland Destiny' in *SCM* 2 (1928), pp. 96–98.

Lulham, Habberton, 'Granny Coombe's cottage' in *The Downland Post* (1 April 1924), pp. 116–18.

Lulham, Habberton, *Songs from the Downs and Dunes* (Kegan Paul, 1908).

Lulham, Habberton, *The Other Side of Silence* (E. Macdonald, 1913).

Lusk, Lewis (Walter Delaplaine Scull), *Sussex Iron: A Romance of the Forest Ridge and the Man who started Shakespeare* (John Ouseley, 1913).

Lusk, Lewis, *Sussex Oak: A Romance of the Forest Ridge of Sussex* (John Ouseley, 1912).

Lycett, A., *Rudyard Kipling* (Weidenfeld & Nicolson, 1999).

Lytton, N. (Earl of), *The English Country Gentleman* (Hurst & Blackett Ltd, 1925).

Lytton, N. (Earl of), *Wilfrid Scawen Blunt* (Macdonald, 1961).

McCann, T., '"A Choice of Strawberries or Peaches": Exploring Sussex with S.P.B. Mais' in P. Foster (ed.), *Sussex Seams Two: A Further Collection of Travel Writing* (West Sussex County Council, 2000), pp. 174–84.

MacCarthy, F., 'Gill, (Arthur) Eric Rowton' in *ODNB* (2014).

McCarthy, J.M., *Green Modernism: Nature and the English Novel, 1900 to 1930* (Palgrave Macmillan, 2015).

McDiarmid, L., 'A Box for Wilfrid Blunt' in *Proceedings of the Modern Languages Association* 120 (1), Special Topic: On Poetry (January 2005), pp. 163–80.

Mais, S.P.B., *All the Days of My Life* (Hutchinson, 1937).

Mais, S.P.B., *Buffets and Rewards* (Hutchinson, 1952).

Mais, S.P.B., *Listen to the Country* (Hutchinson, 1939).

Mais, S.P.B., *See England First* (Richards Press, 1927).

Mais, S.P.B., *Southern Rambles for Londoners: Walk the English Countryside with S.P.B. Mais* (Bloomsbury, 2014, reproduction of Southern Railways 1948 edition).

Mais, S.P.B., 'The Amenities of Southwick' in *SCM* 3 (1929), pp. 535–41.

Malins, E., and J. Purkis, *A Preface to Yeats* (Routledge, 2014).

Mandler, P., 'Against "Englishness": English Culture and the Limits to Rural Nostalgia, 1850–1940' in *Trans Royal Historical Society* 7 (1998), pp. 155–75.

Mantell, G., *A Day's Ramble in and about the Ancient Town of Lewes* (H.G. Bohn, 1846).

Marsh, Edward (ed.), *Georgian Poetry* (Poetry Bookstore, five vols, 1912 to 1922).

Martineau, G.D., 'Out! Out! A Sussex Tocsin' in *SCM* 1 (1926), p. 21.

Marvell, Andrew, *Miscellaneous Poems* (1681) (British Library C.59.i.8).

Matless, D., *Landscape and Englishness* (Reaction, 1998).

Mellor, D., *Paradise Lost: The Neo-Romantic Imagination in Britain 1935–55* (Lund Humphries, 1987).

Meredith, G., *One of our Conquerors* (Chapman & Hall, 1891).

Meynell, E., *Sussex* (Hale, 1947).

Meynell, E., *Sussex Cottage* (Chapman & Hall, 1936).

Meynell, F., and V. Mendel, *The Week-End Book* (Nonesuch Press, 1924).

Meynell, V., *Francis Thompson and Wilfrid Meynell* (Hollis & Carter, 1952).

Mill, J.S., *Principles of Political Economy* (Longman, Green & Co., 1848).

Moggridge, D.E., *Maynard Keynes: An Economist's Biography* (Routledge, 1992).

Montague, C.E., *The Right Place* (Chatto & Windus, 1926).

Moore, J., *The Bloomsbury Trail in Sussex* (SB Publications, 1995).

Morris, A.J.A., 'Raymond, Ernest 1888–1974' in *ODNB* (2014).

Morton, J.B., *Hilaire Belloc: A Memoir* (Hollis & Carter, 1955).

Nairn, I., and N. Pevsner, *The Buildings of England: Sussex* (Penguin, 1965).

Nicolson, A., *Bateman's, East Sussex* (National Trust Guidebooks, 2006).

Nicolson, A., *The Hated Wife: Carrie Kipling 1862–1939* (Faber & Faber, 2001).

Nicolson, N., 'Introduction' in V. Sackville-West, *The Land* (Heinemann, 1926).

Nora, P., *Les Lieux de Mémoire* (Gallimard, four vols, 1999–2010).

Norris, L., *Andrew Young: Remembrance and Homage* (The Tidal Press, 1978).

Noyes, Alfred, *Collected Poems*, Vol. 1 (Wm Blackwood & Sons, 1925).

Noyes, Alfred, *The Elfin Artist and Other Poems* (Wm Blackwood & Sons, 1920).

Oliver, R., *Out of the Woodshed: A Portrait of Stella Gibbons* (Bloomsbury, 1998).

Ormrod, R., *Andrew Young: Priest, Poet and Naturalist: A Reassessment* (Lutterworth, 2018).

Orwell, G., 'Second Thoughts on James Burnham', *Polemic* 3 (May 1946), (http://orwell.ru/library/reviews/burnham/english/e_burnh.html)

Parfitt-King, A., 'Amy Sawyer of Ditchling (1863–1945): Artist, Playwright and Lady of Letters' in *The British Art Journal* 14 (2013), pp. 81–82.

Parfitt-King, A., *Amy Sawyer of Ditchling: Artist, Eccentric and Lady of Letters* (Country Books, 2013).

Pass, G., 'The Sussex Novels of Ernest Raymond: No.1 – the Earlier Novels' and 'No. 2 – the Later Novels' in *SCM* 10 (1936), pp. 395–99, 465–68.

Petre, M.D., *Autobiography and Life of George Tyrrell* (Edward Arnold, 1912).

Pinney, T. (ed.), *The Letters of Rudyard Kipling, Vol. 2: 1890–99* (Macmillan, 1990).

Pinney, T. (ed.), *The Letters of Rudyard Kipling, Vol. 3: 1900–10* (Macmillan, 1996).

Pinto, V. de Sola, *Crisis in English Poetry 1880–1940* (Hutchinson, 1963).

Piozzi, Mrs H.L. (Mrs Thrale), *Anecdotes of the Late Samuel Johnson LLD During the Last Twenty Years of his Life* (Cassell & Co. Ltd, 1887).

Powys, John Cowper, *After My Fashion* (Pan Books, 1980).

Powys, John Cowper, *Autobiography* (Bodley Head, 1934).

Preston, Kerrison (ed.), *Letters from Graham Robertson* (Hamish Hamilton, 1953).

Pryce-Jones, D., *Treason of the Heart: From Thomas Paine to Kim Philby* (Encounter Books, 2011).

Pye, T., 'An Object I Love' in *National Trust Magazine* (Summer 2019), p. 53.

Raymond, E., *Don John's Mountain Home* (Cassell, 1936).

Raymond, E., *Newtimber Lane: Being a Writing of Sir Edmund Earlwin of Cowbourn in Sussex* (Cassell, 1933).

Raymond, E., *Please You, Draw Near: Autobiography 1922–1968* (Cassell, 1969).

Raymond, E., *Tell England: A Study in a Generation* (Cassell, 1922).

Raymond, E., *Through Literature to Life: An Enthusiasm and an Anthology* (Cassell, 1928).

Raymond, E., *We, the Accused* (Cassell, 1935).

Readman, P., *Storied Ground: Landscape and the Shaping of English National Identity* (Cambridge University Press, 2018).

Robertson, W. Graham, *Pinkie and the Fairies: A Fairy Play for Children and Others in Three Acts* (S. French, 1932).

Robertson, W. Graham, *Time Was: The Reminiscences of W. Graham Robertson* (Hamish Hamilton, 1931).

Robson, M., *An Unrepentant Englishman: The Life of S.P.B. Mais, Ambassador of the Countryside* (King's England Press, 2005).

Rose, G., *Feminism and Geography: The Limits of Geographical Knowledge* (Polity, 1993).

Rosenfeld, N., *Outsiders Together: Virginia and Leonard Woolf* (Princeton University Press, 2001).

Rossabi, A., *A Peculiarly English Genius: Or, a Wiltshire Taoist. A Biography of Richard Jefferies, Vol. I: The Early Years, 1848–1867* (Petton Books, 2017).

Rossabi, A., 'Sussex and Richard Jefferies' (1994), (http://richardjefferiessociety.co.uk/articles/76_Sussex_RJ_Rossabi.pdf)

Rowbotham, S., *Edward Carpenter: A Life of Liberty and Love* (Verso, 2008).

Rush, P., *Great Men of Sussex* (The Bodley Head, 1956).

Russell, S., 'There Are More Things in Heaven and Earth' in *SCM* 2 (1928), p. 165.

Ryle, M., 'After "Organic Community": Eco-Criticism, Nature and Human Nature' in J. Parham, (ed.), *Literature and the Environmental Tradition* (Ashgate, 2001), pp. 11–23.

Sackville-West, V., *The Land* (Heinemann, 1926).

Said, Edward, *Orientalism* (Routledge & Kegan Paul, 1978).

Salkeld, W., 'Richard Jefferies in Crowborough' in *The Crowborough Field Society Journal* 1 (1978) and reproduced at http://richardjefferiessociety.co.uk/articles/28_RJ_in_Crowborough.pdf

Samuel, R., *Theatres of Memory: Past and Present in Contemporary Culture* (Verso, 1996).

Sandison, A., 'Kipling: The Artist and the Empire' in A. Rutherford (ed.), *Kipling's Mind and Art: Selected Critical Essays* (Stanford University Press, 1964), p. 147.

Saunders, M., *Ford Madox Ford: A Dual Life, Vol. 2: The After-War World* (Oxford University Press, 1996).

Saunders, M. (ed.), *Ford Madox Ford: Selected Poems* (Routledge, 1997).

Sawyer, Amy, *Sussex Village Plays, and others* (Combridges, 1934).

Sell, R.D., *Trespassing Ghost: A Critical Study of Andrew Young* (Åbo Akademi, 1978).

Seymour-Smith, M., *Rudyard Kipling* (Queen Anne Press, 1989).

Short, B., 'A Man in his Landscape: Peter Brandon 1927–2011' in *SAC* 150 (2012), pp. 193–207.

Short, B., 'Idyllic Ruralities' in P. Cloke, T. Marsden and P. Mooney (eds), *Handbook of Rural Studies* (Sage, 2006), pp. 133–48.

Sidgwick, A.H., *Walking Essays* (Edward Arnold, 1912).

Simpson, Jacqueline, *Folklore of Sussex* (original edition, Batsford, 1973; The History Press, 2009).

Simpson, R., 'Arthur Francis Bell (1875–1918)' in *Times Past* (Storrington and District Museum 39, Summer 2011).

Smith, Charlotte, *Elegiac Sonnets, and Other Essays by Charlotte Smith of Bignor Park in Sussex* (Dennett Jaques, 1784).

Smith, Charlotte, *The Old Manor House* (J. Bell, 1793).

Smith, M., 'Kipling's Sussex (3) – The Very Own House', www.kiplingsociety.co.uk/rg_sussex3.htm (no date).

Smith, M., *Kipling's Sussex* (Brownleaf, 2008).

Soleil, Christian, *Virginia Woolf, la Flâneuse de Rodmell* (Edilivre, 2015).

Speaight, R., *The Life of Hilaire Belloc* (Farrar, Straus & Cudahy, 1958).

Sponenberg, A., *Encyclopedia of British Women's Writing 1900–1950* (Springer, 2006).

Squire, J.C. (ed.), *Younger Poets of Today* (Secker, 1932).

Stansky, P., and W. Abrahams, *Journey to the Frontier: Julian Bell and John Cornford: Their Lives and the 1930s* (Constable, 1966).

Stansky, P., and W. Abrahams, *Julian Bell: From Bloomsbury to the Spanish Civil War* (Stanford University Press, 2012).

Stephens, L., 'In Praise of Walking' in *Studies of a Biographer*, Vol. 1 (Duckworth & Co., 1898), p. 258.

Stevenson, R.L., 'An Autumn Effect' in *The Portfolio: An Artistic Periodical* 6 (1875), p. 53.

Stone, W., *The Cave and the Mountain: A Study of E.M. Forster* (Stanford University Press, 1966).

Taylor, C., 'Wellesley [née Ashton], Dorothy Violet, Duchess of Wellington in *ODNB* (2004).

Taylor, J., *The Sussex Garland: A Collection of Ballads, Sonnets, Tales, Elegies, Songs, Epitaphs Etc. Illustrative of the County of Sussex, with Notices Historical, Biographical and Descriptive* (Newick: printed for the Editor, 1851).

Tennyson, Lord Alfred, 'The Charge of the Heavy Brigade at Balaclava: Prologue' (Dephi Classics, 2013).

Thacker, A., *Moving Through Modernity: Space and Geography in Modernism* (Manchester University Press, 2003).

Thomas, E., *A Literary Pilgrim in England* (Dodd, Mead, 1917).

Thomas, E., 'Book review: *Songs from the Downs and Dunes* by E.P. Habberton Lulham' in *The Morning Post* (25 June 1908).

Thomas, E., *Richard Jefferies: His Life and Work* (Hutchinson & Co., 1909).

Thomas, H., *Under Storm's Wing* (Carcenet, 1988).

Thomas, R.S., *Frequencies* (Macmillan, 1978).

Thoreau, Henry David, *The Price of Freedom: Political Philosophy from Thoreau's Journals* (privately published by D.M. Gross [ed.] 2007).

Thoreau, Henry David, *Walden; or, Life in the Woods* (Ticknor & Fields, 1854).

Thorne, J., *Rambles by Rivers: The Duddon, the Mole, the Adur, Arun and Wey, the Lea, the Dove* (Chas Knight & Co., 1844).

Tolhurst, P., *Virginia Woolf's English Hours* (Black Dog Books, 2015).

Tutté, Francis (ed.), *The Works of William Hay* (J. Nichols, two vols, 1794).

Van den Broek, A., *The Complete Shorter Poetry of George Eliot* (Routledge, 2016).

Vickers, J.A., 'John Drinkwater's Correspondents' in *The Yale University Library Gazette* 48 (1974), pp. 200–10.

Wallbrook H.M., 'A Poet of the South Downs' in *Fortnightly Review* (September 1927), pp. 410–13.

Ward, Rev. F.W. Orde, *Songs of Sussex* (Erskine Macdonald, 1910).

Webb, Mary, *Precious Bane* (Jonathan Cape, 1924).

Wellesley, Dorothy, *Beyond the Grave: Letters on Poetry to W.B. Yeats from Dorothy Wellesley* (C. Baldwin, 1952).

Wellesley, Dorothy, *Letters on Poetry from W.B. Yeats to Dorothy Wellesley* (Oxford University Press, 1940).

Wellesley, Dorothy, *Poems of Ten Years, 1924–1934* (Macmillan, 1934).

Wells, H.G., *Tono-Bungay* (first edition, Macmillan, 1909; Pan Books, 1964).

Wells, R. (ed.), *Victorian Village: The Diaries of the Reverend John Coker Egerton of Burwash 1857–1888* (Alan Sutton, 1992).

Westling, L. (ed.), *The Cambridge Companion to Literature and the Environment* (Cambridge University Press, 2014).

White, D.E., 'Autobiography and Elegy: The Early Romantic Poetics of Thomas Gray and Charlotte Smith' in T. Woodman (ed.), *Early Romantics: Perspectives in British Poetry from Pope to Wordsworth* (Macmillan, 1998).

White, Gilbert, *The Natural History of Selborne* (Everyman's Library edition edited by R.M. Lockley, 1949).

Whittick, C., 'Hurdis, James' in *ODNB* (2008).

Wiener, M., *English Culture and the Decline of the Industrial Spirit 1850–1980* (Penguin, 1981).

Weisenfarth, J., *Ford Madox Ford and the Regiment of Women: Violet Hunt, Jean Rhys, Stella Bowen, Janice Biala* (University of Wisconsin Press, 2005).

Wilkinson, W., *A Sussex Peep-Show* (Geoffrey Bles, 1933).

Williams, R., *The Country and the City* (Chatto & Windus, 1973).

Williamson, E., and T. Hudson, J. Musson, I. Nairn, *The Buildings of England: Sussex: West* (Yale University Press, 2019).

Williamson, H., *Young Phillip Maddison* (Macdonald, 1953).

Wills, Barclay, *Shepherds of Sussex* (Skeffington, 1938).

Wilson, A., *Hilaire Belloc: A Biography* (Mandarin Paperbacks, 1997).

Wilson, A., *The Strange Ride of Rudyard Kipling: His Life and Works* (Secker & Warburg, 1977).

Wilson, J.M., *Virginia Woolf's London: A Guide to Bloomsbury and Beyond* (Tauris Parke, 2000).

Wooldridge, S.W., and F. Goldring, *The Weald* (Collins, *New Naturalist* 26, 1953).

Woolf, Leonard, *Beginning again: An Autobiography of the Years 1911 to 1918* (Harcourt Brace, 1963).

Woolf, Leonard, *Downhill all the Way: An Autobiography of the Years 1919–1939* (The Hogarth Press, 1967).

Woolf, Leonard, *Leonard Woolf. An Autobiography, Vol. 2: Politics, Life, and Literature 1911–1969* (Oxford University Press, 1980).

Woolf, Virginia, *Between the Acts* (The Hogarth Press, 1941).

Woolf, Virginia, *The Death of the Moth and Other Essays* (Harcourt, Brace & Company, 1942).

Woolf, Virginia, *The Diary of Virginia Woolf, Vol. 2: 1920–1924* (edited by A. Bell and A. McNeillie, The Hogarth Press, 1978).

Woolf, Virginia, *The Diary of Virginia Woolf, Vol. 3: 1925–1930* (edited by A. Bell and A. McNeillie, The Hogarth Press, 1980).

Woolf, Virginia, *The Diary of Virginia Woolf, Vol. 4: 1931–1935* (edited by A. Bell and A. McNeillie, The Hogarth Press, 1982).

Woolf, Virginia, *The Diary of Virginia Woolf, Vol. 5: 1936–1941* (edited by A. Bell and A. McNeillie, The Hogarth Press, 1984).

Woolf, Virginia, *The Essays of Virginia Woolf, Vol. 2: 1912–1918* (edited by A. McNeillie, The Hogarth Press, 1987).

Woolf, Virginia, *The Essays of Virginia Woolf, Vol. 3: 1919–1924* (edited by A. McNeillie, The Hogarth Press, 1988).

Woolf, Virginia, *The Essays of Virginia Woolf, Vol 4: 1925–1928* (edited by A. McNeillie, The Hogarth Press, 1994).

Woolf, Virginia, 'The Historian and "The Gibbon"' in *Times Literary Supplement* (24 April 1937), p. 1.

Woolf, Virginia, *The Letters of Virginia Woolf, Vol. 1* (edited by N. Nicolson and J. Trautmann, Chatto & Windus, 1975).

Woolf, Virginia, *The Letters of Virginia Woolf, Vol. 6: Leave the Letters Till We're Dead* (edited by N. Nicolson and J. Trautmann (The Hogarth Press, 1980).

Woolf, Virginia, *The Waves* (The Hogarth Press, 1931).

Woolf, Virginia, *To the Lighthouse* (Vintage, 1927).

Woolf, Virginia, *Virginia Woolf: The Complete Collection* (Oregan Publishing, 2017).

Wylie, J.W., 'A Single Day's Walking: Narrating Self and Landscape on the Southwest Coast Path' in *Transactions of the Institute of British Geographers* 30 (2005), pp. 234–47.

Young, A., *A Prospect of Flowers* (Jonathan Cape, 1945).

Young, A., *A Retrospect of Flowers* (Jonathan Cape, 1950).

Young, A., *Complete Poems* (edited by L. Clark, Secker & Warburg, 1974).

Young, A., *Nicodemus: A Mystery* (Jonathan Cape, 1937).

Young, A., *The Poet and the Landscape* (Rupert Hart-Davis, 1962).

Young, G., *Come into the Country* (Samuel Walker, 1946).

Young, G., *Down Hoe Lane* (Arundel Press, 1950).

Young, G., *The Chronicle of a Country Cottage* (Samuel Walker, 1940).

Young, G., *The Cottage in the Fields* (Samuel Walker, 1945).

Zytaruk, G.J., and J.T. Boulton (eds), *The Letters of D.H. Lawrence*, Vol. 2 (Cambridge University Press, 1981).

ENDNOTES

Editor's Preface

1 In 1992 the North American Association for the Study of Literature and the Environment was initiated. There is now a journal, *Interdisciplinary Studies in Literature and Environment*. And see T. Clark, *The Cambridge Introduction to Literature and the Environment* (2011) and L. Westling (ed.), *The Cambridge Companion to Literature and the Environment* (2014).
2 Jonathan Bate, *The Song of the Earth* (2000), p. 266.
3 Brian Short, 'A Man in his Landscape: Peter Brandon 1927–2011', *SAC* 150 (2012), pp. 193–207. Much is drawn from personal conversations over many years. Thanks also to Joy Hall, who had the presence of mind to record conversations with Peter when he was hospitalised during 2011.
4 S.W. Wooldridge and F. Goldring, *The Weald* (1953), p. viii.
5 P.F. Brandon, 'The Common Lands and Wastes of Sussex' (unpub. PhD thesis, University of London 1963).
6 Brandon, *The Sussex Landscape* (1974), p. 8; *A History of Surrey* (1977); *The South Saxons* (1978).
7 Brandon, *The Sussex Landscape*, p. 8.
8 'The Diffusion of Designed Landscapes in South-East England', in H.S.A. Fox and R.A. Butlin (eds), *Change in the Countryside* (1979), pp. 165–87.
9 Brandon, 'Philip Webb, the William Morris Circle, and Sussex', *Sussex History* 2(1) (1981), pp. 8–14; Brandon, 'Wealden Nature and the Role of London in Nineteenth-Century Artistic Imagination', *Journal of Historical Geography* 10 (1984), pp. 53–74.
10 Brandon, *The South Downs* (1998); *The Kent and Sussex Weald* (2003); *The North Downs* (2005); *Sussex* (2006); *The Discovery of Sussex* (2010).

Introduction

1 Rudyard Kipling, 'A Charm', from his introduction to *Rewards and Fairies* (1910).
2 Richard Jefferies, 'Wildflowers' in *The Open Air* (1885), p. 48.
3 The term psychogeography has been employed to develop ideas about relations to places, particularly as revealed through walking. See J.W. Wylie, 'A Single Day's Walking: Narrating Self and Landscape on the Southwest Coast Path', *Transactions of the Institute of British Geographers* 30 (2005), pp. 234–47.
4 C.E. Montague, *The Right Place* (1926).
5 E. Blunden, *Cricket Country* (1944), pp. 63–64.
6 'Eve of St Agnes', 20 January; 'Eve of St Mark', 24 April.

Chapter 1

1 'Mount Caburn. A Poem. Humbly Inscribed to Her Grace the Duchess of Newcastle, by William Hay, Esquire', British Library, Historical Print Editions (16 March 2011). Poem dated 1730.
2 Alfred, Lord Tennyson, 'The Charge of the Heavy Brigade at Balaclava: Prologue' (Dephi Classics, 2013). This alludes to the autumnal view from Aldworth House, Blackdown, a residence from 1868.

3   A. Bell, 'A Foreword' in C.F. Cook (ed.), *The Book of Sussex Verse* (1920), p. vi.

4   C.E.M. Joad, *Pieces of Mind* (1942), p. 114. Written following his visit in 1936.

5   J. Bate, 'Culture and Environment: From Austen to Hardy', *New Literary History* 30 (1999), pp. 541–42.

6   M. Smith, 'Kipling's Sussex (3): The Very Own House', www.kiplingsociety.co.uk/rg_sussex3.htm). For the concept of sites of memory see Pierre Nora, *Les Lieux de Mémoire* (4 vols, 1999–2010); R. Samuel, *Theatres of Memory* (1996); D. Matless, *Landscape and Englishness* (1998); P. Readman, *Storied Ground* (2018).

7   H. Thomas, *Under Storm's Wing* (1988), p. 50.

8   Arthur Beckett, *The Wonderful Weald* (1911); H. Belloc, *The Four Men* (1912). For Halsham, see P. Brandon, '"John Halsham": the Perfect Countryman', *SAC* 148 (2010), pp. 213–24; Anne Parfitt-King, *Amy Sawyer of Ditchling* (2013).

9   Thorne, *Rambles by Rivers* (1844), p. 88.

10 Laurence Binyon, 'Thunder on the Downs' in *The Cause: Poems of the War* (1917).

11 Reverend F.W. Orde Ward, *Songs of Sussex* (1910). Ward (1843–1922), a clergyman and prolific poet, is buried in Ocklynge Cemetery, Eastbourne.

12 Arthur Beckett, 'Song o' the Sussex Men', based on the climax to Kipling's 'Song of Sussex Men'. 'Bruff' = blunt of speech (*SCM* 1 (2) 1927, p. 84).

13 C. Crocker, *The Vale of Obscurity* (1830 – 3rd edition, 1841).

14 W. Wilkinson, *A Sussex Peep-Show* (1933).

15 M. Wiener, *English Culture and the Decline of the Industrial Spirit 1850–1980* (1981).

16 S. Gibbons, *Cold Comfort Farm* (1932).

Chapter 2

1   William Collins, 'Ode to Pity: Odes on Several Descriptive and Allegorical Subjects' (1746), from Collection of Poems in Four Volumes. By several hands, *Vol. II* (1770), pp. 17–19.

2   Elizabeth Hitchener, 'The Weald of Sussex: a poem' (1822). She was involved in an 'intense platonic relationship' with Percy Bysshe Shelley, who referred to her as the 'sister of my soul' and 'my second self'.

3   P. Cunningham (ed.), *The Letters of Horace Walpole* (1906). Walpole also wrote, with its roads in mind, 'Sussex is a great damper of curiosity' (Vol. 2, p. 42, letter of 26 August 1749).

4   Belloc, 'The Onion Eater' in *The Hills and the Sea*.

5   *Poems, Rural and Domestic* was 'inscribed with humility and gratitude' and dedicated to Mrs Huskisson 'by her highly obliged and very thankful servant'.

6   J. Taylor, *The Sussex Garland* (1851).

7   John Halsham [George Forrester Scott], *Idlehurst* (1898); and see Brandon, '"John Halsham"'.

8   Letter to Georgiana Burne-Jones, 10 January 1883. But he continues, 'Unluckily it is not an interesting town in itself … only not up to its position'. N. Kelvin (ed.), *The Collected Letters of William Morris*, Vol. 2, Part A: 1881–1884 (1987), p. 92.

Chapter 3

1   Robert Bloomfield, 'A First view of the Sea' in H. Bloomfield (ed.), *The Remains of Robert Bloomfield*, Vol. 1 (1824), p. 81.

2   W.H. Hudson, *Nature in Downland* (1925), p. 7.

3   W.H. Hudson, *Nature in Downland* (1925), pp. 6–7.

4   C.F. Cook, *Another Book of Sussex Verse* (1928).

5   Mrs H.L. Piozzi (Mrs Thrale), *Anecdotes of the Late Samuel Johnson* (1887), p. 168.

6   John Keats, 'To Fanny Brawne', *The Complete Poetical Works and Letters of John Keats* (1899), p. 384.

7   Anon. (T.K. Cromwell), *Excursions in the County of Sussex* (1822), pp. 61–62.

8   G. Grigson, 'Hills and Poems', *Geographical Magazine* 29 (1956), pp. 388–96.

9   C.F. Cook (ed.), *The Book of Sussex Verse* (1920), pp. 128–30.

10 Francis Tutté (ed.), *The Works of William Hay* (J. Nichols, 2 vols, 1794).

11 M.A. Lower, *Contributions to Literature* (1854).

12 J. Betjeman, *Coming Home* (1998), p. 156.

13 http://spenserians.cath.vt.edu/CommentRecord.php?action=GET&cmmtid=4200.

14 James Hurdis, *The Village Curate* (4th edition, with an introduction by his sisters, 1813), pp. 69–70.

15 R. Wells (ed.), *Victorian Village* (1992).

16 C. Whittick, 'Hurdis, James' (*ODNB*, 2008).

17 http://spenserians.cath.vt.edu/CommentRecord.php?action=GET&cmmtid=4202; Robert Willmott, 1838.

18 N. Llewellyn, *East Sussex Church Monuments 1530–1830* (2011), p. 38.

19 Charlotte Smith, *Elegiac Sonnets* (1784).

20 J.M. Labbe, *Charlotte Smith* (2003).

21 Valerie Derbyshire, *The Picturesque, the Sublime, the Beautiful* (2019).

22 Smith, 'Beachy Head' (in C. Knowles and I. Horrocks, *Charlotte Smith* (2017), p. 173.

23 Smith, *The Emigrants*, Book 2 (Ibid., p.46).

24 The émigrés: the ousted aristocrats fleeing to England, especially following the execution of Louis XVI in January 1793. In August, her daughter Augusta married the emigrant Alexandre de Foville, with Smith's blessing.

25 Smith, *The Emigrants*, Book 1.

26 Smith, *The Old Manor House* (1793).

27 D.E. White, 'Autobiography and Elegy: The Early Romantic Poetics of Thomas Gray and Charlotte Smith' in Thomas Woodman (ed.), *Early Romantics* (1998), pp.57–69; Scott, quoted in Derbyshire, *The Picturesque, the Sublime, the Beautiful*, p. 2.

28 George Eliot, 'In a London Drawing-Room' (1865) in A. Van den Broek, *The Complete Shorter Poetry of George Eliot* (2016).

29 Richard Jefferies, *Nature near London* (1905), pp. vii–viii.

30 J.S. Mill, *Principles of Political Economy* (1848), p. 113.

31 R.D. Charques, *This Other Eden* (1936), pp. 51–52.

32 William Blake, 'Gnomic Verses' in D.V. Erdman (ed.), *The Complete Poetry and Prose of William Blake* (1988), p. 511.

33 Habberton Lulham, 'To the Hills' in *The Other Side of Silence* (1913).

34 Walter de la Mare, 'Arabia', *Georgian Poetry* (1911–1912), p. 67.

35 V. Gammon, 'Folk Song Collecting in Sussex and Surrey 1843–1914', *History Workshop Journal* 10 (1980), pp. 61–89.

36 G.K. Chesterton, 'The Aesthetes in the Kitchen Garden' in Chesterton, *Ultimate Collection* (e-Artnow 2019), originally in the *Daily News*, 13 and 20 August 1904.

37 H. Heine, *The Prose Writings of Heinrich Heine* (1887), p. 47.

38 R. Jefferies, *The Story of my Heart* (1938).

39 Wilkinson, *Sussex Peep-Show*, p. 39.

40 H. Williamson, *Young Phillip Maddison* (1953), pp. 9–10.

41 D.E. Moggridge, *Maynard Keynes* (1992), p. 403. Keynes was gazetted as Baron Keynes of Tilton in Sussex.

42 Robert Graves, 'To Walk on Hills', *Collected Poems* (1961), p. 85.

43 Mrs Gaskell, *Mary Barton* (1848), p. 269.

44 Henry David Thoreau in D.M. Gross (ed.), *The Price of Freedom* (2007), p. 67.

45 *The Winter's Tale*, Act IV, Scene II, 'A Road near the Shepherd's Cottage'.

46 The coloured third edition one-inch OS sheets were published in the early twentieth century, and that covering Guildford and Horsham, for example, in 1909. After 1918, eye-catching covers were introduced.

47 Thorne, *Rambles by Rivers*, p. 67; Gideon Algernon Mantell, *A Day's Ramble in and about the Ancient Town of Lewes* (1846), p. 135.

48 National Portrait Gallery, www.npg.org.uk/collections/search/person/mp04283/sir-leslie-stephen.

49 L. Stephens, 'In Praise of Walking' in *Studies of a Biographer*, Vol. 1 (1898), p. 258, containing many examples of writer-walkers (pp. 254–85).

50 Indy Clark, *Thomas Hardy's Pastoral* (2015).

51 R.L. Stevenson, 'An Autumn Effect' in *The Portfolio: An Artistic Periodical* 6 (1875), p. 53.

52 Peter Brandon's own preferred walking pattern was essentially thus, as many who have struggled to keep pace can testify.

53 E. Gosse, *Coventry Patmore* (1905), pp. 141, 155, 203.

54 John Burroughs in Charlotte Zoë Walker (ed.), *The Art of Seeing Things* (2001), p. 47.

55 Brandon, *The Discovery of Sussex*, pp. 28, 94, 175. Davidson committed suicide in Cornwall in 1909.

56 Wilkinson, *Sussex Peep-Show*, p. 24.

57 L. Binyon, 'Thunder on the Downs' in *Selected Poems* (1922), p. 69.

58 See D. Davies, 'The Evocative Symbolism of Trees' in D. Cosgrove and S. Daniels (eds), *The Iconography of Landscape* (1988), pp. 32–42.

59 Gilbert White, *The Natural History of Selborne* (ed. R.M. Lockley, 1949), pp. 158–59.

60 Hudson, *Nature in Downland*, p. 22; Eleanor Farjeon, *Martin Pippin* (1921), p. 366.

61 Anthony Mario Ludovici, 'The South Downs' in *The Saturday Review* (27 January 1917).

62 A critique of white, heterosexual masculinist positions in topography is Gillian Rose's, 'Looking at Landscape: The Uneasy Pleasures of Power' in *Feminism and Geography* (1993), pp. 102–30.

63 Noyes, 'The Silver Crook', *The Elfin Artist and Other Poems* (1920), pp. 27–28.

64 A.F. Bell, *The Dear Land of the Heart* (1913).

65 John Halsham, *Lonewood Corner* (1907), p. 193; *Old Standards* (1913), pp. 256–62.

66 Virginia Woolf, 'Evening over Sussex: Reflections in a Motor Car' (1927) in the posthumous *The Death of the Moth and other Essays* (1942), p. 82; and A. Thacker, *Moving through Modernity: Space and Geography in Modernism* (2003), pp. 152–91.

67 Charles Dalmon, 'An English Song Abroad', *A Poor Man's Riches*, p. 18.

68 R. Williams, *The Country and the City* (1973).

69 George Meredith, *One of our Conquerors* (1891), p. 7.

Chapter 4

1   Norman Douglas, *Siren Land* (1911), p. 43.

2   S.P.B. Mais, *See England First* (1927), p. 48.

3   Robert Graves, 'The Cottage' in *The Complete Poems* (2003), pp. 36–37.

4   Thorne, *Rambles by Rivers*, pp. 75–77.

5   W. Cobbett, *Rural Rides* (1830, quotation from the 1967 edition), p. 126; *Cottage Economy* (1823).

6   Alexander Gilchrist (edited by Anne Gilchrist), *Life of William Blake*, Vol. 1 (1880), pp. 149–50.

7   Belloc, 'The South Country' in *Songs of the South Country* (1951).

8   Sir Sydney Cockerell: long-time friend, one-time secretary of Morris's Kelmscott Press and Blunt's part-time secretary. His son invented the hovercraft.

9   J. Aplin, *The Letters of Philip Webb*, Vol. 3, 1899–1902 (2016), pp. 149–50.

10 *The Chronicle of a Country Cottage* (1940); *The Cottage in the Fields* (1945); *Down Hoe Lane* (1950); *Come*

into the Country (1946). His papers are at West Sussex Record Office (AM933) and in the Gerard Young Collection (GY).

11   Binyon, 'The Dream House' in *The Secret* (1920), p. 71.

12   For example, E. Meynell, *Sussex Cottage* (1936), including photos by Haberton Lulham; *Sussex* (1947).

13   F. Meynell and V. Mendel (afterwards Meynell), *The Week-end Book* (1924, and many later editions).

14   This remained the case in 2020 when, despite a warm invitation, the editor was regretfully unable to enter to inspect the library because of Covid-19 restrictions.

15   J.A. Vickers, 'John Drinkwater's Correspondents', *The Yale University Library Gazette* 48 (1974), pp. 200–10.

16   John Drinkwater, 'Of Greatham (to those that live there)' in *Swords and Ploughshares* (1915), p. 37; Coulson Kernahan, *Six Famous Living Poets* (1922), p. 236.

17   G.J. Zytaruk and J.T. Boulton (eds), *The Letters of D.H. Lawrence*, Vol. 2 (1981), p. 276. For the Lawrences and Meynells at Greatham, see K. Cuchman, '"I wish that story at the bottom of the sea": The Making and Re-Making of "England, My England"', *Études Lawrenciennes* 26 (2015), (https://journals.openedition.org/lawrence/235).

18   Zytaruk and Boulton (eds), *Letters*, Vol. 2, p. 282.

19   D.H. Lawrence, *The Rainbow* (1949), p. 464.

20   Lawrence, 'England, My England' in *England, My England and Other Stories* (edited by B. Steele, 1990), p. 11. Lawrence transferred the story location to Hampshire, although he is unmistakably describing the Greatham district.

21   G.H. Ford, *Double Measure* (1965), p. 84.

22   N. Delbanco, *Group Portrait* (1982), especially Chapter 1, 'Figures in a Landscape', and Pent Farm having a 'genius of place' for Conrad (p. 95).

23   M. Saunders (ed.), *Ford Madox Ford, Selected Poems* (1997), pp. 96–97.

24   Stella Bowen, *Drawn from Life* (1940), p. 69. Privacy was also sought from Ford's previous lover, Violet Hunt. See J. Weisenfarth, *Ford Madox Ford and the Regiment of Women* (2005), p. 59.

25   R.M. Ludwig, *Letters of Ford Madox Ford* (1965), p. 94.

26   Ford, *It was the Nightingale*, p. 23.

27   Ludwig, *Letters*, p. 108, to F.S. Flint 30 June 1920.

28   Ford, *No Enemy*, p. 10.

29   Ford, *No Enemy*, p. 23.

30   Ford, *It was the Nightingale*, pp. 107–10.

31   Elgar rented Brinkwells, near Fittleworth, between 1917 and 1922, where he wrote his Cello Concerto as well as other major late works.

32   Saunders, *Ford Madox Ford: A Dual Life*, Vol. 2, pp. 80, 357.

33   Fiona MacCarthy, 'Gill, (Arthur) Eric Rowton', *ODNB* (2014). And E. Gill, *Autobiography* (1940), pp. 205–15.

34   Brandon, *Discovery of Sussex*, pp.177–82. In early 2019, revelations about Gill's perverted sexual proclivities helped to fuel a debate about whether the character of an artist can be divorced from their artistic productions.

35   Anon., 'Art in Ditchling', *Ditchling Parish Council Magazine*, 12 November 2020, p. 16.

Chapter 5

1   W.S. Blunt, 'Possibilities of Peasant Ownership in Sussex', *Nineteenth Century and After*, 59 (1906), p. 955.

2   Neville Lytton, *The English Country Gentleman* (1925), p. 241.

3   E.M. Forster, *Abinger Harvest* (1936, 1974 edition), pp. 297–99.

4   Elizabeth Longford, *A Pilgrimage of Passion* (1979).

5   Lucy McDiarmid, 'A Box for Wilfrid Blunt', *Proceedings of the Modern Languages Association*, 120 (1), *Special Topic: On Poetry* (January 2005), pp. 163–80.
6   Shoon = plural form of shoe.
7   Lytton, *Blunt*, pp. 304–05. Crabbet Park was bisected by the new M23 in 1971 when the horses and stables were sold. For Crabbett, see West Sussex Record Office: Blunt Mss Box 68/Crabbet Stud, covering the years 1889–1919.
8   Blunt, *Poetical Works*, Vol. 2 (1914), pp. 11–13; Lag = a meadow strip along a stream.
9   I. Nairn and N. Pevsner, *The Buildings of England: Sussex* (1965), pp. 321–23; text altered and expanded in the revised edition, E. Williamson, T. Hudson, J. Musson and I. Nairn, *The Buildings of England: Sussex: West* (2019), pp. 587–90.
10 The area west of Horsham around Broadbridge Heath has seen a large expansion of housing since Peter Brandon wrote in 2010, changing the area beyond recognition, and with further housing currently under construction (2023).
11 Blunt, *Poetical Works*, Vol. 2, '*Sed nos qui vivimus*', pp. 33–52, stanza x.
12 Blunt, *Poetical Works*, Vol. 1, 'Sonnet in Assonance', p. 88.
13 Blunt, *Poetical Works*, Vol. 1, 'Worth Forest', p. 23.
14 Blunt, *Poetical Works*, Vol. 1, 'A Day in Sussex', p. 80.
15 Blunt, *Poetical Works*, Vol. 1, 'Chanclebury Ring', p. 87.
16 Edith Finch, *Wilfrid Scawen Blunt 1840–1922* (1938), p. 372; England & Wales, National Probate Calendar 1858–1995.
17 Blunt, *Poetical Works*, Vol. 1, 'Worth Forest', p. 17.
18 Finch, *Blunt*, p. 354.
19 Finch, *Blunt*, p. 345.
20 'Possibilities of Peasant Ownership', pp. 955–67.
21 W.E. Henley and G. Wyndham, *The Poetry of Wilfrid Blunt* (1898), p. v. The reference is from Henley's introduction.
22 Blunt, *A New Pilgrimage and Other Poems* (1889), written in 1881, and see Blunt to Hudson on birds in Sussex, 26 June 1913 (Lytton, *Blunt*, pp. 68–70).
23 Blunt, 'On the Shortness of Time' (*Poetical Works*, Vol. 1), p. 87.
24 D. Pryce-Jones, *Treason of the Heart* (2011).
25 R. Flower, *Napoleon to Nasser* (2011), p. 102.
26 Blunt, 'The Wind and the Whirlwind' (*Poetical Works*, Vol.2), pp. 221–35.
27 Lytton, *Blunt*, p. 84.
28 Blunt, 'A Dream of Good' (*Poetical Works*, Vol. 1), p. 329.
29 Personal communication from Arthur Shopland to Peter Brandon.
30 The Fitzwilliam Museum Cambridge houses the largest single archive of works by, and associated with, Wilfrid Scawen Blunt, including diaries and drafts of major works, together with correspondence with Winston Churchill, Roger Casement, T.E. Lawrence, Oscar Wilde, Lord Alfred Douglas, E.M. Forster and Ezra Pound.
31 Blunt, *My Diaries: Part I* (1922), pp. 240, 376–77. A complete version of the London publication of 1919–20, with an introduction by Lady Gregory.
32 Blunt, *My Diaries: Part I* (1922),
33 Finch, *Blunt*, p. 356.
34 Viola Meynell, *Francis Thompson and Wilfrid Meynell* (1952), p. 178.
35 *The Love-Lyrics and Songs of Proteus* (1892).
36 W. Stone, *The Cave and the Mountain* (1966), pp. 289–90.

Chapter 6

1   Roger Ebbatson, 'Prophecy and Utopia: Richard Jefferies and the Transcendentalists', *The Glass* 19 (2007), reprinted in http://richardjefferiessociety.co.uk/articles/83_RJ_transandentalists_Ebbatson. pdf.

2   Richard Jefferies, *Wildlife in a Southern County* (1879, reprint 2005), p. 141.

3   See Edward Thomas, *Richard Jefferies* (1909) and the *Richard Jefferies Society Journal* for details of his life and work (http://richardjefferiessociety.co.uk).

4   A. Rossabi, *A Peculiarly English Genius*, Vol. 1 (2017). For comparisons with Thoreau see W. Besant, *The Eulogy of Richard Jefferies* (1905), pp. 221–27.

5   *Sussex Daily News* (14 April 1881). Lorna Road was then a new development, part of the Goldsmit Estate.

6   Rossabi, A Peculiarly English Genius, p. 51.

7   W. Salkeld, 'Richard Jefferies in Crowborough', *The Crowborough Field Society Journal* 1 (1978), reproduced at http://richardjefferiessociety.co.uk/articles/28_RJ_in_Crowborough.pdf.

8   Quotation from Besant, *Eulogy*, p. 339, from a letter in November 1885 from Crowborough to C.P. Scott of the *Manchester Guardian*.

9   S.J. Looker and C. Porteous, *Richard Jefferies: Man of the Fields* (1965), pp. 202–03; Rossabi, *A Peculiarly English Genius*, p. 53.

10   A.H. Anderson, 'Richard Jefferies and Sussex', *SCM* 11 (1937), pp. 524–30. And see Rossabi, 'Sussex and Richard Jefferies' (1994): http://richardjefferiessociety.co.uk/articles/76_Sussex_RJ_Rossabi.pdf).

11   Jefferies, 'Wild flowers', *The Open Air*, p. 34.

12   Jefferies, 'Wild flowers', *The Open Air*, p. 39.

13   Jefferies, 'Downs', *The Open Air*, p. 97.

14   Ronald Blythe, Foreword in Peter Tolhurst, *Wessex: A Literary Pilgrimage* (1999), p. 9.

15   Samuel J. Looker (ed.), *The Nature Diaries and Note-books of Richard Jefferies* (1948), pp. 137–39.

16   Richard Jefferies, 'Clematis Lane', *The Life of the Fields* (1884, 1983 edition), pp. 72–73.

17   Looker (ed.), *The Nature Diaries*, p. 139; *The Story of My Heart*, p. 28.

18   Looker (ed.), *The Nature Diaries*, pp. 139, 141, 143–44. The latter also in 'Wheatfields' in *Nature Near London*.

19   Jefferies, *Nature Near London*, p. 75.

20   Jefferies, *The Story of My Heart*, pp. 34–35.

21   Jefferies, 'The Breeze on Beachy Head' in *Nature Near London*, pp. 117–18.

22   Jefferies, 'Under the Acorns', *The Open Air*, p. 57.

23   Jefferies, *The Story of My Heart*, p. 19.

24   Published in two parts on 24 and 31 January 1885 in the *Manchester Guardian* and in *The Open Air*, pp. 94–111.

25   Jefferies, 'The Countryside: Sussex', *Field and Hedgerow* (1948), pp. 100–01.

26   Jefferies, 'The Southdown Shepherd', *Nature Near London*, pp. 110–11.

27   Jefferies, *The Open Air*, p. 98.

28   Besant, *Eulogy*, p. 362.

29   Thomas, *Richard Jefferies*, p. 111; Looker, *The Nature Diaries*, p. 81. Jefferies' influence extended also to the young Peter Brandon (page 13).

Chapter 7

1   Belloc, 'The South Country'.
2   A.N. Wilson, *Hilaire Belloc* (1997), p. 118.
3   For the antisemitism issue, see Chris Hare, *Hilaire Belloc: The Politics of Living* (History People UK, 2022).
4   *The Times* (17 July 1953), p. 8.
5   J.B. Morton, *Hilaire Belloc* (1955), pp. 68–69. Morton also quotes Belloc, 'One of the bores of growing old is that you lose your pleasure in landscape,' – certainly not something that happened to Peter Brandon.
6   Belloc, *The Four Men*, p. 7. All page references are to this 1912 edition.
7   Belloc, *Hills and the Sea*, pp. 197–98. Belloc does not name the place in this essay.
8   Belloc, 'Lift up your Hearts in Gumber' in *Sonnets and Verse* (1923), p. 3.
9   Belloc, 'Ha'nacker Mill' in *Sonnets and Verse*, p. 129.
10 Wilson, *Belloc*, p. 116.
11 E. Thomas, *A Literary Pilgrim in England* (1917), p. 153.
12 Belloc, 'The Weald' in *On Everything* (1909), pp. 174–79.
13 Belloc, *The Four Men*, p. 83.
14 Belloc, 'The Valley of the Rother' in *Hills and the Sea*, p. 237.
15 Belloc, *The Four Men*, p. ix.
16 Belloc's walk was recreated by Bob Copper and published as *Across Sussex with Belloc* (1994). In 2019, Chris Hare's 'Belloc, Broadwood and Beyond' was another example of the revival of interest, with Belloc now linked with the folk song collector Lucy Broadwood, who is buried at Rusper (https:// belloc-broadwood.org.uk/the-four-men).
17 A.H. Sidgwick, *Walking Essays* (1912), p. 208.
18 Belloc, *The Footpath Way* (1911), pp. 1–16.
19 Belloc, 'Stanzas Written on Battersea Bridge During a South-Westerly Gale' in *On Sailing the Sea* (1939), p. 1.
20 Belloc was elected a Liberal MP, representing Salford South from January 1906 until the general election in December 1910, for which, disillusioned with parliamentary politics, he did not stand. He had been elected despite being seen as a French Catholic in a strongly Nonconformist constituency with a temperance tradition. He was, however, generally seen as a loose cannon by his party.
21 E. Raymond, *Through Literature to Life* (1928), p. 242; Meynell, *Sussex Cottage*, p. 186; J. Buchan, *Memory Hold the Door* (1940), p. 56.
22 Belloc, 'Sonnet on being Rich' in *Sonnets and Verse*, p. 88.
23 Belloc, *Emmanuel Burden* (1904), with illustrations by G.K. Chesterton; G. Orwell, 'Second Thoughts on James Burnham', *Polemic* 3 (May 1946) (http://orwell.ru/library/reviews/burnham/ english/e_burnh.html).
24 For the wider context of Distributism among interwar ideas of a return to land-based small communities, including those of the Chesterbelloc, see D. Hardy, *Utopian England* (2000).
25 Jay P. Corrin, *G.K. Chesterton and Hilaire Belloc* (1981), pp. xi–xv *et seq*. Other supporters included Sir Henry Slesser, elected as an MP in 1924 having run a campaign on Distributist lines.
26 Belloc, *The County of Sussex* (1936).
27 Belloc, *The Four Men*, p. ix.
28 Belloc, *The Four Men*, p. 310.
29 R. Speaight, *The Life of Hilaire Belloc* (1958), p. xv.
30 Belloc, 'The Little Old Man' in *On Everything*, p. 22.
31 Belloc, *The Four Men*, p. viii.
32 Belloc, *The Four Men*, p. 309.

Chapter 8

1   I have unfortunately so far failed to trace the source of Peter Brandon's quotation.

2   Carrie: Caroline Starr Balestier Kipling (1862–1939). They married in January 1892. See Adam Nicolson, *The Hated Wife: Carrie Kipling 1862–1939* (2001).

3   M. Smith, *Kipling's Sussex* (2008), p. 39, which is excellent on Kipling and the Sussex landscape.

4   Max Beerbohm, *Cartoons* (1911); A. Sandison, 'Kipling: the Artist and the Empire' in A. Rutherford (ed.), *Kipling's Mind and Art* (1964), p. 147.

5   Tim Pye, 'An Object I Love', *National Trust Magazine* (Summer 2019), p. 53.

6   First published in *Harper's Magazine* (December 1909) and in his *Rewards and Fairies* (1910).

7   Rudyard Kipling, 'The Run of the Downs'. For this and others, see *The Complete Works of Rudyard Kipling* (e-artnow, 2017).

8   Cited in A. Kettle, *Literature and Liberation: Selected Essays* (1988), p. 215.

9   T. Pinney, 'South Africa and Sussex 1900–2' in Pinney (ed.), *The Letters of Rudyard Kipling, Vol. 3 1900–1910* (1996), pp. 1–116.

10   Kipling, *Something of Myself* (edited by T. Pinney, 1990), p. 104.

11   M. Cohen, *Rudyard Kipling to Rider Haggard* (1965), pp. 63, 139.

12   A. Lycett, *Rudyard Kipling* (1999), p. 379.

13   A. Lycett, *Rudyard Kipling*, p. 347.

14   Pinney, *The Letters of Rudyard Kipling, Vol. 3, 1900–1910*, pp. 431–32.

15   'The Land' appears at the end of the short story 'Friendly Brook', from *A Diversity of Creatures* (1917), pp. 35–36.

16   Lycett, *Rudyard Kipling*, p. 436. Members of the Isted and Hobden families were farming locally in the mid-nineteenth century and the names were thus well known around the Dudwell Valley.

17   Although based on a real person, 'Old Hobden' was also Kipling's version of Edward Thomas's 'Lob', the symbolic countryman, and part of an elite cultural literary trope.

18   M. Seymour-Smith, *Rudyard Kipling* (1989), pp. 347–48.

19   Kipling, *Barrack Room Ballads* (1892).

20   First published in the *Metropolitan Magazine* in March 1914, the *Windsor Magazine* in December 1914 and in *A Diversity of Creatures*.

21   Kipling, 'The Floods' in *A Diversity of Creatures*.

22   First published in *Century Magazine* in August 1905, accompanied by the poem 'The Recall'.

23   Kipling, 'An Habitation Enforced' in *Actions and Reactions* (1909), p. 15.

24   Kipling, *Something of Myself*, p. 109.

25   Roger Lancelyn Green, 'Kipling' in D.L. Kirkpatrick (ed.), *Twentieth-Century Children's Writers* (1978), p. 701.

26   R. Vaughan Williams, *Thanksgiving for Victory*, later called *A Song of Thanksgiving*, Catalogue of Works 1944/4.

27   Kipling, *Puck of Pook's Hill* (1906), pp. 13–14.

28   http://www.kiplingsociety.co.uk/rg_habitation1.htm.

29   A point also made by Halsham (page 41).

30   Kipling, *Something of Myself*, pp. 119–20.

31   Dornford Yates: pen name of Cecil William Mercer (1885–1960), a popular interwar novelist.

32   Pinney, *The Letters of Rudyard Kipling*, Vol. 3, 1900–10, pp. 150–51.

33   Smith, *Kipling's Sussex*, pp. 63–75.

34   Peter Brandon thought this might be a reference to the Roman Stane Street, but I am happy to go with Michael Smith's interpretation as the Roman Greensand Way, running parallel along the foot of the Downs escarpment (Smith, *Kipling's Sussex*, p.56). R. Thurston Hopkins, *Kipling's Sussex Revisited* (1929), pp. 46–47, favours Shipley; Smith suggests Sompting Abbots.

35   Kipling, *Traffics and Discoveries* (1904), pp. 315–16.

36 Kipling, 'The Deep-sea Cables', first published in *English Illustrated Magazine* (May 1893). The first successful transatlantic cable was in service by 1866.
37 Adam Nicholson, *Bateman's, East Sussex* (2006).
38 Seymour-Smith, *Rudyard Kipling*, p. 338. But the book otherwise provides little elaboration on this important theme.
39 Cohen, *Rudyard Kipling to Rider Haggard*, p. 138. 'The Ballad of Minepit Shaw' from *Rewards and Fairies*.
40 Kipling, 'The Way through the Woods' in *Rewards and Fairies*.
41 A. Wilson, *The Strange Ride of Rudyard Kipling* (1977), p. 285.
42 A. Wilson, *The Strange Ride of Rudyard Kipling*, pp. 327–31.
43 Edward Said, *Orientalism* (1978), pp. 226–28.
44 Seymour-Smith, *Rudyard Kipling*, pp. 7–11, 114–15.
45 Lycett, *Rudyard Kipling*, pp. 590–91.
46 P. Rush, *Great Men of Sussex* (1956), p. 109.
47 Hopkins, *Kipling's Sussex Revisited*, p. 24.

Chapter 9

1   Habberton Lulham, 'To Each his Own', *Songs from the Downs and Dunes* (1908), p. 84.
2   See his photographs illustrating Adelaide Gosset, *Shepherds of Britain* (1911). This also includes Lulham's 'The Shepherd and his Lore' from *Songs of the Downs and Dunes*.
3   Edward Thomas, 'Book review: *Songs from the Downs and Dunes*, by E.P. Habberton Lulham' (*The Morning Post*, 25 June 1908).
4   Latterly, a school for children with special educational needs.
5   In 1888, W.G. Grace came as captain and secretary to the London County Club and would presumably have played with Lulham. The club wound up in 1908 having played first-class cricket for some years.
6   Lulham, *Devices and Desires* (1904). Lulham received a complimentary acknowledgement from A.E. Houseman on receiving a copy of the book. Houseman thought several of the poems very good, although he rather disliked the rhyming of 'morn' and 'dawn'! See A.E. Houseman (edited by A. Burnett), *The Letters of A.E. Houseman* (2007), p. 159. Thomas Hardy sent 'limited compliments' in late 1905, T. Hands, *A Hardy Chronology* (1992), p. 110.
7   N.P. Blaker, *Sussex in Bygone Days* (1919), p. ix.
8   Lydia Lidstone, 'Habberton Lulham, Sussex Poet', *SCM* 4 (1930), p. 544.
9   *Rendcomb College Magazine* (1936, Vol. 5 [1]).
10 Lewes County Grammar School for Girls opened in 1913, followed in 1930 by the boys' grammar school. The schools merged to form the modern Priory Comprehensive School.
11 *The Barbican*, June 1936, Easter Term Lectures; *The Cranleighan*, December 1938, p. 151.
12 Lulham, 'Downland Destiny', *SCM* 2 (1928), pp. 96–98.
13 Lidstone, *Habberton Lulham*, p. 544.
14 '"Slip out of Life" – Sussex Poet's Letter to the Coroner', obituary in *Sussex Express and County Herald* (15 July 1940), p. 8.
15 A wooden box of his slides was recently found in Eastbourne containing many images of gypsies in Sussex (www.memorywall.org.uk/documents/Hidden_Photographs_of_a_Hidden_People.pdf). Some of the slides were taken by other photographers but probably used by Lulham in his lectures.
16 Lulham, 'On the Downs', in *Downs and Dunes*, p. 17.
17 Barclay Wills' *Shepherds of Sussex* (1938). Four photographs by Lulham, including one of Jim Fowler.
18 Lulham, 'Stray Memories' in Wills, *Shepherds*, p. 100.
19 Gosset, *Shepherds of Britain* (1911).

20 Probably New Barn Farm, now an equestrian and livery centre.

21 Lulham, 'Amberley and her Wild Brooks', *SCM* 13 (1939), pp. 598–603.

22 Lulham, 'Foreword' in Blaker, *Sussex in Bygone Days*, p. xi. The practice of putting bells on sheep is retained in other parts of Europe. Canisters or cluckets were the primary types. Canister bells are the oldest type, having the same width from shoulder to mouth with a flat crown. The specimen at the Museum of English Rural Life (University of Reading) actually comes from Ditchling.

23 'To the Hills' in *The Other Side of Silence*, p. 59.

24 Michael Fairless (Margaret Fairless Barber 1869–1901), *The Roadmender* (1911).

25 Lulham, 'Granny Coombe's Cottage' in *The Downland Post*, 1 April 1924, pp.116–18.

26 *Downs and Dunes*, p. 85.

27 Lulham, *The Other Side of Silence* (1913). The poem 'Number 4' may have referred to his younger days, 'my never-failing sanctuary' at No. 4 Hill Crest Road, Sydenham.

28 Candida Lycett Green (ed.), *John Betjeman Letters 1926–1951* (1994), p. 308.

Chapter 10

1 Virginia Woolf, *The Diary of Virginia Woolf, Vol. 2: 1920–1924* (edited by Anne Olivier Bell and Andrew McNeillie, 1978), Saturday, 10 April 1920.

2 Within the huge industry of interpretations of her life and work is Hermione Lee, *Virginia Woolf* (2006). The voluminous papers of both Virginia and Leonard are among the Bloomsbury Archives in the Special Collections, University of Sussex (The Keep, Falmer).

3 Jane Brown, *Spirits of Place* (2002), p. 30. In Firle, Little Talland House was named after the holiday home in St Ives, where the family stayed between 1882 and 1894; Nigel Nicolson and Joanne Trautmann (eds), *The Letters of Virginia Woolf, Vol. 1* (1975) p. 476.

4 Originally spelt 'Asheham' but now more generally 'Asham'. L. Woolf, *Beginning Again* (1963), p. 56. See http://thresholds.chi.ac.uk/the-story-behind-the-asham-trust. In 1932, a cement works was begun here, with the house used for a quarry manager. The quarry expanded but later became a landfill site. The house was demolished in 1994.

5 Virginia Woolf, *Virginia Woolf: The Complete Collection* (2017), p. 4047.

6 Judy Moore, *The Bloomsbury Trail in Sussex* (1995).

7 E. Bishop, *A Virginia Woolf Chronology* (1989), pp. 107–08.

8 *The Diary of Virginia Woolf*, a five-volume set covering 1915–40 (1977), variously edited by Ann Olivier Bell and Andrew McNeillie.

9 Virginia Woolf, *Virginia Woolf: The Complete Collection*, Virginia to Vanessa Bell, 25 June 1938; 20 January 1939; 12 July 1940.

10 Quentin Bell, *Virginia Woolf*, Vol. 1 (1976), p. 148.

11 Virginia Woolf, *The Waves* (1931).

12 Virginia Woolf, *The Waves*, p. 199.

13 Virginia Woolf, *Virginia Woolf: The Complete Collection*, p. 4436.

14 Virginia Woolf, *Virginia Woolf: The Complete Collection*, p. 3341.

15 McNeillie (ed.), *The Essays of Virginia Woolf, Vol. 2: 1912–1918* (1987), p. 40.

16 Jasper Botten, dairy farmer at Place Farm, Rodmell.

17 Virginia Woolf, *Virginia Woolf: The Complete Collection*, p. 1622.

18 Virginia Woolf, *Virginia Woolf: The Complete* Collection, p. 2418.

19 For Virginia Woolf's relationship to the Sussex countryside and elsewhere, see Peter Tolhurst, *Virginia Woolf's English Hours* (2015).

20 Virginia Woolf, *Virginia Woolf: The Complete Collection*, 1 March 1937; *The Diary of Virginia Woolf, Vol.5: 1936–1941*, p. 99.

21 5 September 1928; Jean Moorcraft Wilson, *Virginia Woolf's London* (2000), p. 10. Her walking and observing in both town and countryside led to the description of her as a '*Flâneuse*', Christian Soleil, *Virginia Woolf, la Flâneuse de Rodmell* (2015).

22 Now the Campaign to Protect Rural England.

23 Virginia Woolf, *The Diary of Virginia Woolf, Vol. 3: 1925–1930* (edited by Bell and McNeillie, 1980), 25 September 1927, p. 158. Reverend James Hawkeford was rector from 1896 until his death in January 1928.

24 Virginia Woolf, *The Diary of Virginia Woolf, Vol. 3: 1925–1930*, 22 September 1928.

25 Virginia Woolf, *The Diary of Virginia Woolf, Vol. 5: 1936–1941*, 26 April 1938. For the work on Monk's House, see N. Hancock, 'Elusive Encounters: Seeking out Virginia Woolf in Her Commemorative House Museum' in J. Dubino et al. (eds), *Virginia Woolf: Twenty-First-Century Approaches* (2015), pp. 34–50.

26 Virginia Woolf, *The Diary of Virginia Woolf, Vol. 4: 1931–1935*, 26 November 1934.

27 Virginia Woolf, *The Diary of Virginia Woolf, Vol. 3 1925–1930*, 8 September 1930.

28 Virginia Woolf, *The Diary of Virginia Woolf, Vol. 4: 1931–1935*, 8 February 1932.

29 Virginia Woolf, *The Diary of Virginia Woolf, Vol. 5: 1936–1941*, 8 October 1938.

30 Bell, *Biography*, Vol. 2, p. 210.

31 Nicolson and Trautmann (eds), *The Letters of Virginia Woolf, Vol. 6: 'Leave the Letters Till We're Dead'* (1980), p. 425.

32 Nicolson and Trautmann (eds), *The Letters, Vol. 6*, p. 460.

33 Virginia Woolf, *The Diary of Virginia Woolf, Vol. 3, 1925–1930*, pp. 197–98.

34 Nicolson and Trautmann (eds), *The Letters, Vol. 6*, p. 12.

35 Nicolson and Trautmann (eds), *The Letters, Vol. 6*, p. 416.

36 For her participation in the WI, see C. Jones, *Virginia Woolf: Ambivalent Activist* (2015).

37 K.C. Hill-Miller, *From the Lighthouse to Monk's House* (2001), p. 8; G. Beer, 'Virginia Woolf and Pre-History' in E. Warner (ed.), *Virginia Woolf: A Centenary Perspective* (1984), pp. 99–123. Virginia's interest in Darwin, and natural history more broadly, is in C. Alt, *Virginia Woolf and the Study of Nature* (2010).

38 McNeillie (ed.), *The Essays, Vol. 2: 1912–1918*, p. 41.

39 O.G.S. Crawford and A. Keiller, *Wessex from the Air* (1928); G. Holleyman, 'The Celtic field-system in South Britain' in *Antiquity* 9 (1935), pp. 443–54.

40 Virginia Woolf, *Between the Acts* (1941), p. 8.

41 'The Historian and "The Gibbon"', *Times Literary Supplement* (24 April 1937), p. 1. This was marking the bicentenary of Gibbon's birth in 1737.

42 Woolf, *Between the Acts*, p. 13.

43 Virginia Woolf, *The Diary of Virginia Woolf, Vol. 5: 1936–1941*, pp. 133, 135. The spelling was initially variable before settling on Pointz Hall.

44 Virginia Woolf, *The Diary of Virginia Woolf, Vol. 5: 1936–1941*, pp. 197 and 346.

45 Woolf, *Between the Acts*, p. 93.

46 Woolf, *Between the Acts*, p. 34.

47 Nicolson and Trautmann (eds), *The Letters, Vol. 6*, p. 449.

48 Alexandra Harris, *Virginia Woolf* (2013), p. 153.

49 Natania Rosenfeld, *Outsiders Together* (2001), p. 169. Quote from Leonard in *Woolf's Downhill all the Way* (1967), p. 254.

50 Virginia Woolf, *Diary, Vol. 5: 1936–1941*; Monday, 24 March 1941.

Chapter 11

1   S. Kaye-Smith, *The Ploughman's Progress* (1933), p. 26.
2   Kaye-Smith, *Three Ways Home* (1937), pp. 11–12.
3   The Sheila Kaye-Smith Society was formed in 1987 (www.sheilakayesmith.org.uk); S. Cooper, *The Shining Cord of Sheila Kaye-Smith* (2017). In the 1939 register, she is returned as 'novelist' but Penrose is a 'poultry farmer'.
4   M. Cowley, 'The Women of Thornden', *Dial* 67 (1920), pp. 259–62, writing of *The Challenge to Sirius* (1917) and *The Four Roads* (1919).
5   Kaye-Smith, *The Treasures of the Snow* (1950), p. 40.
6   Kaye-Smith, *Sussex Gorse* (1916), p. 41.
7   Kaye-Smith, *Joanna Godden* (1921), p. 10.
8   Kaye-Smith, *Sussex Gorse*, p. 462.
9   Kaye-Smith, *The End of the House of Alard* (1923); R. Thurston Hopkins, *Sheila Kaye-Smith and the Weald Country* (1925).
10 Kaye-Smith, *Little England* (1918), p. 293.
11 Kaye-Smith, *The Village Doctor* (1929).
12 Kaye-Smith, *Ploughman's Progress* (1933).
13 Kaye-Smith, *The Valiant Woman* (1939), p. 4.
14 Kaye-Smith, *The Treasures of the Snow* (1950) p. 27.
15 Kaye-Smith, *The Challenge to Sirius* (1917), p. 1.
16 Kaye-Smith, *Joanna Godden Married and Other Stories* (1926).
17 The neglect or criticisms of Kaye-Smith are addressed in D. Head, *Modernity and the English Rural Novel* (2017), pp. 60–66.
18 Eleanor Farjeon, *Edward Thomas: the Last Four Years* (1958), p. 129.
19 Presumably, Farjeon refers to the popular story of Sir John Mandeville, supposedly a knight from St Albans, who set off to the Holy Land, Asia and Africa in 1332.
20 Farjeon, *Martin Pippin in the Apple Orchard*, pp. 212–13, 267–68.
21 In the 1939 registration enumeration, Joe was living in East End Lane, Ditchling, and described as 'Author'.
22 Annabel Farjeon, *Morning Has Broken* (1986), p. 131. Eleanor's poem, set as a children's hymn 'Morning has broken' remains widely sung today. For her later years, see Denys Blakelock, *Eleanor: Portrait of a Farjeon* (1966).
23 Peter Brandon here references the work of Anne Harvey, executor of the Farjeon estate, who has undertaken much research and given talks on Eleanor Farjeon. See her edited *Like Sorrow or a Tune* (2013).
24 Originally written for adults, *Martin Pippin* became more widely known as a children's book following the illustrated edition of 1925 (A. Sponenberg, *Encyclopedia of British Women's Writing 1900–1950* (2006), pp. 88–89). The Children's Book Circle presents the prestigious Eleanor Farjeon Award annually to individuals or organisations for outstanding commitment to children's books. Farjeon herself received several awards although she refused an OBE, explaining that she 'did not wish to become different from the milkman' (www.childrensbookcircle.org.uk/pages/the-eleanor-farjeon-award).
25 According to the 1939 register, taken on 29 October, Eleanor's household at Laughton with George also included at least three Jewish refugees, including one retired Hungarian teacher. Eleanor's father, Benjamin, was Jewish.
26 'Eleanor Farjeon: The writer who left a permanent mark on the South Downs', *Sussex Life*, 10 April 2017. And see H. Coffey, 'Eleanor Farjeon and the South Downs National Park', www.southdowns.gov.uk/eleanor-farjeon-and-the-south-downs-national-park [accessed 6 September 2022].
27 Eleanor Farjeon, *Magic Casements* (1941), pp. 27, 37–42. In fact, a blister proved too much and she

took the train to Petersfield (Farjeon, *Edward Thomas*, p. 139). *Magic Casements* also recounts the walk with Lawrence.

28 Farjeon, *Edward Thomas*, p. 158.

29 Republished as a facsimile by the Snake River Press.

30 Naomi Lewis, 'Introduction' in *The Eleanor Farjeon Book* (1966), p. 4.

31 P. Holliday, 'Eric Gill, Amy Sawyer and the "Gladys Panel"' in Holliday (ed.), *Eric Gill in Ditchling: Four Essays* (2002), pp. 68–82.

32 Anne Parfitt-King, 'Amy Sawyer of Ditchling (1863–1945): Artist, Playwright and Lady of Letters', *The British Art Journal*, 14 (2013), pp. 81–82; and *Amy Sawyer of Ditchling*. Anne's great-aunt was companion and housekeeper to Amy Sawyer in later life.

33 Amy Sawyer, *Sussex Village Plays*, and others (1934).

34 Maisie Robson, *An Unrepentant Englishman* (2005), https://literaryreview.co.uk/ an-unrepentant-englishman-the-life-of-s-p-b-mais-ambassador-of-the-countryside.

35 There is a plaque on the Hall – 'S.P.B. Mais 1885–1975, novelist, travel writer, Champion of Cricket lived here 1927–1932'. The plaque was unveiled in 1997 by his daughters, Imogen and Lalage.

36 Timothy McCann, '"A Choice of Strawberries or Peaches": Exploring Sussex with S.P.B. Mais' in Paul Foster (ed.), *Sussex Seams Two* (2000), pp. 174–84.

37 www.kingsengland.com/an-unrepentant-englishman-c2x8930497; West Sussex Record Office, ACC 10887. Photocopy of the script *c.* 1940.

38 S.P.B. Mais, *Southern Rambles for Londoners* (1948) 2014 reproduction, p. vi.

39 S.P.B. Mais, Southern Rambles for Londoners, p. i.

40 Mais, 'A day with the hikers' in *Listen to the Country* (1939), pp. 221–25.

41 Mais, *All the Days of My Life* (1937), pp. 182–83. A second autobiography, *Buffets and Rewards* was published in 1952.

42 Mais, 'The Amenities of Southwick', *SCM* 3 (1929), pp. 535–41.

43 G.J. Johnson, 'Ernest Raymond' in G.M. Johnson (ed.), *British Novelists Between the Wars* (1998), pp. 265–75.

44 E. Raymond, *Tell England* (1922). Rather like Stella Gibbon with *Cold Comfort Farm*, this novel subsequently overshadowed all his later work.

45 Ancestry.co.uk: see his entry in *Kellys Directory*, 1938, for Haywards Heath.

46 Raymond's *ODNB* entry makes no mention of his Sussex writing (A.J.A. Morris, 'Raymond, Ernest 1888–1974' [2014]). But see G. Pass, 'The Sussex Novels of Ernest Raymond: No.1 – the Earlier Novels' and 'No. 2 – the Later Novels' in *SCM* 10 (1936), pp. 395–99, 465–68.

47 I have made minor editorial adjustments to Raymond's list according to details in the British Library catalogue. In 1932, Raymond published *Once in England*, which incorporated *A Family That Was* and *Mary Leith*.

48 Raymond, *Newtimber Lane* (1933). Sir Edmund was based on Raymond's father, George Blake.

49 Raymond, *We, the Accused* (1935); *Please You, Draw Near* (1969), p. 36.

50 Johnson, 'Ernest Raymond' in G.M. Johnson (ed.), *British Novelists Between the Wars*. The book was adapted for BBC television in 1980, starring Ian Holm.

51 Raymond, *Don John's Mountain Home* (1936).

52 Gibbons, *Cold Comfort Farm*. The prize had been won in 1926 by Mary Webb for *Precious Bane* (1924), ironically one source of caricature by Gibbons. In 1928, Sussex resident Virginia Woolf won the prize for *To the Lighthouse*. Woolf continued to maintain, however, that Stella Gibbons was a poor choice by the judges.

53 *Christmas at Cold Comfort Farm* (1940); *Conference at Cold Comfort Farm* (1949), *The Matchmaker* (1949).

54 Oliver, *Out of the Woodshed*, pp. 200–02.

55 Oliver, *Out of the Woodshed*, pp. 120–21.

56 *Cold Comfort Farm*, p. 16.

57 Faye Hammill, *Women, Celebrity and Literary Culture Between the Wars (2007)*, pp. 152–78.

58 *Cold Comfort Farm*, pp. 8–9. All page numbers are taken from the Penguin 1977 edition.
59 *Cold Comfort Farm*, pp. 32–33.
60 *Cold Comfort Farm*, p. 86.
61 *Cold Comfort Farm*, p. 45.
62 Hammill, *Women, Celebrity and Literary Culture*, pp. 152–78.
63 *Cold Comfort Farm*, p. 65.
64 *Cold Comfort Farm*, p. 55.
65 Williams, *The Country and the City*, pp. 302–03.

Chapter 12

1 Arthur Bell, 'Song of Praise to West Sussex', in Bell, *The Dear Land of the Heart*.
2 Leonard Clark (ed.), *Andrew Young: Prospect of a Poet* (1957), p. 89.
3 A.S. Cooke, *Off the Beaten Track in Sussex* (1911); H.M. Wallbrook, 'A Poet of the South Downs' in *Fortnightly Review* (September 1927), pp. 410–13.
4 Roger Simpson, 'Arthur Francis Bell (1875–1918)' in *Times Past* (Storrington and District Museum 39, Summer 2011).
5 Bell, 'The Happy Phantom' in Cook, *The Book of Sussex Verse*. The poem 'Song of Praise to West Sussex' is dedicated to C.F. Cook, who included praises to Bell in the brief biographical notes concluding his *Book of Sussex Verse*, pp. 206–07.
6 Bell, 'Song of the Sussex Coast' in *The Dear Land of the Heart*.
7 University of St Andrews Archive, ms 38761/4. Petre's two-volume biography of Tyrrell was placed on the index of forbidden books: M.D. Petre, *Autobiography and Life Of George Tyrrell* (1912); Bell dedicated 'Last Night' to Petre, who became a very active member of the Storrington community.
8 Bell, 'The Happy Phantom'.
9 See, for example, his 'Parson Herrick's Muse', *The Yellow Book 3* (1894), pp. 241–42.
10 For a tribute to Dalmon's poetry, see Anon., 'The Sussex Poetry of Charles Dalmon', *SCM* 1 (1927), pp. 593–97.
11 Dalmon, *A Poor Man's Riches*.
12 The tracing of Dalmon's identity is further confused by variable spellings of his name: his birth in the Old Shoreham baptismal register is recorded as 'Dolman', and his father's in 1840 as 'Dalman'.
13 Dalmon, 'Milking-time at a Wealden Farm' in *A Poor Man's Riches*, pp. 67–68.
14 'The Call of the Blood' in *A Poor Man's Riches*, p. 49.
15 'Cure [or care] of souls' – without his own parish.
16 Dalmon to Walt Whitman, 27 September 1888 (the Walt Whitman Archive: https://whitmanarchive. org/biography/correspondence/tei/loc.01437.html). Whitman had moved to Camden, New Jersey, in the last years of his life.
17 At South Square, his boarder, Frank(lin) Dyall (1870–1950), was returned in the 1901 census as an actor, whose later son was the better-known film and radio star Valentine Dyall (1908–85).
18 George Cockman, 'Charles Dalmon' (www.edward-thomas-fellowship.org.uk/Newsletter%20PDF/ Newsletter%2045%20August%202001.pdf).
19 https://lansburyslido.blogspot.com/2010/05/god-is-only-landlord.html [accessed 8 August 2022].
20 www.bfi.org.uk/films-tv-people/4ce2b6a5e39fb; Dalmon, 'Art direction in British Film Studios', *The Bioscope British Films Supplement* (July 1920), p. xv.
21 *A Poor Man's Riches*, p. v.
22 George Cockman, *Charles Dalmon: the Forgotten Poet Laureate of Sussex* (Horsham Museum Society, 2015).
23 Charles Dalmon, 'Summer Evening in an old Sussex Garden'. A slightly different version was

published as 'The Sussex Muse'. And see Brandon, *Discovery of Sussex*, p. 158 for Dalmon's *Singing as I Go* (1927).

24 He is credited with the words to 'What if the Fowler my Blackbird has Taken' (also known as 'The Royal Blackbird'), a popular 'street song' and see *Song Favours* for many examples (https://mudcat.org/Detail.CFM?messages__Message_ID=3880871).

25 British Library C.59.i.8: Andrew Marvell, 'The Garden' (*Miscellaneous Poems*, 1681), pp. 48–51.

26 Ormrod, Andrew Young.

27 Andrew Young, *A Prospect of Flowers* (1945), p. 132.

28 Roger D. Sell, *Trespassing Ghost: A Critical Study of Andrew Young* (1978).

29 Young, *Complete Poems* (ed. L. Clark,1974), pp. 15–25.

30 University of Edinburgh: E93.58, Folder 2: Andrew Young Papers: Correspondence 1943–70.

31 L. Norris, *Andrew Young: Remembrance and Homage* (1978).

32 L. Clark (ed.), *Andrew Young*.

33 Young, *A Prospect of Flowers* (1945) and *A Retrospect of Flowers* (1950).

34 Ormrod, *Andrew Young*, p. 113.

35 Young, *Nicodemus: A Mystery* (1937), broadcast on the BBC Home Service at 9.30 p.m. on 23 January 1944 (*Radio Times*).

36 Young, 'In the Fallow Field' (*Anthology of Twentieth Century English Poetry* [1960], Smithsonian Folkways Recordings, 2004).

37 Ormrod, *Andrew Young*, pp. 183–84, 'Old and New Assessments'.

38 The University of Sussex Library has several of Young's books of poetry, bequeathed from the library of Bishop Bell in 1968, and signed by Young himself.

39 Young, *The Poet and the Landscape* (1962). But nothing in the book touches directly on Sussex.

40 Peter Stansky and William Abrahams, *Julian Bell* (2012).

41 Peter Stansky and William Abrahams, *Julian Bell*, p. 88.

42 The poems 'Brumaire' (23 October to 21 November) and 'Frimaire' (21 November to 20 December) were named from months in the French Revolutionary calendar but nevertheless portray downland scenes.

43 Stansky and Abrahams, *Journey to the Frontier* (1966), p. 72.

44 Julian Bell 'London I' in *Work for the Winter and Other Poems* (1936), pp. 23–24.

45 Bell, 'Return' in *Work for the Winter*, p. 31.

46 Reproduced in J.M. Keynes, 'Foreword' in Quentin Bell (ed.), *Julian Bell: Essays, Poems and Letters* (1938), p. vi. Originally from the Annual Report, King's College Cambridge, 13 November 1937.

47 Bell, 'Arms and the Man' in M. Roberts (ed.), *New Signatures* (1932).

48 Nigel Nicolson, 'Introduction' in Sackville-West, *The Land*.

49 Letters exchanged between Yeats and Wellesley from 1935 to 1938 are collected in Wellesley, *Letters on Poetry from W.B. Yeats to Dorothy Wellesley* (1940) and see her *Beyond the Grave* (1952).

50 V. Sackville-West, *The Land* (1926), p. 45.

51 Virginia Woolf, *The Diary of Virginia Woolf, Vol. 3, 1925–1930*, pp. 191–92.

52 Vita wrote Wellesley's original *ODNB* entry ('sources: private information, personal knowledge'). It is now revised by Clare Taylor, 'Wellesley [née Ashton], Dorothy Violet, Duchess of Wellington' (2004).

53 Wellesley, *Poems of Ten Years, 1924–34* (1934).

54 W.B. Yeats (ed.), *Oxford Book of Modern Verse 1892–1935* (1936).

55 Kathleen Raines, 'Letters on Poetry from W.B. Yeats to Dorothy Wellesley' as cited in E. Malins and J. Purkis, *A Preface to Yeats* (2014), p. 156.

Chapter 13

1   Peter Brandon did not attempt to distinguish between 'fairy' and 'faery', using the words somewhat interchangeably, despite the latter being seen as a more mischievous or malicious presence than the helpful and beautiful spirit of the fairy.

2   Rudyard Kipling, 'Puck's Song', in *Puck*.

3   Charles Lamb, *The Works of Charles Lamb* (1838), p. 106.

4   For recent scholarly interest, see the University of Chichester Centre for Fairy Tales, Fantasy and Speculative Fiction and an annual publication, *Gramarye* (www.sussexfolktalecentre.org). The Folklore Society was founded in 1878.

5   Jacqueline Simpson explains in *Folklore of Sussex* (1973), that by the Victorian period, Sussex speech frequently used a 'reduplicated plural' such as 'wapses' or 'ghostses'. So, we get 'fairises' and hence, by confusion, the biblical 'Pharisees'.

6   Lulham, 'On the Downs' in *Songs from the Downs and Dunes*.

7   Lulham, 'On the Downs', 'Love's Neophyte' and 'Will there soon be Nine?' in *Songs from the Downs and Dunes*.

8   Bell, 'A Sussex Shepherd's Song' in *The Dear Land of the Heart*, p. 24.

9   Maurice H. Hewlett, *Open Country* (1909), p. 116.

10   A.S. Cooke, 'The Song of the Harebells' in Cooke, *Songs of the Sussex Downs*, pp. 14–15.

11   Dalmon, 'Milking-time at a Wealden Farm'.

12   Dalmon, 'The Olden Harpers' in *Flower and Leaf* (1900), p. 59.

13   Dalmon, 'O Never Say that Pan is Dead' in *Flower and Leaf*, p. 23.

14   Richard Realf, born in Framfield in 1832, published a book of poems, *Guesses at the Beautiful*, in 1852, containing fairy poetry. He emigrated to the USA shortly afterwards, serving in the Union Army in the Civil War. After the war, he established a school for freed slaves and resumed his old life as journalist and lecturer, but, with a complex private life, committed suicide in California in 1878 (http://theweald.org/N10.asp?NId=1405).

15   Dalmon, 'The Sussex Muse' in *Song Favours*, pp. 52–59.

16   The high concentration of downland references can be seen in the map of Sussex fairies and folklore at www.sussexfolktalecentre.org/wp-content/uploads/2015/06/folklore-map-prototype4.pdf.

17   https://johnirelandtrust.org/john-ireland-by-ian-lace.

18   Noyes, 'The Tramp Transfigured' in *Collected Poems*, Vol. 1 (1925).

19   W. Graham Robertson, *Time Was* (1931), pp. 296–97. His full name was Graham Walford Robertson.

20   Robertson, *Pinkie and the Fairies* (1932).

21   For some of Robertson's voluminous correspondence see Kerrison Preston (ed.), *Letters from Graham Robertson* (1953).

22   *Time Was*, p. 292. 'Old Chiddingfold' is now in the National Trust Library (NT 3129871) at Smallhythe Place, Kent, Ellen Terry's sixteenth-century house.

23   Blunden, *Undertones of War* (1928), p. 307.

24   Blunden, *Edmund Blunden* (1962), p. 22. Locketts Farm and Little Locketts are on the high ground of Itchingfield, between Blunden's old school at Christ's Hospital and Stane Street. At Denne Park, south of Horsham, the avenue of lime trees, although damaged by the 1987 storm, still lead to the early seventeenth-century mansion, now converted to apartments.

25   Blunden, 'A Southern Pilgrim' in Clark (ed.), *Andrew Young*, p. 107.

26   S. Russell, 'There Are More Things in Heaven and Earth', *SCM* 2 (1928), p. 165.

27   For fairies in late-nineteenth and early twentieth century imagination, see Tracy C. Davis, 'What are fairies for?' in T.C. Davis and P. Holland (eds), *The Performing Century* (2007), pp. 39–52. For fairies in Sussex, see also www.sussexarch.org.uk/saaf/fairies.html.

Chapter 14

1   Henry David Thoreau, *Walden; or, Life in the Woods* (1854), p. 196.

2   Belloc, *Short Talks with the Dead and Others* (1926), p. 125.

3   W.H. Auden, *Poems* (1930).

4   T.S. Eliot, 'The Waste Land' in *The Criterion* (1922).

5   Edward Marsh (ed.), *Georgian Poetry* (five vols, 1912 to 1922).

6   Auden (ed.), *A Choice of de la Mare's Verse* (1963), Introduction.

7   V. de Sola Pinto, *Crisis in English Poetry 1880–1940* (1963), p. 117.

8   *SCM* 1 (i), 1926.

9   G.D. Martineau, 'Out! Out! A Sussex Tocsin', *SCM* 1 (i) (1926), p. 21.

10 F.R. Leavis, *The Common Pursuit* (1952), pp. 182–203 for the relations between literature, history and sociology. The journal *Literary Geographies* is one example, begun in 2015, of an attempted integration of literature and social science. See N. Alexander, 'On Literary Geography', *Literary Geographies* 1 (2015), pp. 3–6.

11 https://agendapoetry.co.uk/documents/NotesforBroadsheet7.pdf, p. 131.

12 Stanley Baldwin, 'England: An Address' at the annual dinner of the Royal Society of St George at the Hotel Cecil, London, on 6 May 1924. And see Alun Howkins, 'The Discovery of Rural England' in R. Colls and P. Dodd (eds), *Englishness: Politics and Culture, 1880–1920* (1986), pp. 62–88.

13 Paul Fussell, 'Arcadian Recourses' in *The Great War and Modern Memory* (1975), pp. 231–69.

14 For the variety of Belloc's writing, see Speaight, *The Life of Hilaire Belloc*, pp. 489–505.

15 Clark (ed.), Introduction to *Complete Poems: Andrew Young*, pp. 15–25.

16 Edward Carpenter, *My Days and Dreams* (1916), p. 27; Sheila Rowbotham, *Edward Carpenter* (2008), p. 20.

17 Richard Lebeaux, *Thoreau's Seasons* (1984), pp. 305–06. Quotation from Thoreau's journal for 1858.

18 Alexandra Harris, *Romantic Moderns* (2010), pp. 12–14. And see David Mellor, *Paradise Lost* (1987).

19 Op. 27 (1940). Concerts in 2019 and 2020, and on Classic FM on 6 October 2022. She moved to Buxted in 1939 and later lived in Seaford, where she died in 1998.

20 The resurgence is illustrated by the acclaimed exhibition at the Pallant Gallery, Chichester, in 2022–23, 'Sussex Landscape: Chalk, Wood and Water', including print, sculpture, photography and digital works. Badmin is unfortunately missing from the exhibition.

21 Lewis Lusk, *Sussex Oak* (1912). Lusk was the pen name of Walter Delaplaine Scull (1863–1915), who moved to Crowborough from London by 1897. He died at The Pines, the home he built in Crowborough. He also published the novel *Sussex Iron* in 1913, as well as books on local history under his own name (http://theweald.org/d10w.asp?BookId=scull001).

22 *The Atheneum* (21 September 1912), p. 309.

23 Connolly, *The Unquiet Grave*, p. 1.

24 Richard Church, 'The Poetry of Andrew Young' in *Speaking Aloud* (1968), p. 206.

25 Jefferies, *After London*.

26 Jefferies, *The Story of My Heart*.

27 Carpenter, *My Days and Dreams*, p. 139; 'Desirable Mansions' in *England's Ideal* (1887), pp. 62–78.

28 Carpenter, *Civilisation: Its Cause and Cure*, p. 39.

29 Blunt, 'The Love-Sonnets of Proteus, Part 3: Gods And False Gods'; and 'On Reading the Memoirs of M. D'Artagnan', *Works*, pp. 1, 72.

30 Belloc, *The Servile State*; and see Speaight, *Hilaire Belloc*, pp. 316–20.

31 Halsham, *Lonewood Corner*, p. 182.

32 Ford Madox Ford, *The Soul of London* (1905); G.K. Chesterton, *The Napoleon of Notting Hill* (1904).

33 See Brandon, *The Discovery of Sussex*, pp. 183–92, 209–20.

34 Woolf, *Essays, Vol. 4: 1925–28* (ed. McNeillie, 1994), p. 290; Leonard Woolf, *Leonard Woolf: An Autobiography*, Vol. 2 (1980), pp. 104–05. *Comic Cuts* was a British comic book magazine published from 1890 to 1953. 'Lyons' should not have merited an apostrophe as given in the quotation.

35 Since Peter Brandon's death in 2011, the concerns about eco-destruction have multiplied, for example, with the rise of Green politics, in television documentaries, and the anxieties about climate change and the existential human future expressed, for example, in the controversial Extinction Rebellion movement.

36 Bate, *The Song of the Earth*, p. 283. And see D. Farrier, *Anthropocene Poetics* (2019); J.M. McCarthy, *Green Modernism* (2015) as well as Head's *Modernity and the English Rural Novel*.

37 R.S. Thomas, 'The Small Country' in *Frequencies* (1978), p. 19.

Chapter 15

1 Robert Frost, 'The Road Not Taken' in *Mountain Interval* (1916).

2 D. Hardy and C. Ward, *Arcadia for All* (1984).

3 For the late Victorian and Edwardian period, see Colls and Dodd, *Englishness*, and for the twentieth century, see Matless, *Landscape and Englishness*.

4 R.G. Collingwood, *The Principles of Art* (1938), p. 88.

5 John Cowper Powys, *After my Fashion* (1980); and *Autobiography* (1934).

6 M. Ryle, 'After "organic community": Eco-criticism, Nature and Human Nature' in J. Parham, (ed.), *Literature and the Environmental Tradition* (2001), pp. 11–23.

7 Raymond, *Don John's Mountain Home*, pp. 261–65.

8 Brit. Parlt Papers 1919 (9), Report by B.H. Holland to the Commission on Wages and Conditions of Employment in Agriculture (May 1918).

9 P. Mandler, 'Against "Englishness": English Culture and the Limits to Rural Nostalgia, 1850–1940' in *Trans Royal Historical Society* 7 (1998), p. 166. For the obfuscating tradition of the 'rural idyll', see Brian Short, 'Idyllic Ruralities' in P. Cloke et al. (eds), *Handbook of Rural Studies* (2006), pp. 133–48.

10 Mrs Henry Dudeney (ed. Diana Crook), *A Lewes Diary 1916–1944* (1998), p. 62.

11 See J. Carey, *The Intellectuals and the Masses* (1992), pp. 3–22.

12 Thomas Hardy, *Tess of the d'Urbevilles* (1891,1974 edition), p. 163.

13 F.R. Leavis and D. Thompson, *Culture and Environment* (1891, 1974 edition), p.163.

14 H.E. Bates, *The Blossoming World*, p. 91, cited in Head, *Modernity and the English Rural Novel*, p. 142.

15 I. Finlayson, *Writers in Romney Marsh* (1986), p. 20.

16 I. Finlayson, *Writers in Romney Marsh*, pp. 22–23.

17 I. Finlayson, *Writers in Romney Marsh*, pp. 178–202; R. Dellamora, *Radclyffe Hall: A Life in the Writing* (2011), p. 203.

18 H.G. Wells, *Tono-Bungay* (1909, 1964 edition), p. 59.

19 D. Cody, 'Kipling's Imperialism' (The Victorian Web, www.victorianweb.org/authors/kipling/rkimperialism.html).

20 Wilson, *Hilaire Belloc*, p. 191. Cecil was G.K. Chesterton's brother.

21 In July 2018, University of Manchester students painted over a mural of a poem by Rudyard Kipling, arguing that he 'dehumanised people of colour'. The issue remains highly contentious.

22 V. Woolf, *To the Lighthouse* (1927), p. 166.

23 Woolf, *Essays, Vol. 3: 1919–1924* (edited by McNeillie, 1988), p. 142.

24 R. Barthes. 'The Death of the Author' in *Image, Music, Texts/Roland Barthes* (1977), pp. 142–48.

INDEX

Page numbers in italics refer to figures in the text; numbers in bold refer to colour plates